The Spirit of

INDIAN
PAINTING

ADVANCE PRAISE FOR THIS BOOK

'Professor Goswamy's book meets a long-felt need. In all the years that I have been involved with Indian art I have repeatedly been asked to recommend a book which covers the whole subject. This is it. This is it. This is it' SIR HOWARD HODGKIN

'With his thoughtful selections and wonderful writing Professor Goswamy makes us first of all see and understand; and then, understand and see. Quietly—without insistence—he leads us to gaze upon now an orchid, now a lotus bloom; fragrant roses and eye-filling narcissi. There is more than spirit in this "introduction": there is deep knowledge and gentle passion. All this, and finally—and above all—a book to make both layman and connoisseur alike realize why pre-modern Indian painting is one of the great arts of the world' NEIL MACGREGOR

'A tour de force! B.N. Goswamy brings to this remarkable publication the insights of a connoisseur, a *rasika*, with the erudition of a discerning scholar . . . He unravels these [paintings] one by one and layer by layer to reveal not only their intrinsic beauty but the historical circumstances which shaped them. . . . A delightful addition to the vast oeuvre of an art historian par excellence, this book serves to engage and "open the eyes" of the viewer to the incredible visual wonders hidden within these rare gems of art' GULAMMOHAMMED SHEIKH

'B.N. Goswamy is probably India's most admired art historian. He combines the eye of the aesthete, the discrimination of a connoisseur and the soul of a poet with the rigorous mind of a scholar and the elegant prose of a gifted writer. *The Spirit of Indian Painting* is the summation of a lifetime's loving dedication to his subject. It may well be his most beautiful and is certainly his most heartfelt work' WILLIAM DALRYMPLE

'This is a remarkable book by a great art historian and critic. B.N. Goswamy's work has a broader significance in matters of art and what he has to say is applicable not only to classical Indian art and miniature painting but to a great deal of art being executed today . . . He writes eloquently on the many aspects which manifest themselves gradually and combine to yield a lasting sense of delight . . . Such is the power of art and the elements which comprise it' KRISHEN KHANNA

'No one knows more about Indian painting than B.N. Goswamy, and in *The Spirit of Indian Painting* he shares a lifetime of knowledge and insights in a lucidly written text and on a captivating selection of paintings. From Mughal India to the Deccan and Rajput courts and beyond, Goswamy provides ways of seeing and reading Indian paintings that are unparalleled' GLENN LOWRY

'Close to half a century ago, it was B.N. Goswamy who revolutionized our perception of Indian paintings, taking these "miniatures" not simply as decorative items produced for some royal patron's fancy, but as master-works in their own right, in the process restoring to the artist the honour that belonged to him. He taught us to see with greater clarity, revealed to us things that lay hidden behind small and seemingly simple surfaces. The astonishing thing is that—as *The Spirit of Indian Painting* establishes—he continues to do so even now, tirelessly and in his inimitable voice' EBERHARD FISCHER

'Drawing from a life of immense learning and experience, B.N. Goswamy has created a book wholly accessible to the general reader, yet essential for the specialist. In "A Layered World", he explores why certain pictures are great, showing us how to look closely at images that for many will be unfamiliar. But he also wants the reader to understand the lives out of which these images emerged, and why those lives are important. His ability to relate the work of artists to the world around them—to religions, literatures, historical events, social situations—is unrivalled. This is the best possible introduction to the richly varied traditions of painting in India' MILO BEACH

The Spirit of
INDIAN
PAINTING

Close Encounters with 101 Great Works
1100–1900

B.N. GOSWAMY

ALLEN LANE
an imprint of
PENGUIN BOOKS

ALLEN LANE

Published by the Penguin Group

Penguin Books India Pvt. Ltd, 7th Floor, Infinity Tower C, DLF Cyber City, Gurgaon 122 002, Haryana, India

Penguin Group (USA) Inc., 375 Hudson Street, New York, New York 10014, USA

Penguin Group (Canada), 90 Eglinton Avenue East, Suite 700, Toronto, Ontario, M4P 2Y3, Canada

Penguin Books Ltd, 80 Strand, London WC2R 0RL, England

Penguin Ireland, 25 St Stephen's Green, Dublin 2, Ireland (a division of Penguin Books Ltd)

Penguin Group (Australia), 707 Collins Street, Melbourne, Victoria 3008, Australia

Penguin Group (NZ), 67 Apollo Drive, Rosedale, Auckland 0632, New Zealand

Penguin Books (South Africa) (Pty) Ltd, Block D, Rosebank Office Park, 181 Jan Smuts Avenue, Parktown North, Johannesburg 2193, South Africa

Penguin Books Ltd, Registered Offices: 80 Strand, London WC2R 0RL, England

First published in Allen Lane by Penguin Books India 2014

Text copyright © B.N. Goswamy 2014
Page 538 is an extension of the copyright page

Generous grants from

Jñāna-Pravāha, Varanasi   IndiGo Airlines   The Raza Foundation

have supported the publication of this book at a special price

ISBN 9780670086573

Front cover: detail from 'Raja Balwant Singh Examining a Painting with Nainsukh'
Back cover: detail from 'The Virgin and Child'

Book design by Aparajita Ninan
Typeset in Baskerville by R. Ajith Kumar, New Delhi
Printed at Thomson Press India Ltd, New Delhi

A PENGUIN RANDOM HOUSE COMPANY

for
little Madhav
who is all spirit, all light

CONTENTS

Contents

Contents

Contents

The Spirit of
INDIAN
PAINTING

a LAYERED WORLD

There are things, some of them passing strange, that happen when you confront a work of art: (i) unfolding of the heart; (ii) its expansion; (iii) its agitation; and, finally, (iv) vibration.

—From a reading of *Kavyartha*

I

Indian paintings have been variously described: as layered objects in which one thing, or thought, is gently laid upon another; like schist rocks, foliated and iridescent; like a couplet in Persian or a *doha* in Hindi, terse but meaningful; like a great floral carpet that lies rolled up but can be spread out endlessly, revealing new things with each mellow unfurling.

Each description is seductive, and contains much truth. They are also in their different ways saying a single thing—a painting presents to us a layered world of meaning. One needs to, thus, make an effort to receive from it all the riches that reside within. We must first summon *utsaha*—energy, enthusiasm, the excitement of anticipation. Then we need to make what can only be described as a visual immersion in the work. Thereon much can be expected—the joy of discovery, stimulus to reflection, visual excitement and, finally, heightened delight.

To attain delight one must then learn to read a painting. To begin with—oddly, to be sure, for this book is about painting—a relatively small south Indian bronze of c. fourteenth century, that the noted art historian Stella Kramrisch called 'The Tree of Life and Knowledge'. There is allure in the form: a tree with a slender, straight trunk from which curving branches issue forth with symmetry and evenness, first dipping low as if borne down by their weight and then rising slightly at the bud-like tips. Each branch is connected to the one above or below it by carefully spaced single, flame-like leaves, creating a latticework effect. In the centre of the tree's crown sits a curled *naga* with many hoods. Just below the *naga*, but also set against the trunk is a layered, ribbed disc, looking like the solid wheel of a chariot.

Lower down stand two crowned monkey figures, clinging to the trunk but each with one hand raised, a wondering finger to the lips. And at the base two small cows, one on either side, flank the trunk. Higher up, almost merging with the swelling bud-tips, sit small *hamsa* figures at the very edge of the branches, as if weightless, their upraised tails brushing against the buds.

It takes a while to take in the form in its entirety, and its grace and sophistication. Then one begins to wonder what the figures on the tree stand for. What did the maker of this bronze have in mind? Is the mythical many-hooded *naga* in the tree one of those serpents celebrated in the Puranic texts: Vasuki, Shesha, Muchalinda? Is the disc the Sudarshana *chakra* of Vishnu? Where do the crowned monkey figures come from—the Ramayana? Are the cows at the base of the tree waiting for Krishna?

The *hamsa* figures eventually intrude upon these questions. By including the birds in the bronze, is the sculptor drawing our attention to the old myth where the *hamsa* is the ultimate symbol of discernment? In traditional belief, the bird has the *neera–ksheera viveka*—the ability to separate milk from water, drinking only the milk, and leaving the water behind. Or do the *hamsa*s

Tree of Life, Indian, probably Tamil Nadu, late sixteenth to seventeenth century, Vijayanagar
(1336–1672) or Nayak (seventeenth to eighteenth century) period; Bronze, 24 × 23 inches
(61 × 58.4 cm); Courtesy: The Nelson-Atkins Museum of Art, Kansas City, Missouri; Purchase:
William Rockhill Nelson Trust, 41-35 A, B; Photo: Jamison Miller

allude to some yogic practice, the syllables *ham* and *sa* standing for incoming and outgoing breaths?

Many such questions arise, as one stands looking at the sculpture, admiring its skill. But *are* there any answers? Was the maker of this piece creating a riddle for his audience to solve? Was its description by Stella Kramrisch as 'The Tree of Life and Knowledge' purely intuitive, or was it based on some obscure text that only she knew of? One does not know, but one is repeatedly drawn back to the bronze, as one is drawn back to all great art: with the hope of understanding it yet being ready for failure.

Abu'l Hasan, that great painter at the Mughal court—Nadir-al Zaman is the title that the emperor Jahangir conferred upon him, meaning 'Wonder of the

Age'—moved away in one of his works from the glitter of power and opulence to paint an old, fragile man (see at left and p. 498). The tone of the painting is hushed and one falls silent looking at the lone, hesitantly moving figure. The man—an old pilgrim perhaps or, possibly, a mendicant who has seen better days—stands barefoot, leaning on a thin, long staff.

The body bears marks of the ravages of time: the hunched back, the stooped shoulder, the snow-white beard, the lean, desiccated frame. But one can see, from the look in the eyes, that the mind is still keen and the bent of mind religious—he holds prominently a rosary of beads in his bony right hand and wears one round his neck. There are signs of indigence everywhere. The lower part of the body is bare, the feet are unshod, and the coarse apparel he wears consists mostly of a rough cloak used as a wrap, a folded shawl-like sheet thrown over the left shoulder, and an unadorned tightly bound turban.

Technically, the work is brilliant. One notices the roughness of the skin at the knees; the thinness of the fingers; the rendering of the beads in the rosary, each shrivelled and varying in size; above all, the face with its lines of age and experience. The painting, though, is as moving as it is skilful and it fills the viewer with questions. What did Abu'l Hasan intend by this picture? Did he know his subject? It is most unlikely that the painting was done *for* the man, but then—used as he must have been to royal commissions and grand themes—why did Abu'l Hasan pick him?

Was it simply a portrait or was the artist addressing an abstract idea? Whatever the case, Abu'l Hasan seems here to infuse a universality of feeling into this figure. Poets have spoken much about old age. It is the time when the meaning of things begins dimly to unfold, when the hollowness of life makes itself manifest. For the man of God, it has been said, there comes a time when he has to sit out his years with submission rather than defiance, for he knows that this edifice of life is built on walls that are but sand, and rests on pillars fickle as the wind. Is this Abu'l Hasan's response to the subject, a painter's intimations of mortality?

Now to a celebrated early *Bhagavata Purana* series, datable to the first half of the sixteenth century. The series as such is well known even though where it was made, who its painters were, and its precise date have been the subject of debate among scholars for years. What has never been questioned, however, is its remarkable quality: the verve, the spiritedness, the devotion, the emotional fervour, the glow of the painters' conviction that what they were visualizing is the only way things must have happened in the past.

Each leaf is a celebration of the life and the deeds of Krishna and is accompanied by an excerpt from the original text of the Purana on its verso. To identify a scene, therefore, is easy. What is less easy is to decipher the visual language and the vocabulary that the painter/s use. For they play and trifle with natural appearances and abandon them at will in favour of poetically conceived conventions. It is all done assertively and with flamboyance—the lines soar, the colours sing.

Boldly distinctive figural types are established both for men and women—sharp profiles, large, languid eyes, heroic chests in the case of men, full ripe breasts in the case of women; generally lithe forms, cadenced stances, clear gestures that seem to come from the world of dance. The painters claim for themselves complete freedom in the rendering of dresses, furnishings and architectural details; sky and water and rocks are all depicted in an imaginary way; backgrounds are established through seemingly arbitrarily chosen colours. It is the sum of these parts which makes for the magical effect. They beckon and lead us in, challenge our ideas about the nature of appearances, establish startlingly different ways of seeing, and all the while quietly illumine the viewer's surroundings with the glow and intensity of colours.

In this particular painting Krishna, having accomplished his mission on this earth by having killed Kamsa, decides to not return to Vraja to his beloved *gopi*s but sends his close friend Uddhava instead with his message. It says that they will have to forget him, for he is not going to return to them. Uddhava's therefore is not an easy task. When he breaks the news to Krishna's many beloveds, they complain and shed bitter tears. How can He do this, they ask? Do you think that it is easy to let go of memories of Him?

In this painting Uddhava appears twice: once on the right and then again on the left, as if turning to listen first to one *gopi* and then to another, for each of them has her own thoughts, her own pain, to share with him. The two *gopi*s on the right make emphatic gestures and even show him the footprints He

Folio from a pre-Mughal *Bhagavata Purana*; possibly Delhi–Mathura region; second quarter of the sixteenth century; 18.5 × 23.5 cm; Courtesy: The Sarabhai Foundation, Ahmedabad

had left behind as a promise, close to the trunk of his favourite tree. Two other *gopi*s follow Uddhava as he is led away by another *gopi*. She is pointing to a cow that is standing atop a rocky ridge, craning her neck as if searching for Krishna.

For anyone who understands the context, especially for a devotee of Krishna, there is great beauty in the rendering. But the painting has also to be read with care. It is all emphatically but very subtly done, the painter taking every possible liberty in the process. The verdant groves of Vrindavan are reduced to three elegantly articulated trees. The Yamuna flows at the bottom of the page, astir like a pond with aquatic birds and blooming lotuses. The monochromatic colours in the background change from blue to orange to green in order to establish different spaces. The women are as beautiful

9

and stately as ever, and the dark sky with its wavy horizon holds everything together. Floating above everything, however, the mauve-pink rocky ridge with its scalloped ends stands suspended in the air, asking pointed questions.

As a last instance, in this attempt at emphasizing the need to look at paintings with more care, and greater intent, than we generally do, one can turn to a leaf from a celebrated eighteenth-century *Gita Govinda* series from the Pahari area. Jayadeva's poetic text in Sanskrit is famous for its celebration of the love of Radha and Krishna. 'If remembering Hari enriches your heart / if his arts of seduction arouse you,' the poet says at the beginning, then 'listen to Jayadeva's speech / in these sweet soft lyrical songs.'

Countless people, over the centuries, have listened. This leaf (see p. 468) comes almost at the beginning of the poem. Nanda, Krishna's foster-father, is out grazing cows when he suddenly sees 'clouds thicken the sky / *tamala* trees darkening the forest', and becomes concerned about young Krishna, for the thunderstorm and the approaching night might frighten him. He asks Radha, who is a little older than Krishna in this narrative, to take 'the boy' home. But then, as the two head homeward along the banks of the Yamuna, their love begins to unfold, their 'secret passions . . . triumph'.

In the painting, stars have begun to appear in the darkening sky, the Yamuna, almost unnoticed, flows quietly in the background, the dark forms of the '*tamala*' trees and palms loom over the scene. Against this are placed the illuminated forms of the two lovers (see detail on p. 11). Krishna has thrown his left arm around Radha's shoulder and gently reaches out to touch her breast with his right hand; she makes futile gestures, restraining his left hand and pointing with her own right hand towards the path that they should take. But there is no conviction in her resistance. She turns back, and gazes lovingly into Krishna's eyes, standing elegantly like a dancer, left leg lightly crossed against the right, one toe barely touching the earth. It is a wonderfully quiet moment. Time seems to have come to a stop, nothing else seems to exist for the two lovers.

The stillness is strangely affecting. As a narrative strategy, the painter's decision to devote a whole page to this quiet, tender moment is brilliant, for soon energetic, frenetic passion will take over. There is going to be talk of the '*tamala* trees' fresh leaves absorbing strong scents of deer musk', of 'budding mango trees trembling from the embrace of rising vines', and of 'yellow silk and wild flower garlands'.

We too get lost in the moment: the unfailing sense of colour, the fluency and the elegance of line, the unlikely mix of precise detail and loose brushwork, all create an image of great vividness. But there is more in the painting that needs absorbing. Against all laws of nature, while darkness falls everywhere, the forms of the two lovers, standing as if in a masque, remain dazzlingly lit. The painter, too, is playing with the forms of the trees. The tree in the back has its trunk split into two, each limb moving closer to the other and entering into a gentle embrace next to where the lovers stand; one of them lighter in skin than the other. Radha, gleaming like lightning, and Krishna, dark as a cloud.

II

Very few documents deal directly or at length with Indian painting. From time to time one comes upon references to painting and painters—in stray colophons, in contemporary chronicles, occasionally in memoirs. Some works have survived in which one can see painters at work or come upon signatures, as well as attributions by scribes or librarians. But there are no exhaustive accounts. Art historians have to mostly make their insights by having a broad cultural understanding of the period, but they are working with very little material.

They are challenged, too, by the fact that historically, artists have been mostly anonymous in India, something that has been sought to be understood and explained in different ways. Some scholars have worked hard and with remarkable patience, piecing together lists of artists from scraps of information, going to unconventional sources for unearthing names and constructing genealogies, or—more recently—identifying the work of a whole range of master painters based upon their styles. But it still remains, by and large, a world of silence in which one has to strain very hard to pick up whispers from the past.

Fortunately for us, something of the texture of the times, of the thoughts in a painter's mind, can be felt when one listens to the occasional accounts that the painters of today—inheritors of old traditions—narrate, or from passing references contained in some texts. How true these stories are, we will never know yet they are embedded with precious things: values, judgements, an understanding of modes of working and insights into social relationships.

There is, for instance, an engaging story of the painter who was asked by his patron, a raja, to paint a portrait of his rani for her birthday. This story must have circulated in different versions earlier but was narrated to me by a Pahari painter recently and it truly carries the flavour of the hills.

The commission given to the painter had one major challenge: he was not supposed to see the rani in real life, she being in purdah. Thus, the 'portrait' he was to execute was, clearly, to be an idealized one.

The painter went about his task with enthusiasm, summoning to his aid all the time-honoured descriptions of feminine beauty—eyes that resembled those of a doe, eyebrows that took the shape of a stretched bow, nose like the beak of a parrot, lips like a bimba fruit, full breasts, narrow waist, ample hips, and the like. It turned out, like it was intended to, as a portrait endowed with all the *lakshanas* or characteristics appropriate to the delicate form of a *padmini* woman.

But, as he was giving the finishing touches to the work, a tiny black dot of paint fell from the brush tip on to the rani's body. Upset by this but unable to remedy it, the painter hoped that the tiny dot would not be noticed. The next day the painter presented the painting to the raja. The raja was greatly pleased with the portrait but when he examined it with the kind of care that the work demanded, his eye fell upon the tiny black dot which happened to be on the thigh of the rani. Knowing that the rani had a mole on her thigh at exactly the same spot, the raja became suspicious and wondered whether there was a secret liaison between the painter and his wife.

Angrily, he ordered the painter to be thrown into prison. The following night, however—so the story goes—Devi, the Great Goddess, appeared to the raja in his dream and chided him for having been unfair to the painter. The painter, the Goddess told the raja, was a great devotee of hers, and it was she, sitting on the tip of his brush, who had made that little black dot fall on the rani's body for the portrait to gain a closeness to reality. The next day the repentant raja ordered that the painter be released and allowed to return home, loaded with honours.

The story has undoubted charm but it also tells us some important things— the nature of 'portraiture' as it was understood in that society; the relationship between painter and patron; the religious belief of the painter; trust in divine inspiration behind works of art.

Of a different flavour are passages from scattered Mughal sources that speak of connoisseurship. The emperor Akbar's great interest in the art of painting, and his determined efforts to found an imperial atelier—often in the face of the orthodox Islamic view against the making of images—we know from Abu'l Fazl's enthusiastic account. But of connoisseurship we hear from his son Jahangir, who writes in his memoirs:

> As regards myself, my liking for painting and practice in judging it have arrived at such a point that when any work is brought before me, either of deceased artists or of those of the present day, without the names being told me, I say on the spur of the moment that it is the work of such and such a man. And if there be a picture containing many portraits, and each face be the work of a different master, I can discover which face is the work of each of them. If any other person has put in the eye and eyebrow of a face, I can perceive whose work the original face is, and who has painted the eye and eyebrow.

The Khan Khanan, Abdul Rahim, a grandee held in high esteem at the Akbari court, was also known to be a patron of many painters, and this casual reference in a later work, the *Kalimut-ush-Shuara*, relates to his discerning eye:

> When the Khan Khanan was going to the court of the Emperor, a painter came to him and handed over to him one of his pictures. The scene depicted there was of a lady who was taking her bath and that a maidservant was rubbing the sole of her foot with a pumice stone. The Khan Khanan looked at the picture for a moment and then, putting it in

his palanquin, went away to pay homage to the Emperor. When he returned, the painter reappeared. He ordered that a sum of rupees five thousand be paid to him. The painter said, 'My picture is hardly worth more than five rupees, but there is one artistic skill which I have employed in it. If Your Honour has remarked that, then I shall be glad to accept your reward, for then I shall have the satisfaction that Your Honour has really appreciated my work.' The Khan Khanan said, 'Your skill lies in that you have expressed in the lady's face the feeling which is produced by the rubbing of the sole with a pumice stone.' The painter was much delighted . . .

There is every possibility that the writer, who was relating an event much before his time, got it slightly wrong and that the painting was a visualization of a well-known *doha* in Hindi—a language that the Khan Khanan knew well. In it the poet speaks of his beloved's tender foot and the delicate pink of her sole. Mistaking it for a stain, the maidservant keeps trying to rub the pink out of her foot and the effect is of course the opposite—the more she rubs the deeper the pink becomes.

There is another version of the same 'story', told in the Pahari area, of a painter dejected at seeing that his royal patron has not noticed the elegant variation he has produced on a known theme. Instead of showing the lover bending at the feet of his angry beloved, hoping to placate her by massaging them—which is the traditional image—the painter had depicted the lover using a rose so as not to hurt her. Fineness of feeling is all.

That there was great value attached to the artist's precision in workmanship and to minuteness in detail is evident in other ways, especially during the Mughal period. A letter written by the emperor Humayun to a friendly Central Asian chief, Rashid Khan of Kashgar, found its way into the memoirs of a contemporary, Bayazid Biyat.

'From among those matchless artists,' the letter said,

> who had presented themselves before me in Iraq and
> Khurasan and were generously rewarded, a group came and
> joined my service in Shawwal A.H. 959 [September–October
> 1552]. One of them is the painter Mir Sayyid Ali, the nadir
> al-asr, who is matchless in painting [*taswir*]. He has painted
> on a grain of rice a polo scene—two horsemen stand within
> the field, a third comes galloping from one corner, while a
> fourth horseman stands at one end receiving a mallet from
> a footman; at each end of the field are two goalposts; and
> at each corner of the rice is written the following couplet:
> 'A whole granary lies within a grain / and an entire world
> inside a bubble.' And at the bottom he has written, 'the
> humble servant Sayyid Ali, in the month of Rajab A.H. 959
> [June–July 1552]. Another of these rare craftsmen is Maulana
> Fakhr, the book-binder, who has made twenty-five holes in
> a poppy seed . . . and there is the unique craftsman Ustad
> Wais, the gold-wire drawer [*zar-kash*], who has made twenty-
> five gold and silver wires so thin that Mulla Fakhr could
> draw them through the holes in the poppy seed. These few
> things made by these talented people are being sent.

Other documents surface occasionally giving us tantalizing glimpses
of the lives of artists. Thus, a painter's plaintive petition to his royal patron
asking for leave to depart; a powerful noble's instructions to a subordinate
asking him to intervene so that 'his painter' is absolved of the charges
levelled against him; a *qazi*'s adjudication in the matter of a theft that a
painter was accused of.

At the same time, far away from princely courts, too, one hears meaningful
voices. Like that of the celebrated Pahari painter Nainsukh, who made

this entry in his own hand in the register of a family priest at the great
pilgrimage centre of Haridwar which he visited carrying the ashes of his
princely patron.

> Of the Sandal sept. Written by Naina [Nainsukh], carpenter-
> painter, native of Guler. Son of Seu, grandson of Hasnu,
> great-grandson of Bharathu. Great-great-grandson of Data.
> The maternal ancestry also written. Purohit Hariram
> recognized [as the family *purohit*]. Maternal grandfather: Das.
> Maternal great-grandfather: Chuhru. Maternal great-great-
> grandfather: Hariya. If the writing of [my] brother Manaku
> [in proof of recognizing a *purohit* as the family *purohit*] turns
> up with [in the register of] another purohit, that writing will
> be taken as genuine. This entry has been made with this
> reservation. Written on the first of the month of Jyeshtha
> [May–June] of the Samvat 1820 [1763 CE].

Nainsukh drew a remarkably delicate drawing of Shiva and Parvati beside
his entry but it is the text, and its lucky survival, that is more striking. Nothing
quite like this—giving the genealogy of a remarkable family of painters—has
surfaced elsewhere in India.

To go back to stories, however. There is one, handed down from generation
to generation within a family of artists, which has as its theme the
assertive nature of the artist. A painter—he remains unnamed—was once
commissioned by a raja to paint murals in a newly built temple in his capital.
The work involved was extensive, and he was advanced some money for
procuring materials and making other necessary preparations.

Several months passed after the task had been assigned, but there was no
sign of any work having been started in the temple. The raja had all but
forgotten the commission, but several people, including jealous rivals, carried

complaints about the painter to him, suggesting that months had been idled away and the money advanced to the painter had been misappropriated.

Incensed at hearing this, the raja decided to visit the painter in his home rather than summon him. When he entered the painter's house, he found him sitting in the courtyard, grinding some pigment on a stone slab. The painter did not even notice the raja's arrival with his entourage until his name was called out. Then he looked up.

The raja angrily demanded to know why no work on the temple had been started but the painter made no reply. Instead, he picked up a round, hard clod of earth that lay by his side. Then, still not uttering a word, and with everyone watching, the painter mixed the pigment that he was grinding with some liquid, dipped his brush in it, and with it drew a line around the clod. With a stone he struck the clod, splitting it open.

He then held up the two parts for the raja to examine, pointing out that the pigment that he had applied around the clod had permeated just halfway through its thickness. He would have started the work, he said, only when the mineral he was now working with had been ground to a fineness that would permit the colour to permeate all the way into the centre of the clod of earth. But, the story continues, he added that now that doubt had been cast upon his honesty, he would return all that he had received from the raja, and abandon the commission.

Like the other stories, this one is entertaining but it also communicates attitudes, and contains intimations of other matters: the manner in which works were commissioned, rivalries between artists, the occasional acts of boldness on the part of the painters, and the value attached to proper methods and materials.

All of this, each scrap of information, each story or document, is meaningful: it allows us to feel the breath of those times—even if lightly—upon our skin.

But it still amounts to very little, for there are no connected accounts, no biographies, no detailed chronicles.

One has, therefore, to fall back upon one's own resources: the patience to piece things together, the willingness to construct a narrative, the imagination to flesh it out. For gaining a deeper understanding of it all, one can turn with profit, even if briefly, to ideas that are woven into the fabric of our thoughts: those, for instance, that deal with Time and Space and with *rasa*.

III

The idea of *rasa* lies at the heart of the Indian theory of art. The concept is old, going back at least to the *Natyashastra* of Bharata, that extraordinary work on the arts of the theatre which is generally placed close to the beginning of the Common Era.

In his work, where he clearly acknowledged his debt to older masters, Bharata enunciated and applied the *rasa* theory to the arts of the stage, incorporating dance and music (*natya*). But, as the great art critic Ananda Coomaraswamy commented, the theory is 'immediately applicable to art of all kinds'. This has been argued earlier. For writers such as Vishwanatha, fourteenth-century author of the *Sahitya Darpana*, a celebrated work on poetics, the very definition of poetry involves invoking *rasa*. His dictum is often quoted—'Poetry is a sentence the soul of which is rasa.'

The term *rasa* in itself is difficult to translate: among the variants used are 'tincture', 'essence', 'flavour', 'relish' and, most often, 'sentiment'. Aesthetic experience is described as *rasasvadana*, 'the tasting of flavour'. The taster or the 'knower', in other words, the viewer or the reader, most specifically a scholar or connoisseur, is referred to as a *rasika*; a work of art possessing *rasa* is designated as *rasavat* or *rasavanta*.

In its most obvious sense, the sense in which it is still employed most widely in daily parlance in India, *rasa* means the sap or extract of plants. In this sense the word means the same thing to nearly everyone. In its secondary sense, however, *rasa* signifies the non-material essence of a thing, 'the best or finest part of it', like perfume, which comes from matter but is not so easy to describe or comprehend. In its tertiary sense, *rasa* denotes taste, flavour; the relish or pleasure related to consuming or handling either the physical object or taking in its non-physical properties.

In its final and subtlest sense, however—and this is close to the tertiary sense in which the word is applied to art and aesthetic experience—*rasa* comes to signify a state of heightened delight, in the sense of *ananda*, the kind of bliss that can be experienced only by the spirit.

Over centuries, the *rasa* theory became more refined and complex. But whatever philosophers and theoreticians might have to say, the common person uses the word frequently, often with remarkable accuracy. Great works insist that the justification of art, its raison d'être, lies in its service of the fourfold purposes of life: right action (*dharma*), pleasure (*kama*), wealth (*artha*) and spiritual freedom (*moksha*). But, without reference to those leaps of thought, at the ordinary level it is understood that art must result in an experience of *rasa*. It must yield delight.

It is possible that the concept of *rasa* would have been more familiar to persons who came from the Hindu–Buddhist–Jain tradition rather than, say, to those from the Islamic. It may thus have been spoken of more in relationship to Rajput works—Rajasthani or Pahari—than in relationship to the Islamic Mughal or Deccani works. But even in the latter tradition, the idea of works of art yielding heightened delight, not simply pleasure, was not unfamiliar. Or else one would not hear, in the context of art, words like *soz* and *gadaz*, meaning, literally, 'burning and melting' that one comes upon so frequently in the Persian–Urdu tradition.

How *rasa* comes into being, or is experienced by the viewer, is a matter of importance and has been sought to be explained by many. It is causally related to *bhava*—the term has been translated generally as 'mood' or 'emotional state'—of which, according to Bharata, there are eight dominant types, and each has its equivalent *rasa*. The *rasa*s, 'everyone knows' as they say, are *Shringara* (the erotic), *Hasya* (the amusing), *Karuna* (the compassionate), *Raudra* (the furious), *Vira* (the heroic), *Bhayanaka* (the fearsome), *Bibhatsa* (the odious), and *Adbhuta* (the marvellous). To these, over time, was added a ninth: *Shanta* (the quiescent). Even though in its essence *rasa* is one and undivided, it is through one or the other of these nine *rasa*s that an aesthetic experience takes place. This is because out of these nine, one sentiment or flavour dominates a work of art and propels a spectator towards, or becomes the occasion for, a *rasa* experience.

Bhava—mood or emotional state—has several components: those that determine it, those that follow it, others that give rise to complementary emotional states, each having specific Sanskrit terms. Physical stimulants or surroundings, gestures, movements, all come into play for bringing a dominant emotional state into being. While a performance is being watched—the original context is, after all, that of theatre—all these things are being registered upon the mind of the viewer. With it a 'churning of the heart' takes place, as the phrase has it.

The conversations around *rasa* take a more ambiguous and subtle turn hereon. The argument runs thus: as a result of this 'churning of the heart', this coming together of different elements, a dominant or durable emotional state emerges in the mind of the viewer. This state transmutes itself into a rasa. '*Bhava*,' it is said, 'is the flower and *rasa* the fruit thereof.' Now, if the circumstances have been right, if the performance is of the proper order, and if the viewer is cultured and sensitive enough—is, in other words, a *rasika*—a spark will leap from the performance to the viewer, resulting in an experience that will suffuse his entire being.

21

The experience might possess the suddenness of a flash of lightning (*chamatkara*), leaving the viewer unprepared for the moment and unaware of the swiftness with which it comes. This is the moment when, as a later writer put it, 'magical flowers . . . blossom' in the viewer's awareness and *rasa* is tasted. The experience is genuine and definable but cannot be predicted, there being so many variables. It just simply happens, comes into sudden bloom.

Vishwanatha's definition of the nature of the aesthetic experience has such authority and value that it is still quoted:

> Pure aesthetic experience is theirs in whom the knowledge
> of ideal beauty is innate; it is known intuitively in intellectual
> ecstasy without accompaniment of ideation, at the highest
> level of conscious being; born of one mother with the
> vision of God, its life is as it were a flash of blinding light of
> transmundane origin, impossible to analyse, and yet in the
> image of our very being.

There are so many aspects to *rasa* that it has continually been debated among the learned. Is the number of *rasa*s fixed, for instance; is the experience in the nature of a revelation or is it the coming into being of a state that did not exist before? How does aesthetic experience differ from experience of the kinds of emotions which are part of our real, everyday life? How can the states of sorrow or fear or disgust yield pleasure? Are there any impediments to *rasa*? And so on.

And yet to return to an earlier point, one is struck by how readily people even today use the term to describe their experience of a work of art. It was *sarasa*, a person might say after having heard a music recital, or *neerasa*: meaning, respectively, 'full of delight' or 'devoid' of it.

This is not far removed from the manner in which, in literary works of old, one reads about praise being lavished upon a work of art because of the delight it has yielded. When suddenly moved—reading a passage, seeing a performance, listening to a poem—a person would involuntarily experience a heightened state, and would speak of having *romaharsha*, meaning, literally, 'the hair on my body has become happy'.

For all the meanings that *rasa* yields, this popular view of the effect of great art upon the viewer remains at its centre. In essence, *rasa* points to the relationship between art and its audience, and about the states that are awakened in the viewer. The *rasika*—he who is *sahridaya*, meaning 'of the same heart'—must be competent, deserving, knowledgeable; who can bring *utsaha* to the act of viewing. And with this one comes back to the idea spoken of at the very start: that we can take from works of art only according to our own energies, or capacities.

IV

In countless Indian paintings one sees the same figure/s appearing more than once within the same frame. This can be regarded simply as a useful, visually economical convention that grew over a long period of time. But clearly there is more to it than that. For it is rooted in, or at least related to, an understanding of time and how subtly it works in the visual arts of India.

One speaks here not of different 'categories' of time, if one can call them that: thus, of 'psychological time' which a work of art demands; or the time taken to carefully regard a work of art, 'ruminative time', in other words. One also knows that each work of art comes out of a particular time and always, consciously or unconsciously, references it. The issue is how one has to come to terms with time that is inherent in the work itself. In this sense, incomprehensible as it may sound at first, time becomes a specific component in the structure of a work of art, even though it does not appear uniformly. For the understanding, even the awareness, of time varies greatly, each culture having developed its own view of it.

There are extraordinarily subtle, abstruse speculations about the nature of time in Indian philosophical thought: those about maya, the very nature of illusion, for instance, or about cosmic cycles of time that comprise *yuga*s and *kalpa*s. The term Kalachakra—'wheel of time'—subsumes within itself all kinds of time—cosmic, mythic, sacred, astrological, as well as calendrical. In India, the popular perception of time is that it is cyclical and never comes to an end. Its *gati*—gait, in other words—is different.

Take the way time figures—subtly, almost unnoticed—in well-known mythological stories. It is at that level initially that abstract ideas become embedded in popular culture. In an episode in the *Vishnu Purana*, for instance, one reads of the great god Vishnu accompanied by the divine sage Narada stopping at one point in the course of his wanderings, and asking Narada to fetch some water from a nearby village. While he waits at the edge of the forest, Narada goes to the village, knocks at a door, falls in love with the young woman who answers, marries her, founds a family, and lives happily with his wife and children for many long years until a flood comes and inundates the village, sweeping everything away. Narada too is washed away by the current which throws him at exactly the spot where he had parted company from Vishnu. As he lands, and opens his eyes, he is greeted by the god who asks him, simply: 'Son, have you brought me the water that I had asked you to get?' The pace at which time has moved for Vishnu and for Narada is utterly different.

In the *Krishnakarnamritam*, a widely known devotional text by Lilashuka, dating to the fourteenth century, there is a famous verse in which Yashoda, Krishna's foster-mother, recites the story of the Ramayana to baby Krishna while putting him to bed. The narrative reaches the point where the demon Maricha, in the guise of a golden deer, lures Rama away from his forest hut in the hermitage, leaving Sita exposed to danger. As Yashoda speaks animatedly of the scheming Ravana's arrival on the scene to abduct Sita, suddenly baby Krishna, half asleep by now, jerks into wakefulness and shouts out: 'Lakshmana! Where, oh where, is my bow?' It is as if the memory of his earlier incarnation as Rama, the seventh incarnation of Vishnu, overtakes Krishna in his present life, as the eighth incarnation. Suddenly, time has moved in a loop.

Another Puranic story speaks of the humbling of Indra's pride. The king of gods sits majestically in his assembly, self-satisfied and aware of his own importance. Into this assembly comes charging in a phalanx of ants, a virtual army. Astonishment, even alarm, overtakes everyone. But one person in the assembly, a young sage, seeing this strange vision, laughs aloud. When asked by Indra what causes him this amusement, the sage says he recognized that each of these ants was an Indra in a former birth. Countless cycles of time are hinted at in the story.

In the *Bhagavata Purana*, Narada, visiting Krishna's kingdom at Dwarka, enters the palace's inner apartments to greet the god. As he approaches Krishna's seniormost queen, he finds her attending upon the Lord with a fly whisk in her hand as the Lord sits, eating his food. Greeting the divine pair, Narada withdraws and moves into the next chamber to pay his respects to the wife of Krishna next in seniority, only to find her playing a game of dice with Krishna. In another palace he sees one of Krishna's queens massaging the soles of the Lord's feet as he lies in bed. Amazed, Narada moves further on, and finds, in each chamber, a queen in Krishna's company, serving him food, helping him with oblations, and so on. In chamber after chamber, Krishna greets him as if he has seen the sage for the first time.

One sees here the simultaneous presences of the same person at different places. There are other tales such as these, embodying the many aspects of time. In them, Time moves in a cyclic fashion, making bends and loops, turning back upon itself, rising spiral-like, splitting itself, assuming different speeds for different people. In short, mercurial, illusive, elusive.

The Indian painter would have grown up with this view of time. One does not think of him as being a philosopher, but as one who was part of the Indian tradition, and thus as one who not only imbibed these ideas but also contributed to them in his own manner. At the subtlest level, his view of time affects the view that he takes of several things. But the most dramatic reflection of his understanding of time lies in his adoption of continuous pictorial rendering. He simply presents, within the same frame, the same figure or set of figures more than once, establishing a sequence of events but not necessarily separating the different moments.

This goes back to a very early tradition in sculpture. There, for example, within the same frame or panel one might see, in a Jataka representation, the Buddha in a former birth take on the appearance of a deer who is first trapped, then aimed at by a hunter and finally released from the trap with the aid of another friendly animal. The three renderings, different moments of time and therefore sequential, are set next to each other, without being separated. The sculptor is clearly relying upon the viewer for decoding the narrative, and working out his own sequence. In painting, the Rajput painter,

for instance, does exactly the same thing. On the same leaf we can see a painter entering the palace of the raja at the top-left, then going into the inner apartments at the bottom-right, and then at work in the centre of the painting finishing off a fresco on the palace wall. Or, in a forest setting, one might see a tiger appear at the top-right, leap into the air in the middle of the painting, and then fall dead at the bottom-left, hit by the bullet of a hunter concealed in a tree (see p. 374 and detail on p. 26).

Paintings such as these are not philosophical statements made by the painter, nor are they naive. They simply reflect the fact of his being completely at home with the notion of time as manipulable and elusive. Coomaraswamy was alluding to this when he said: 'Where European art naturally depicts a moment of time, an arrested action or an effect of light, Oriental art represents a continuous condition.'

There are other absorbing instances where the artist can be seen working out his own method for using time. One sees him sometimes bringing the narrator of the story into the painting itself. This is done with much aplomb in the *Laur Chanda* series of the sixteenth century, which tells a popular lovers' tale; or in the seventeenth-century *Sur Sagar* leaves visualizing the devotional poems of the great blind poet of Mathura, Surdas.

The introduction of the author, or the narrator, into each leaf can be seen as a flashback: a way of suggesting perhaps that not only is the composition free of the bonds of time but so is its author. In most leaves of the *Laur Chanda* series, the author, Mulla Daud, can be seen seated in a small rectangular box panel, rosary in hand, reading from his book resting on a *rehal*-stand in front of him. The rest of the page is filled with a rendering of the scene or the passage described in the composition written on the verso of the page in beautiful calligraphy. But the Mulla is usually there, reading, in one corner or another.

In the *Sur Sagar* series, too, the blind poet always appears, seated at the bottom-left or -right corner of each leaf, playing upon his pair of golden cymbals, apparently singing or composing the song that is illustrated on the page (see p. 428). As a variant, when a long tale is being told, the narrator and the listener are both included in the scene as in the early *Aranyaka Parvan* manuscript—a part of the great epic the Mahabharata.

There are other fascinating variations. Where the narration is very long, and there is an extended dialogue, the painter sometimes renders two very similar—almost identical—scenes with only the smallest variations being introduced—a change in the position of objects around the persons conversing, for instance, or replacing day with night. This suggests that much time has elapsed in the course of the conversation, from the preceding folio to the present one. In the series of drawings of the Ramayana by Ranjha where this device is used, even an informal 'explanatory' note has been put in the margin by a pandit or a senior artist saying, *'bhava vartalapa da'*, meaning that much time has passed in this conversation.

Clearly, the artists kept forging, over a period of some two thousand years, different strategies for coming to terms with time. In working out these strategies, they kept taking something from the tradition and, in turn, giving something back to it.

Interestingly, while the device of continuous representation is employed almost routinely in paintings that spring from the Hindu–Buddhist–Jain tradition—seen for the most part in Rajput painting—it barely appears in mainstream Mughal painting. One has to look truly hard for examples of Mughal painting in which the same figure appears more than once.

There is a painting, altogether rare, of a murder scene in the Jahangir album, for instance, where one sees this. An armed intruder sneaks into a house by breaking a brick wall, attacks a man sleeping in the courtyard under a

canopy even as a woman looks on, breaks his neck, and then climbs up a tall
tower from whose height he throws the severed head down where a horrified
crowd of men has gathered. The severed head is that of the man who was
asleep inside; and the intruder is seen twice—even if one does not see his
face clearly: once as he kills the sleeping man and then atop the tall tower
from where he throws the severed head, his trophy perhaps, down to the
ground. We know this because he wears exactly the same clothes—brown
tunic, red knee-length tight *paijama*, large shield tied to the back—which
would be a requirement of continuous narration.

Another example is from a folio of the *Hamzanama* where a man first appears
outside a fortress and then, again, is seen scaling its wall. It is possible that if
one keeps looking, one might find a few other examples in so-called 'Muslim'
painting, but the number would be small. There can be little doubt that this
stems from the view that the Mughal painters had of time. To a Muslim
painter, working within the Judaeo-Christian tradition, it would simply be
'illogical' to render the same figure twice within the same painting.

Of course, not all Mughal painters were Muslims—a very large number
of them were drawn from the Hindu fold—but everyone working in a
Mughal atelier, one imagines, must have had to conform to the belief or
the discipline of the *ustad*, the master painter, who virtually ruled over
the atelier. From the names that have come down, it can be gathered that
the *ustad*s were all Muslims and it is to the Islamic view of Time that they
must naturally have leaned. It would not have been easy for a painting
employing the method of continuous pictorial rendering of the 'Rajput
kind' to slip through the net.

V

Space, like Time, has occupied the Indian mind for a very, very long time.
Great myths speak of the sky and the earth being separated by Indra for

space to come into being, of space being not fixed but expanding and shrinking, of space as *Vishnu-nabhi*, emerging from the navel of Vishnu as he lies resting on the waters of eternity. But it is issues relating to its treatment in painting which are of concern here, above all those of perspective and depth.

The term perspective generally refers to 'any graphic method, geometrical or otherwise, that is concerned with conveying an impression of spatial extension into depth, whether on a flat surface or with form shallower than that represented'. In painting it often translates into 'the sense of diminution in size of objects at a distance and the convergence of parallel lines in recession from the eye'. When one explores the area of landscape in which perspective often becomes a central point of understanding or discussion, one finds that in Indian art, for the most part, different understandings and different strategies were at work.

For one, in early Indian art, as in so many other cultures, landscape as such—'that type of pictorial representation in which natural scenery is the subject, or at least prevails over the action of the figures'—would be hard to find. This is not for want of a real feeling for nature. Indian literature is remarkably rich in its celebration of nature; one finds evocations of it in words both delicate and passionate. But the emphasis always remains on human action. The painter, on his part, constantly refers to nature, drawing upon its details to echo human emotions—branches drooping, streams in flood, trees ablossom, rocks uneasily piled one upon another, and the like— but seldom, if ever, does nature come to occupy the foreground in his work.

One can take as an example the range of paintings that go under the theme of Baramasa, poems about the twelve months of the year. Poet after poet kept writing of the seasons and their majestic cycle, and painter after painter kept creating 'equivalents' in visual terms. But, without exception, the context of the poems and paintings remained that of a conversation between lover and beloved. Come the month of Chaitra or Shravana, for example, and the beloved turns to her lover, pointing out to him how beautiful the month is and why should he, surrounded by such beauty, even be thinking of leaving her and going on his travels again? The month changes, but the beloved's plea does not, for she points out to him again all the alluring sights and sounds that the new month has brought, and asks him once more to stay by her side. The poetry has a great lilt of its own and the descriptions of nature are seductive. However, the sights recede into the background or turn into small vignettes while the lover and beloved claim most of the viewer's attention: seated on a terrace watching the clouds in the sky, clinging to each other under quilts while a brazier of coals burns next to them, leaning down from a balcony to watch young men and women smearing each other's faces with coloured powder during Holi.

Again, painters enthusiastically render episodes or scenes from another great favourite of theirs, the *Gita Govinda*, that classic *kavya*, in which nature figures so prominently. For here 'wind perfumes the forests with fine pollen / shaken loose from newly blossomed jasmine'; and one hears the 'crying sounds of cuckoos, mating on mango shoots / shaken as bees seek honey scents of opening buds'. In this richly imagined landscape, the painter knows that 'gleaming saffron flower pistils' turn into 'golden sceptres of love', and 'flame-tree petals' are but 'shining nails of Love'. With this in his mind, he focuses on the figures of the two lovers, Radha and Krishna. At times he even innovates and introduces visual passages that do not belong strictly to the text. He plays, for example, with the current of the Yamuna which flows in every single folio of this series, for it is essentially on its banks that the drama unfolds. But we see the river differently each time: now flowing quietly, now moving in a sudden zigzag, now splitting into two streams, now rising and overflowing its banks. Clearly, here the painter introduces the river and its different states as a vivid metaphor for moods or states, for the eye keeps getting drawn to the figures of the lovers, and it is only slowly, upon ruminative viewing, that one takes in these wonderful details.

Occasionally one comes upon what can be called a 'pure landscape', in which no figures appear, nothing else 'intrudes'. A startling example is the 'view' of the 'soft sandal mountain winds' caressing 'vines of love' that the painter Manaku brought to an early leaf in his *Gita Govinda* series of 1730. The text does not require it, for it has only the briefest mention of 'sandal mountains'. In creating this unusual masterpiece, Manaku was drawing upon the legend that snakes are greatly drawn to the fragrance of sandal and remain coiled around the trunks of sandalwood trees. One can be certain that the Pahari artist had never seen sandalwood trees, growing as they do in the distant south. Visually, it is a dazzling leaf (see below): piled one upon another, crystal rocks of incredible hues—yellow and brown and green and magenta and orange—rise steeply on either side of a ravine full of trees. Those growing on the left half are all 'sandalwood', bearing snakes of all descriptions—spotted, plain, blue and white and red and green—and those on the right half of the leaf all ablossom, topped with spiky, flowering shoots. The 'spring's mood is

Folio from a *Gita Govinda* series, painted by Manaku; 1730 CE;
Courtesy: The National Museum, New Delhi

rich here', as the text says, but the sight that Manaku creates could never have greeted his eyes. Observation is not at work here, imagination is.

To understand the way the painter's mind would have worked, one can turn to another painting. This is from a southern manuscript—from Mysore—and is a rendering of the Ganga following Bhagirath who, from his chariot at the bottom-right, directs its course. One sees the great milky-white river in flow, splitting and winding down the mountain and through the plains like a giant serpent. The river itself is filled with life—fish and crabs and other aquatic creatures. All that one sees on either side are hillocks, interspersed occasionally with small groves. The soil turns from yellow to orange and red along the rolling slopes, and on the top of the painting is a strip of blue, intended to represent not the sky but a sea with little islands in it. The painting is of course based in mythology, and indeed the whole scene is visualized as if in a dream.

Historically, this is how Indian painters depicted landscape, and only occasionally is a brief illusion of space, of planes being established in a methodical if not quite scientific manner, allowed into their work. From the sixteenth century some things begin to change, beginning for the most part with Mughal painting late in that century. Evidently, the coming in of European works, informed by the use of 'scientific' perspective, led to this development. 'True landscapes' are yet to be seen, for even in Europe these do not appear before the seventeenth century. But a breath of 'naturalism' starts entering Indian painting from this point. We begin to see observation in the depiction of nature and the occasional realistic use of landscape. Indian painters were highly skilled at making copies—the evidence in this regard is overwhelming—and we can see them picking up elements from different sources, working out different approaches. Thus, passages from European paintings—distant views of European towns, atmospheric effects, and the like—are lifted and incorporated in backgrounds, and depth is sometimes introduced, persuading the eye to enter the painting and explore space.

None of these developments, though, move in a linear fashion. The same artist who seems in one painting to be enthusiastic about the 'European way' of doing things, easily shifts gear to move into his own ways in another. Even in the work of Keshava Das or of Abu'l Hasan—two of the most gifted Mughal painters—whose prodigious skills enabled them to absorb and copy European works, Christian themes and all, with relative ease, there is no evidence of a complete 'conversion'. Things are changing, but no artist appears to be in any hurry. Carefully, very carefully, each one makes his choice. Only those elements that they can, or will, integrate with their own vision are incorporated.

Mughal work is not an exception in this regard. One begins to see similar things happening in paintings in Rajasthan and in the Pahari area, though perhaps at a different pace. There is no commitment to a given way of doing things, but an awareness of it is palpable. For the painter, these techniques are new weapons to use in his armoury as and when he chooses.

Why is naturalism/realism merely one among different aesthetic choices for the Indian painter? The answer lies in the way they understood space. Linear perspective, vanishing points, aerial perspective, were for them only some of the many devices used for establishing relationships between objects and distances. They are in fact 'tricks', for creating illusions of space within works of art, for presenting three-dimensional reality on a two-dimensional surface.

If an early artist could clearly communicate to the viewer that in a scene things that were at the top of the work were further away than those in the middle or bottom, then he had created a logic to his work. This might be different from what has erroneously come to be called 'scientific perspective', but it was a logic all the same. There are no fixed points in space, the artist seems to say. If one were to actually move in space from one point to another, perceptions of relationships between objects and places would necessarily change. In a work, space—*aakash*, *kham*, whatever name it be given—can be, most often needs to be, manipulable. In the *Shvetashvatara Upanishad*, an early text which goes back to a few centuries BCE, the sage speaks eloquently of space that man can roll up like a deer-skin, wrap round his loins, and walk away with:

Yadaa charmavad aakasham veshtayishyanti manavah

The image of some yogi seated in meditation on a deer-skin comes to mind.

So often in Indian painting, within the same work, points of view, lines of sight, are changed, all according to the needs of the situation. While a garden is represented as it would be seen by a person from a distance—lines converging, space receding, and so on—the perspective changes when it comes to showing a pool with a fountain in the same garden, or a carpet spread on the grass. These are rendered as if seen directly from above, completely flat like a perfect square or rectangle. Again, at the lower end of a painting, a person might be standing outside a wall built around a palace beyond which, at eye level, nothing would be possible to see. Yet in the middle of the painting, the point of view shifts and what lies inside the walls becomes perfectly visible. It is as if, for seeing, one had moved on to a high balcony somewhere outside. The striking aspect of these constant shifts is that there is no discomfort or disorientation felt by the viewer. For everyone understands—from artist to viewer—that there is no rigidity; nothing is immutable. It brings to mind *syaadvaada*, the Jain doctrine that all judgements are conditional, and that the ways of looking at things are infinite in number.

VI

Like landscape, portraiture in Indian painting has not been a subject of great attention, but it needs to be examined and understood. Its existence is noticed, and where princely or other prominent figures appear reasonably identifiable, there is some discussion. Personages that figure in history and art are looked at with a certain amount of care and interest when they appear in narrative works or illustrations of 'historical' texts; or when one encounters them in the usual durbar scenes or processions. But what view this culture took of portraiture in general is what is not frequently discussed.

This may be less true of Mughal painting than, for example, of the Rajasthani or Pahari schools. In studies of Mughal painting, portraiture has always occupied substantive space and its obviously high quality attracted attention from early on. The fineness of workmanship, combined with psychological insights, gave Mughal portraiture a decided status not only in the art of India but of the world. It is the portraits that may loosely be called more 'Indian' that have remained on the periphery of vision. This may partly be due to the fact that early voices like those of Coomaraswamy did not see the making of portraits as a serious activity by the Rajput painter, and also because these portraits do not fit easily into generally accepted notions of what portraits are supposed to be. The Rajput painter was interested in portraiture but of a kind that corresponded to his received notion of its purpose. This was to capture an inner reality, the essence of the person rather than the accident of his appearance.

In early India, emphasis was on capturing the *lakshana*s of an individual, his characteristic or cognitive attributes. This does not mean that there was any lack of observation on the part of the Rajput painter but that he was only interested in one salient aspect, especially where portraits of rulers were concerned. The Mughal painter was also interested in types, and one can see a great number of characters cast in set moulds in Mughal painting: face in true profile, gaze directed straight ahead, and so on. But the painter looked unblinkingly at a person when he wanted to take a likeness. Within the limits of his own style and its conventions he came very close to naturalism, while his Rajput counterpart by and large tended to stand aloof from this approach.

The point can perhaps be made with the help of some examples. Consider, thus, this description of his late father, the emperor Akbar, by Jahangir in his memoirs.

> In his august personal appearance he [Akbar] was of middle height, but inclining to be tall; he was of the hue of wheat; his eyes and eyebrows were black, and his complexion dark than fair; he was lion-bodied, with a broad chest, and his hands and arms long. On the left side of his nose he had a fleshy mole, very agreeable in appearance, of the size of half a pea. Those skilled in the science of physiognomy considered this mole a sign of great prosperity and exceeding good fortune. His august voice was very loud and in speaking and explaining had a peculiar richness. In his actions and movements he was not like the people of the world, and the glory of God manifested in him.

One notices, in the passage, the references to convention, hints of what was considered auspicious or discreet, and flattering details. But one gains at least some idea of what the great emperor looked like.

Contrast this with the seventh-century description of another great emperor, Harsha, as given by Bana, his court poet, in the *Harshacharita*, in which we come as close as possible to the opportunity that a poet and chronicler might have had to describe his royal patron. From his observations of Harsha from close quarters, Bana paints a picture that is nothing but conventions. The emperor's toenails were like 'the ten directions of space impersonate', he writes; the brightness of his teeth came through when 'easy jests' flashed from his mouth; 'his two thighs were two ruby pillars, set to bear the weight of the earth which rested on his heart, like two sandalwood trees with their roots shining with the rays from the crest jewels of the serpents clustered around them'; his broad forehead was 'reddened by the pink of his crest ornaments, as if it were the lac-dye of Lakshmi's feet which had clung to it, when he sought by prostration to appease her jealousy at the preference shown to Saraswati'; and so on.

Bana also gives a picture of Skandagupta, one of Harsha's generals, along much the same lines. He is represented as possessed of 'a natural unbending dignity, an air of command'. We hear of 'his swinging arms, which reached his knees and dangled as he moved', of 'a somewhat full and pendulous lip, sweet as ambrosia'; 'a nose as long as his sovereign's pedigree', 'a pair of long eyes, exceedingly soft, sweet, white and large, as if they had drunk the Milk Ocean', 'a forehead full and wide beyond even Meru's flank', and 'his hair, very long, naturally curling and rejoicing in a soft dark colour as if from growing in perpetual umbrella shade'.

It is obvious that the descriptions of both Harsha and Skandagupta, the general, follow a given pattern. We are here in the area of iconography. What appear at first sight to be individual characteristics—broad forehead, sharp nose, flashing teeth, full lips, brightness of appearance, long arms, shiny hair, glistening toenails—are features that one comes across again and again in Indian texts dealing with *lakshana*s of the gods and of great men like a Chakravartin, an 'All-conquering, Wheel-turning Master'.

In the *Citralakshana* of Nagnajit, a very early text, the appearance of the Chakravartin (meant very likely in this case to be the Buddha) is described at length. The text also describes various kinds of eyes: those resembling a bow made of bamboo, or an *utpala* petal, or the belly of a fish, or the petal of a *padma* lotus, or a cowrie shell. The iconographic–iconometric text moves on to other parts of the body: teeth, nails, hair, arms, hands, etc.

Evidently, a total picture is sought to be evoked through these descriptions, a picture that combines beauty of person with majesty of bearing. The text describing the Chakravartin ends with the following passage:

The Great Man turning the Wheel should be represented
like the molten gold of the Jambu river, like the hollow stem
of a lotus in full bloom, like the bright magnolia, saturated
with colour. One should know that the King of Men should
be represented with the gait of the King of Elephants, the
leader of the herd, with the gait of the Wild Goose, of the
Chakravartin. He has the rank and the great power of the
King of Elephants, the sharpness of mind of the leader of
Bulls, of a ruler, the strength of a King of Lions, the majesty
of a King of Wild Geese; such is the outward appearance of
the Master of Men.

It is easy to see a connection between passages like these and descriptions
such as those of Harsha and Skandagupta given by Bana.

The descriptions that these writers employ are not always easy to visualize.
Why then were they used? To really understand this, one must be acquainted
with the idea of *sadrishya*, one of the 'six limbs' of painting—differentiation
of forms, scale and measurements, depiction of emotion and so on—that
one comes upon in early texts. *Sadrishya*, in fact, seems to be the key in the
context of 'Indian' portraiture. For it is not to be understood as 'resemblance'
or 'verisimilitude' in the usual sense of the term: it points instead to analogies
and similes. One can here take the help of a series of illustrations that
Abanindranath Tagore got made by his pupils at Calcutta and Santiniketan,
delineating the stylization of the parts of the human body, and the body as a
whole (see p. 40).

While texts speak of 'types' of men and of women, they were differentiated by
their *lakshana*s through which persons, and their essence, could be recognized.
The artists working in the Rajput—as distinct from the Mughal—tradition,
while fitting their subjects into different types, would concentrate upon some
telltale detail. Apparently insignificant details such as the manner of sitting or

Illustrations delineating the stylization of the human body, made by the pupils of Abanindranath
Tagore at Calcutta and Santiniketan; Courtesy: Visva-Bharati, Santiniketan

standing, of dressing, of carrying an object like a staff or a pen case, would indicate the rank of the person and his or her profession or function in a given setting.

The intention was to achieve clarity. Observation was subordinated not to rules—sometimes one gets startlingly graphic details as in Bana's description of an ascetic, in the same setting as he describes Harsha, his king—but to situations. The need of each situation determined the painter's approach.

In early literature, there are countless references to 'portraits' being made, but there was no 'observed' portraiture in the art of India before the advent of the Mughals. Individualized features were rarely to be seen, whether in the so-called 'portraits' of kings or queens or donor couples. What prevailed, as an idea, was 'idealized' or 'conceptual' portraiture. It is only from the time of Akbar onward that what can be called 'true portraiture' in the sense best understood in Western terms comes into its own in India.

The great Abu'l Fazl has left us with a useful description of what went on in the area of portraiture at Akbar's court. Starting from the observation that 'drawing the likeness of anything is called *taswir*', he goes on to write, 'His Majesty himself sat for his likeness, and also ordered to have the likenesses taken of all the grandees of the realm. An immense album was thus formed: those that have passed away have received a new life, and those who are still alive have immortality promised them.' The large number of portraits from the Akbar period that have survived, and their high quality, bears this out. From that reign onward, portraiture kept gaining momentum in the Mughal setting. And one sees it attaining great heights in the reigns that follow, of Jahangir and Shahjahan.

Developments in the Rajput domains are not so linear. In painting generally there was much imitation of the Mughal style, and, in portraiture, of the Mughal mode of naturalism and observation. However, the Rajput painter,

41

once asked to take a likeness, or drawn to the idea of portraiture on his own, seems frequently to dip into his reservoir of concepts and ideas that go far back into the past, and resort to the more 'Indian' notion of what a portrait should be. Likenesses cast in the *lakshana* mould were produced by him at several centres, and some truly remarkable works which can be characterized as portraits in the Indian tradition were created between the seventeenth and nineteenth centuries.

'Normal', or observed, portraits existed side by side with them, and the Rajput painters both in Rajasthan and in the Pahari states created images of great power and vitality. They seem to be saying that this was the proper manner in which kings ought to be seen. Detaching their figures frequently from their backgrounds, which are rendered in strong, flat colours such as pure yellow or sage green, the figures of these rulers of men occupy the entire space of the picture, dramatically conveying an impression of monumentality. Even though the size of the paintings remains small, the images appear to be larger than life, the contours of the form occasionally nudging the borders, and some little detail such as a weapon spilling out.

As examples one can take some portraits from even small centres of painting like Mankot or Mandi or Basohli in the Pahari area. From Mandi, towards the end of the seventeenth century—when elsewhere, as at the Mughal court, highly refined observed portraiture was the norm—one gets several portraits of its famed ruler, Sidh Sen (see p. 358). In each one of them the painter sees and presents him as a larger-than-life figure, like some *yaksha* of old. Whether seated or standing, he towers over everyone in sight. One sees him walking with a firm step with a retainer behind, dressed in a large *chogha* carelessly thrown open in the front to reveal his hairy chest and a pair of striped drawers that enclose his pillar-like legs; striding towards a temple carrying a large platter of offerings, or seated majestically in a durbar, planning a campaign with his generals. Virtually in each of these paintings, one can spot clearly identifiable objects associated with him: a dagger with a tiger-shaped hilt, a peculiar *huqqa*, an amulet around his neck. We even see his face pockmarked. But what strikes one most is the height of the figure, and the length of his arms, which the painter has extended to make them long enough to reach down to his knees, one of the most characteristic *lakshana*s of a great man in the tradition. Quite obviously, the painter was presenting him as a legendary figure, and when one sees him in a 'portrait' cast as Shiva himself, with four arms carrying iconic objects, the picture becomes complete. It is as a deified king, a *devaraja*, that the painter wishes us to see him.

The painter's view of Sidh Sen conforms to what is remembered of him till today in Mandi: a devout man, a great believer in Tantra and in Shiva and the Devi, possessing a magical *gutka*, wearing which he would fly off to the source of the Ganga each morning to take a ritual bath and return to Mandi in time for attending to the business of state. In respect of his physical powers, it is 'remembered' that he could take a coconut in the palm of his left hand and crush it instantly to pieces. The portraits aim then at catching as much the essence of his being as his appearance.

Much the same thing happens in the small state of Mankot and at Basohli. Aquiline noses, arched eyebrows, large lotus-like eyes, broad chests and narrow waists are to be seen in portrait after portrait of rulers, whether seated or standing against flat backgrounds that yield no place to anything, not even to the sky at the top. It is as if the painter had never forgotten formulae and prescriptions as old as a thousand years or so, telling him how to render great men.

Nothing of course stays like this forever. Even as portraits of this character and this power were being made in one part of the Pahari area, sharply observed and sensitively drawn portraits were being painted in another. Points of view vary, attitudes differ, demands change. Nothing is as simple or linear as it appears to begin with. When entering Indian painting, one knows one is entering a layered world.

VII

To understand the world of Indian painting, one has to try and reconstruct three different but related areas—patrons, painters and the technique of painting. There is very little documentation so one must piece together a few facts and combine these with some speculation. Quite naturally, the three overlap, move in and out of one another, but it is of interest to go into them one by one.

Not much is recorded about the early patrons of painting. But past the days of the great mural cycles at Ajanta or Bagh, which ended by the seventh century, and with the beginning of painting in miniature on small surfaces— palm-leaf first, followed by paper in the fourteenth century—works of art turned into objects that could be owned and transported.

It was, naturally, men of means or power or influence who emerged as patrons. A monk could ask a follower to get a text written and painted for a monastic establishment; so could a princely figure with taste, or an affluent merchant or householder. The themes being religious, initially at least, there was both merit and fame, apart from genuine delight, to be gained from this act.

How painters and scribes were located or selected, what terms were negotiated, or what conversations took place, remains unknown. What we get to know, from whatever colophons that have survived, are, most often, names of patrons rather than those of the painters. The 'lotus feet' of a prelate might be mentioned; all the 'choicest blessings of heaven' might be invoked upon a patron. But the men who produced the work lurk in the shadows for the most part. From the eleventh century onward, this remains the situation for close to five hundred years. It is hard to imagine that professional groups of painters/scribes remained permanently attached to establishments or to princely figures. At the same time, it is unlikely that illustrated manuscripts could be bought and sold in the market. There probably were guilds or families that patrons would call in for commissions and specific tasks.

It is interesting that until the very end of the fifteenth century there are no images of patrons, observed or idealized, that have come down to us. If, on a Jain *patli*—a wooden book cover—two learned monks, Devasuri and Kumudchandra, appear, engaged in disputation, it is not to be assumed that the manuscript which these wooden painted covers guarded were made for either of the *muni*s or that the way they are represented is the way they looked in real life. The far greater likelihood is that the likenesses are idealized and that it was the community that had commissioned the manuscript. This, after all, is about the time that Muslim Sultanates had started being established in north India. Much of the work was being done for these Sultans and—with exceptions like Nasir-ud Din Khalji, for whom the *Ni'matnama*, the 'Book of Delicacies' of c. 1500, was produced—these Muslim patrons would have been reluctant to have themselves 'portrayed' in deference to the orthodox Islamic view.

Much changed, however, in the sixteenth century. The Mughals, who stamped their authority over the major part of the land from the mid-sixteenth century onward, were to emerge as a dynasty of men of remarkably refined taste. They had obvious fondness for painting and emerged as the most discriminating patrons of the art. The great Akbar's father, Humayun, we know, brought back with him some of the great masters of the Safavid court in Iran when he returned to India from his forced exile. We also know the great delight he took in sending examples of the sophisticated work done for him by his craftsmen to a chief in Kashgar, and we see him, in one work by the artist 'Abd-al Samad, examining a painting made by his young son while seated in a tree house. His wife, Hamida Banu, who gave birth to Akbar, also commissioned at least one Ramayana manuscript and a *Dvadasha Bhava* series based on a mythological/astrological text.

It was with Akbar, however, that an unprecedented fillip was given to painting. Abu'l Fazl's evidence on the subject is overwhelming. He writes of how a great atelier under master artists was founded, how the emperor countered the orthodox objection of the mullahs to painting, with what sharpness of eye he was able to spot talent, how he 'weekly' examined the work of his major artists, and how he commissioned his men to undertake and accomplish great projects in painting, including the *Hamzanama* extending to 1400 painted folios. This degree of enthusiasm for the art, and this level of discernment, sent clear messages to nobles at the court, to men in authority manning outlying parts of his empire, and to those at its periphery. A truly great patron of painting had emerged.

Of his son Jahangir's passion for painting and the pride he took in the work of his painters a great deal is known. He wrote in his memoirs about the gifted men whom he used to take with him on his travels, on whom he conferred glittering titles—Nadir-al Zaman, Nadir-al 'Asr, and the like, meaning 'Wonder of the Age', 'Rarity of the Times'. He inscribed notes in his own hand on their work, and summoned them in haste to record anything new or different that he saw, from a dying man to a rare flower, or a bird of rare plumage.

'On this date,' he would write with unbridled enthusiasm in 1618,

> Abu'l Hasan the artist, who had been awarded the title of Nadir-al Zaman presented a painting he had made for the opening page of the *Jahangirnama*. Since it was worthy of praise he was shown limitless favours. Without exaggeration, his work is perfect, and his depiction is a masterpiece of the age. In this era he has no equal or peer. Only if Master Abdul Hayy and Master Bihzad were alive today would they be able to do him justice.

One finds similar passion in an account of the Mughal grandee, the great Khan Khanan, Abdul Rahim, and the artist he patronized, Miyan Nadim:

> He was a slave of the Commander-in-Chief . . . He was so skilled in drawing and painting that, since the days of Mani

and Bihzad, none has been born who can rival him. He acquired this proficiency in the library, and in the service of this Commander-in-Chief. In fact, the exalted Khan Khanan himself raised him to this high level. Thus, under the training of the Khan Khanan, he became a peerless master in his art. He breathed his last in the service of his master. He had a comfortable and carefree life, as he was handsomely paid by the Khan Khanan.

It is not difficult to imagine what patronage such as this, at the highest level—there were other grandees like Mirza Aziz Koka, Nawab Bahadur Khan, Prince Daniyal—must have meant to the painters who worked for the emperors. They must have worked harder than ever before, and vied with one another to catch the emperor's eye. To be able to attach sobriquets like 'Humayun Shahi', 'Jahangir Shahi' to their names in inscribed paintings would have been high reward in itself.

To be working directly for the emperor brought to the painter evident prestige, but there would have been great honour even in working at the sub-imperial level. The tone of the relationship between painters working for the emperor and others who worked for grandees is hard to guess at, and one does not even know if an 'imperial' painter was occasionally given permission to work for a prince or a highly placed noble. But the sense one gets from the period is that in Mughal India it was at the court and in the courtly circles where painting had come to 'reside'.

In the rest of India—the Mughals were powerful overlords but did not directly rule over all areas—the situation as far as patronage is concerned must also have started taking on something of the hue of the prestigious imperial centre. However, at the Rajput courts—in Rajasthan and the Pahari region—and at the Deccani courts, the atmosphere is likely to have been different. For one thing, there were no 'workshops' there of the kind that one reads about at the Mughal court—no halls or buildings situated in the capital city where stern *ustad*s sat presiding over all that happened, and artists from diverse backgrounds sat working together. Work for the Rajput courts was done within families of painters, in 'family workshops', so to speak, not necessarily located in the state capital or nearby, and not made up of artists from different backgrounds or extraction. Obviously, here too there were seniors and juniors, authority and obedience, and one can visualize deference being paid to masters who headed the family. But the tone of the relationship must have been that between members of a family.

It is difficult to gain an idea of how comfortable the painter was in the presence of his imperial master at the Mughal court, how freely he was able to speak to him, or discuss a point. But one has the feeling that it is likely to have been a relationship of the kind between an exalted master and lowly painter, in which there was little relaxation and much formality. At the Rajput courts, in contrast, the atmosphere, it appears, was quite different. Undoubtedly, there were hierarchies here too and a sharp consciousness of rank and status. But when one sees paintings of durbar scenes one notices that everyone, or nearly everyone of any status, sits, like the ruler, on the carpeted floor, in fairly close proximity, eyes at the same level. One gains the impression therefore that here things might have been more relaxed, and the relations between patron and painter might not have been overly affected by the tensions of formality.

The impression is strengthened by the stories that one hears from painters belonging to the tradition: of rajas walking into the homes of painters to check on the progress of commissioned work, or of painters declining to part with paintings that they thought had not truly been 'understood' by the patron. The occasional document that surfaces also points to this: a patron intervening on behalf of his painter who had been involved in a case of alleged murder, or a painter accompanying the ashes of his patron for immersion in the Ganga.

In situations such as these, it is easy to imagine informal conversations between patron and painter, even discussions about specific plans. One can almost see a painter being 'ordered' by his patron, the Maharana of Mewar, to prepare for him a Book of Darshans, 'auspicious sights', that he would like to gaze at each morning before the business of the day began, and the painter humbly asking in turn detailed questions about those sights or visions before beginning his work. Likewise, one can almost hear the painter Devidasa explaining to Kripal Pal of Basohli why he was inclined to replace the figure of Krishna in the *Rasamanjari* series with that of a *nayak*, a mortal lover; and the raja turning around to ask him, or the learned pandit seated next to him, if this would still be in consonance with the spirit of the text.

In the Rajput or Deccani setting, one does not hear of the ceremony with which grand titles were conferred upon painters by their Mughal patrons. The evidence we have shows that payments too were relatively modest in these kingdoms. It is also likely that painters could move between courts without displeasing their patrons. A painter like Chokha could move between Mewar and Devgarh without much problem, it seems; Kripal or Devidasa could move from Nurpur to take up an assignment at Basohli; the same master painter could work both for Maharao Kishor Singh of Kota and the prelate of Nathdwara, Dauji.

Certainly loyalties could have been formed and closeness could have grown, as between Balwant Singh of Jasrota and his painter Nainsukh (see p. 362) who had apparently free access to his patron and painted him in all kinds of situations: listening to music, having his beard trimmed, writing a letter sitting on a camp bed wrapped up in a quilt, stalking a duck or standing, umbrella in hand, supervising construction.

For painters, there must have been other patrons too: members of the royal household or fraternity, heads of religious establishments, even affluent merchants. In the nineteenth century, in fact, one knows of painters, like those from Kashmir, picking up occasional commissions while doing the rounds of the countryside; also of painters sitting, as at Kalighat, working for pilgrims; and at given centres, in the 'Company' phase, producing albums for East India Company's 'sahibs' and 'memsahibs'. When, over time, the old mould of patronage broke, painters began to 'hawk' their wares, and an open market for their work began to grow. But by and large, the paradigm that had emerged in the sixteenth century held firm for centuries. Painters were retained men who worked for patrons, mostly of the royal class, and payments in one form or the other underlay relationships.

Clearly, we have some information, but there is so much more that we don't know. How, for instance, did painters perceive their role—as that of servants or slaves—once they entered royal service? What freedoms, if any, did they have? Were they bound by the tastes and preferences of the patron or could they produce work of their own accord? Were individual works of art discussed and commented upon by the patron? Again, did every court have an atelier of its own? How did patron and painter come together in the first instance, and how did they part? Did the most affluent patrons attract the best talent among painters? Were there disagreements? Was there disenchantment? Did painters have the luxury of making choices as far as patrons were concerned?

Questions like these are not easy to answer. But two statements, each in its own way, tell us something. One: 'We are like sunflowers,' remarked a painter who came from a family that had worked in the tradition for ten generations or more. And the second is a witty but meaningful prayer in the scribal colophon of a manuscript: 'Protect me, Lord,' pleads the manuscript, 'from oil, from water, from fire, and from poor binding. And save me from falling into the hands of a fool!'

VIII

We know so little about the Indian painters of the past that it is tempting to stand E.H. Gombrich's famous dictum on its head—'There really is no such thing as Art; there are only artists'—and say, of the art of India, that 'There really are no artists; there is only art.' This might be something of an exaggeration because, of late, energetic efforts have been made by scholars to accord primacy to artists: to dig out names, compile lists, put together genealogies, reconstruct styles and speculate on contexts. Till close to half a century ago, the artist was taken for granted, anonymity was believed to be the natural condition of Indian art, and no artist was written about because one did not know much about him. Today, hundreds of names can be cited; directory-like works containing names and the barest of facts or speculations have been compiled. All the same, our information remains thin. It does not go much beyond a few signatures, a handful of inscriptions containing facts, passing notices, attributions made by past librarians or today's scholars, names gleaned from registers at pilgrimage centres or storekeepers' records, or land grants. As noted earlier, no biographies or long accounts of painters have come down; when, and if at all, patrons or chroniclers speak of artists, they do it only briefly and in their own voices.

A few documents have surfaced and been published: a grant of land given to a painter by his patron; a petition made by a painter begging for his emoluments to be raised; an entry made by a painter in the register of a priest at a centre of pilgrimage; a letter written by one member of a painter's family to another; a colophon recording a date, a name, a place. But, even as one gratefully reads and ponders over all these, one is left with the feeling that the information they yield is still scrappy and partial. A rough outline emerges, not a complete picture.

Of all the periods, or schools, of Indian painting, it is the Mughal which appears to be the richest in information. Even here, however, there are no continuous accounts, and no more than passing bits of information. There are mentions of his most gifted painters—Abu'l Hasan or Mansur or Bishan Das—by the emperor Jahangir in his memoirs, but they are brief and have the general air of reminiscence about them. From the earlier reign, that of Akbar, one gets a whole chapter on the 'Arts of Writing and Painting' by Abu'l Fazl, that tireless chronicler. The account has promising statements, like there being 'more than a hundred painters [who] have become famous masters of the art'. But when it comes to writing specifically about any of those whom the writer designates as 'the forerunners on the high road of art', even the great Persian masters Mir Sayyid Ali and Khwaja 'Abd-al Samad find only brief and somewhat desiccated mention. The longest entry on any painter by Abu'l Fazl is this:

> Then there was Daswant, the son of a palanquin-bearer (*kahar*), who was in the service of this workshop and, urged by a natural desire, used to draw images and designs on walls. One day the far-reaching glance of His Majesty fell on those things and, in its penetrating manner, discerned the spirit of a master working in them. Consequently, His Majesty entrusted him to the Khwaja ('Abd-al Samad). In just a short time he became matchless in his time and the most excellent (*sar-amad-i ruzgar*), but the darkness of insanity enshrouded the brilliance of his mind and he died, a suicide. He has left several masterpieces.

The information is tantalizing and one just begins to sense the presence of a real person. So also with the master 'Abd-al Samad, who, in a note he inscribed on his painting of two camels fighting (see p. 290), speaks of his 'now being at the infirm age of five and eighty years', when his 'faculties have become feeble', his 'brush has slowed down', and his 'remarkable sight grown dim'. But that is all the information about himself the aged painter gives, for he then moves on to say that his work is intended for his 'knowledgeable and astute son, Sharif Khan . . . who understands the subtleties of the most obscure points of awareness', and upon whom blessings are invoked.

Silence still largely surrounds the painters of the past. It is still not possible to feel the texture of these people's lives or the grain of their thought, or to enter with confidence the world of their religious beliefs, their joys and aspirations, the pains they lived with, the 'slings and arrows' they had to bear. One is not far off the mark when one compares the situation of the Indian art historian searching for firm 'facts' with that of the *abhisarika nayika*—the classical heroine of literary descriptions—who steps out on a stormy night into the darkness of the forest to keep her tryst, her path lit only by an occasional flash of lightning in the sky.

Things were of course different for painters working at different courts, or centres. At the Mughal court where talent seems to have been recognized and rewarded by discerning patrons, competition among artists must have been fierce and master artists must have controlled their workshops with iron hands. In that situation, no one could have assumed that employment in the studio would be in perpetuity.

No painter, however meritorious, could have taken it for granted that his son would find similar employment or that he would inherit his mantle. Artists must have had to fight to keep their jobs, and sons of gifted fathers must have had to earn their way into the favour of the court on the strength of their own talent. One reads about some fathers and sons making good together or one after another—'Abd-al Samad and his son, Sharif Khan, for instance; Basawan and his son, Manohar; Aqa Riza and his two immensely talented sons, Abu'-l Hasan and 'Abid; Bhawani Das and his son, Govardhan; Mahesh and his son, Miskin. In general, however, positions in the imperial ateliers were not filled on the basis of lineage or heredity.

At the Rajput courts where things worked differently, on the other hand, a painter might have been able to assume that his children would also be entitled to the same patronage as he himself. The pattern that obtained there was of 'family workshops', most painters living not at the court, or in the capital town, but in their village homes on pieces of land granted to them by the patron virtually in perpetuity. Painting was a hereditary profession there. This must have made it possible for painters to have had a greater sense of security and, in that situation, equally possible, in generation after generation, for young talent to be nurtured along different lines, work to be distributed, continuities to be maintained, memories to remain strong and members of the family to keep painting—if not for the same royal house, then for another branch of it or for another court.

One can take as an example the 'history' of the family of Pandit Seu of Guler in the Pahari region. The pandit's two sons—Manaku and Nainsukh—were painters with greatly celebrated talents. Manaku's two sons, Fattu and Khushala, were painters as were all four of Nainsukh's sons—Kama, Gaudhu, Nikka and Ranjha. The line passed on, we know from records kept in the registers of priests at pilgrim centres, with nearly everyone continuing to paint. Not everyone could possibly have had the same gift, nor could every single person have painted at the same level. But patrons continued to patronize the family and the tree kept being watered, as the local saying goes, even when the leaves began to fall. The last scion of this family, Chandu Lal, was painting into his last days less than a generation ago, and still had in his possession sketches and drawings that went back to the times of Manaku, some seven generations before him.

As regards the general status of the painter in earlier times, whether at court or in society, the evidence we have access to does not appear to be consistent. One cannot see it with clarity even at the Mughal court. On the one hand one reads about truly gifted artists receiving great favours, being honoured with seductively phrased titles: Nadir-al Zaman, Nadir-al 'Asr in the case of painters; Zarrin Qalam (of the golden pen), Mushkin Qalam (of musk-like pen), 'Anbarin Qalam (of amber pen) and the like in the case of calligraphers.

The very same painters, on the other hand, would refer to themselves as *ghulam* (slave), *banda-i dargah* (humble servant of the exalted house) or *kamtarin* (the lowliest of the low) while signing their works. One can see that courtly custom is at work in these usages, and attitudes of great humility are assumed, not just by painters but also by nobles and grandees at the court. But in life, there was material difference between the two. Painters wielded no power, unlike those grandees; and their daughters did not marry into the royal family. The painters' description of their humble status in their signatures might therefore have been not far from the way it actually was.

When, on occasion, we see a painter induct himself into a durbar scene or a gathering, we see him standing in an obscure corner, like a retainer, recognizable either through a tiny inscription or through the tools of his trade that he carries: a brush case tucked into the waistband, a satchel with an album slung across the shoulder, or a painting in his hand.

We hardly ever see the highly regarded Abu'l Hasan standing in close proximity to his patron, whether Jahangir or Shahjahan; and when he refers to himself in a 'signature' as *kamtarin-i khanazadan* (the lowliest among those born in the imperial household), one begins to wonder about his real position. Probably the most telling of images as far as the status of the painter at the Mughal court goes is that of Keshava Das, without doubt among the greatest of Mughal painters, standing, bent with age, with a petition addressed to his patron, the emperor Akbar, in hand. The image is often published showing Keshava Das alone, standing by himself. But it is a detail and tells only a part of the truth. In the complete painting, the emperor is seen at some distance, far above, speaking with someone, while a minor court functionary, an *akhta-begi* according to the inscription, appears below, advancing towards the aged painter, chastising rod in hand, shooing him away.

There is nothing conclusive about any of this, but it is not too unlikely that even though relationships at the Rajput court may not have been as hierarchical as at the Mughal court, the painters often refer to themselves as *das* (lowly servant), *chakar* (menial) or *nafar* (humble commoner). Perhaps everyone, not only the painter, found himself in this position vis-à-vis the ruler.

A most interesting insight, however, is provided by a chance discovery—a letter or representation made by a painter, Shiba, to one of the best-known patrons of the arts in the Pahari region, Sansar Chand of Kangra. This is how the letter, written in very neat Takri characters—Takri is the general script of the Pahari area—on a sheet decorated with daintily executed lotus leaves and flowers all along the margins, reads:

> Om. To the illustrious Rajadhiraja, Maharaja, Parambhattaraka, Shri Shri Shri Sansar Chand (may peace be upon him!) from his humble servant, the painter Shiba. Every day he [Shiba] salutes you with 'Jai Deya'; pray grant acceptance of his touching of your feet. Now be it known that owing to the righteous rule of the Maharaja, this humble servant is happy. May the Lord of the World [literally, 'the master'] [rule] in safety and joy, that your countless subjects may be blessed.
>
> Further, O Maharaja, this is my humble submission: that you had said [to me]: 'Do not go back to your home; if you do, I will punish you. Stay you now by my side in future.' I believe, O Maharaja, that it was truth indeed that you spoke for, first, I am without food; I am, in fact, dying. Secondly, truly did you show great kindness to me, your humble servant. So much so that you granted me employment by the side [under the care of] Gaudhu. But the reality of that 'employment' is that the accountant, Sardaru, does not give me anything out of that. He offers me taunts instead: he does not take [enrol?] your humble servant.

You had said that I should bring my family over. It is good that I did not do that, for just as your humble servant here has fallen on bad days and is without food, so would they [my family] have suffered. Your servant has been living on debts [of several rupees] that he has incurred here. Now, however, no one gives [a loan?] any more.

The thing that matters is one's own self [literally, 'belly']. All rights or wrongs that anyone does, he does for his own dear self, and not without a cause. Do be kind, O Maharaja, and allow this humble servant of yours now to depart. He is helpless for here he goes without food. And forgive, please, the sins and faults of this humble servant.

Several things can be read in this letter: a painter from elsewhere taking up employment in the royal court; the threat of punishment; the existence of a supervisory mechanism, among other things. In the context of the painter's status or position, one notices that notwithstanding his relatively lowly station—consider the salutation, the touching of the feet, the repeated references to 'this humble servant', the asking for forgiveness for all 'sins and faults'—Shiba has written a bold letter. It may be couched in politic language, but it is also candid and caustic. There is no knowing what this letter led to, for nothing else has survived. We only have this outburst of dismay and anger.

There are other instances of painters lamenting their state: the petition that, in a portrait of his, Mir Musavvir, aged father of the master artist Mir Sayyid Ali, is seen holding in his hand; the representation made by the painter Saudagar to the Rani of Garhwal after her husband, the artist's original patron, had died. Keshava Das was probably trying to make his representation to the emperor towards a similar end. They are all importuning the patron for enhanced emoluments.

One does not know what these painters were paid, for no figures have come down. It is possible that a few, perhaps very few, of the painters, apart from being highly honoured with titles and the like, or appointed to positions of rank—as at the Mughal court—lived lives of comfort. But in general the depressing feeling one gets is that the Indian painter's life was one of hardship, if not penury; one can almost hear the blunt pounding of the hammer of want in the background.

The picture painted by the French physician Bernier, who travelled through parts of India in the second half of the seventeenth century, during the emperor Aurangzeb's reign, might be a bit exaggerated, for he speaks almost with anger of the destitute state of the artists working in the grandees' *karkhana*s, always living in fear of the *korrah*—whip—and yet there might be a core of truth in what he says.

In general, at least in the Pahari area from which we have a measure of hard evidence, retained painters seem to have been 'paid' in three different ways. One, through the conferment of a small piece of land for building their homestead and living off its produce; two, by being paid in cash, something like a salary per month; and, three, by being given rations in kind, in the nature of a daily allowance, whenever they were away from home and doing duty at court. The first must obviously have operated in a situation where the painter was not only offered employment and attached to the court, but his successors also stayed in service, as hereditary artists running a 'family workshop'; and the third introduces the idea that painters ordinarily lived in their own homes, however modestly, and left them only from time to time to be present at the court, when required, or when an occasion arose.

This at least is the sense one gets from a small group of documents that have survived from the first half of the nineteenth century. They relate to members of a family of Pahari painters who moved to the plains of the Punjab for taking up employment under Sikh nobles, or with the maharaja at Lahore. The family to which these painters belonged had, earlier, been given a piece of land by the Raja of Chamba to live on, but that state having now become subject to Sikh control, the painters had sought and received employment in the plains of the Punjab where power resided.

The land they lived on was in the nature of a small *jagir*, but all *jagir*s have to be reconfirmed whenever one rule succeeds another. One of these documents speaks in tones of authority to the present and future *'amil*s of the *taaluqa* of Haripur and Guler' to hand over the *jagir*, valued at 100 rupees per annum, conferred upon the painter Gokul as a retainer for his services, and 'not to offer any obstruction in this matter'. Another document states that from the date mentioned in the month of Jyeshtha of the year 1843, the same painter, 'Gokul, son of Nikka, son of Nainsukh', is to be treated as an employee on the following terms: 'Rations: six and a half seers; Payment per mensem: rupees thirty; Jagir land; as before [?]'. The orders are that this fact be entered in the records.

Documents like this may not tell us as much as we might want to know, but they do illumine a shadowy area. It is clear that one has to reconstruct, piece together a picture, and for that it is necessary to read between faint and broken lines. Equally necessary perhaps is to speculate upon the circumstances, whether formal or private and intimate, in which a painter grew up and trained. Once again, there are only shreds of information, but every little thing helps.

From the Mughal world there are some indicators. There, it seems, the master–pupil relationship was of a stern, and possibly very rigid, nature. The *ustad* was an *ustad*: no questions asked. Whether he ruled over a studio or instructed a student in private, his authority was unquestioned. There is a very revealing leaf from an illustrated manuscript of the *Akhlaq-i Nasiri*, a compendium of rules and conduct belonging to the Jahangiri period, in which the theme treated of is the nature of authority and how it is wielded.

The painter responsible for illustrating this chose to depict a studio where painters and calligraphers are at work. At the top sits an *ustad*, with one cautionary finger raised, instructing a princely figure who is writing; other men, at least two of them painters, sit a little below, painting; one man is busy burnishing a sheet of paper; servants and attendants stand about. The text speaks of the *ustad*—he who is 'capable of imagining the end from within himself'—and his pupils, those who, initially at least, are 'totally lacking in the capacity for invention', but preserve 'the directions of the master craftsman on the matter in hand, carefully follow them out so that the task is completed'. It is easy to read meanings into the painting.

Then there is a remarkable painting—again from the Mughal period—showing a young scholar seated alone while below him, on the ground, lie a wooden tablet and a scroll (see p. 286). On the tablet is inscribed a short verse, a well-known Persian aphorism perhaps, which reads: 'On the tablet [of the heart] are to be written these words in letters of gold / "The sternness of a master is far above a father's fondness".' If, as has been suggested, the work is a self-portrait of the great master Mir Sayyid Ali, at an age when he must have still been a pupil himself, it is not unlikely that he might have brought these words in as a reminder to himself.

From the Rajput world too one comes upon instances of the sternness with which master artists treated their pupils, but somehow one gets the feeling that the impersonal, and possibly distant, relationships that one associates with Mughal workshops did not exist here, largely because it was within families of artists that instruction and training took place. The routine here too must have been rigorous and demanding. But for a young boy growing up and learning, there must have been the warmth of natural affection within a family which, like a large wrap, would have been all around him.

There may not have been much rest, or periods of relaxation, for the work in hand was always demanding, but one can see young members of the family initially being given, somewhat lighter tasks: cleaning brushes, turning twigs slowly over fire for preparing charcoal sticks, making *waslis*—layered sheets of paper—and the like. Traditional painters speak about young pupils being asked to repeatedly draw figures and patterns with charcoal sticks on wooden tablets covered with a thin, dried layer of clay dissolved in water and, later, graduating on to doing the same thing on paper, which was not always available in abundant quantities.

The next task would have been to hold the brush firmly in one hand, the other pressing the paper down on a tablet resting on a flexed knee. 'Draw for me folded hands one hundred times, first as seen from left, and then as seen from right' is what one painter of today recalls having been instructed to do by his father. 'Now draw the trunk of Ganesha curling towards the left, one hundred times, and then, the same number of times, curling towards the right.' And so on. Thus would pass years before real painting began; and that was another regime of hard training and practice.

It was not only technique or skill, one imagines, that was being passed on from generation to generation. There was also constant enrichment of the mind. No didactics were involved here, but almost unnoticed—for it was all in the form of stories, whether from the Puranas or from the epics—characters and situations would come to life for the young learner. Some of the characters may have appeared so real that they could be walking by his side, weaving themselves into his thoughts. Quite naturally, boys and girls in the family would sit huddled up around a grandmother, listening and absorbing. There would also, one imagines, have been occasions when they would listen to senior members of the family discussing works. Old drawings would be taken out of battered iron boxes and looked at with interest and reverence, for they were heirlooms, material remains of the thoughts of an earlier generation. How a pigment behaves, or what goes wrong while making a brush, and other such matters are likely to have been discussed. Formal education—reading and writing, interpreting texts, etc.—would have been entrusted to a family pandit, or someone in the neighbourhood. Perhaps the young boy would, in the course of this, even pick up some knowledge of and taste for poetry.

All this while the grind of household routine would have continued. The young boy would also be feeding the family cow, running errands in the village bazaar, fetching water from the river, and so on. Following family tradition, he would also be learning how to sit at prayers, memorize *shlokas* and mantras, making sure to wash his hands and feet before sitting down to draw, watching a senior sit in meditation. All these things would imprint themselves upon the young mind: it is not only the task at hand, but thinking about it that makes for better work; withdrawing into oneself cleanses the mind; constantly seeing work done in your family and by others sharpens the eyes; and the like. There was always thus a gathering of thoughts and impressions, a shoring up of the riches of the mind. Later, life would take its own course, bringing its own stresses and challenges, but these years were critical.

None of this is recorded, and most of these speculations come from conversations with present-day members of old painter families, mostly from the Pahari tradition. But one imagines that—mutatis mutandis—things must have proceeded elsewhere in much the same way within families or groups that practised other faiths or had different cultural leanings.

IX

However imperfect the description might be, works on paper that make up the vast majority of Indian paintings go by the name of 'miniatures'. They can vary greatly in size—from being smaller than postcards or, in some cases, not appreciably larger than outsized postage stamps to being close to a metre in height. Yet the label remains. It is retained possibly for good reasons, serving as it does at least three purposes: establishing that these paintings do not belong to the mural category, and come after the great age of mural painting in India had passed; drawing pointed attention to the technique involved in making them; and, above all perhaps, emphasizing the preciousness of their character.

Like a book, a miniature was meant to be taken in the hand and seen—'read' might describe it better—from close, so that the eye could move lingeringly over its small surface, take in its luminous colours, absorb every subtlety of detail, every pressure on the brush, and be led through it to the matrix of thoughts and images from which it had sprung.

The earliest 'miniatures' in India that one can speak of—at least from those that have survived—go back to the eleventh century, and are to be found in books written on palm-leaf, the paintings either integrated into the text scripted on loose leaves, or made on the inside of the wooden covers that held the book together. Later, the physical connection between paintings and books became thinner, or loose, for other formats like portfolios came in. But the connection with books did not ever completely die. Like finely handwritten books, paintings would be kept tucked away as precious objects, taken out only from time to time, to be read and shared; and, like books, they would be admired not only for their content, but also for their form. Fineness of workmanship was almost always admired, for it was, as they say, 'a delight for the eye, a comfort to the mind'.

A great artist like Mir Sayyid Ali might paint a polo game in progress on a grain of rice, but even when he would be involved in painting a folio of the *Hamzanama*, nearly a metre in height, the workmanship in it remained of the same order—in every single detail, from jewel-like tile mosaics to dainty patterns on textiles and the tongues of fire emitted by snarling dragons— refined and precise and meticulously executed.

Almost always, the field belonged to professionals. One hears of course of skilled amateurs—princes and princesses with leisure on their hands, and the like—but the field was not theirs. The rigour of the discipline, the knowledge needed of technical intricacies, was something that came from years of practice, whether working under an *ustad* or in a family workshop. The range of materials that the painters used, and the elaborate processes that painting a miniature involved, must have differed from region to region and from one painting tradition to another. But nowhere does there seem to have been any substitute for working, practising, day after day, year after year.

There were treatises that spoke of technique and materials—from the early world in India, works like the *Chitrasutra*, the *Manasollasa*, the *Shilparatna*; or from the 'Islamic' tradition, works like the *Qanun al-Suwar* of Sadiq Beg—but knowing them or reading from them could not have served the professional painter in the manner or to the extent that doing things did. There was valuable information in the texts, and yet some of it was so complex or obscure that only working under a guru or *ustad* could unlock it. *Shastra* (theory) is one thing, as they say, and *prayoga* (praxis) another.

On early surfaces for writing and painting alone—birchbark, coarse cotton cloth, wooden panels, leaves of the talipot palm or palmyra, *sri-tada* and *khar-tada* respectively, for example—a great deal can be said: their innate nature or *svabhava*, preparing them to receive ink or pigment, the use of brush or iron stylus, and so on. Or on paper again—which came into use in India somewhere between the thirteenth and fourteenth centuries—one can go into countless details: differences in its nature and quality depending on the centre where it was produced, the raw material used to make it, processes like sizing, burnishing. There is then the whole field of pigments and brushes and binding media; and the methods of working.

Fortunately, a few paintings have survived, most of them from the Mughal period, in which one can catch a glimpse of the materials and techniques used. These are essentially portraits of painters—Daulat, Govardhan, Manohar, Abu'l Hasan, Bishan Das—seen seated, working, with their tools, brushes, pigment-containing oyster shells, brush cases, and so on, lying by their side. These are not complete paintings in themselves and can be seen on the margins of a page of calligraphy in the Gulshan album, or following or accompanying colophons at the end of great manuscripts. But they clearly evoke an atmosphere. On the last page of a *Khamsa* of Nizami, for instance, a calligrapher and a painter appear together—the calligrapher 'Abd-al Rahim 'Ambarin Qalam, absorbed in writing, and the painter Daulat, with a *takhti*-tablet resting on his knee, dipping his brush in a little cup by his side. For those searching for clues about the life of painters, and the manner in which they worked, the entire manuscript suddenly comes to life. But one also begins to wonder how many pens or brushes there are in that pen case, or what else there is in that album on the carpet, close to Daulat.

The making of brushes, like so much else, was the domain of the painter himself. While some texts speak of brushes made from fine hair taken from the inside of a calf's ears, or from a horse's tail, the finest ones were made from the soft hair taken from a squirrel's tail. Each hair was inserted, one at a time, gently tapped through the thin, hollow tube of a bird's feather which led to its coming out on top, as Sadiqi said in poetic terms in his *Qanun-al Suwar*, like a dainty bud. The most refined of the brushes, as a Mughal legend has it, was made of a single hair—the *yak bal qalam*—and could be used only by the greatest of masters.

On pigments that the painters used, or preferred, different accounts have been written. Early texts speak of there being only 'five colours'—red, blue, yellow, black and white—through which a range of colours 'without number' could be obtained. The colours were obtained from both the mineral and vegetal world. White came from white lead or zinc; sometimes also from burnt conch shells or kaolin. Black was obtained, for the most part, from lamp black, for the preparation of which old formulas were laid down and known; there is mention also of a mineral source for black called antimony. Red, a favourite of painters, came from diverse sources: crude cinnabar, red ochre, lead oxide, red arsenic, lac resin and the kermes insect. Blue was obtained mostly from minerals—lapis lazuli or azurite—but also from indigo.

Yellow had arguably the most 'interesting' sources. It usually came from orpiment or turmeric, or, from saffron and flowers of the *palash* tree; but the most Indian and brilliant of all yellows, that went under the name of *peori* or *gao-goli*, came from—as painters are very fond of telling, although this is contested—the urine of a cow that had been fed on mango leaves or had an affected liver. Green, the most problematic of colours—for if made from acetate of copper it starts eating into paper after some time—could of course be obtained from mixing the primaries, blue and yellow, but terre verte, malachite and verdigris are mentioned prominently as its source.

Then, there was gold—'that fount of brilliance, descended from the sun'— and silver, the making and application of which required great patience and skill. It was a master artist who would tell the pupil if the sizing, generally gum arabic, mixed with gold was too little or too much. Too little and the gold would not stick to the painting. Too much, and it would lose its lustre and be hard to burnish. The technique of applying gold had clearly been known and mastered since very early times as can be seen in the generous use of the colour in Jain paintings to sumptuous effect.

Painters speak of 'recipes' of colours preserved since 'olden times' and kept as secrets within families. Preparation was the key and it was not easy. From a recipe for preparing lac dye to be used in painting, as recorded in a text, one can judge the intricacy of the method and the need for experience.

> Pure water should be made to boil at a high temperature.
> In this bubbling hot water, the powder of lac resin should
> be gradually mixed. The water should be stirred all the
> time to prevent the resin from turning solid. After this, the

temperature of the water should be raised further, and at brief intervals, powders of lode and borax should be thrown in. To ascertain whether the colour is ready, a simple test can be applied. Dipping the pen in the solution, a few lines should be drawn upon paper. If the ink does not split, the colour is ready.

In general, the technique used in nearly all Indian paintings is described as gouache, sometimes as 'opaque watercolour on paper', and there are many stages through which the making of a painting passes. The first step is to draw, in rough outline, a sketch with a charcoal stick with only the rudiments of a composition being brought in. If a pounce or stencil is used for producing a copy or version of another, earlier painting, the outline is still drawn with a charcoal stick. The initial drawing is then firmed up in sanguine with a brush, and some details are introduced. This is followed by a thin coat of priming in white. The priming must be truly thin, for the 'under-drawing' has to show which, in the next step, is firmed up with a black line. Blemishes are taken out and some burnishing done to turn it into a ground on which colours are applied.

The first coat of pigments is thin, but the order in which colours are applied varies, some artists preferring to use only lighter shades first. There is variation, too, in the direction in which colours are applied, most artists preferring to work from the top downwards on a page. Pigments are applied in stages, layer after layer, and after each coat is applied, the painting is placed face down on a flat surface—one hears of ivory sheets, now of glass panes—and burnished from the back with an agate stone or a conch shell, using some pressure. This process does two things at once: it fuses the pigments to the surface and imparts upon the painting a measure of lustre.

Thus far the work looks somewhat bland and uninteresting. Then come the final steps, the first being *khulai*, literally, 'opening up'. Every outline turns

The different stages (from left to right) in the making of a painting by Sharda Prasad of Benares;
Courtesy: The Museum of Fine Arts of the Panjab University, Chandigarh

crisp, every detail comes to life. The work begins to open its eyes, as it were. If one were to see the different stages through which a painting goes—the same scene or motif repeated but moving from one state to the next—the experience is like that of a polaroid film slowly developing in front of us, like a bud unfolding its petals one by one (see above).

Other processes follow: *pardaz*, meaning fine shading, is done and of this there are several kinds, each bearing a distinct name; stippling, where needed, is done; gold is applied but, unlike different pigments, never burnished from the back with the painting placed face down, for that could damage it. Whatever burnishing is needed is done from front, often with a small, pointed stone called *gholti*, or, if available, with a boar's tusk. The final, absolutely the last stage, apart from the colouring of the borders and margins, is called *moti mahavar* (pearl and henna) work, in which the minutest of detailing is painted in: impasto is applied on ornaments and jewellery, 'tooling' is done, lips and fingertips reddened.

One can see that the process is extremely refined and detailed, and painters often speak of how fragile it is, for anything can go wrong at any stage. Drawing is one matter, but painting is another—it is time-consuming and when we come, occasionally, upon an *ustad*'s instruction, directing a pupil to finish a particular painting within 'five and a half days', one knows that the pressure on the painter must have been enormous. As a matter of course, assistance was required in any case. Tasks like the preparation of *wasli*s, the grinding of pigments, the filling in of minor but routine details—adding blossoms to a creeper, making patterns on a carpet, decorating a border with an oft-used motif, and the like—were given to young boys and women of the household in 'family workshops', and to paid assistants in atelier situations. What did not change, however, was the fact that the overall control of the main work stayed with the master artist.

Another kind of collaboration—the one that was more public, though not too common—was that of more than one artist working on the same painting. Since the processes were of different orders, and bore different names in the Mughal tradition—*tarah*, meaning drawing, *'amal* meaning the application of colours, *chehra*, meaning the putting in of faces—one gets inscriptions sometimes in the form of librarians' or recorders' notes that assign credit to different artists who had worked on the same painting. Thus, in an Akbar-period painting, the inscription at the bottom of a page might read: *tarah-i Basawan, 'amal-i Mansur*, meaning the drawing in this work was

69

by Basawan and the colouring was Mansur's work. On occasions, a further refinement was added, the *chehra-i naami*—the principal or most important face—might be in the hand of an artist other than the one who worked on the remaining *chehra*s. In the making of a whole book, of course, several specialists were needed to collaborate: the *warraq* (page maker), the *jadwal-kash* (line drawer), the *hashiya-kash* (margin maker), the *katib* or *khushnawis* (scribe or calligrapher), the *musavvir* (painter), the *mudhahhib* (illuminator) and the *mujallad* (binder).

A far less visible but real collaboration—something that is not often spoken of and is documented even less—must have existed between painters and men of learning who knew literary texts and the subtleties of language. Stories that were to be painted—'illustrated' is the usual but unfair expression often used—might have been known to the painter, and royal durbars and processions might not have to be 'understood'. But when it came to poetic works, for instance, surely the painter would have needed help in understanding words and expressions, for upon that understanding would depend the subtlety and refinement that he could bring to his work. At the Mughal court, to take an example, if a painter were to be asked to illustrate the verses of Hafiz, or the poetry of Anvari—filled with puns and metaphors and literary conceits—he would necessarily have sought help from men learned in these texts or literature in general. Likewise, if in a Rajput setting the Sanskrit text of Bhanudatta's *Rasamanjari* or the laconic but power-charged *dhyana*s of the Goddess were to be given visual form, surely the words and their meanings, both obvious and obscure, would have had to be elaborated upon for the painter by some scholar.

Fortunately, there is some surviving evidence that points towards such collaboration. In the preliminary drawings of the famous *Nala–Damayanti* series from the Pahari area, one finds brief notes on the margins of some folios, containing comments or instructions for the painter when he turns to making paintings based on these drawings. Thus, upon seeing a drawing, someone—a pandit perhaps, or a senior and learned member of the family who knew the complex Sanskrit text on which the series was based—would write, briefly, that when finished, the pomegranate tree at the back of the garden should be shown laden with fruit, for it is that sight of the tree which reminds Nala, the hero, of his beloved's luscious, full breasts as he sits ruminating in his palace garden. And so on. Again, in the extensive series of drawings of the Ramayana by the painter Ranjha, there are notes on the margins instructing the painter to add something he had missed out or correct an error of interpretation that he had made. These isolated examples, in themselves, might not amount to much, but they are more than illustrative: eloquence resides in them.

How a painting was made is possible to track. How it truly came into being, however, remains obscured from our view. We can only guess at what must have gone on in the painter's mind: the thinking, the search for references, the gathering together of memories, the summoning of energies, the choosing of the moment that he could seize and then 'throw it clear beyond the reach of time'.

X

The story of miniature paintings can be told here only in the barest summary, but it needs to be told, for the paintings that are drawn upon for telling it have to find their place in it. Much in the story will continue to remain obscured from view, but one thing is clear: by the time that painting in the small, portable format comes in, the great mural tradition as seen at Ajanta, Bagh, Badami, for example, had all but dried up, though there was some later work on walls in pockets such as Alchi, Lepakshi, Tanjore, Mattancheri.

Early texts do speak of paintings on a small scale—the series of portraits of eligible princes that Chitralekha painted for her friend, the princess Usha, in the story of Usha and Aniruddha, serves as an example—but nothing of the kind has survived. The only painted works in 'miniature format' that can be dated before 1000 CE—seventh to eighth century is the date generally assigned to them—are the wooden book covers of what have been called the Gilgit manuscripts. Appropriately perhaps, some romance belongs to their discovery, for it was in 1931 that some cattle grazers in the Gilgit area suddenly chanced upon them.

The two manuscripts were both Buddhist-*sutra* texts, one written on palm-leaf and the other on birchbark. The discovery created a sensation, for nothing as early as these had till then come to light. They began to be spoken of as 'among the oldest manuscripts in the world' and 'certainly the oldest manuscript collection surviving in India'. The restoration and reading of the texts took a long time, but what interested scholars of painting from the outset were the wooden covers within which the leaves had been secured, for they were painted on both sides, the outer side covered with lotus scrolls and the inner with images of Buddhist deities: Avalokiteshvara Padmapani, the Buddha himself, the *dhyani* Buddha, Amitabha, and some devotees in acts of prayer or receiving blessings.

The style in which the figures were painted linked the covers to the wider world of Buddhism—Kashmir and Central Asia. But the fact that they were found on Indian soil and had obvious Indian links was significant. Some sixty years later, more manuscripts on birchbark turned up, again by chance. This time they were seen on the international market. They were said to have come out of war-torn Afghanistan and discovered by some refugees from the Taliban regime. The state in which they were found has been graphically described: they looked, when first found, like 'badly rolled up cigars', almost impossible to separate without their breaking into small fragments.

These 'Dead Sea scrolls of Buddhism' were soon picked up by collectors and institutions—some went to Norway, others are now in the British Library—and are currently the subject of intensive study. Scholarly opinion inclines to the view that these manuscripts, written in what is now beginning to be called the 'Gandhari script', and evidently belonging to some monastery, could go back to the first or second century. This would make them, in all probability, the oldest Buddhist texts ever found, as well as the earliest surviving manuscripts in any Indic language. There were, however, no paintings that accompanied them.

From the eleventh century onward, some kind of a narrative of Indian painting—of 'miniatures' if one prefers to so term them—is often constructed. One starts speaking of 'schools' and 'styles', both terms used rather loosely. Very very briefly—sketchily, in fact—one speaks, early on, of two separate streams or schools of manuscript painting: the eastern Indian or Pala, and the western Indian, sometimes also referred to simply as Jain. The first refers for the most part to the regions of Bengal and Bihar, and consists almost exclusively of Buddhist work, and the second to areas in Gujarat and south-western Rajasthan where Jainism had established itself as a major faith.

With the coming in of Islam, and the increasing establishment of large pockets of Islamic power in the northern parts of India from the thirteenth century onward, what is designated as Sultanate painting comes in, its main centres being Delhi, Jaunpur and Malwa, with some scattered activity visible in other areas. Most interesting developments are seen in the period of the Sultanates, Islamic texts in Persian being increasingly 'illustrated' on the one hand and local styles interacting with them to create a sizeable body of work that leans on two disparate, almost opposing, styles.

From the sixteenth century one enters more secure ground, for dated materials come one's way. The middle of the century sees the founding of the celebrated Mughal school, patronized by the emperors themselves, from Humayun through Akbar and Jahangir and Shahjahan, down to the early years of the eighteenth century. Alongside the Mughal school—both contributing to it and taking from it—rose the equally celebrated Rajput school, with its two major expressions in Rajasthan and in the Pahari areas, now parts of Himachal Pradesh and Jammu and Kashmir. In the same period, in southern India, painting with a Deccani slant begins to flourish—with major centres in the Sultanates of Ahmednagar, Bijapur and Golconda. The coming of the British leads to the birth of what has been called the 'Company School'—Indian artists working mostly for British patrons, officers of the East India Company. There are of course other schools or styles—Mysore, Maratha, Kutch, Sikh, Kashmir, Assam, Delhi, among others—but they have, at least till now, not been seen as a part of the mainstream, and have remained on the periphery.

Broadly speaking, from the eleventh century to the nineteenth, painting in India keeps running in different courses, at different paces, with varying energies. These developments, as noted before, are not linear. It is not as though one style died and was replaced by another. In the world of Indian painting, several streams ran parallel to each other.

To go back to the narrative. Painting in eastern India consisted chiefly of manuscripts in which as much regard was paid to calligraphy as to illustrations. Scribes, as the art historian J.P. Losty has remarked, seem to have taken great pains to produce 'beautiful and measured harmony with their pen, to invest the page with dignity through the use of majestically large and separate letters or of lines proceeding in measured, rhythmic tread across the great width of a page'. The emphasis on calligraphy—whether on palm-leaf or, later, on paper—is understandable because the subject of the manuscripts was sacred, the text meant to be revered by devotees who included members of the Pala royal dynasty. The work arising from eastern India had a deep connection to the work in Nepal where calligraphy was also viewed with great respect. One can speak of a stylistic complex in this region of which, culturally, Nepal, Bengal and Bihar were parts. They were connected by religion, too. In fact, many of these illustrated manuscripts were later taken to neighbouring Nepal during the Islamic invasions of the eastern regions of India.

The Tibetan historian of Buddhism, Taranath, writing as late as the early years of the seventeenth century, was aware of the reputation of the work in this region for he spoke of it in his own fashion. 'In the times of kings Devapala and Srimant Dharmapala [eighth to ninth centuries],' he wrote, 'there lived in Varendra [northern Bengal] an especially skilful artist named Dhiman. His son was Bitpalo. Both these produced many works in cast metal, as well as sculptures and paintings which resembled the works of the Nagas.' Whatever value is placed on Taranath's account as an authentic record of things as they once were, one knows that in eastern India where Buddhism—first of the Mahayana order and later of the Vajrayana—flourished, a great corpus of illustrated manuscripts was produced. Among the most widely copied and illustrated texts was the *Ashtasahasrika Prajnaparamita*—literally, 'The Perfection of Wisdom in 8000 Sections'—an abstruse work filled with discussions of wisdom, of Buddhahood, and of Bodhisattvahood. They also contain *sadhanas*—chants and invocations intended to protect the devotee, the chanter.

The text lent itself more to single, iconic images of the various deities rather than to narrative. Power had to be packed into the image. The devotee's attention was almost forced to linger on the attributes of the figure, which often occupied a small space in the centre of the leaf for the texts were written mostly on palm-leaf of a limited height, and in the horizontal *pothi* format. Several manuscripts of this text are known, among the earliest of them being two, both from the reign of King Mahipala: one datable to c. 983, now in the Asiatic Society, Kolkata, and the other, now in the University Library at Cambridge, with a date that works out either to c. 1000 or close to it, depending upon the reading.

There are others, of course, among them the famous Vredenburg manuscript (see p. 128) dated c. 1118, 'in the 36th year of the reign of king Ramapala', now in the Victoria and Albert Museum, London. The Vredenburg manuscript is considered 'the most classically perfect of the great manuscripts associated with the name of Ramapala'. Besides its high quality, the manuscript has information of value, for it mentions that it was prepared at the expense of one Udayasimha for the benefit of his parents' souls. Originally, the manuscript had close to 179 folios, of which eighteen had miniatures.

But, barring the painted pages, the manuscript is almost completely lost. The images we have are celebrated for the quality of their workmanship. Nine of them are of Bodhisattvas, drawn, as Losty says, 'with a perfectly controlled line fully expressive of volume, so that even where the paint has flaked on the yellow and white Bodhisattvas, the figures still seem fully modeled'. The image of Prajnaparamita herself is missing, but there are superbly painted images of the red-coloured Amitabha Buddha, and of Vajrasattva.

There are other manuscripts of this particular text which have a larger repertoire of images: events from the life of the Buddha, terrifying divinities of the northern Buddhist pantheon, and some more Bodhisattvas. Some of the wooden book covers of the folios are also superbly painted. Whether produced at Nalanda or Vikramashila, or at centres in Bengal, other Buddhist texts like the *Pancharaksha*, the *Karandavyuhasutra*, the *Vasudharadharani* were also taken in its sweep by the 'eastern Indian' school.

What is remarkable about this school, spread over two centuries or more, is that the style seems to have 'descended' from the mural tradition. The images are redolent of Ajanta: the same sinuousness of line, the same softness of expression, the same fullness of forms, the same eloquent gestures, the same delicacy in the rendering of hands. Quite naturally, the compositions are not as elaborate and detailed, for the themes do not require this and the surface spaces were limited. The Mahashri Tara from the Vredenburg manuscript, if enlarged, could be easily mistaken as being from Ajanta. It is as if there was once a pan-Indian style that ranged over vast areas of the land.

Manuscripts like these—sacred in themselves—earned for the scribe/painter/donor/patron spiritual merit, and when they were donated to a monastery, the merit was all the greater, for there they would confer benefit upon many others too. The *dana pushpikas*—colophons recording details of donation—that occur at the end of several manuscripts leave one in no doubt about this kind of intent. But it all came virtually to an end in the thirteenth century with the coming in of Muslim invaders, committed to iconoclasm. There are records of staggering destruction. When the Tibetan monk Dharmaswami visited eastern India between 1234 and 1236 he found that the famous Vikramashila *mahavihara* on the banks of the Ganga had been razed to the ground and its stones thrown into the river. Likewise, Nalanda, that other great centre of Buddhist learning, was almost completely destroyed in 1205 by the Muslim armies of Sultan Muhammad Bakhtiyar Khalji. Monks were slaughtered, books burnt, structures demolished. The eastern Indian style survived only in Nepal and, farther off, at another remove, in Tibet.

———————

At the other end of India, in the west, where the so-called western Indian style of painting flourished for three hundred years or more, it was Jainism that provided the chief impetus to painting. The flavour of the work done in this area—Gujarat and western Rajasthan for the most part—is different from that in the Buddhist east, but the activity is intense. Here too, as early as the eleventh century, there is evidence of sacred manuscripts being scripted and painted—in the early phase on palm-leaf and later, when paper was introduced, on paper.

One of the earliest illustrated manuscripts here is from Jaisalmer, the *Oghaniryukti*, a philosophical text, bearing the date 1060. There are not many illustrations on the folios, but in this early period, in Jain manuscripts in general, one turns to wooden book covers, *patlis*, to be able to form an idea of the quality of work the painters were capable of. An astonishing example is the *patli*—referred to before—which depicts and celebrates a famous theological debate that took place in 1124 at the court of a Solanki prince at Patan. Two highly revered monks, Muni Devasuri and Muni

Kumudchandra—the first belonging to the Shvetambara sect of Jainism and the latter to the Digambara—had engaged in a prolonged debate. Muni Devasuri emerged as the winner (see p. 278). The *patli*, generally dated c. 1130, is almost a historical record of that event. But it was the sacred texts—the hallowed written word—that provided the theme par excellence to scribes and painters, and among them stood out the *Kalpasutra*, the most venerated of all canonical works of Jainism.

That text consists of three sections—the *Jinacharita* which covers the lives of four of the most prominent among the twenty-four *tirthankaras*, from Mahavira, who was a historical figure, going back to Parshvanatha, Neminatha and Rishabhanatha; the *Sthaviravali* which is the succession list of Jain pontiffs; and the *Samachari*, rules for monks. The *charitas*—life stories focusing essentially upon the most important events of their lives—naturally lend themselves to narrative treatment and it is these stories that the painters illustrated in manuscript after manuscript. To this day, the *Kalpasutra*, as a text, is venerated among devout Jains, the mere *darshan* of it bringing merit. Very often, another text is appended to the *Kalpasutra*—the *Kalakacharya Katha*—which is a non-canonical but extremely popular work. This tells a highly engaging and edifying story with a great teacher, the monk Kalaka, at its centre, and characters like the monk's sister and an evil king, and an alliance with a Shaka chief. Everything of course leads in the end to faith in the Jain doctrine.

A number of other Jain texts were written and painted over the centuries, among them the *Parshvanatha Charita* as an independent text, the *Adipurana*, the *Uttaradhyayanasutra*, the *Prabandhachintamani* and the *Kathakosha*. But when one thinks of Jain painting, it is the *Kalpasutra* and the *Kalakacharya Katha* that stand out. The Jain community, being among the most literate, and also the most affluent, of all communities in India, underwrote the writing of a very large number of manuscripts of the *Kalpasutra*. Legend has it that King Siddharaja Jayasimha of Patan (1094–1143) employed 300 scribes to copy books for the royal library, and that Kumarapala (1143–74) established twenty-one libraries, in each of which he placed a copy of the *Kalpasutra* written in gold.

The great Jain *bhandar*s, repositories of ancient texts and other sacred objects, like the one at Jaisalmer, are filled, shelf after shelf, with manuscripts. The early manuscripts, from the eleventh to the thirteenth centuries, all on palm-leaf, were very sparsely illustrated, much of the painting concentrating on decorative designs on the margins or on occasional single figures. The *Oghaniryukti* manuscript, dated 1060, has a folio containing a taut representation of the goddess Shri and Kamadeva, but also, on the colophon page, depictions of well-rounded elephants. The challenge that the grainy surface of palm-leaves offered to painters was absent on wood of which book covers, *patli*s, were made, and that is how some of the most elaborate early Jain paintings are to be found on them.

Things changed with the coming of paper to India around the fourteenth century. Palm-leaf was abandoned, slowly at first but rapidly later, as a writing surface. The possibilities that paper offered of altering the old format—narrow and horizontal, dictated by the nature of the material—were not exploited, however. It was the *pothi* format—horizontal leaves, generally unstitched—that continued to be used. The earliest *Kalpasutra* manuscripts go back to the middle of the fourteenth century, but from then on they started being produced in large numbers. In the western part of India, apart from major centres like Patan and Ahmedabad, one finds in the fifteenth century great *Kalpasutra*s being produced at centres as far from each other as Mandu (dated 1439) and Jaunpur (dated 1465).

In respect of the style that one associates with Jain painting, with all its characteristics and peculiarities, its hieratic character, one cannot do better perhaps than cite Coomaraswamy's eloquent description:

The art is one of pure draughtsmanship; the pictures are brilliant statements of the facts of the epic [the life of Mahavira], where every event is seen in the light of eternity. To call this pure drawing implies that it is an art of symbols and indifferent to representation. On the other hand, it is not calligraphic, that is to say that elegance or an elegant combination of lines is not deliberately sought, and in this sense is more like script [such as that of the accompanying text] made to be clearly and easily read. There is no preoccupation with pattern, colour, or texture for their own sake; but these are achieved with inevitable assurance in a way that could not have been the case had they been directly sought. The drawing has in fact the perfect equilibrium of a mathematical equation, or a page of a composer's score. Theme and formula compose an inseparable unity, text and pictures form a continuous relation of the same dogma in the same key.

The human form in Jain painting—this 'formal art of hieratic traditions'—stands out in particular: the angularity of features; the face seen in true profile but the chest seen in three-quarters and so full that it is not always easy to distinguish the male from the female; the narrow lion-waist; the large eyes that extend almost to the ears. The most characteristic feature is the eye, stretching beyond the contour of the face, appearing to hang in the air. This peculiar and archaic feature—the 'inevitable stigmata of time and place'—stays in Jain art for a long period, disappearing, when it does, slowly and reluctantly.

Meanwhile, in these paintings, light remains perfectly even and never changes, the space at the back hardly ever opens up, objects like canopies hang in the air without any support, persons attending on the main figure seem sometimes to levitate in the air, patterns on textiles keep getting

richer with time. There are elements of abstraction in the style that take some getting used to, but there is brilliance in them, for they are 'the direct expression of a flashing religious conviction and of freedom from any specific material interest'.

For the most sumptuous example of Jain painting, one cannot do better than to turn to the manuscript that belonged to the Devasano Pada Bhandar at Ahmedabad and consists of the combined texts of the *Kalpasutra* and the *Kalakacharya Katha* (see p. 136 and detail above). The work remains undated but comes possibly from the last quarter of the fifteenth century. The colophon page as it exists today only mentions that it was prepared at the request of Sana and Jutha, obviously wealthy men, who lived in the port of Gandhar near Broach in Gujarat. Against the ultramarine ground of nearly all the folios, the gold with which the text is written shimmers; and one sees in the *Kalaka* section several innovations that the painter brings in: dancing female figures occupying vertical panels at the side margins; lively renderings of animals, mythical beings with wings, horsemen, ships; elements of design imported from the Islamic world. Jain paintings continued to be made into the eighteenth century, but the winds of change, one senses, were already beginning to blow by the sixteenth century.

Jain painting, although it figures so largely in the area, was not all that goes under the name of western Indian style, for there were devotional texts embedded in Hindu belief—the *Balagopalastuti* of Bilvamangala, the *Bhakti Ratnavali*, the tenth canto of the *Bhagavata Purana*, the *Devi Mahatmya*, for instance—as well as poetical works like the *Gita Govinda* of Jayadeva and the *Vasanta Vilasa* that shared some of its artistic features. Of some of these

texts, more than one illustrated version has come down. But easily the most typical of these non-Jain texts is the unique *Vasanta Vilasa*, in the form of a scroll on cloth, close to twelve metres long, now in the Freer-Sackler Galleries in Washington DC (see p. 412 and detail on p. 82).

Painted in 1451, for an aristocrat named Chandrapala, it is a *phagu*, a long uninhibited poem describing the glories of spring in which 'lovers please one another', and the mere recitation of which 'blesses men of discrimination'. In image after image, interspersed with the text of the poem, one finds damsels pining and waiting for their lovers, joined with them in union, seeking the company and advice of their confidantes, while the scent of fresh mango blossoms and the sounds of humming bees waft in the air. The artistic vocabulary is much the same as that of many Jain texts, but the feel of the work is different: more open, celebratory, charged with eroticism. But everything stays within visual conventions that had been worked out much earlier.

A great deal of work of different kinds—hieratic, iconic and canonical on the one hand, and non-hieratic, non-canonical and 'secular' on the other—belongs to the Sultanate period, meaning, in the time after the coming of Islam to India and the establishment of centres of Islamic power, but before the arrival of the Mughals. This needs to be distinguished from what is generally referred to as 'Sultanate painting', which consists essentially of work done for the Sultans or for highly placed patrons who were rooted in Islam, who valued classics of the Islamic world and commissioned them.

Sultanate painting is a brief but complex chapter in the history of Indian painting, and its picture is far from complete in our minds. In it surface contradictions, like those reflected in the attitude of orthodox Islam towards the art of painting in general and the patronage of that art at the same time. There is also a coming together, at times, of different streams of art. Orthodox Islam was in general distrustful towards any kind of figural work in painting, and yet we see patronage from the Muslim elite at this time. There is also a coming together, on occasion, of different streams of art—Hindu–Buddhist–Jain on the one hand and Iranate on the other. These two tensions, of philosophies and styles colliding and merging, is what makes Sultanate painting particularly fascinating.

The opposition to the art of painting, to any kind of figural work, gets summed up in the evidence we have from the reign of the zealous Sultan Feroze Tughlaq (1351–88). In his own words, in the *Futuhat-i Feroze Shahi*, the Sultan states:

> In former times it had been the custom to wear ornamented garments, and men received robes as tokens of honour from kings' court. Figures and devices were painted and displayed on saddles, bridles and collars, on censers, on goblets and cups and flagons, on dishes and ewers, in tents, on curtains and on chairs, and upon all articles and utensils. Under Divine guidance and favour I ordered all pictures and portraits to be removed from these things, and that such articles only should be made as are approved and recognized by the Law. Those pictures and portraits which were painted on the doors and walls of palaces I ordered to be effaced.

The same Sultan also ordered a Brahmin, who was reported to him as carrying with him a wooden tablet 'covered with paintings of demons and other objects', to be burnt alive if he were not to accept conversion to Islam. At the same time, there are references to paintings in the palace of Sultan Iltutmish, and of Sultan Ala-ud Din Khalji summoning a painter, bestowing upon him his own cloak, an elephant and a horse, and ordering him to take a likeness of the princess Chhitai, daughter of King Ramadeva Yadava.

Clearly, much was going on in the Sultanate world and it was not a world only of confrontation or contradiction. Native Indian elements come to merge with the work of the Islamic world—Persian, Inju, Mamluk, among others—making it interesting, even possible, to distinguish, say, an illustrated *Shahnama* of Persian origin from one painted on Indian soil with local elements entering into it. Losty has grouped Sultanate manuscripts into three different categories. The first is 'work in basic Iranian styles' of which there are two parts—the earlier represented by a small group of manuscripts of Persian classics in a clearly provincial version of Persian work, like the Jules Mohl *Shahnama* in the British Library; and the second by manuscripts that are demonstrably connected with specific centres of Sultanate power, works like the *Bustan* in the National Museum at Delhi, the *Ni'matnama* painted for the Sultan of Mandu in the India Office Library, the *Iskandarnama* of Sultan Nusrat Shah of Bengal, or the *Nujum al-Ulum* now in the Chester Beatty Library. These Losty treats separately, because of the pronounced Indian characteristics they possess. The second group, by this classification, consists of works 'not connected with any Muslim court but produced for other patrons', showing clear traces of fourteenth-century Mamluk and Inju styles mixing with medieval Indian characteristics and best represented by the Chandayan manuscript in Berlin, the dispersed *Khamsa* of Amir Khusrau, and the now vanished *Iskandarnama*. The third group, finally, consists of manuscripts like the *Laur Chanda* in the Prince of Wales Museum, Mumbai, and the *Chandayan* in the John Rylands Library in Manchester. These, according to him, are works in which 'Persian and Indian elements are thoroughly synthesized'.

Some of the work is of great interest for two reasons: for enabling us to trace the initially uneasy coming together of two styles based in different artistic traditions, and for the visual delight that resides in them. One knows that 'foreign' elements had already started entering even such 'sacred' Jain texts as the *Kalakacharya Katha*—the introduction of three-quarter profiles, the costumes of the Shahi figures in them derived obviously from Islamic models, the elements of decorative designs—but here are works that appear consciously to integrate two visions. In some, like the vanished *Iskandarnama* or the Berlin

Hamzanama, there is a clear folkish element. The figures are summarily treated, the backgrounds remain unexplored or opened up, the horizon is pushed to the very top if it features at all, and so on. In others, like the *Ni'matnama* or the Prince of Wales *Laur Chanda*, the figures are decidedly more sophisticated but come as much from Persian sources as from Indian. The elements of design, especially in architecture, are emphatically Islamic, marked by domes and arabesques and lattice patterns. The foliage or birds, on the other hand, bear a clearly 'native' look. The confluence of cultural streams is reflected, most spectacularly, in the way the text appears on each painted folio of a *Laur Chanda* manuscript. The text is in Avadhi Hindi, the script is Persian with the Avadhi verses bearing, at the top, captions in Persian.

Possibly the most exciting—intriguing?—of all Sultanate manuscripts is the now dispersed 'Jainesque Sultanate *Shahnama*', of uncertain origin, undated, but painted close to 1450 (see p. 140 and detail above). The text, as expected, is in Persian—a selection from Firdausi's great classic—and the calligraphy and the late owner's seal suggest the patron was a Muslim. The text is written in four columns on large sheets of the codex format but the paintings, however—richly coloured, with highly detailed costumes and ornamentation on architecture—are all in the horizontal *pothi* format. Close study of the work leads one to believe that the work was assigned to a painter who was rooted in the western Indian tradition, possibly even Jain, and knew remarkably little of the Persian classic which he might have been asked by a Muslim patron to illustrate. It is likely that the story was narrated to the painter by his patron, the characters outlined and identified, the action explained. The painter seems to have struggled, however, to render Iranian figure types, clothing them in Central Asian costumes that one sees some of the Shahi figures wear in late *Kalakacharya Katha* manuscripts, and bringing in foreign-looking accessories and the like, so as to give it an 'authentic' Islamic look.

But there are signs everywhere of markedly Indian features in the paintings: scaling of figures according to their importance, in other words, hieratic; the diaphanous clothing and the jewellery that the women wear; the curving bulge of the chest in the figures of men even when shown frontally; the sharp *mudra*-like gestures of the hands; the rendition of fire which rises in sharp-edged spiky flames rather than in the decorative, Chinese cloud-like formation seen in Persian work; the long scrolls held by courtiers or generals that serve as letters or *farman*s, reminiscent of the way they are seen in western Indian paintings; the narrow, decorative bands above arches or on throne-coverings; the extraordinarily rich range of textiles which are woven, brocaded, printed or embroidered in patterns and motifs immediately associated with Indian workshops; the division of an occasional page into clearly demarcated registers; the small settees with their backs shaped like flattened melons; above all, the occasional projecting eye that one sees on some faces.

The list is long and may sound a bit dreary but the paintings pulsate with life, making them works not only of uncommon beauty but also of real historical significance. There is boldness in the work and the compositions are so self-assured, so instinctively right, that one is taken by surprise. But in many ways, elegantly combining simplicity with sophistication, the painter seems to anticipate the justly lauded 'early Rajput' work which was just round the corner, especially in respect of the manner in which he displays his ability to engage with his characters, his desire to enter their minds and feel the grain of their emotions as they are caught up in various situations.

————————

To the early Rajput style—between 1450 and 1550—belong a number of manuscripts, or series, of great brilliance. In the broadest terms these works are spoken of as being in the *Chaurapanchasika* style, the name—'Fifty Stanzas of the Love Thief'—coming from a Sanskrit text by the poet Bilhana (see p. 416 and detail below). The series based on this theme must originally have consisted of fifty folios, but less than half of them have survived and these belonged once to the N.C. Mehta Collection now in Ahmedabad. It is not that the *Chaurapanchasika* leaves are the finest among this group of paintings, but the name has come to stay. By now a number of other works done in or affiliated to this style are known. Thus the *Aranyaka Parvan* of the Mahabharata in the Asiatic Society of Bombay; the *Devi Mahatmya* in the Himachal Pradesh State Museum at Shimla; the *Laur Chanda* series shared between the Lahore Museum in Pakistan and the Government Museum at Chandigarh; a single *Ragamala* leaf—Ragini Bhairavi—formerly in the J.C. French Collection and now in the Victoria and Albert Museum; and an extensive *Bhagavata Purana* series, now completely dispersed.

Virtually nothing can be said with certainty about the place or area from which these different works come. One of them, the *Devi Mahatmya*, bears in its colophon the name of 'Jaisinghdeva-nagara'—almost certainly the modern Jaisinghpur in the Kangra region of Himachal Pradesh, for it came from the collection of a family living in a place very close by. Another, the *Aranyaka Parvan*, mentions that it was executed at the '*jala-durga*'—literally, 'water-fort'—of Kachhauva which scholars have placed somewhere in the Delhi–Agra region. These places are very far apart, and one has no evidence from any other work of this group about a place of execution or acquisition.

There is similar uncertainty about the dating of these works. The *Devi Mahatmya* has a date in the form of a complicated chronogram which places it in the third quarter of the sixteenth century; the *Aranyaka Parvan* has a clear date—the equivalent of 1516, in the reign of the 'victorious Sultan Sikandar' (Lodi). None of the other works, including the *Chaurapanchasika*, provides any clue about a date. The *Bhagavata Purana* may have been painted c. 1525 if, as is being conjectured, it was made either for Vallabhacharya, the great Vaishnava teacher who founded the Vallabha *sampradaya*, or his son, Vitthalnath, both of whom were located in the Mathura region and were passionate devotees of Krishna. But nothing can be said with assurance and it is perhaps safe to place this entire group between 1450 and 1550. All these uncertainties notwithstanding, however, one's attention goes eagerly to this group of works because of their astonishing quality.

It would be excessive, given the silences of the past, to try and identify a family workshop or guild of where they came from. Two names, 'Sa Mitha' and 'Sa Nana', one finds inscribed on several pages of the *Bhagavata Purana* series, but whether they are the names of painters remains uncertain. However, certain features bind the works of this group together even as differences can be discerned. If, for instance, one notices the feature in the *Aranyaka Parvan* in which the narrator and the listener of the epic tale appear, page after page, tucked away in some corner of the leaf—in defiance of time as we ordinarily understand it and making the viewer a witness to the events as they unfold, much as the narrator and the listener sit envisioning them—the only other series in which something approaching it is seen is the *Laur Chanda* of Lahore/Chandigarh in which the author, Mulla Daud, appears on every single known folio, sitting in a corner, reading from a text. In no other work of this group is this to be seen. In the *Chaurapanchasika*, the relevant verses in Sanskrit are inscribed inside a top register on every single folio series but this feature is not to be seen anywhere else in this group. Strategies vary, and the logic of the situation dictates itself to the painter each time.

Yet the same bodily types—full breasts, narrow waists and ample hips, with fleshy faces seen in true profile, large unblinking eyes, sharp noses; men with athletic forms, broad chests and lion-waists—appear nearly everywhere. In some instances, as in the *Chaurapanchasika* series, these forms and conventions stop just a bit short of being extreme, but the basics remain the same. Gestures remain remarkably sharp, inviting the eye to travel in given directions. The device of continuous pictorial narration, the same figure/s appearing freely within the same frame, remains a constant.

Flat coloured backgrounds dominate with colours changing almost without notice, the painter often using the logic of changing colours to hint at changed spaces. There is very little interest in depth, and things stay as close to the surface as possible; the conventionally treated horizon always remains high, barely being allowed into the page; the architecture freely combines Hindu and Islamic features; things and figures are often placed in compartments that take the form of horizontal registers or vertical columns; nothing that does not contribute either to understanding or to the situation is brought in. There is an economy to the style and the air is almost always dramatic, one suggestion being that the style draws freely upon folk theatre. There is no attempt at creating any slickness of surface, or any 'effects', and the execution appears to be almost rough at times.

But what stands out in these series of paintings or manuscripts is the deep emotion they are capable of stirring within the viewer. Belief and conviction reign. When, in a *Bhagavata Purana* folio, Krishna and Balarama take the cows grazing, the animals, unable to believe their good fortune, do not simply walk, but prance with dancer-like agility. When the poet-thief Bilhana recalls the sight of his beloved, 'with her eyes closed in the ecstasy of love, and all her limbs relaxed . . . [but] her garments and tresses strewn in disorder', one can almost see her through his and the painter's eyes from the way the page is set up, and the eyes travel along every bend, every sinuous line of the body.

As seen in the *Laur Chanda*, these works possess boldness but also a 'noble artificiality'. The sharp observation—faces, stances, gestures, characters, objects, and the like—is always subordinated to a great, soaring sense of design. Atmosphere is created with ease and elan, the painter not having to wait for an especially poetic description or passage to come along to 'take off' in his own language: he seems to have the ability to do this even in the most prosaic of contexts—like that of rendering a 'view' of the town of Govar over which a princely character in the tale ruled. With all this brilliance around, how one wishes that one had access to more information, some evidence, about precise dates and places and names.

With the coming of the Mughals, however, things change, and one enters, in a sense, more secure territory. This, because the documentation suddenly picks up, both contemporaries and later researchers availing themselves of the records, names, colophons, scribal notes that, however speckled, belong to the period. We may not have the levels of information as we have on painting in Europe during the same period, for instance, but there is enough to build some structure upon, to speculate and ascribe. One owes a measure of this to Akbar's great chronicler, Abu'l Fazl—with all our reservations about the eulogistic tone which came naturally to him—and to an emperor, Jahangir, who not only was a patron but also found time to make occasional but astute notes on painting and the painters of the time in his memoirs.

In the *Ain-i Akbari* which is appended to his chronicle, the *Akbarnama*, Abu'l Fazl has a whole chapter on the 'Arts of Writing and Painting'. In it he places the art of calligraphy above that of painting in the Islamic world, saying:

> A letter is the portrait painter of wisdom; a rough sketch from the realm of ideas; a dark night ushering in day; a black cloud pregnant with knowledge; the wand for the treasures of insight; speaking, though dumb; stationary, and yet travelling; stretched on the sheet, and yet soaring upwards.

Despite this preference, he does write about the art of painting and the great interest that his patron took in it. 'Drawing the likeness of anything,' he says, beginning from the beginning as it were,

> is called *taswir*. Since it is an excellent source, both of study and entertainment, His Majesty, from the time he came to an awareness of things, has taken a deep interest in painting and sought its spread and development. Consequently this magical art has gained in beauty. A very large number of painters has been set to work. Each week the several *daroghas* (supervisors) and *bitikchis* (clerks) submit before the king the work done by each artist, and His Majesty gives a reward and increases the monthly salary according to the excellence displayed . . . The *Chingiz-nama*, the *Zafar-nama*, this book, the *Razm-nama*, the *Ramayan*, the *Nal Daman*, the *Kalila wa Dimna*, the *'Iyar-i Danish* and other books have been illustrated, His Majesty himself having indicated the scenes to be painted.

Whether or not the emperor examined each week the work of his painters, one gets at least a clear sense of a system, of the existence of an atelier, of the kinds of projects undertaken. The chronicler also lists, as we have seen earlier, some painters—Mir Sayyid Ali, 'Abd-al Samad, Daswant, Basawan, Kesudas, among them—and even takes notice of the great *Hamzanama* series which kept painters busy for upwards of a decade.

Abu'l Fazl provides in addition most profitable insights into the debates that still raged about the right of painting to exist as a legitimate activity in Islam. The early Mughal emperors clearly stood on one side of the debate. Humayun, the emperor's father, was an enthusiast for painting and was responsible for bringing back with him to India some of Iran's finest painters; his wife Hamida Banu Begum favoured the art and commissioned texts to be illustrated with paintings, and Akbar himself, while still a young boy, had taken lessons in painting from great masters.

And yet the orthodox must have continued to fulminate against painting, making Abu'l Fazl feel the need to cite the position taken by the emperor and include his ringing statement:

> There are many that hate painting, but such men I dislike. It appears to me as if a painter had quite peculiar means of recognizing God; for a painter in sketching anything that has life, and in devising its limbs, one after the other, must come to feel he cannot bestow individuality upon his work, and is thus forced to think of God, the giver of life, and will thus increase in knowledge.

Painting flourished. One knows of a host of illustrated manuscripts and series—chronicles like the *Tarikh-i Alfi*, the *Chingiznama*, the *Tawarikh-i Khandan-i Timuriya*, the *Baburnama* and the *Akbarnama*; books of tales and works of wisdom, like the *Tutinama*, the *'Iyar-i Danish*, the *Kalila wa Dimna*, the *Anvar-i Suhaili* and the *Hamzanama*; Hindu epics and other sacred works, including the Ramayana, the *Razmnama* being a version of the Mahabharata, the *Jog Bashisht*; poetic works, like the *Gulistan*, the *Diwan-i Anvari*, the *Khamsa* of Amir Khusrau.

The list is almost endless, and when one adds to it the countless portraits which must have been made—one recalls again Abu'l Fazl's words about an immense album of likenesses commissioned by Akbar—as also the work done for great nobles like Khan Khanan, 'Abd-al Rahim, Mirza Aziz Koka, Nawab Bahadur Khan, Shaikh Farid Murtaza Khan Bukhari, one knows that the world of painting was astir with activity.

Undoubtedly, the greatest of these undertakings was the painting of the *Dastan-i Amir Hamza*—*Hamzanama* for short—a classic tale of unlikely adventures and pitched battles, love and intrigue, magic and sorcery, heroism and deceit. It was conceived and executed on a large scale: 1400 folios, each, almost in defiance of established norms for miniature painting, nearly 64 cm in height and 50 cm in width. Between 1562 and 1577, it is estimated, a host of painters worked on the 'manuscript' in the imperial atelier. The work is a benchmark in the annals of Mughal painting not simply because of its daring extent, or for the vigour one can feel in its folios, but also because it drew upon different, almost opposed, artistic streams—Iranian on the one hand and native Indian on the other—and brought them together (see pp. 148 and 152).

The Mughal style, one knows, did not come to rest at one point. It kept moving, absorbing, expanding, almost mirroring the very nature of the empire that it grew in. There is, for example, the phenomenon—it is certainly more than an interlude—of European works coming into India, first in the baggage of Jesuit missionaries who were given charters by the emperor to settle in India and follow their own faith, and then brought by travellers and ambassadors. The arrival in Akbar's India of the eight-volume Royal Polyglot Bible illustrated with engravings is well documented. Engravings like these, or paintings on wood or paper, were naturally seen by the emperor himself who, it is recorded, went to the chapel established by Christian missionaries in Agra and was very taken up with them, reflecting as they did a different way of seeing and rendering reality: almost, in fact, a different view of the world.

Intrigued, the emperor ordered exact copies of some of these works by his own painters, who not only executed those commissions but also absorbed elements from them which could inform their own work: distant townscapes seen through atmospheric haze, figures in the far distance diminishing, objects seen as possessed of weight and volume, things seen from a fixed point of view, for example.

Great painters like Keshava Das or, later, Abu'l Hasan, were quick to absorb and adapt, and exact copies that they made of European works have survived. Abu'l Fazl noted and remarked on this development:

> Such excellent artists have assembled here (at the Imperial court) that a fine match has been created to the world-renowned unique art of Bihzad (the great Timurid artist, an icon in the Islamic world), and the magic-making of the Europeans. Delicacy of work, clarity of line and boldness of execution, as well as other fine qualities have reached perfection, and inanimate objects appear to have come alive.

A reign later when Sir Thomas Roe arrived in 1615 as ambassador from King James I to the emperor Jahangir's court, he was to discover for himself the prodigious skills of Indian painters. His record of an 'event' at the court in his own words is both amusing and instructive. 'The business,' he writes in the record of his embassy,

> was about a picture I had lately given the King (Jahangir) and was confident that noe man in India could equall yt. So soone as I came hee asked mee what I would giue the paynter that had made a coppy soe like it that I should not knowe myne owne. I answered: a painters reward: 50 rupies. The King replied his painter was a cavallero, and that too smalle a guift; to which I answered I gave my picture with a good

95

hart, esteeming it rare, and ment not to make comparisons or wagers: if his servant had done as well, and would not accept my guifte, His Maiestie was most fitt to reward him . . . At night hee sent for mee, beeing hastie to triumph in his woorkman, and shewed me six picturs, five made by his man, all pasted on one table, so like that I was by candle-light troubled to discerne which was which; I confesse beyond all expectation, yet I showed myne owne and the differences, which were in the arte apparent, but not to be judged by a common eye. But for that at first sight I knew it not, hee was very merry and joyful and craked like a northern man.

By the time Sir Thomas Roe arrived Jahangir—'Shah Salim', while still a prince—who had once rebelled against his father, the ageing Akbar, and had set up an independent court at Allahabad with very gifted artists working for him, was very much his own man. The empire was his and so were its inexhaustible resources. The high degree of refinement that one sees in the last phase of painting under Akbar was taken to a yet higher level under his discerning eye, and in his court names of great painters floated about—Aqa Riza, Abu'l Hasan, Bishan Das, Bichitr, Govardhan, Manohar, Balchand, Hashim, Ghulam, Daulat. Each of them, it seems, kept trying to rise to the demanding taste of his patron.

The claims that the emperor made for himself in his memoirs about his 'practice in judging' painting might have a trace of vanity, and yet, they could be close to the truth. Consider the description of a turkey cock, an unusual and little-seen bird, in his own words:

> One of these (uncommon) animals in body is larger than a peahen and smaller than a peacock. When it is in heat and displays itself, it spreads out its feathers like the peacock and dances about. Its beak and legs are like those of a cock.

Its head and neck and the part under the throat are every minute of a different colour. When it is in heat it is quite red—one might say it had adorned itself with red coral—and after a while it becomes white in the same places and looks like cotton. It sometimes looks of a turquoise colour. Like a chameleon it constantly changes colour.

That gifted painter of flora and fauna, Ustad Mansur, who had earned from Jahangir the title of Nadir-al 'Asr, did an extraordinarily sensitive study of the bird, which has fortunately survived. The painter Bishan Das, 'unequalled in his age for taking likenesses' in the emperor's own words, was sent by him with an embassy to the court of Shah Abbas of Iran, possibly only to bring back portraits of the Shah and other men of his court. Jahangir knew, through intense observation, the strengths of his men and assigned them tasks accordingly.

The interest in the illustration of manuscripts—so strong in the Akbari period—it would seem, slowly declined during Jahangir's time, even though a few were painted in the early years of his reign. There was of course, his own memoir, the *Jahangirnama* or the *Tuzuk*, to which illustrations were added. It was instead individual paintings, especially portraits and durbar scenes, that now came into favour, many of them ending up in exquisitely assembled albums, two of the most distinguished being now in Berlin (the Jahangir Album) and Tehran (the *Muraqqa-i Gulshan*).

Of uncommon interest, and of the highest quality, is a group of 'allegorical' paintings showing the emperor in different situations, with him naturally at the centre of all things: embracing Shah Abbas; feasting with Shah Abbas; preferring a Sufi Shaikh to kings; taking aim at poverty (see pp. 322 and 326, and details on p. 98), among them. The statements made in them are as much aesthetic as political. All objects and personages in the works are included with clear intent: thrones, angelic figures, the hourglass, the sun and the moon, the lion and the lamb, a globe, Manu on a fish, the bull

supporting the earth, the chain of justice. Whatever was happening during this period to the structure of the empire, Jahangiri painters kept trying to rise to the demanding taste of their patron and to match in their work the great sparkle of the court.

The heightened activity in Jahangir's court was, however, only a preparation for what was to follow in the succeeding reign. Shahjahan's court has been more celebrated for its great architecture than for its painting, yet the *Padshahnama*, the most sumptuous of all Mughal manuscripts, emerged from here. Now in the Royal Library, Windsor Castle (see pp. 342 and 346), it is a fragment of its original and the ordering of the surviving leaves has been the subject of much discussion. But whatever its state, or its present extent, it stands out as a dazzling document. All the glitter of the imperial court and all its ceremony seem to be compressed into its gleaming pages. Quite appropriately, it opens with a double *shamsa*, that symbol of royalty and divine light, and has as its frontispiece a richly illuminated double page with Shahjahan seen seated on the page at left facing the founder of the Mughal dynasty, Amir Timur, at right, who holds up the dynastic crown in one hand as if to offer it to the emperor across the divide of the double page. There is clear meaning in this. The legitimacy of succession is sought to be established at the same time through the respective titles of the two rulers: Timur as 'Sahib Qiran', the 'Lord of the Auspicious Planetary Conjunction', and Shahjahan as 'Sahib Qiran-i Sani', the 'Second Lord of the Auspicious Planetary Conjunction'. What follows is, in appearance, an account of the different events of the reign but is, in fact, a celebration of it.

Durbar scene follows durbar scene—Rajput rulers offering their submission with crowds of nobles and courtiers standing in respectful attendance, Shahjahan as Prince Khurram being received by his father or joined to his sons, the emperor being weighed against gold and precious stones on his birthday, and so on. There are scenes reconstructing sieges and battles, great victories and the capture of rebel chiefs. Weddings and festivals are celebrated in all their colour and glory. If the chroniclers speak of Arabs and Turks, Tajiks and Kurds, Ethiopians and Circassians; or of Ranas and Raos and rajas of different clans from the lands of the Rajputs— Rathore, Sisodia, Kachhwaha, Hada, Chauhan, Jhala among them—being in constant attendance at the durbars, it is in these pages that we see them. There is here, in the leaves of the *Padshahnama*, a clear sense of 'a court petrified by opulence and ritual'.

There was of course much other work done for and at the Shahjahani court: albums were prepared, portraits were painted, events like the accession to the throne were recorded by great painters. But one cannot escape the feeling that here was an artistic tradition nearing the end of its life. Under Aurangzeb, painting continued but truly little stands out; and, after him, but for a brief spark under Muhammad Shah, it went into decline. Painters working in the style remained and some of them continued working into the nineteenth century. Yet of the great Mughal style what remained was a memory. But a part of that memory must include the fact that painting under the Great Mughals did not only reflect 'an interest that is exclusively in persons and events', and that it was not 'essentially an art of portraiture and chronicle'. It was that, but it was also more than that.

———

Rajput painting, in contradistinction to Mughal, was little known, at least to the outside world, till the beginning of the twentieth century. It had a history that went back to pre-Mughal days, but it lay in obscure and unexplored, even if royal, corners till Ananda Coomaraswamy rediscovered it, gave it a name, and published distinguished examples of it in the early years of the twentieth century. His work, *Rajput Painting, Being an Account of the Hindu Paintings of Rajasthan and the Panjab Himalayas*, published from Oxford in 1916, came as a revelation and has stayed as a classic, for in it he distilled for the 'world out there' the essence of Rajput work. 'Their ethos is unique:' he wrote introducing the subject,

> what Chinese art achieved for landscape is here accomplished for human love. Here if never and nowhere else in the world the Western gates are opened wide. The arms of lovers are about each other's necks, eye meets eye, the whispering sakhis speak of nothing else but the course of Krishna's courtship, the very animals are spell-bound by the sound of Krishna's flute and the elements stand still to hear the ragas and raginis. This art is only concerned with the realities of life; above all, with passionate love service, conceived as the means and symbol of all union.

And then continued:

> Rajput art creates a magic world where all men are heroic,
> all women are beautiful and passionate and shy, beasts both
> wild and tame are the friends of man, and trees and flowers
> are conscious of the footsteps of the Bridegroom as he passes
> by. This magic world is not unreal or fanciful, but a world of
> imagination and eternity, visible to all who do not refuse to
> see with the transfiguring eyes of love.

These words—unmatched in their eloquence incandescent with perception—
still give shape to our understanding and appreciation of Rajput work. Apart
from interpreting its spirit, however, Coomaraswamy also pieced together a
history of Rajput painting, which now seems very dated, considering all the
fresh material that has been discovered since—a quantum of new works, new
approaches to classification, the linkages with other styles and regions. This
is especially the case in the marked distinction the great art historian drew
between Rajput and Mughal painting. The difference between the two was a
recurring theme in his writing. 'Mughal art,' he wrote initially,

> is one of miniature painting, as Persian is an art of illumination.
> In the rare cases where Mughal work is executed on palace
> walls, it has the character of miniatures enlarged. Mughal
> art is at home in the portfolios of princely connoisseurs, but
> Hindu paintings have stepped from the walls of shrines and
> palaces and public buildings where their traces linger still.
> Mughal art is secular, intent upon the present moment, and
> profoundly interested in individuality. . . . It is dramatic
> rather than static; young, fond of experiment and ready to
> assimilate. It is splendid and attractive, but it rarely touches
> the deep springs of life. Its greatest successes are achieved
> in portraiture and in the representation of courtly pomp

and pageantry. All its themes are worldly, and through sheer intensity of observation—passionate delineation—sometimes raises individual works such as the 'Dying Man' . . . to the highest possible rank, yet the subject matter of Mughal art, as such, is of purely aristocratic interest: while that of the Rajput painters is universal. The distinction of Mughal from Rajput painting is indeed nowhere more apparent than in the fact that the former is aristocratic and professional, while the latter is at once hieratic and popular, and often essentially mystic in its suggestion of the infinite significance of the most homely events. Mughal courtiers would not have been interested in an art about herdsmen and milkmaids, nor Vaishnavas in pictures of elephant fights.

In his 1927 *History of Indian and Indonesian Art*, Coomaraswamy spoke about the distinction again, calling attention to the fact that the approach of the Mughal painters was personal, with 'names of at least a hundred Mughal painters . . . known from their signatures, while of Rajput painters it would be hard to mention the names of half a dozen, and I know of only two signed and dated examples'. He also spoke of Mughal painting being 'academic, dramatic, objective, and eclectic; Rajput painting is essentially an aristocratic folk art, appealing to all classes alike, static, lyrical, and inconceivable apart from the life it reflects'.

However, here his approach to the subject of distinction, one realizes, was more nuanced than before. For, in a footnote, he explained:

It is unnecessary here to discuss in detail the Rajput elements present in true Mughal painting. These Indian elements are apparent in several directions, (1) the illustration of Hindu themes in the first quarter of the seventeenth century, (2) the adoption of Hindu costume at the courts of Akbar and Jahangir in the 'Rajput period', (3) the fusion of themes and styles in the eighteenth century, especially in Oudh, producing mixed types, and (4) the fact that more than half of the Mughal painters were native Hindus. All these conditions create resemblances between Mughal and Rajput painting, quite superficial in the case of 1 and 2, more fundamental in the case of 3 and 4.

In the light of the considerable additions to our information since this was written, and of having gained a somewhat fuller understanding of the cultural situation that prevailed, some things need to be said. The relationship between Mughal and Rajput painting, it seems, was more of a circular nature—one feeding into the other, and in turn being enriched by it—than of being the opposites of each other. With the great prestige of the empire, and the fact that it was the dominant power in India, the style of the Mughals came to set certain standards. It was natural for influences to travel from the imperial court to different parts of the country, and for it to set trends. At the same time the Mughals—whose painting almost from the days of the foundation of the imperial atelier under Akbar had started absorbing elements of the 'Indian' styles—were always recruiting talented artists who must have brought with them their own understanding and their own energies.

Insights can be gained from a range of facts. A host of Muslim artists were at work in Rajasthani courts, working on what can be called 'Hindu' themes—Nasir Din and Sahib Din at Mewar, Arif and Rahim and Ghulam Ali at Jodhpur, extended families of Muslim *ustad*s at Bikaner, to take some prominent examples. Mughal paintings kept landing up in Rajput collections: the great Akbar-period Ramayana and *Razmnama* in the *pothikhana* of Jaipur, for instance; and portraits of individuals that were copied in their own surroundings by Rajasthani artists. Constantly, it appears, different strands were being woven together.

103

The history of the *Ragamala* painted at Chunar near Benares in 1591 is a brilliant example of how territories were transgressed, objects moved, styles spread. This *Ragamala* was painted by three sons of Shaikh Bahlul, pupils of the Mughal masters Mir Sayyid Ali and Khwaja 'Abd-al Samad. The series is believed to have been acquired by a Hindu chief, Rao Surjan of Bundi, while acting as governor of that region on behalf of the Mughal overlord, and taken to Bundi where it became a model for some superb *Ragamala*s painted there by local artists. Clearly, the processes at work were complex, and fruitful.

Coomaraswamy applied the term 'Rajput Painting' to painting that flourished in two different areas—Rajasthan and the Pahari region—far apart from each other in terms of distance but all under the rule of Rajput chiefs, and bound together by a common culture, of which Hindu thought and literature in Indian languages was such a substantive part. That Rajput painting was 'the counterpart of the vernacular literature of Hindustan' is largely true—texts like the *Sur Sagar* of Surdas, the *Rasikapriya* and the *Kavipriya* of Keshavadasa, the *Satsai* of Bihari were common currency. But there were also all those great works in Sanskrit: sacred texts like the Ramayana and the Mahabharata; the Puranas such as the *Bhagavata*, the *Skanda*, the *Harivamsa*, and the *Markandeya* with the *Devi Mahatmya* embedded in it, with all their wonderful stories and their stirring strain of devotion. Then there were the authoritative and emotion-charged poetic texts like the *Rasamanjari*, the *Gita Govinda*, the *Naishadhacharita*; rhetorical works that dealt on the one hand with music, like the *Ragamalas*, and on the other with *Nayikabheda*, the classification of *nayak*s and *nayika*s. Remarkably few chronicles were at hand, but there was an abundance of romantic tales told in a folk manner—*Madhu Malati*, *Dhola Maru*, *Sohni Mahiwal*, and the like. This was a world barely entered, if ever, by the painters of the Mughals; but durbar scenes, processions, entertainments, hunting scenes, portraits, were areas that were clearly shared by both.

Rajasthan covers an enormous area and it was dotted with many kingdoms, some remarkably large and others relatively smaller but equally proud—

Mewar, Marwar, Bikaner, Bundi, Kota, Kishangarh, Jaisalmer, Sirohi, Amber/Jaipur, among them—ruled by dynasties that claimed descent from mythological ancestors, although connected accounts of their histories can be traced to somewhere between the fifteenth and sixteenth centuries. Following the norms of good kingship as laid down in authoritative texts, each ruler was a patron and a supporter of the arts. The region was rich therefore in painting activity, each state or *thikana* having families or groups of painters working for the royal house or members of the high nobility.

A large number of names of highly gifted artists have emerged from Rajasthan over the years: Sahib Din, Manohar, Bagta, Chokha, Nihal Chand, Bhawani Das, Rukn-ud-din, Jagannath, Sahib Ram, Nathu, Harji, Qasim, among them, and their hands have been identified. It would be hard here to list even in brief the outstanding series or works associated with each centre. But one can at least recall to one's mind the great flair of the work in Mewar, the abstractions of Jodhpur, the cool precision of Jaipur, the elegance of Kishangarh, the poetic resonance of Bundi, the energy of Kota.

The range of themes treated in Rajasthani work, the variety of styles, the approaches taken by the artists, all make for a world saturated in colours and singularly rich in imagination. Here lovers cling to each other in abandon, surrounded by a mosaic of cushions and bolsters; elephants run amok and dart under arches scraping their sides; armies of monkeys and bears turn into a vast cloud as they advance upon Lanka; the universe comes into being before one's eyes as matter begins to form from void; a tiger shot in a forest tumbles nineteen times over before it falls to the ground; a blind poet envisions baby Krishna waking up; princes stand on marble embankments feeding crocodiles; the Goddess impales the buffalo-demon on her trident even as she smiles; turbans adorning royal heads rise vertically in the air; boats ply on gentle waters while lovers escape to fragrant arbours. There is so much to see here, and savour, as painters play around with time and keep manipulating space at will: a world of 'imagination and eternity' as it was once described.

————————

At some distance from Rajasthan, but joined to it in spirit, is another fragrant world: the northern 'branch' of Rajput painting known as Pahari, meaning, literally, of the hills. A large number of big and small states make up the area—once called the 'Punjab Hills'—on either side of the river Ravi: Jammu, the largest in the group to the west of the river, along with Basohli, Mankot, Bandralta, Jasrota; and Kangra, the largest in the group to the east, with Nurpur, Guler, Chamba, Mandi, Kulu, Bilaspur, and others.

The fact that Jammu and Kangra were the premier states of the region in terms of size and resource led Coomaraswamy to associate them with two principal styles—one marked by the vigour and abandon of the primitive, and the other tender in spirit and fluent in line. This classification, based on the idea that each state had a style of its own, has only been challenged some fifty years ago. Today's scholars argue that it was not the state that determined the style but the artist family—the *gharana*, as in the world of Indian classical music—which was its basis.

This paradigm had larger implications, for it could be relevant for understanding how things worked outside the Pahari area as well. However, this way of approaching styles could work only if more information about families and, wherever possible, artists, could be gathered first. For the art of the Pahari region, this problem was addressed by going to unusual and almost never used sources for collecting information and constructing genealogies: locating it in the *bahi*s of the *panda*s—records kept by priests in their registers at major centres of pilgrimage—and in the governmental records of land rights.

A sizeable body of information was thus gathered, ordered and analysed. Names of artists emerged from these; family relationships could be established and genealogies constructed; native places were determined; some dates appeared; occasionally, connections with patrons could be tracked; in a few cases, even swiftly made drawings by painters in the registers of the priests surfaced. With the help of this body of information, the putting together of genealogies of some significant families of artists in the Pahari region—such as those of Pandit Seu of Guler, of Kripal of Nurpur, and of Purkhu of Kangra, to take just three examples—became possible.

The beginnings of Pahari painting are not easy to determine and the subject has been one of debate and disagreement. The earliest dated document to be found in the area—the date is in the form of a chronogram that can be read in two different ways, but both readings place it in the third quarter of the sixteenth century—is a superbly painted manuscript of the *Devi Mahatmya*, consisting of eighteen double-sided *pothi*-format folios, each with the text written in the centre of the page and paintings in the margins. The work seems to be stylistically affiliated to the celebrated *Chaurapanchasika* group which has never been associated with this region till now. All the same, it is there, and seems to have intrinsic evidence that it was painted, or at least scripted, at Jaisinghpur in the Kangra region.

Not far removed from this in time, from the first half of the seventeenth century, is a body of highly accomplished work that seems to have been painted in Mandi in a style that leans upon the Mughal in different ways. The work includes portraits of a ruler, large-sized leaves from a *Bhagavata Purana* and a Ramayana series, and isolated images of the Goddess. In the third quarter of the seventeenth century the painter Kripal of Nurpur painted a brilliant group centring on aspects of Devi, the Great Goddess, and a series based on a Sanskrit classic, the *Rasamanjari*; and, towards the end of that century—in 1694–95—Kripal's son, Devidasa, painted another version of the same text for a patron in Basohli.

In the little principality of Guler was active, at least from the opening of the eighteenth century, the immensely gifted family of Pandit Seu from whose hands have come some of the most brilliant works that one associates with the Pahari area: a Ramayana of c. 1720 by Pandit Seu himself; a *Gita Govinda* series dated 1730 by his elder son, Manaku (see p. 464), as also a very extensive series of finished paintings and drawings of the *Bhagavata Purana*; from c. 1740 onward, a large body of most delicately painted and drawn portraits and records of private moments in the life of his patron, Balwant Singh, by the pandit's second son, Nainsukh (see p. 362 and detail above). And in the hand of the next two generations of the same family, were executed some of the most celebrated series of Indian paintings, all ascribed to 'Kangra' once: a *Gita Govinda*, a *Bhagavata Purana*, a Ramayana, a *Nala–Damayanti* and an *Usha–Aniruddha* group, a Bihari *Satsai*, a *Ragamala*. Families of painters active at other centres in Mankot, Bandralta, Chamba, Bilaspur, Bahu, Kulu were also engaged in turning out, between 1700 and 1825, great amounts of work, now flamboyant, now delicate, but almost always steeped in feeling. Styles vary as do approaches, but it all keeps moving between hot intensity and cool elegance. Some of the work, as in Kripal's *Rasamanjari* series (see pp. 204, 456 and 460), gives one the feeling that it is a visual counterpart of that concentration, that single-minded focusing of the mind, that a devotee aims for as he sits down to meditate. Thoughts of the outside world, of all things that could distract, are pushed out and a fine, pointed ray of light is trained at the centre. On the other hand, in work like Nainsukh's there is gossamer lightness. Idioms seem not to dominate his work and conventions are but handmaidens. What shines forth is the painter's ability to seize a detail, a most mundane detail sometimes, and with incredible grace exalt it.

———

At the very time that major developments were taking place in the north—at the Mughal court as much as in the Rajput world—activity was under way south of the Vindhyas, most of it at the Deccani courts ruled by Muslim Sultans: chiefly Ahmednagar, Bijapur and Golconda. There is a somewhat different flavour to this work, but Deccani is now spoken of in the same breath as the major schools and styles of the north. Names of great patrons— Murtaza Nizam Shah of Ahmednagar, Ibrahim Adil Shah II of Bijapur, Quli and Abdulla Qutb Shah of Golconda—are, or need to be, as much on the horizon of our awareness as those of the great patrons in the north.

It all starts a bit mysteriously, though. At the end of the sixteenth century perhaps, one suddenly comes upon different but seriously dispersed series of *Ragamala* paintings: with long inscriptions in Sanskrit at the top—the text paraphrased or reduced to captions in Persian—and with superbly painted images of Ragas and Raginis, Hindol, Varari, Gauri, Trivani. The musical modes are seen in lush but highly stylized garden settings: elegant women— tall and lissom, narrow-waisted and ample-hipped though not always full-breasted—dressed in *choli*-blouses and *ghaghra*-skirts with flamboyant *orhani*-veils that almost trail on the ground, move about, singing, making music, clinging to lovers while seated on swinging beds.

There is an unearthly air about these folios—abstract half-moon patterns mark the ground partly obscured by palm-like trees in some; in others the earth—if it is the earth at all—is covered by cotton-like pink-coloured shapes that now look like clouds, now like rounded rocks; figures seem to float in the air; and, above everything else, peacocks take to wind, their tails brushing treetops (see pp. 420 and 424). Where these *Ragamala* leaves come from it has not been possible to determine exactly. They are placed sometimes in Ahmednagar but, more often, generally in the 'northern Deccan' region, possibly on account of the proximity of that region to the few remaining Hindu centres of power, and because of the occurrence of meticulously composed Sanskrit texts that appear on them. But one does not know this with any certainty.

At Ahmednagar, in any case, there were signs of an early flowering of painting, important illustrated works such as the *Tarif-i Hussain Shahi* appearing there as early as 1565. Among the earliest Deccani works to draw attention to itself, however, was a portrait of a prince seated on a delicately crafted throne, issuing instructions to a courtier while a retainer stands behind, waving a long cloth fly whisk even as a young boy approaches the prince with what looks like a *paan* in hand. The painting, dated generally to c. 1575, believed to be a portrait of Sultan Murtaza Nizam Shah of Ahmednagar, and now in the Bibliothèque Nationale in Paris, is brilliantly painted: crisp and colourful and slightly enigmatic. But it also affords us clear views of some details or characteristics that become recurring features in Deccani work: men wearing nearly transparent *jama*s that almost sweep the ground; the long and flamboyant *patka*-waistbands with their double strands appearing a little agitated as they hang in front; the metal belt at the waist with a curiously shaped purse-like golden object suspended from it, stroking the thigh; above all, the fact that a long piece of muslin cloth, rather than a *chauri* or peacock's-tail fly whisk, is waved over the Sultan's head. The last-mentioned feature is charged with political meaning: in the uneasy situation that existed between the Deccani Sultans and the all-powerful Mughal emperors in the north, the use of the traditionally 'higher' forms of fly whisks would have been tantamount to a declaration of 'sovereign status'—something the Sultans did not enjoy vis-à-vis the Mughal emperors, and would thus have invited serious displeasure.

The Deccan Sultanates, established in the fourteenth century, always maintained direct contact with centres of Islamic power outside India, such as Iran, and there was much coming and going between them. The work done by the painters for the Sultans therefore frequently bore the impress of work in those distant lands. But it also sprang from the cultural complex that Deccani society was, consisting as it did of Hindus, Muslims, Arabs, Persians and imported slaves. There are no great works that deal with historical themes in the Deccan, nor much interest in ceremonials and processions of the Mughal kind. On the other hand, there is a celebration of the joys of life, wine and poetry often leading the way. In general, there is about Deccani work, as the collector and art historian Mark Zebrowski put it, the 'fantastic mood of a mirage', for the painters were able to create 'a restless opulence and a romantic nostalgia for another time and space'.

Nowhere was this seen better than in the work done under Ibrahim Adil Shah II (1579–1627) at Bijapur. The Sultan was a man of remarkable taste and catholicity of outlook. There appears to have been something mystical in his nature, for poet, musician, writer, that he was—the famous *Kitab-i Nauras* was his composition—he appears to have attracted talent from all

over the world—not only because he had something to give but also because he always wanted to receive and gain. Zuhuri, the celebrated poet, was at his court, as was the greatly talented painter Farrukh Hussain (or Farrukh Beg), who appears to have moved between the Mughal court and Bijapur. The glitter of this Sultan's persona and of the talent of his painters is reflected in several of his portraits: standing holding castanets, playing on the *tambur*, hawking, riding an elephant. To his reign belong also some stunning renderings of dervishes and *yogini*s (see detail at right and

p. 514) men and women who had cut their ties with the world. Some of the studies of dervishes from the Deccan—inwardly turned men living almost in penury but visited by men of rank and power—are moving. And the *yogini*s whom we see in Deccani painting—young and attractive women, sometimes of princely background, wandering about, ash-besmeared, part ascetic, part sorceress, possessed of strange powers—leave one at once seduced and mystified.

At Golconda again, where for some time almost purely Safavid and Turkish elements dominated, the court resounded with the sounds of music and recited poetry. Local tradition speaks sometimes of their Sultan, Muhammad Quli Qutb Shah (1580–1612), in the same breath as Ibrahim Adil Shah II of Bijapur. The Sultan was himself a poet, often celebrated as the first great Urdu poet who wrote in the 'Dakhani' idiom, and his *Kulliyat*, or 'Complete Works', continues to be published even today. His artists painted for him images to accompany his verses, and much more. Fantastic landscapes were created and among the most intriguing works attributed to this Sultan's court is 'The Speaking Tree', a visualization of the tree at the island of Waqwaq which Alexander the Great is believed to have seen: made up of countless figures of animals and humans hidden inside or suspended from leafy branches while the trunk of the tree is made up entirely of writhing, intertwined snakes. It is a disturbing but dazzling work, mystifying by intent, surreal in effect (see p. 164 and detail on p. 112). Succeeding reigns after that of Quli Qutb Shah saw continued activity and there are some affecting portraits, some flamboyant, others more restrained, of rulers and their mentors. But what is of compelling interest from the Golconda workshops are some studies of courtesans or *nayika*s, their bold coyness captured with great elan by the painters.

The course of things in the Deccan changed with Hyderabad coming under Mughal hegemony, as well as Bijapur and Golconda, which were annexed by Aurangzeb. There seems to have been a dispersal of Deccani painters to other centres of painting in the north, many of them moving to courts in Rajasthan. The Deccani style did continue here, however, some of it innovative, some rooted in memories of the past.

To the late eighteenth and the nineteenth centuries belong a range of styles, most of them subsumed under the somewhat awkward but now established title, 'Company Painting'. The 'Company' referred to is, of course, the East India Company—in local parlance often called the 'Company Bahadur'—which had taken control of large parts of the country by then. Many of its officers turned to 'native' painters to create works, sometimes whole series, that recorded for them the 'fact of India'. For many of them this 'fact' consisted of a record of all the trades and professions and callings which they could see around them in this land, but which would be unfamiliar to those who were 'back home'. For others, people and customs and manners were of interest; still others wanted to preserve a memory of the sights amidst which they were living while in India. A small number—connoisseurs, amateur artists, collectors—took genuine interest in Indian art, and some even developed a measure of respect and admiration for the Indian mind, wanting to approach it through images.

The motives that led to the founding of the Company School were thus mixed: curiosity; creation of a record in the absence of photography which came in only—and hesitantly—towards the middle of the nineteenth century; real delight in art. A Mrs Fay, who landed in 1780 in Madras where some European buildings had by then been built, was struck by the sights: 'Asiatic splendor, combined with European taste is exhibited around you on every side, under the forms of flowing drapery, stately palanquins, elegant carriages, innumerable servants, and all the pomp and circumstance of luxurious ease, and unbounded wealth.' Another lady, Maria Nugent, noticed bazaars where 'copper vessels, crockery, rice, sugar, gods and goddesses, knives, muslins, silks . . . were all displayed together—all sorts of coloured turbans and dresses, and all sorts of coloured people—the crowd immense—the sacred Brahmin bull walking about and mixing with the multitude'. On the other hand, a highly cultivated civil servant like Mountstuart Elphinstone was taken in by 'the mosques, the minarets, tombs and gardens of so many Mohammedan cities, the marble courts of the Palace of the Moguls, peopled with the recollection of former times, and surrounded with the remains of fallen greatness'. These made a vivid impression and, as he wrote, 'could not but affect the imagination'.

From all this, a number of situations emerged, somewhat naturally. With the Mughal empire having nearly collapsed and many 'native states' having shrunk in resources and power, the painters traditionally bound to those centres of power had by then started looking for opportunities elsewhere. A number of British civilians, keen on art on the one hand and on creating a visual record on the other, were in search of local artists who could work for them or assist them. Despite their reservations about the way the Indian artist worked—'they have a slender knowledge of the rules of proportion, and none of perspective', one of them wrote; another remarked that 'they are very unsuccessful in the art of shading', while yet another rued that the art of the Indians was 'conducted by no scientific principles, and the effect produced is the result of patient exactness, or a happy knack, rather than of a well-conceived design'—they attached Indian artists to themselves.

The artists were recruited for various ends. Some were employed as draughtsmen on official surveys; others to make copies of ornamental details on monuments, or to do specialized work for institutions such as the Botanical Gardens or a menagerie in Bengal, to document flora and fauna. For the Indian artists this was an opportunity to learn different techniques, ways of seeing and rendering things. As the art historian Mildred Archer noted:

> Stimulated . . . by apprenticeship to Company servants, the deliberate copying of British originals, the study of prints and water-colours, and even by direct instruction, Indian painters began to modify their traditional techniques in a British direction. They gave up using gouache, which Europeans found hard and dry, and began to paint in water-colour on European paper. They ceased to paint on a prepared ground and learnt to draw in pencil or sepia wash directly on to the paper. They modified their colour, tempering brilliant reds, oranges and pinks with sombre sepia, indigo blue and muted greens.

In the welter of 'Company' works, the range is wide and can be a bit disconcerting at times. Dreary sets of 'trades and professions' jostle with superbly executed natural history drawings; unfeeling likenesses stand next to sharply observed and subtly rendered portraits. Important centres of Company work emerged—Tanjore, Benares, Patna, Murshidabad, Calcutta,

Agra, Delhi, Lahore, among them. Discerning patrons—like Chief Justice Sir Elijah Impey and his wife, Lady Impey, and, a bit later, William and James Fraser and Col James Skinner—commissioned extensive series. And the names of some outstanding artists stand out—Ghulam Ali Khan, Ghulam Murtaza Khan, Zain-al Din, Bhawani Das, Ram Das, Shaikh Muhammad Amir, among them. The intensive effort that has gone into researching Company work—as much of interest to British scholars as to us here—has thrown up material that is now a part of the mainstream of Indian painting. What emerges is a school of painting which went beyond its official intent—to document—and created instead an often moving style of European technique combined with Indian sensibility.

Consider, for example, the series of portraits—some of individuals, but many of groups of people—that painters working for the Fraser brothers created (see p. 386). So acutely studied are the faces and the costumes, and so sharp is the delineation of personalities, the understanding of character, that it almost takes one's breath away. Portraiture was not unknown to Indian painters and, at the Mughal court, it had attained great heights, as one knows. But this work has a different flavour: an uncommon blend of Mughal reticence and European naturalism, something done in 'anticipation of photography' to use Stuart Cary Welch's phrase. Nearly every figure is frontally seen, full faces looking intently at the painter, in all honesty, with not a trace of artifice. There are portraits, too, of people of ordinary or no rank: a foot soldier, a messenger, a peasant, a village guard, and so on. And then, as if for the first time, we see portraits of women: demure courtesans and seductive public performers, but all specific individuals, looking out of the frame directly at the viewer, with ease in their stances and an air of insouciance all around them (see p. 402 and detail on p. 116). Clearly, by the end of the nineteenth century, one can sense a different wind blowing throughout India and through the world of its painters.

––––––––––

This, very briefly, is the story of Indian painting from the twelfth century till the end of the nineteenth century. Whether or not from it emerges a sense of there being a specifically Indian 'aesthetic' can be argued. But what does emerge is that to look at an Indian painting is to enter a layered world that does not reveal all its treasures immediately. 'Reading' an Indian painting can be likened, perhaps, to watching a Rajasthani *phada*—the large painted textile that tells a detailed and complex tale—being unrolled and installed, as the viewer sits on a sand dune on a dark night, waiting for the performance to begin. Then, the *bhopa*-singer begins to sing the epic tale, following his assistant who, oil lamp in hand, moves in front of the painted images on the scroll, now illuminating one episode and now another, proceeding in a non-linear fashion. Slowly, bit by bit, segment by segment, areas light up, and things begin to fall in place. The work begins to 'speak' to the engaged viewer, leading him to new ways of seeing as he experiences the delight of discovering all that lies embedded in it. And when that happens, 'the flame', as aestheticians of old say, 'leaps from the object to the viewer'.

CLOSE ENCOUNTERS *with* 101 GREAT WORKS

A Note on Selection and Arrangement

There is an old Bengali saying that goes '*baansh boney dom kaana*', meaning, 'In the forest of bamboos, the bamboo cutter goes nearly blind', not knowing what to cut and what to leave behind.

It is not easy to cull 101 works from several thousand works one knows well. Such a selection has to be personal. The 101 works that follow are included, first and foremost, because each one of them speaks to me with a strength and clarity I cannot ignore. Others may, of course, see and hear these paintings differently. In my selection, I have also tried to represent the different periods, the subjects and themes that inspired painters, the range of regional styles, historically important works, those influenced by foreign traditions, and the works of some great masters—all of which I have written about in the introductory essay. Though each of these paintings is, in my opinion, a great work, this is not to say that they are the greatest masterpieces of Indian painting. There are many others, and I hope this book will inspire the reader to seek them out and explore them.

As with the selection, so with the ordering of these 101 works—it has not been easy. The intention in this volume is not to present yet another history of Indian painting, but to bring readers/viewers into close contact with each work, and to make them feel the texture of its form and thought, to taste its essence or *rasa*. The paintings are arranged not in chronological order but in four different groups—Visions, Observation, Passion, Contemplation. These must by no means be seen as rigid categories, for their boundaries are fluid. Visions can be informed by passion; observation can lead to contemplation. It can, equally, be the other way—or any other way— around: contemplation can spring from visions, and observation can be expressed in terms of passion. There is, however, a thinking behind this organization.

The paintings that come under 'Visions' are chiefly those that envision sights and events unseen, but that have for long been part of our 'awareness' and imagination. Thus, it includes images of abstraction like Hiranyagarbha, the Cosmic Egg, floating on the waters of eternity, or the golden mount, Meru. Here, too, are iconic images of goddesses bestowing grace or striking fear, and of divine couples looking down from snowy peaks. Then there are works relating to mythologies or heroic tales: the Ramayana, the *Bhagavata Purana*, the Speaking Tree. Krishna holds a mountain aloft on the palm of his hand; seven-storeyed vehicles rise in the air; trees speak; cows levitate in the air; the great hero Hamza battles dragons breathing fire; and Neptune roars through the oceans.

'Observation' is perhaps somewhat misleading as a title for a group of paintings. For in these works, imagination and idealization mingle with clear-eyed observation. The paintings in this section are mostly based on real sights, people and scenes, seen or imagined by the painter, and some of them especially commissioned by the patron. Naturally, portraits figure large in this group, as do scenes of palace life and princely pursuits, even though these are sometimes modified, reconstructed and given an unusual twist: the emperor Jahangir looking at a portrait of his father in one, shooting arrows at 'Poverty' in another; a rendering of the emperor Akbar, breaking the conventions of royal portraiture, with his eyes lowered in repose; a towering Raja Sidh Sen of Mandi striding forth like a *yaksha* of old. Some of these 'observations' capture an inner reality: a dying Inayat Khan gazing into nothingness; a hunter becoming the hunted as a lion pounces on him; a chameleon sitting utterly still yet casting a sly eye at everything around him.

The paintings under the section titled 'Passion' are largely those inspired by poetic texts like the *Gita Govinda*, the *Rasamanjari*, the *Sur Sagar*, the *Rasikapriya*. There are a few, too, from the *Ragamala* series, which depict musical modes and the emotions they evoke. The paintings here depict an intensely poetic world; in them, passions rise sometimes gently, sometimes in a frenzy. Lovers cling to each other against a landscape glowing with the exuberance of spring; languid *nayika*s lie lost in thoughts of absent lovers; Radha and Krishna gaze silently into each other's eyes on the banks of the river Yamuna; Princess Champavati with her exquisite 'lotus face' confuses the bumble bees who, instead of heading to the lotus pond, swarm around her.

Finally, the serene world of 'Contemplation'. Intense, private and quiet— these works are relatively rare and thus especially striking. A saintly figure in a European chair quietly ponders over life, like Hamlet with a skull in his hands; 'Bu Ali' Qalandar, wearing a Sufi's woollen robe, sits under a tree in the wilderness, turning his head gently as if straining to hear an unstruck sound; sadhus sit in a circle around a pile of smouldering ash, each lost in his own thoughts; a regally attired *yogini*, her back turned towards her past, stands as if sharing her innermost thoughts with a mynah bird; an old pilgrim in tattered clothes moves haltingly forward, his expression suggesting he is reflecting over his life and the one hereafter.

Each person, however, has to approach all these works, and these sections, in his/her own way. They are assembled in this fashion to urge viewers to explore them with their eyes, mind and heart fully open. As the great poet Ghalib said:

Sad jalwa ru-ba-ru hai jo mizhgaan uthaaiye
Itna hai bas ki deed ke saamaan laaiye

There are sights without number out there;
If you would but lift your eyelashes a trifle,
And then, if you would but have the vision to see.

Visions

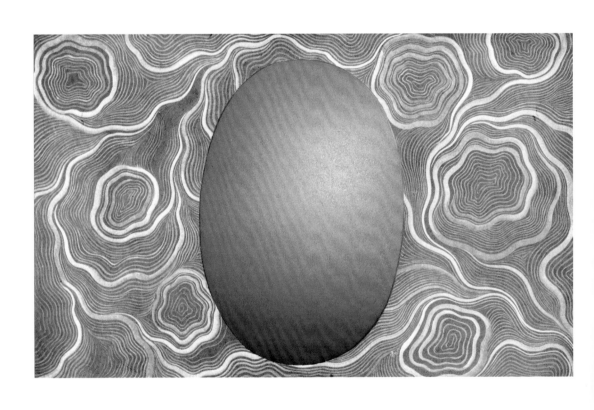

HIRANYAGARBHA
THE COSMIC EGG

Folio from a *Bhagavata Purana* series
Opaque watercolour and gold on paper
Pahari, by Manaku of Guler; c. 1740
21.8 cm × 32.2 cm (outer)
17.6 cm × 28 cm (inner)
Bharat Kala Bhavan, Varanasi

Among the many speculations about the Origins of Creation, the Beginnings of it All—something that Indian thought is rich in—there are references to the wondrous, mysterious Hiranyagarbha, literally, the 'golden womb' or 'golden egg'. In that ancient text the *Rigveda*, there is a whole composition named *Hiranyagarbha Sukta*, in praise of a single, supreme creator deity. The text is both fascinating and, in many ways, uplifting. Here is how it describes Hiranyagarbha:

Hiranyagarbha was present at the beginning; when born, he was the sole lord of created beings; he upheld this earth and heaven. . . . (he) is the giver of soul, the giver of strength, whose commands all (beings), even the gods obey, whose shadow is immortality, whose (shadow) is death . . . Who, by his greatness, has verily become the sole king of the breathing and seeing world, who rules over this aggregate of two-footed and four-footed beings . . . through whose greatness these snow-clad (mountains) exist, whose property men call the ocean with the rivers, whose are these quarters of space, whose are the two arms . . . by whom the sky was made profound and the earth solid, by whom heaven and the solar sphere were fixed, who was the measure of the water in the firmament . . . Whom heaven and earth established by his protection, and, shining brightly,

regarded with their mind, in whom the risen sun shines forth . . .
When the vast waters overspread the universe containing the germ
and giving birth to AGNI, then was produced the one breath of
the gods.

Let us offer worship with an oblation to the divine KA.

There are descriptions of the Golden Egg in other ancient texts as well. An
Upanishad says that the egg floated around in emptiness and the darkness
of non-existence for a long time, and then broke into two halves. One of
the oldest Puranas, the *Matsya Purana*, has this account of the beginnings
of creation: after Mahapralaya, the great dissolution of the Universe, there
was darkness everywhere and everything was in a state of sleep. Then
Svayambhu, the Self-Manifested Being, arose—a form beyond senses. It
created the primordial waters first and placed the seed of creation into it.
The seed turned into a golden womb, the Hiranyagarbha. Then Svayambhu
entered the egg.

The *Bhagavata Purana*, centring
as it does predominantly on the
deity Vishnu-Narayana, states
that in the beginning there
was Narayana alone: multi-
headed, multi-eyed, multi-
footed, multi-armed, multi-
limbed. This was the Supreme
Seed of all creation, subtler
than the subtlest, greater than
the greatest, larger than the
largest, and more magnificent
than even the best of all things,
more powerful than even the
wind and all the gods, more

resplendent than the Sun and the Moon, and more internal than even the mind and the intellect.

In the course of painting his great *Bhagavata Purana* series, the painter Manaku (see p. 108 in 'A Layered World') would surely have sat down to visualize the Hiranyagarbha. He must have struggled to come to terms with the thoughts behind the concept: reading about it from whatever might have been available to him, asking seniors in the family, a learned pandit perhaps, and then come to a decision. What he turned out, after all that, is a dazzling image. Those 'primordial waters' that the texts speak of, he spread over the entire surface of the page. There are no waves here, no great commotion, only concentric whirlpools and eddies, like giant rings of time on timeless waters. And in their midst, unmoving, completely still, floats the great golden egg, a perfect oval, seed of all that there is going to be.

––––––––––

A fascinating detail about this painting: when one sees the painting laid flat, the egg appears a bit dark, almost dominated by browns. It is when you hold the painting in your hand, as it was meant to be, and move it ever so lightly, that it reveals itself: the great egg begins to glisten, an ovoid form of the purest gold; true hiranya, *to use the Sanskrit term for the precious metal.*

A BODHISATTVA, POSSIBLY RATNAPANI

Detail from an *Ashtasahasrika Prajnaparamita* manuscript
Pigments on palm-leaf
Eastern India; Pala period; c. 1118
6 cm × 7.2 cm
Victoria and Albert Museum, London

Meditate upon the words AH-VAM-SA
As the jewels spin their webs around you
They will cause a rotating wheel of energy to swirl around you
As you follow the golden and dark waters
To their source deep below
Neither dark nor light
Yet shining with unearthly brilliance

Pass by the sandy shores of a river, friend
For many beings are there, dancing and luring
All passing travellers into their weaving games
From whence they never escape

Prajnaparamita—literally, the 'Perfection of Wisdom'—represents the oldest of the major forms of Mahayana Buddhism. The name denotes the female personification of wisdom, sometimes called the Mother of All Buddhas. The main creative period of Prajnaparamita thought extended from perhaps 100 BCE to 150 CE. The best-known work from this period is the *Ashtasahasrika Prajnaparamita (Eight Thousand–Verse Prajnaparamita)*.

Countless texts were scripted under the title *Ashtasahasrika Prajnaparamita*, and this image comes from one of the best known of those—the Vredenburg manuscript (see p. 75 in 'A Layered World'), now housed in the Victoria and Albert Museum in London. Only six of its original 179 folios have survived, and for the art historian they yield valuable information, as well as some stunning images.

The manuscript, according to the partial colophon that has survived, was copied in the thirty-sixth year of the reign of King Ramapala, of the Pala dynasty, but was paid for by a man called Udayasimha who had it scripted and illustrated 'for the benefit of the souls of his parents'. More recently, the covers of this manuscript appear to have been located in the collection of a Japanese scholar, and it is on them that an image of the personified Goddess of the Perfection of Wisdom has survived. Her representation on the cover makes perfect sense for she was the one who would protect the text inside.

She, it is believed, also symbolizes the direction of space from which the sun rises, the beginning of a path that, in a section of the text, Sadaprarudit was told to take. When he, the text says, found himself in the seclusion of a remote forest, a voice in the air said to him: 'Go east, son of good family! There you shall hear the perfection of wisdom.'

The folios from the manuscript contain only images of the Bodhisattvas, nine of them in all. Here, in this detail from a folio with neatly written text occupying most of the space on it, is seen a Bodhisattva, identified tentatively as Ratnapani, the one who bears the wish-fulfilling gem. With a smile hovering on his lips, head slightly inclined towards the right, torso bare, the lower part of the body clothed only in a brief wrap, the Bodhisattva sits in a 'stance of ease', as it is called, a large bolster cushion behind, one leg bent at the knee and placed flat on the ground, the other also bent at the knee but raised and inclined to the right.

One hand with exquisitely tapered fingers holds possibly a lotus; the other hand rests in the lap, but also holds an object that in the present state of the folio is not easy to determine. The figure is ensconced within a nearly circular frame, reddish orange in colour—plain and flat except for the richly decorated nimbus that throws the head of the Bodhisattva in relief. There is profuse jewellery on the body—a golden tiara-like crown, large circular rings in the ears, armlets, wristlets and bangles, even anklets, apart of course from the broad, delicately crafted waistband of gold.

The delicately modelled figure exudes serenity, but powers of 'compassionate destruction' are suggested by the presence of the Tantric figure of Hayagriva, seated to his left—wrathful and red, eyes fiercely open, limbs wrapped in tiger skin. The very presence of figures such as these made the manuscript a source of power and energy, conferring upon it a sacred status.

What strikes one also—something that one sees in many other illustrated manuscripts from the eastern region—is how this kind of work is so reminiscent of murals so far away from this region: Ajanta, Bagh and the like. It is as if the two were *sahodara*—'born of the same womb'—even if their scale is so different and so many centuries set them apart. But then who knows how things happened in those distant times—how movements took place, how images moved about, what channels existed.

THE GODDESS GREEN TARA DISPENSES BOONS

Detail from a folio of an *Ashtasahasrika Prajnaparamita* manuscript
Eastern India, Bengal; Pala period, early twelfth century
7 cm × 41.9 cm (size of folio)
The Metropolitan Museum of Art, New York

In the eastern part of India what might be called 'manuscript painting' blossomed and flourished, even though chronologies are difficult to establish, and names of artists or scribes hard to locate. The great age of wall paintings—at Ajanta and Bagh, for example—had come to an end well before the beginning of the second millennium, but traces of their style lingered, and one finds them in very small format on the surfaces of palm leaves in Bengal, Bihar and areas bordering Nepal.

Buddhism had begun to retreat in the rest of India but was still a dominant force in these regions, and it is this faith that provided the occasion, or the impetus, for these extraordinary illustrated manuscripts. The images are not necessarily illustrations for the actual text. They exist—Buddhas and Bodhisattvas, goddesses of different hues and fearsome divinities—to offer 'protection' to scribe and painter, donor and reader, text and repository. Spiritual merit resided in these manuscripts and the images of deities made the manuscript almost a sacred *mandala*-circle. The images were thus not mere adornment: there was magic in them, as it were. Each written and painted manuscript was therefore regarded with an exalting mix of reverence, affection and fear.

Among the most popular texts illustrated at this point of time—between the eleventh and twelfth centuries—was the *Ashtasahasrika Prajnaparamita*, 'The Perfection of Wisdom in 8000 verses'—a work of 'the most abstruse metaphysics' but containing images of a diversity of Buddhist deities and goddesses who had come to populate Mahayana belief, including frequently the goddess Tara who personified that wisdom. Tara was an embodiment of universal grace—born of the compassionate tears of Avalokiteshvara—the one who could take the devotee across the ocean of existence, her very name originating from the root *tri*, to cross.

This image is just a detail, no more than 7 cm in height, from a palm-leaf page that it shares with sacred text. It belongs to one of the most richly embellished *Ashtasahasrika Prajnaparamita* manuscripts that has survived. The manuscript itself is now dispersed, most leaves shared between the Metropolitan Museum in New York and Lhasa in Tibet. It cannot be dated with certainty, although stylistically it can be placed in the early years of the twelfth century, and it is presumed to have belonged once to one of the great monasteries of eastern India. But it has a colophon leaf which mentions that it was 'the pious gift of the queen Vihunadevi', a personage difficult to place. How many images figured in the manuscript would be difficult to guess at but here one sees Tara, in her green version, standing with a *chhatra*-parasol over her head, distributing boons, as is her generous wont. The devotees who crowd around her scramble to receive the gifts even when they know that her bounty is without limit. The old and the young, men and women, the infirm and the healthy, stand with hands outstretched, even as the goddess's two female attendants stand close by her side and gaze at her with eyes of wonder.

There is remarkable richness of colour and tone in the image and the line is impeccable—sinuous and flowing, able to achieve volume on its own. The goddess stands, legs firm, body flexed, one delicately painted hand held above her head as if in benediction, the other extended to give. The expression on her face is gentle as she lowers her gaze to look at the faithful. So much in the articulation of her form reminds one of the grace and fullness and gravity that one sees in Ajanta. There are also those same riches of decoration: strings of pearls and diaphanous clothing, elegant foliage and an ornate halo. It is as if the early style had taken a leap across space, landing on a remarkably small surface without losing any of its power or seductive charm.

At the same time, however, one begins to wonder if the style is not near to turning brittle. And whether, in the distance, there is a danger of clichés taking over.

A small group of 'illustrated' manuscripts from the eastern Indian school are known, nearly all of them Buddhist in theme, a few of them dated, and very few of them with narrative content. This particular manuscript has been attributed by John Guy to the 'Mahavihara Master'. Other masterly works include the famous Vredenburg manuscript in the Victoria and Albert Museum, London (see previous painting and pp. 75–76 in 'A Layered World'). It has been surmised that the work might have been done by a monk. It may also possibly have been commissioned at one of the famous monastic universities in the eastern part of India, such as Nalanda or Vikramashila.

THE HEAVENLY COURT OF INDRA

Folio from a *Kalpasutra* and *Kalakacharya Katha* manuscript
Opaque watercolour and gold on paper
Western India, Gujarat; c. 1475
11.3 cm × 26.8 cm
San Diego Museum of Art, Edwin Binney Collection

A famous scene in the canonical Jain text, the *Kalpasutra*, describes the chief of the gods descending from heaven and kneeling with an offering before Vardhamana Mahavira, the founder of Jainism. The scene is a very moving one, and Ananda Coomaraswamy observed that it was of 'cosmic and not merely temporal significance'. Surely, he went on to argue, that 'like Blake, the poet artist thought that there were listeners in other worlds than this'.

The episode from the life of Mahavira seen here, part of one of the most sumptuous manuscripts of the *Kalpasutra*, once housed in the Devasano Pado Bhandar (a famous Jain library), is close in spirit to the scene described by Coomaraswamy. It was an episode much loved by illustrators of the text, for it offered to them a whole range of pictorial opportunities. The news of the impending descent to earth of the great saviour, Mahavira, reaches every corner, and Indra, king of the gods, seated in his heavenly court, hears of it too. In his mind, an entire chain of events is going to follow, for he will order that the embryo which is to become the future *tirthankara* be transferred from the womb of a Brahmin woman to that of Queen Trishala, wife of the Kshatriya king Siddhartha.

Here, however—in a painting that occupies, in uncommon fashion, the entire surface of the page, with none of the usual text around it—the theme is simply the glory of the court of Indra, 'Wielder of the Thunderbolt', 'Destroyer of Ungodly Cities', 'Performer of a Hundred Sacrifices', as the text of the *Kalpasutra* describes him.

We read that when he heard the joyous news of the impending descent of Mahavira to earth, he was sitting in the celestial sphere, Sudharma, his body glowing with light, a wreathed crown on his head, a garland of wild flowers hanging down his chest, 'his garments spotless as the sky'. As usual, the king of gods was enjoying 'great heavenly pleasures amidst surroundings that reverberated with the sound of song and dance and of music made by strings, hand cymbals, horns, the deep-toned *mridanga* drum and the soft-voiced *pataha* drum'.

The painter sets out here to capture the joyous atmosphere of the heavenly court, filling the shimmering page not only with the looming, lustrous figure of Indra—attended upon by fly-whisk bearers and receiving the homage of two men who await his orders—but with row upon animated row of women dancers and musicians.

In his articulation of the scene, there is no real departure from the rigorous conventions of the style that the painter was working in. See the treatment of figures, the emphatically flattened space, the hieratic scaling, the levitating *chhatra* topped by *hamsa* figures, the fluttering scarves, for instance. But within these limits he creates a page filled with great movement and variation and rhythm.

The beautiful lapis lazuli blue that one sees used so profusely in this exquisitely scripted and illuminated manuscript forms the ground upon which each head is limned, surrounded by a nimbus of red. The movements and gestures of the dancers—some thirty-one of them—are most subtly varied; and there is great delicacy in the figurative patterns that one sees on the garments worn by everyone, especially by Indra. Everything combines to bathe this folio in an other-worldly light.

———————

Sadly, the Devasano Pado manuscript is now widely dispersed. For all its lavishness, it does not appear to have been done for any royal personage, or even for the head of a monastery. Two names, Sana and Jutha 'of Gandhara Bhandar', near Broach in Gujarat—possibly affluent merchants and certainly devout Jains—figure in the manuscript as persons who commissioned this copy of the revered text. However, no date is mentioned in the manuscript: it is only on stylistic grounds that it is generally given the date c. 1475. That period, towards the last quarter of the fifteenth century, seems to have been rich in sumptuous manuscripts, some of them, like the Narsinghji Pol Kalpasutra, *almost indistinguishable in quality from the Devasano Pado manuscript.*

بیسجیل دلما بکفتاد آرای | بیه سوی بهرام دار بدی چه | نمار هم اید دیا یدبت | بیه سازم لکنر بدیر کنل
از ترد دید دخن نامول | سیاه دخل لکنر بجخون درنر | موا ملء سیا ه دنریر درنر | دو خر زید تا بنله بخو دبت
موم همان لشکر نامول | زنده با کرت بند بو بزد | برفت سیا بان ستخر وکله | دو بجیل طوس بهبد رنشاه
نشاه میا دخل درخل ناه | | | دو با کار نامه یکا و ثاه
بر لند ذکی یم لند ذتاج | | مل شن میا دخل ذدا به جیحون | و دینی میا دخل یکر بنتر
نو کفنی عز و رسا بنتخن | سه بهر ها ه جنان جنان بجاح | د دین بیران دلزا سیاب | دو لد برز مد درم بهام دکوی
زو دلد لد انجا دجند کمان | جنت سا بیفنان نا بیان یاند | بان بهار لزیز از ذکر بی | بهر منز لی دی ها ه حود حوی

جو کاری ی اللدیر بر سل نل | زه خیشان کزیر کزک بیر هام | مه سرکشان یا تیره یا تلود | بیره یالد یفرصه صه یا تا ب
بیار رسل لی دخوان جل سیبل | یکی نهاکل بریز ل محنت | میدا ره کرد کبیر نویل | ارنشان ر بان مشکفه ارخت
بمرله زدین بوسی نفش | ابا تحن نبین سه بید کر | دو با فته بر نای درش | بیها یا بامه سه د بیس
نبا جه برا انبا کر کی بهر | حدلب کر نا یه بادزیر ی | یا با یست ردی نسیر ارتهم | مرح سراس بزد وکمر
میاد نور جه بشید کا ه د بیا ک | ارزش مبداد بیران شکاه | بیره غدی یا ل شکا ه | حود نیبا ز زیان یا بان سیل
یدد نبر ارود کرنتی کنان | بروکت کای بهوان بیا ه | بهر مید لزو نامود نهر باد | جلا بخ زکی یا ی دوار یرولو

RIVAL ARMIES MEET ACROSS THE RIVER

Folio from a Jainesque Sultanate *Shahnama*
Central India, possibly Malwa; mid-fifteenth century
11.8 cm × 19.8 cm
Museum Rietberg, Zürich, Gift of Balthasar and Nanni Reinhart

This richly coloured and startlingly stylized folio comes from a now dispersed manuscript of the *Shahnama*, Firdausi's great Persian epic. Nothing quite like it is known. The work bears no date, except that on the seal of a late owner; there is no indication of where it was written or painted; no name of painter or patron appears. The text is all in Persian, written in four columns on pages of a vertical, codex—Islamic?—format, yet the style of the paintings is far from Persian. The manuscript raises important questions of context and attitudes and might have a deep bearing on our understanding of what was happening in the world of painting during the Sultanate period, a time which has been relatively less explored by art historians.

The *Shahnama* as a text must have been widely known and copied—almost always for Muslim patrons—in the Sultanate period. Those works undoubtedly bore marks that showed its descent from the Persian tradition of painting. This work, however, has a distinctly different flavour and has many elements of style that come from a pronouncedly Indian—'native'—source, almost certainly Jain.

While the characters are all from the Persian epic, at every step in the folios from this manuscript one is reminded of things Indian. The projecting-further eye that one sees on some figures, the *chhatra* with *torana*-like fringes levitating in the air, thrones with no high backs or armrests, fly whisks held over princely figures, finely etched fingers of hands, tassels tied to the ends of hair, small settees with flattened melon backs, exquisitely patterned

141

textiles, full-bosomed women—all appear to come from Jain works as seen in *Kalpasutra* manuscripts.

Other conventions that one sees in various folios of this manuscript—the basket-weave pattern used in the river, the delineation of fire in the form of spiky flames, the little mango-stone circle marking the chin, the absence of pupils in the eyes of the dead or the dying, for instance—are a far cry from images painted in the Iranate tradition.

Almost certainly a Muslim patron, eager to have a copy of the *Shahnama* made, had the right scribe but could only find a painter from the Jain tradition. The painter was thrown a challenge and this exciting work, surprising in its quality, was what he created. Possessed of an air of freshness and energy, the work is bold, combining simplicity with sophistication, in a remarkably self-assured composition.

The *Shahnama* is a long tale of kings waging endless battles. In this picture, the young prince Siyavash of Iran, to the left of the image, arrives with his contingent to meet Afrasiyab, king of Turan, who with his companions stations himself on the other bank of the river Jihun. Negotiations are in progress, as indicated by the hands which are extended as if in conversation.

Nothing in it is quite like what one is used to seeing in the usual *Shahnama* illustrations. The delineation of the river reduced here to a slim stream, the toy-like horses, the uniform direction of glances, the unblinking eyes, the parasol held over old Afrasiyab's head, the helmets with camails and corselets of chain mail are all very different. The colours glow, the forms appear heroic, and the tension of the moment is palpable.

————————

Much remains obscure about the manuscript from which this painting comes and the fact that the folio is now widely dispersed does not help. It is unclear where it was made—art historians have claimed a range of places from Gujarat and Malwa to Jaunpur and Ahmednagar on stylistic grounds. We are on surer ground with the date. The mid-fifteenth century is generally agreed upon because of its closeness to work in the high period of Jain painting. Persian seals through the manuscript bear the name Muhammad Fazil and different dates ranging from 1696 to 1718 CE. These seals clearly belong to a late owner rather than to the manuscript itself.

KRISHNA SUBDUES TRINAVARTA, THE WHIRLWIND DEMON

Folio from a dispersed *Bhagavata Purana* series
Northern India, possibly Delhi–Mathura region; pre-Mughal, second quarter of the sixteenth century
18 cm × 23.5 cm
Freer Gallery of Art, Washington, Smithsonian Institution

'Oh learned sage,' the king Parikshit says at one point to Sukadeva in the course of the dialogue that serves as a frame to the *Bhagavata Purana*, one of the most sacred of all texts for Vaishnavas, 'be pleased to do me the favour of recounting to me the glorious exploits of him [Krishna] who has assumed human form through his Maya-power, and who pervades all sentient beings, and who, as the Controller of Self and as the Destroyer of the Time-Spirit, confers Liberation upon the spiritually minded, releasing them from the cycles of birth and death.'

The passage is from the opening chapter of the Tenth Book of the Purana, and sets the stage for Krishna's story. The words of this account are soaked in veneration, charged with the warmth of human emotion, and astir with action. There would scarcely be a true Vaishnava who is not deeply moved by this sacred tale.

The 'dispersed *Bhagavata Purana*', as this extraordinary series is often called, matches in many ways the telling of the tale. As if in a tapestry, dramatic episodes are woven with philosophical utterance, spirited action is succeeded by quiet, lyrical passages, signifying complete submission to the will of the Lord. So complete is the understanding of the Purana text by the painters that one cannot escape the feeling that they must themselves have grown up and worked in an atmosphere of devotion, even guided perhaps, while working, by superior minds who had felt the texture of the tale and plumbed its depths.

Among the countless episodes from the life of Krishna—the series might well have consisted originally of 300 folios if not more—the painting here deals with Krishna's defeat of Trinavarta, the demon who comes at the behest of the evil-intentioned Kamsa in the form of a whirlwind. Trinavarta has been sent to kill the infant Krishna as he plays in the courtyard of his parents' home.

Arriving with a gust of force, the text says, the demon 'enveloped the whole of Gokula in a cloud of dust, blinding the eyes of all inhabitants. . . . The quarters and intermediate points' trembled with his 'extremely terrible roar', and the whole village was covered in a cloud of darkness. In this confusion, the demon picked the baby Krishna up, and flew away to the skies only to start feeling, in the next instant, the weight of the divine child who had held him by the throat. Unable to breathe, the demon fell to the earth, all his limbs shattered by the fall 'like the cities cleft by the arrow of Rudra'. The baby remained completely unscathed. Yashoda, Krishna's devastated mother, and the rest of the village had witnessed a miracle.

The conventions of the *Chaurapanchasika* style (see p. 417, 'Remembering That Fawn-Eyed Beauty', and pp. 90–91 in 'A Layered World' for an explanation of the style) are all in place—for this *Bhagavata Purana* series falls squarely within that style. Soaking the page in dazzling colours, the painter produces here, daringly, what is his own version of the episode. He completely discards the idea of rendering the demon in his anthropomorphic or demonic form and turns him into a roaring swirl that rises and hangs over the scene, now looking like smoke, now like an unruly cloud, now like a cosmic vine throwing out shoots of diverse colours. No head or rakshasa's horn is seen and yet we know, much as the painter knew, that this is Trinavarta himself. Inside the maelstrom, Krishna plays, unconcerned, descending to reassure his distraught mother that all is well.

This is the way it proceeds in this remarkable series. The lines in Sanskrit inscribed at the back of the folio faithfully follow the text, but the painter/s continually bring in their own ideas. This, they seem to say, is how *we* see it.

———————

This series, of which only some 200 folios have survived, has been the subject of intensive study, especially by Daniel Ehnbom. So little, however, do we know about its date, authorship, place of painting and patronage, that it has been named differently at different times: the 'Palam Bhagavata', the 'Khajanchi Bhagavata', the 'Mitha-Nana Bhagavata', even the 'Scotch-tape Bhagavata'. The reference is, respectively, to the name of the village close to Delhi where a scholar said he had seen a colophon page; the person who once owned a sizeable segment of the series; the names of two men found on some of the leaves and assumed to be of the painters; and the fact that at one time Scotch tape was used to paste the crumbling leaves together. Opinion veers towards the series being painted for the great Vaishnava teacher, Vallabhacharya, or his son, Vitthalnath, who were active at this time in the Mathura region.

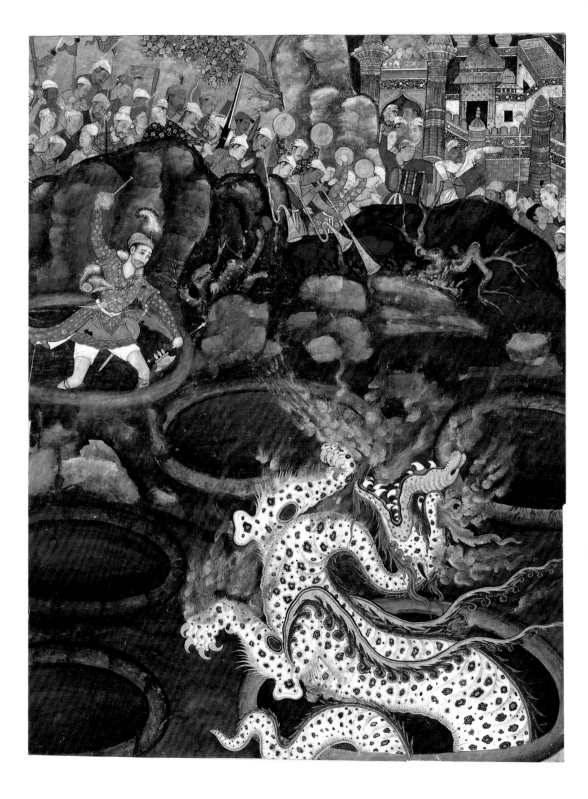

UMAR SLAYS A DRAGON WITH NAPHTHA

Folio from a *Hamzanama* manuscript
Mughal; c. 1567–72
61.9 cm × 51.2 cm
MAK, the Austrian Museum of Applied Arts, Vienna

> It is now seven years that the Mir [Sayyid Ali] has been busy in
> the royal bureau of books as commanded by His Majesty in the
> decoration and painting of the large compositions of the story of
> Amir Hamza and strives to finish that wondrous book which is one
> of the astonishing novelties that His Majesty has conceived of. Verily,
> it is a book the like of which no connoisseur has seen since the azure
> sheets of the heavens were decorated with brilliant stars, nor has the
> hand of destiny inscribed such a book on the tablet of imagination
> since the discs of the celestial sphere gained beauty and glamour
> with the appearance of the moon and the sun.

This is from a note by the sixteenth-century writer Mir Ala-al Dawla, who
was writing a commentary on poetry and an anthology of biographies of
poets active in Iran and in India. The 'Mir' he refers to is the celebrated
painter Sayyid Ali, one of the master painters and also a poet, who followed
Humayun to India when he returned from Iran.

'His Majesty' is evidently the emperor Akbar to whose court the writer had
attached himself, and the manuscript he describes is the *Hamzanama*, one of
the most exciting, and extensive, manuscripts ever to be painted in India,
and one of the key documents of Mughal painting.

The *Hamzanama* is a long and heroic tale of adventures and sorcery, chivalry
and sly magic, involving an incredible range of characters—from Amir
Hamza, the Prophet's uncle, and Umar, the gifted trickster, to Landhaur the

warrior and Zamurrud Shah, gigantic king of the East. Battles are fought, spells are cast, tricks are played, dragons are slain; human courage and divine intervention are interwoven; three-eyed winged horses gallop along and armies fly through the air riding on urns. Appropriately perhaps, therefore, the tale was chosen to be told—or rather, illustrated—in a manuscript of heroic proportions. Some 360 stories were told over 1400 folios, each close to a yard and a half in height, with painters and gilders and illuminators and binders all working together.

The two great Persian masters—Mir Sayyid Ali and Khwaja 'Abd-al Samad—directed and supervised the massive project, and a host of greatly gifted painters, drawn from the Indian tradition, collaborated on it. Intricate design and bold invention, close observation and soaring imagination came together. Descriptions of the manuscript vary—with respect to size, extent, the time taken, the cost of the entire enterprise—but there is no disagreement about the quality of the work. It is, in one word, breathtaking.

In this folio, Umar the sprightly *ayyaar*, on his way to deliver a message to an adversary king, confronts a great dragon. Snorting and emitting noxious vapours, the dreaded creature emerges from one of the dark pits that dot the bleak tract of land that is his home and advances towards the intruder. Umar has to fall back upon his wits to get out of this. He pulls out a vial of naphtha that he is carrying and throws it at the dragon which bursts into flames and is soon reduced to cinders. At this, the populace gathered to see this fight, from just outside the palace at the top of the painting, breaks into jubilant music.

The energy in the page and the manner in which the painter/s have set the scene up are striking: the dark and ominous ground is contrasted with the brilliantly lit form of 'one of the finest dragons in all of Islamic art'; the athletic figure of Umar emanates confidence yet his face reveals anxiety. The range of expressions on the faces of the curious but timid men taking refuge behind the painted rocks is astonishing. But the viewer is also invited to contemplate upon all those dark and open-mouthed pits from which this great dragon has emerged. Could something else be lurking in those too?

———————

The Hamzanama *is no longer intact, most of its 1400 or so folios now lost. Most of those that have survived are distributed between the Austrian Museum of Applied Arts in Vienna and the Victoria and Albert Museum, London. Only a very few are in private hands, and almost none in India. This folio has been attributed by John Seyller to the painter Daswant who, he believes, was assisted by Tara, another painter who came from the Indian tradition.*

THE PROPHET ILYAS RESCUES A PRINCE

Folio from the *Hamzanama* manuscript
Mughal; c. 1567–72
67.4 cm × 51.3 cm
The British Museum, London

Akbar's *Hamzanama* series (see previous painting) contains a few paintings about a young and handsome prince called Nur-ud-dahr. In one of them, a fragment of inscription has survived. It reads: 'When the demon threw Prince Nur-ud-Dahr into the sea, St. Elias the prophet took him out of the water. Nur-ud-Dahr wound up on an island.' The inscription doesn't say much but the story of the prince can be reconstructed through the works that come before and after it.

The prince whose name translates into 'The Light of Eternity' was the son of Prince Badi'uz Zaman and was of surpassing beauty. He used to sit close to the foot of a tree, and people from far and near would gather simply to gaze at him and marvel at his appearance. Among his admirers was an 'infidel' girl who heard from a demon that he had kidnapped the young prince in the night and thrown him into the sea.

Upset by this news she reported the matter to the ever resourceful *ayyaar*, Umar. However, it was not Umar but divine intervention that saved the young prince. The agent of providence was the Prophet Ilyas—the same as Elias and Elijah in the Biblical and Hebrew traditions—who, as the crisis prophet, suddenly appears on the scene in times of difficulty, 'with thunder on his brow and tempest in his voice'. He arrived and helped the hapless young prince reach the safety of the shore.

The way in which the painter approaches this scene is ingenious. He splits the page into two almost equal halves, the lower half where the drama of

rescue unfolds, and the upper half where nature opens herself up as it were, lush and verdant and peaceful.

The sea is rough and dangers lurk in it in the form of alligators and diving fish, but around the prophet, who comes walking on water, there is an air of calm reassurance. His head is surrounded by a fiery aureole as in the Islamic tradition, and he looks gently back, throwing his scarf to the drowning prince and pointing towards land with his right hand. The young prince, body nearly submerged in water, a tiger-skin wrap over his shoulders, looks helplessly up at the prophet as he seizes the scarf.

The forest shimmers above, in contrast to the turbulent sea and the tense drama of the rescue. Exquisitely painted trees fill this top half of the painting, with their leaves glistening, their edges limned in golden yellow. Flowering bushes lean on rocks, peacocks perch on high branches or roam through the forest, weaver birds build their nests, *chakor* birds look longingly at each other. There is remarkable freedom in the treatment and also genuine, delicious delight. The painter has succeeded in creating a true haven.

———————

The folio, as John Seyller remarks, has been 'attributed to as many as four unidentified painters working together, as well as to Mir Sayyid Ali and Miskin'. In his view, however, it is to Basawan that the page ought to be attributed. In support of his argument, he cites the handling of nature, especially the trees with their 'heavily painted and knotted trunks' and the wet tufts of vegetation, which are typically Basawan. He adds, though, that possibly it was another artist who supplied the three peacocks. Uncertainty remains; the only thing certain is the superb quality of this exceptionally well-preserved page.

THE GREAT GODDESS IN HER CHAMUNDA FORM

Leaf, possibly a fragment from a scroll of the *Devi Mahatmya*
Opaque watercolour on fine cloth
Mughal, Akbar period; c. 1565–75
15.1 cm × 21 cm
Government Museum and Art Gallery, Chandigarh

A little like the Goddess herself, the intriguing group of paintings from which this magnificent leaf/panel comes takes time to reveal itself. The Central Museum at Lahore originally had the six paintings in its collection—three are now in Chandigarh—when S.N. Gupta's catalogue was published in 1922. There they were described as 'once belonging to a manuscript', illustrating 'passages from the *Chandi* which describes the destruction of the demons by Durga, Tara and other *rajasic* forms of the goddess'. Gupta noted that 'the pictures show a mixture of the elements of the Persian style with those of the Hindu style'. They were also assigned a date: 'Late 17th or early 18th century'.

The paintings might have belonged to a Tantric series since the Goddess appeared in different *rupa*s, like an iconic figure, occupying the very centre of the page in all the six paintings.

But a seventh painting from the group was subsequently discovered several decades after 1922, with a clearly narrative content—the Goddess reducing a demon, possibly Dhumralochana, to ashes while her mount the tiger kills another demon close to her. This has led scholars to think that the series comes possibly from a now lost *Devi Mahatmya*—also called the *Chandi Saptashati*—manuscript series. If so, this would be the only *Devi Mahatmya* series ever to have been painted during the Akbar period.

157

The images are riveting. In this painting, the artist clearly sets out to establish the annihilating power of the Great Goddess. In this form, nothing can withstand her, neither god nor demon, Time nor Space. Angry and terrible, she destroys and devours. Her garment is made up of the severed heads of the countless demons she has slain. Her earrings are half-burnt corpses, and among her weapons she carries a skeleton as a staff. In one hand she carries her food: meat and bones, pecked at by a crow.

Eight-armed, naked and shrivelled, with a hideous grinning expression and dishevelled hair, she stands amid the scene of her carnage, poised as if about to break into a slow dance. All around her are carrion birds and scavenging animals—crows, jackals, dogs. Blood spurts from dismembered bodies and the sound of crunching bones can almost be heard.

But the devotee remains aware that even in her terrible aspect, she remains the Mother of the Universe—'who has created this world of the real and the unreal and who, by her own energy, with its three modes, protects it, destroys it and plays [with it]', as the text says.

Stylistically, this work and the remaining six paintings in this group do not fall in any other known group. They appear as if they were 'on their way to somewhere else'. They contain elements that put one in mind strongly of the work done in the early Akbari workshops: the treatment of space, the figures of the demons, the turban worn by the one 'secular' man, the rendering of fire, the slender-pillared pavilion in one of the paintings. On the other hand there are elements that come from the so-called Rajput context and remind one strongly of the *Chaurapanchasika* style of work (see also p. 417, 'Remembering That Fawn-Eyed Beauty', and pp. 88–91 in 'A Layered World'). Nothing fits snugly, therefore, into a known category or group. But that uncertainty does not dim the splendour that these images are bathed in.

There are many unanswered questions that the paintings of this group raise. How extensive was this group of paintings, one wonders, for instance? Why does not any text appear on the sheets of paper that form the backing of these paintings? Were there any other paintings done in the style of these works? Where were these works made? Were they commissioned by someone completely outside the imperial circle? Are they, in their own fashion—without being imperial Akbari works—drawing upon the sources on which works like the Hamzanama *and the* Tutinama *did? Was the 'Akbari' style worked out necessarily, and only, in the imperial workshops? Perhaps there will be some answers, some day.*

Quem penes arbitrium ... as ti manet æquoris oræ   Da facilem ratibusq, viam facilesq, recursus
Per tua, Neptune ô, regna tridente potens.   Hanc Deus humanis adyce rebus opem.

NEPTUNE, LORD OF THE SEAS

Mughal, by Abu'l Hasan; 1602
21.5 cm × 26 cm
The Goenka Collection, Mumbai

This bare-bodied, angry-looking rider astride a fish-tailed, lobster-clawed horse galloping furiously through the waves comes from no Indian sea. He is Neptune, the Roman god of the seas. Images of him had been sculpted and painted for centuries in Europe, and at least one of them seems to have reached Indian shores at a time when curiosity about the Western world was high. Whether it came in the baggage of a trader or a diplomat or a Christian missionary remains unknown, but one knows from the inscription in Persian at the bottom the name of the painter who copied that image—Abu'l Hasan, later to be honoured by his patron, the emperor Jahangir, with the title of Nadir-al Zaman, 'Rarity of the Age'.

But this grand title was only to be bestowed on the painter several years later, and his patron was still only a prince, then known as Salim, the heir apparent to the Mughal throne, who had defiantly set up an independent court of his own at Allahabad, far from his father Akbar's capital. The inscription therefore simply reads: *'aml-i Abu'l Hasan ibn-i Riza, murid-i padshah Salim, sinn-e 1101* [sic]*'*. (Painted by Abu'l Hasan, son of [Aqa] Riza, devout follower of Padshah Salim. The year 1602 [equivalent of AH 1011].)

Why would Abu'l Hasan be drawn to a subject, an image, such as this? Was he *asked* to paint it? Was he, by electing to copy a European painting on a completely unfamiliar theme—done in an unfamiliar technique—trying to teach himself? Or was he setting himself a challenge? Could he have been planning perhaps to surprise his patron or his father—an accomplished painter himself?

It is hard to know. But one thing is certain: Abu'l Hasan was very young at this time, just fifteen years old. We know this from a stunning brush drawing he had made two years earlier, inscribed with a dated note giving his name and stating that he was thirteen years of age then. That image was of the figure of St John standing at the foot of the Cross, excerpted from a Dürer engraving. European works clearly fascinated Abu'l Hasan, perhaps especially so because of his youth. The wonder of the new might have seemed even more wondrous to his eyes.

This precocious work of art is astonishingly accomplished. The wild grandeur in the figure of the naked and muscular trident-bearing god, mane flowing like that of his lively mount, bearing an expression that says he is the complete master of this domain; the rhythm in the waves, the sea astir with creatures gazing at the sea lord with fear and amazement—he appears to have caught everything to perfection.

There is refinement in the workmanship and exquisite attention to detail—the dolphins with their mouths open as if to 'speak' in unison, the pelican swooping close to the god's head, and the angle at which the right hand holds the dreaded trident. The young artist might have had a problem handling, in his own defined, linear manner, the clouds which seem to have something of the aspect of muscular biceps, but those hardly enter the viewer's awareness. It is the roaring sea that one hears and the godly hubris that one sees.

––––––––––

Some other things in the work compel attention. The four lines in Latin at the bottom, a laudatory verse invoking the god of the seas, which Abu'l Hasan appears to have copied exactly, stroke by stroke, loop by loop, without knowing a word of the language or the script. The inscription in Persian contains a courtly refinement: the words 'Padshah Salim' at the very top in the midst of clouds are to be read as if following the word 'murid-i', for the emperor's name cannot possibly be allowed to mingle with that of his 'devoted follower'. Finally, the year of execution that appears at the end of the inscription reads in the original as '1101' which must have been a mistake. Abu'l Hasan was left-handed as we know from a portrait of his in which he is seen painting, and while intending to write '1011', he appears to have got the order of the digits wrong.

THE SPEAKING TREE

Deccani (or Mughal?); early seventeenth century
14.6 cm × 9.5 cm
Islamische Museum, Berlin

Among the legends popular in the Islamic world was one about the Speaking Tree which bore human fruit and was to be found in mythical lands or on an island by the name of Waq Waq. The great Firdausi speaks of it in the *Shahnama*; so does Nizami in the *Iskandarnama*, one of the five poems in his celebrated work, the *Khamsa*. In both these works, Alexander—Sikandar as he is known in Islamic texts—figures not only as a conqueror but also as a philosopher-king, full of questions, always curious to learn. The story of him standing at the foot of a tree that talks has fascinated writers and painters alike.

Firdausi writes of Alexander reaching the end of the world where he encounters a tree with two trunks. Male heads sprout from one trunk and speak during the day in a voice that strikes terror, and female heads from the other trunk talk sweetly at night. The male heads warn Alexander that he has already received his share of blessings, and the female heads urge him not to give in to greed; but both predict that his last days are near: 'Death will come soon: you will die in a strange land, with strangers standing by.' This is exactly what happens. Alexander dies in Babylon, far from his home.

The fascination with the legend has persisted over centuries even as it changes in different lands, and in different hands. Liberties are taken. Sometimes one sees Alexander on horseback close to the foot of the tree, straining to listen; at others, the conqueror is nowhere to be seen and only the tree appears, with human figures suspended from its branches. The tree is sometimes a symbol of prophecy; in other works it represents our inability to comprehend the mysteries that surround us.

The painter of this mystifying, somewhat eerie, work creates a surreal world in which, to begin with, nothing is quite what it appears to be. The tree, teeming with figures of humans and beasts—one can see heads of leopards and horses, deer and elephants, rams and foxes peeping through the leaves— is made up of a trunk that is nothing but snakes, intertwined and slithering, even as they turn into branches. What appear like bushes, close to the foot of the tree, bear heads of other animals rather than flowers; and resting their heads on a rock are fish that seem to have come from nowhere.

Here is the American poet Muriel Rukeyser describing the Speaking Tree very similarly in her poem:

> The trunk of the speaking tree looking like a tree trunk
> Until you look again.
> There people and animals
> Are ripening on the branches, the broad leaves
> Are leaves; pale horses, sharp fine foxes
> Blossom; the red rabbit falls
> Ready and running.

She continues:

> The trunk coils, turns,
> Snakes, fishes. Now the ripe people fall and run . . .
> flames that stand
> Where reeds are creatures and the foam is flame.

Close to the end of the poem come these lines:

> This is the speaking tree,
> It calls your name. It tells us what we mean.

This striking painting must have challenged the painter almost beyond straining point. It is generally regarded as coming from Golconda in the Deccan, although a Mughal ancestry cannot be ruled out. The Qutb Shahi Sultanate of Golconda was founded by Turkmen princes, and during the early years of their reign, Turkmen artists seem to have settled in the region as well. They laid the ground for the style that came later to flourish in that soil.

———————

The Speaking Tree as a theme appears to have fascinated painters all over the Islamic world, and vastly differing versions of it were painted, some stark and sparse, others rich and flamboyant. It figures in Arabic texts as well as in Persian ones. There is even a Thai version of the motif which has survived.

THE VIRGIN AND CHILD

Leaf from a Jahangir album
Opaque watercolour and gold on paper
Mughal, late Akbar period; c. 1590
21.7 cm × 13.7 cm
San Diego Museum of Art, Edwin Binney Collection

> The first thing he [the emperor Akbar] did was to go into the Church
> [set up in Fatehpur Sikri], which was well appointed with its perfumes
> and fragrance. On entering he was surprised and astonished and
> made a deep obeisance to the picture of Our Lady that was there,
> from the painting of St. Luke, done by Brother Michael Godinho, as
> well as to another beautifully executed representation of Our Lady
> by Fr. Martin de Silva from Rome, which pleased him no end.

This is what one of the Jesuit fathers who had come to the court of Akbar
wrote in a letter to his principals in Goa. The letter goes on to say that
after stepping outside briefly to discuss these pictures with his attendants,
the emperor returned with his 'chief painter' and others, and 'they were all
wonderstruck and said that there could be no better paintings nor better
artists than those who had painted the said pictures'.

This letter reflects some of the cultural aspects of Akbar's court: the liberal
monarch's interest in, and respect for, other faiths; the excitement in the early
years about the arrival of medieval Christianity in Mughal India; the coming
of European paintings and other artefacts; and the seductive opportunities
this encounter with them opened up for the painters working in the imperial
atelier.

The chronicler Abu'l Fazl's remark, in his chapter on the 'Arts of Painting'
in the *Ain-i Akbari*, in praise of the great Mughal artists can be seen in this

context. Their masterpieces, he wrote, 'may be placed at the side of the wonderful works of the European painters who have attained worldwide fame'. The implication is that European paintings had, in their own manner, set a standard, or at least thrown a powerful challenge to the artists of the Mughal court.

This painting, clearly based upon—if not exactly copied from—a European work is, though unsigned, clearly from the hand of one of the great Mughal artists—Keshava Das, Basawan, Manohar, among them—who were most drawn to the exciting new works which would occasionally arrive from Europe. Whatever its authorship, the painting is exquisitely executed.

The Madonna, in repose, with her Botticelli face and heavy-lidded, downward-turned eyes, reclines against a large bolster. She has a child at her breast, gently steadying him with a delicate hand. By her side, on a cushion placed on the intricately patterned carpet, lies an open book from which she has obviously been reading; a candle stand is next to the book. At the foot of the carpet, on the grassy ground, a gold carafe stands close to a flat golden bowl that captures the interest of an alert cat. A goat rests peacefully in the background, mirroring the repose on the Madonna's alabaster face.

There are suggestions and symbols here, but also 'effects'. In the background, virtually unrelated to its immediate surroundings, we can see a part of a building with heavy drapes tied at the side to reveal a vista in the far distance: at left a lone tree rises above a thatched structure, a masonry well and vines trained on a trellis. The sky above this vignette at top-left is filled with clouds against which tiny birds can be seen in flight.

The exact source of this painting remains difficult to establish, but the impact of Europe is evident everywhere: the Christian subject apart, one sees it in the Madonna's and the child's faces and figures, the rich oil-like colouring, the clothing, the treatment of the structure at the back, the drapery, the forms of the goat and the cat, the open book. But, engagingly, the sum of all these parts seems, somehow, to have a very Indian air. Although there is a great crispness of detail, everything is bathed in a melting warmth.

Of special interest is the fact that the Persian verses in the cartouches at the top and bottom—beginning with the words, *mahi dar husn az khurshid zadeh*—seem not only to be related to the image but inspired by it in some manner. Roughly translated, they read:

> A beauteous moon has been born of the sun
> And feeds upon the milk of its breast;
> A dainty bud floating upon the surface of the spring
> Of beauty with which the very face of heavens is washed.

———————

This painting, hough unsigned, has been attributed differently by scholars. In the notes in Edwin Binney's hand on this painting in the San Diego Museum of Art, the attribution is to Basawan, the great painter at the Akbari court. John Seyller, however, argues for its being attributed to Manohar, Basawan's son, suggesting that the painter was leaning here upon his father's work for some details and manner of treatment.

THE GODDESS SARASWATI ENTHRONED

Leaf, possibly meant for an album
Opaque watercolour and gold on paper
Deccani, by Farrukh Hussain; c. 1600
23.6 cm × 15.8 cm
City Palace, Jaipur, Sawai Bhawani Singh Collection

An uncommon range of images and ideas come together on this sumptuous page. The three names that find mention in it—'Sarsuti', 'Ibrahim' and 'Farrukh'—in the remains of inscriptions scattered through the page, help us in piecing some things together. The first two belong together and can be read in the narrow floral panel that runs more or less across the page, just above the broad, elaborately gold-embroidered textile that hangs *chhatra*-like on the upper half of the page, and is held up by the two winged *peri*s who stand at either end of it.

It reads: *'Ibrahim ko kot pita, dev Ganpati mata pavitra Sarsuti.'* This means, roughly: 'Ibrahim has countless fathers; his deity is Ganpati [that is, Ganesha], and his mother the pure and sacred Sarsuti [that is, Saraswati].' The words are in Hindi or Dakhani, but written in the Persian script. This might be a line from one of Ibrahim Adil Shah II, the Sultan of Bijapur's own Dhrupad compositions. The highly cultivated king, who presided over an extraordinary and culturally eclectic court, was passionate about Hindustani classical music. He wrote the *Kitab-i-Nauras*, a book on music, and composed Dhrupads that he sang himself to the accompaniment of his favoured instrument which he had named Moti Khan.

That he, a devout Muslim, paid open tribute to Hindu gods and goddesses was a fact known throughout his kingdom, and celebrated. For him to refer to Saraswati—the goddess, in fact, the very embodiment, of music and learning—not only as pure and sacred but also as his mother, seems then

173

completely in keeping with his personal belief, for it is her blessings that he always sought.

The painting is, however, not about the Sultan himself—it is about the 'pure and sacred' goddess. Bejewelled and majestic, seated on a magnificently carved golden throne, Saraswati, holding the double-gourded *veena* and a *mala* that are parts of her iconography, appears to be completely lost in herself, and her music. There is a youthful innocence on her face and great delicacy of expression.

She seems to be utterly unaware of her surroundings: the young attendant with that typically rich Deccani *patka* who stands next to her, probably holding some objects of worship; the two winged peris who appear above and behind her, standing at some distance, their enormous, sweeping wings forming a triumphal arch above her; even the peacock, her *vahana*-vehicle, that moves gently from right to left in front of her throne, its magnificent tail in full view.

The page is rich, almost over-rich, packed with expansive decorative detail. At the very top in the spandrels, very Persian- looking simurgs (mythical birds) and clouds in gold fly or float about. On either side of the goddess's throne stand tall Chinese-looking vases, with bouquets of flowers filling their mouths. At the very bottom appears an icon flanked by two aquatic birds. But, in the midst of this, one's eye lands upon the small, squarish painted panel, just under the cusp of the arch at the top, showing a rider on an elephant. If one knows something about Deccani painting, one would instantly recognize a reference here to another well-known painting showing Ibrahim Adil Shah riding his favourite elephant, Atash Khan.

On the steps, in a tiny hand, appears the name of the painter who painted not only this rich and absorbing work but also the the famous painting of the monarch riding his elephant. It is the great Mughal artist Farrukh Husain, who in the imperial court in the north was known as Farrukh Beg. The inscription here, in Persian, states that this is 'the work of Farrukh Hussain, *musavvir*' who describes himself as 'Ibrahim Adil Shahi', meaning owing allegiance to that Sultan of great taste.

———————

Its evident quality apart, this work is of key importance in terms of art history. For one, it reconfirms that the great painter Farrukh Beg worked in the Deccan for Ibrahim Adil Shah and also at the Mughal court where he was known as Farrukh Husain. This is also possibly the only painting in which he addresses a 'Hindu' theme. It is evident that he has struggled with the iconography—the many arms of the goddess, in particular—and with presenting the interior of a temple, but there is no denying the valiant nature of his effort and the delicacy of his workmanship.

THE HOUSE OF BIJAPUR

Leaf, possibly from an album
Opaque watercolour on paper
Deccan, Bijapur, by Kamal Muhammad and Chand Muhammad; c. 1680
41.3 cm × 31.1 cm
The Metropolitan Museum of Art, New York

Succession and legitimacy seem never to have been far from the thoughts of kings and princes, for thrones were often contested and potential conflict always hung in the air. Documents attesting to the legitimacy of succession were therefore always being created. Take, for instance, the famous painting now in the British Museum, of the princes of the House of Timur, all shown together, generation after generation of rulers seated next to one another. Even in the tiny state of Guler, a series of paintings was made showing the ruler on elephant back and his heir apparent—in fact, the one who succeeded him even if he was not the heir apparent—seated behind him. The intent was the same: to establish that the throne had passed legitimately to the one who actually did succeed to it.

This work, showing us successive Sultans of Bijapur together, needs therefore to be seen essentially as a document of state. A message is being sent out, issues of legitimate succession being settled. But its beauty is impressive.

There are two key figures in the painting: the founder of the Adil Shahi dynasty, Sultan Yusuf, seen seated in all his majesty on the throne in the centre, and the young boyish figure, Sikandar Adil Shah, for whom the painting was evidently made, seated at the end of the group of four at the right. Sikandar had come to occupy the throne at a very young age, and his situation was insecure. His inclusion in the image is thus deliberate.

177

Now to the other figures. The person standing at the back of the entire group, and merging with or emerging from the light pink ground that keeps rising upwards and ends in those fanciful rocks, remains unidentified. But his presence is essential to understanding the image, for he appears to have just handed over to the enthroned Sultan a golden key—*kaleed-i-saltanat*, as it might have been called—a symbol undoubtedly of authority and power.

Who exactly he is remains uncertain but the two theories are that he represents either Shah Ismail, the Safavid ruler of Persia from whom the Sultans of Bijapur had received the title of 'Shah', 'an act of great cultural importance for the dynasty'; or, just possibly, the Sufi ancestor of the Safavid line. The other personages, all seated on the brilliantly painted carpet, are more securely identifiable.

In the group at left are the Sultans Ismail Ibrahim I and Ali I, and in the group at right Ibrahim II, Muhammad, Ali II and the boyish Sikandar. But one needs to remember it is not the collective auspiciousness of the group that the painter was invoking here—it was the line of succession. If one reads the painting carefully, one can see that each Sultan is seated on a throne— by no means as majestic as that of the founder of the dynasty, but still a throne—the arched finial of which rises and frames the head.

The workmanship here draws attention to itself, for it is refined and reminds one constantly of the Persian origins of this style. The elaborately patterned carpet; the medallion at the feet of the central figure, eclipsed slightly by the sphere on which a foot firmly rests; the floral motifs in gold on a blue ground; the pink-mauve rocks atop which little shrines appear—all these point eloquently to their source.

At the same time, the usual conventions—two guards resting their hands on long staffs; a groom with a horse, the hind part of which is cut by the border, all at the bottom of the page—have been incorporated by the painters. In general, the horse with the groom is to be read as a sign of recent arrival in paintings such as these. If that is the case here too, is it perhaps the horse that the young Sikandar has ridden to be able to join this distinguished group?

———————

There are two inscriptions on the work, one misleading, the other completely credible. The first, merging with the clouds at the top, put in by a late hand, states that this is the image of Shah Abbas, king of Iran, which clearly the main figure is not. The other, written along the border at left and in very minute characters, says that the painting is the work of 'Kamal Muhammad and Chand Muhammad'. Not much is known about these painters, and whether they were related to each other is also not clear, but the information is certainly of interest.

RAMA, SITA AND LAKSHMANA IN EXILE

Folio from a Ramayana series
Opaque watercolour and gold on paper
Mughal, sub-imperial; c. 1595–1600
28.8 cm × 19.8 cm
Sir Howard Hodgkin Collection

It is not easy to make out what scene this painting depicts. That the page is from a Ramayana series—fragmentary now and widely dispersed, the folios partially damaged as the edges show—is clear. The three figures seen here—Rama with his dark, bluish complexion, Sita and Lakshmana do not seem to be in Ayodhya but in exile. For, apart from the fact that the two brothers are not dressed as princes, rarely if ever would have one seen them together like this had they been in Ayodhya.

There appears to be some concern, perhaps even anxiety, in the air. Rama and Sita are in conversation, he turning his head to look back at her as she speaks; at a slight distance Lakshmana, Rama's devoted brother, looks away to his right as if trying to see or identify something in the distance. An approaching demon, perhaps? It is just possible that the moment the painter has chosen to depict is when Maricha, disguised as the golden deer, suddenly appears.

Sita falls instantly in love with him and asks Rama to capture him for her sake. Rama suspects that the deer is in fact a demon who has taken this form with some fell intent. But Sita insists and the two converse animatedly about the matter. Lakshmana, on his part, is as mistrustful as Rama and therefore keeps an eye out.

Eventually, Rama yields to Sita's insistence and goes in pursuit of the 'deer'. What follows is of course all too well known: Rama is lured further and further away by the 'golden deer', Maricha is killed, Lakshmana has to rush to the aid of the 'wounded' Rama, and eventually Sita is abducted by Ravana, king of Lanka, who had hatched this entire plot to avenge the disfiguring of his sister, Surpanakha. Grave and dramatic consequences follow.

If one is right in reading the painting in this manner—it has also been seen as a scene of the new home built in Panchavati by Lakshmana as a dwelling for the exiles—the gestures and the positioning of the three figures fall more easily into place.

Regardless of what this scene depicts, however, one is struck by the gorgeous setting: superbly designed tiles in blue and white—rows of small squares below and large pieces with circular patterns in a broad frieze—making up the floor; the facade of a chamber with a *mihrab*-like red door set into a richly decorated wall with floral patterns; a slender column supporting a scalloped arch; and topping everything a white dome dotted with sparsely placed floral designs. Clearly, this is not the kind of opulence that exiles usually dwell in.

The only sight we have of a forest is the patch of green in the background and two trees, one partially obscuring the column and the other seen in half at top-left. It is all a bit confusing, possibly the work of a painter who is passionately partial to tile designs and cannot resist bringing them in, whether here or in another folio from the same series (in the Goenka Collection), where King Dashratha sits with his wives and sons.

These contradictions between setting and scene have to be set aside, however, for there is so much to see and admire in this page of dazzling colour and design: the superbly articulated figures—real and yet stylized—of Rama, Sita and Lakshmana, the sharply observed stances and the attention to detail. One notices little things like the wisp of hair escaping from the bun at the back of Rama's head, the lightness and the transparency of Sita's clothing and Rama's scarf, the alert gestures, the firm manner in which the two brothers grasp their bows, the sense of engagement in the moment. This

182

is the work of a master painter, although we do not know if the series is in the hand of an artist from the imperial atelier or comes from a sub-imperial workshop. The narrow frieze at the bottom of the 'door' with its 'Persian' clouds, the flat band of gold at the top, clearly show an awareness of high Mughal work. But there is something distinctly 'Rajput' in the colour and the rich patterning.

———————

There is no dearth of Ramayana manuscripts or series from this period, made for Mughal patrons, for everyone from Hamida Banu Begum, Akbar's mother, to the emperor Akbar himself, on to the Khan Khanan, Abdul Rahim, had them painted and treasured them. This series, however, inscribed with Sanskrit text at the back, seems to have been prepared for some Hindu noble or prince.

KING KAMSA IN HIS INNER APARTMENTS

Folio from a dispersed *Bhagavata Purana* series
Opaque watercolour and gold on paper
Pahari, possibly from a Mandi workshop; c. 1650
49.5 cm × 35 cm (outer)
45.5 cm × 32 cm (inner)
Private Collection

The small group of paintings from which this work comes raises, in respect of style, dating, authorship and so on, the same set of issues which another work here, a Ramayana leaf, 'The Celestial Chariot' (see p. 193), does. We are on fairly sure, but by no means absolutely certain, ground. There is, and has been, much room for fine and detailed argument, so much of it that it almost comes in the way of savouring these works. One needs to learn to live with uncertainties, for there is much to be gained in turning to the paintings themselves, and moving inside them in a leisurely fashion, lingering over every nuance.

In this painting, which relates evidently to the Tenth Book of the *Bhagavata Purana*, in which the story of Krishna is told, the painter takes us to the inner apartments of a palace where the princely figure whom one can identify as Kamsa is seen conversing with an old woman seated close to his feet. Maids and attendants stand around, flanking the two central figures: three at right and three at left. Behind the latticed screens more women, evidently belonging to the royal household, can be seen even if hazily, and in the spacious carpeted courtyard leading out from Kamsa's chamber a large group of women musicians—as many as twelve—can be seen playing on instruments or singing. Further down, a fountain plays and water courses down a channel, on either side of which we see glimpses of a rich garden.

185

The remarkable thing, however, is that with all this happening—royal instructions being issued, music being played, whispered conversations behind latticed screens, water gurgling down marbled channels—there is an air of hushed silence in the painting, possibly because the moment is such. For, as far as one can read this scene, the story has reached a point where Kamsa, having heard a prophecy that speaks of his impending death at the hands of the child to be born of Devaki's womb, is quietly taking preventive measures by issuing instructions to an old woman.

One cannot be certain, but a specific passage from the *Harivamsa*—that other great Vaishnava text—might have been on the painter's mind. After the sage Narada had left, having warned Kamsa of what he must fear, that text says, Kamsa first laughed, making light of the threat, but then decided to take prudent measures. He called his closest advisers into his private apartments and informed them of the sage's warning. Therefore, he said, 'You must help me kill her [Devaki's] children. Devaki will be confined to her rooms and though permitted to conceive, she will be very carefully watched when she is with child.' And then added: 'I shall instruct my woman to count the months from conception so we may know when she is to give birth.' Almost certainly this is the moment that the painter is rendering: quiet instructions being issued to the old duenna-like woman who must have been the one entrusted with counting the months from Devaki's date of conception.

The painter creates architectural detail and soft furnishings of remarkable richness: marble everywhere, from walls to courtyard; the scalloped arch under which Kamsa sits and the delicately carved niches with decorative objects at the back; the stunningly executed tall lattice screens made of what appears like Kashmiri *pinjra*-work, behind which the clearly articulated figures of palace women can be seen. Note, too, the rolled-up curtains featuring floral sprigs echoing the design on the *jama* worn by Kamsa, of the kind that one sees in Shahjahani *pietra-dura* work at Agra; the fountain playing at the very heart of the painting with water swirling all around and a strong jet holding aloft a single rose delicately poised at top; exquisitely painted panels featuring *shikargah*-like flora and fauna that flank the fountain; the two short flights of marble steps; the cypresses in the garden patches; the doorway in the outer wall in which a woman guard stands questioning a visitor or petitioner.

There is subtle detail everywhere if one pays close attention. The women who stand around Kamsa and the old duenna form two groups very carefully distinguished as regards their respective status. Again, the two ladies of the royal household who appear behind the latticed screen at left are but partially visible through an opening in the screen, having a quiet conversation between themselves, the one standing possibly relaying to the other the snatch of conversation she has overheard between the king and the duenna. Their interest and concern are noticeable. And then of course there are those two astonishingly engaged—as also strangely engaging—groups of women musicians. Nearly all of them are looking upwards, intently, for that is where their patron, the princely figure, sits, and each one has a different instrument. The rendering of the instruments by the painter alone elicits admiration, for not only is each one—percussion or stringed—keenly observed and executed, but so also are the hands of the women, perfectly attuned to what they are doing.

This is the kind of detail that by itself can resonate within the alert viewer.

KAMSA ATTEMPTS TO KILL THE
NEWBORN CHILD

Folio from the same dispersed *Bhagavata Purana* series as the previous painting
Opaque watercolour and gold on paper
Pahari, possibly from a Mandi workshop; c. 1650
50.5 cm × 35 cm (outer)
48 cm × 32.5 cm (inner)
Private Collection

Having been informed of the birth of Devaki's child, the heartless Kamsa arrives, full of apprehensions that the sage Narada's prophecy of his death at the hands of one of Devaki's children will come true (see p. 186). He dismounts from the royal elephant, enters the cell where the child is and, ignoring the piteous pleas of his sister, picks up the infant, intending to kill it by dashing it against a slab set up in the courtyard.

The painter sets up the scene perfectly for the miraculous happening about to take place, unknown to Kamsa. The courtyard which the cell of Krishna's parents abuts is shown as a trapezoid space with a high outer wall; another chamber with a half-open door is at the left, and a protective wall at the back. The ground is coloured a silken-smooth light jade green for everything to show up with perfect clarity against it. In the middle of the courtyard a platform appears, low but broad, on which Kamsa is to mount to perform his ghastly deed. A few men, trusted courtiers and soldiers, are allowed inside the courtyard, and they stand in rows or twos, in perfect discipline but with anxiety on their faces. Each person knows exactly what is going to take place.

Against the dark opening of the cell, the figures of Vasudeva and Devaki stand out sharply, Devaki seated on the floor with her head bent in utter despair. Outside, at the lower end of the painting, men stand around, some with heads slightly bent as if to hear the sounds that might be emerging from inside. The richly caparisoned royal elephant, having brought his master to the spot, stands still at right, with a mahout and an attendant still positioned on his ample back. Another group stands at left: a horse held by a syce, two men bearing colourful triangular pennants—ensigns of royalty—marked by cloud patterns in gold stamped on orange-red ground. Nobody moves.

And, suddenly, in a moment of intense drama skilfully created by the painter, Kamsa is inside the courtyard. Clad in a brilliant golden *jama*, he mounts the platform. Left hand resting on the hilt of his sword, he takes the infant in his right hand and dashes it against the slab. But, miraculously, the infant slips from his hands, and rises heavenwards, exactly as Vishnu had described, 'to a place of eternal glory'.

And now, the infant—the one that Krishna had been exchanged for by Vasudeva—is visible in her real, goddess form up in the sky, surrounded by a cloud, an aura of sheer dazzling gold. She is eight-armed, clad in a red garment, holding in her hands the emblems of Vishnu—discus, conch shell; and those of Shiva—trident and club; and of the Great Goddess herself— sword, shield, arrow. The cloud of gold in the heart of which the goddess, Yoga Maya, now stands has risen from a trail, the thin lower end of which, a mere wisp, one can track down to Kamsa's disbelieving hand. And up there, flanking the place where the goddess stays suspended, as if dancing in space, natural clouds part and take on different hues, from smoky black and rich blue to pink and mauve, their rims limned with gold.

Interestingly, no one on the earth below looks up at this heavenly phenomenon, not even Kamsa, for it has all happened in a trice, but the viewer's eyes naturally move upwards to take in the glorious sight. One can almost hear the goddess's stern words as she addresses Kamsa: 'What have you gained, you dunce, by killing me? Your destroyer, your adversary in a former birth, has been born and is alive, but lives now in a place unknown to you.'

There is sheer radiance in the rendering of the scene. While on the one hand one is reminded of the virtuosity with which so many of the leaves of the Mughal *Padshahnama* were painted—the colouring, the grouping of figures, the individuation of characters, the studied stances and attitudes, the awareness of ranks and stations, the compositional devices—one knows on the other hand that this is a different mental space and that what one is witnessing is much more than an earthly happening. At no point in the telling of the tale does the painter falter as far as attention to detail is concerned. The expressions and the varying attitudes of the men both inside and outside the courtyard tell their own story: eyes downcast or chins resting on staff, ears sharply cocked, and so on. Where Devaki sits huddled, eyes unable to lift themselves, an expression of anguish on her face, there is a sense of deepening gloom. But where the keepers of the elephant and the horse, or bearers of arms and pennants, stand, there is almost complete lack of concern at what is happening: they are here because this is where they are meant to be, performing ordained duty. One is lost in awe at the way each studied detail has been captured.

THE CELESTIAL CHARIOT

Folio from a dispersed Ramayana series
Opaque watercolour and gold on paper
Pahari, possibly from a Mandi workshop; c. 1650
43.5 cm × 33.6 cm
San Diego Museum of Art, Edwin Binney Collection

Everything about this 'chariot' is celestial: it is made of glittering gold, as described in the Ramayana, rising to countless storeys, festooned with garlands and strings of pearls, capable of flying and moving with 'the speed of mind'. Belonging to Kubera, the lord of untold wealth, the chariot was summoned to Rama's presence when, with Ravana slain, Sita freed and reunited with him, and the fourteen long years of exile coming to an end, he decided to return to Ayodhya.

The moment is one of rejoicing, but also of the sadness that descends at moments of leave-taking. Vibhishana, devotee of Rama and now crowned king of Lanka in place of his slain brother, asks Rama for words of advice and hears them with great reverence. Then he begs to be allowed to accompany the Lord to Ayodhya, together with Lakshmana, Sita and Hanuman, and the elect among the monkey and bear troops. Everyone then enters the celestial *vimana*, the flying chariot Pushpaka. As it rises in the air, scattering the clouds and startling the birds, the citizens of Lanka, men, women and children, come out of the golden walls of their city and bid farewell, hands folded, heads bowed.

There are different, wondrous domains in this brilliantly composed folio. There is one inside the great chariot where Rama, at last reunited with Sita, sits in the uppermost chamber and begins to point out all the places that he had been to during his tormented search for her after her abduction. Vibhishana, Hanuman and others sit in one chamber; the monkey and bear

193

chiefs huddle together in unfamiliar surroundings or look out of the windows with mounting curiosity.

On either side of the *vimana*, enveloped in a haze of golden dust as it rises in the air, is the exquisitely painted world of cloudy skies in which great birds fly about. Below, in the great ocean, creatures emerge from the deep to look up with amazement at this golden citadel in the sky. The world outside the walled city of Lanka is filled with men and women, eyes lit with adoration, surprise and relief still written on their faces.

And then there is the world of all those wonderful animals, bears and monkeys, which the painter renders with uncommon empathy. There they are, crowding the great bridge that joins the golden island with the mainland, or scampering about on either side of it. The monkeys, true to their playful nature, run around, leaping, diving, swimming. The bears, the painter wishes us to know, are not that comfortable with water, and even as they jostle each other on the bridge, some of them are kept busy rescuing those that have fallen into the water. It is a joyous, frolicsome world, coloured by the delight of victory and the promise of homecoming.

The painting, like the rest of the series from which it comes, is grave and joyous at the same time—and ambitious in scale. But where is it from? Opinion among scholars is sharply divided: some are inclined to see it as a Rajasthani work, from Bikaner to be specific; others place it in Mandi, in the Pahari area.

Not a great deal is known about early Mandi painting, which carries traces of a Mughal connection, but evidence seems to be mounting that this series does indeed come from that matrix. The Mandi stream to which they belong appears to have dried up over the years, for work in that region later took on a very different aspect. Without going into the argument in any detail, it is relevant to point out the painter's preference here for showing his figures as very small, and for bringing in a marked reddish tint on the cheeks—which characterizes nearly all the other leaves from this series. One painting, in the same style, now in Vadodara, carries on its back a brief inscription in Takri, the script of the hills virtually unknown anywhere else.

———————

The most consistent work on this and the related series from Mandi has been by Catherine Glynn who has recently written another densely argued essay on the subject. It would appear that it was not only the Ramayana and the Bhagavata Purana *that were painted by these painters active at Mandi in the middle of the seventeenth century but also a number of others, now widely scattered over different collections in the world, both public and private.*

KRISHNA LIFTING THE MOUNT GOVARDHAN

Folio from a *Bhagavata Purana* manuscript
Opaque watercolour and gold on paper
Rajasthan, from a Bikaner workshop, by Ustad Sahib Din
29.7 cm × 38 cm (outer)
22 cm × 30.6 (inner)
The British Museum, London

The tale is much loved, and has been told countless times. When, says the *Bhagavata Purana*, despite protestations from the elders of the village of Gokula, Krishna stopped his kinsmen from continuing to worship Indra, the presiding deity of rains, and urged them to begin worshipping instead the Mount Govardhan which in truth sustained them and their cows, Indra was greatly incensed. Flying into a rage he 'instructed the host of clouds called *samvartaka* which can bring about the destruction of the universe' to go and shatter 'the arrogance of those foolish cowherds', and destroy all of their cattle with incessant rain. 'I shall myself,' said the Rain God, 'follow you, riding my elephant Airavata, accompanied by the troop of *maruts* [storm deities who are Indra's attendants] of enormous prowess.'

The clouds obeyed and set forth, unleashing upon the villagers rain 'dazzling with flashes of lightning and thundering with the roar of thunderbolts and accompanied by tempestuous winds and hailstones'. Never having witnessed such a terrifying deluge before, everyone in the village—men and women, cows and their young ones—ran towards Krishna for help for he alone could save them, they knew. Krishna reassured them, saying that 'with all the yogic powers at my command, I will protect this Gokula . . . This is the eternal vow taken by me.'

And then, even though still a child, he 'uprooted the Mount Govardhan with one hand and held it up as if it were a mushroom'. Then, asking them to shed their fears, he asked everyone to take shelter under the mountain which he held up 'for seven days and did not move from his position'. Seeing this, Indra was astounded, his pride shaken; and he instructed the *samvartaka* clouds to restrain themselves. Then, seeing that the sky had cleared, and the sun had risen, Krishna asked everyone to emerge from under the upheld mountain and go home with their belongings and their cattle, 'even as he sportfully placed the mountain in its previous position'.

Yet another miracle, the text says. Krishna was flooded with affection and gratitude from all sides. The cowherd women offered him worship, and everyone in his own family 'embraced him and showered him with benedictions'. In the heavens, the celestials, *siddhas*, *gandharvas* and *charanas*, broke into music. Kettledrums and conches were sounded in triumph and celebration.

The painter, Sahib Din—or Shah Din, by another reading—takes the viewer straight into the heart of the action. Krishna, not a child but a very young figure, occupies the centre of the page, body at ease, left hand raised to support the mountain, the right still holding his beloved flute. Gently, he turns his head towards his right, gazing at the bevy of beautiful women— one of them carrying a baby in the crook of her arm—who stand praising him, bringing him gifts, plying him with a fly whisk even as streams of water fall from the mountain above. Two cows look up at him with adoring eyes. At right, another small group of equally beautiful women stands, while a group of cowherds sits on the ground, possibly taking a breather after having helped support Krishna's effort to raise the mountain with their cowherds' staffs held aloft.

The mountain—a vision in pink and grey and mauve—is surrounded by brilliantly rendered dark, rumbling clouds all around it. Among the clouds one discerns, at an angle, the figure of Indra riding his great Airavata elephant, his legs partly obscured by banks of rolling clouds—this because he had promised his clouds that he would personally follow them to the spot. In the far distance at left, visible just above the cover of the foliage, is a town.

The painting follows the text in so many ways but also departs from it. The sizeable number of women who stand flanking Krishna, each more elegant than the other, are brought in evidently to stand for the *gopis* who will all fall madly in love with Krishna as time moves ahead. There are no elders to be seen, neither Nanda nor Yashoda, nor Rohini. The four men talking to each other, seated at right directly under a steady stream of water, represent presumably all the 'menfolk' of the village.

At the same time, the painter reserves special attention for the foreground where he introduces delightful little vignettes: a cow suddenly gives birth to a young one at left, evidently because of the fearsome noises that the thunderbolts produced. Two cows sit calmly as if they already know the outcome of these dramatic events. Two cowherds keep watch, wearing as protection blankets over their heads. One little snow-white calf nestles up, mistakenly perhaps, to a grey cow hoping for milk and protection. The drama in this sumptuously coloured and drawn painting is evident, but so are the gently slipped in human touches with which the painter invests it.

———————

With time, and across space, the story kept on being embroidered by poets and painters alike. The text, for instance, does not say anything about Krishna holding up the great mountain on the little finger of his left hand, and yet one sees this again and again in paintings. In some works—even though not in this one—Indra is seen twice, once riding his elephant mount arrogantly in the skies and a second time descending to the earth, touching the earth with his forehead in homage, all pride humbled.

THE DEVI RIDES IN STATE

Folio from a Devi series
Opaque watercolour and gold on paper
Pahari, attributed to Kripal of Nurpur; c. 1670
18.5 cm × 27.2 cm
Museum Rietberg, Zürich; on loan from Eberhard and Barbara Fischer

> Mind and words are powerless
> to encompass your glory
> whose extent is as immeasurable
> as that of cosmic space
> The myriads of galaxies
> you set in motion
> move with precipitous speed
> Were the earth to be split into atoms
> and set end to end
> that immense distance would be equal
> to that you have placed
> between universes,
> O beautiful One!

The words are those of the Tamil poet Subramania Bharati, which he sings in praise of Devi, the Great Goddess, whose vision as the Divine Mother he tried, like many others, to capture. However, for the true devotee, Tantric in belief or not, the Great Goddess cannot be described, for she is immeasurable, elusive, ineffable.

When the painter of the great Tantric series on the Goddess—to which this painting is clearly related even if slightly different in format—sat down to envision her, he must have done so with great intensity. One can sense that these paintings are the visual counterpart of that concentration, that single-minded focusing of the mind, that a devotee aims for while seated in meditation. Essentially a visualization of *dhyana shlokas*—meditative formulaic verses—these paintings conjure up successive visions of the Goddess, in one *shloka* after another. The text from which these *dhyana shlokas* are taken has so far not been identified, but clearly it is Tantric in its intention and meaning. The devotee—in this case the viewer—is helped to envision, through the paintings, images of the Goddess, changing slightly from leaf to leaf, in her countless aspects: Bhadrakali, Kalaratri, Indrakshi, Bhagavati, Bhuvaneshwari, Varahi or Siddha Lakshmi.

Most often, in this series, she appears as Bhadrakali—dark-bodied, all-powerful, full of energy. Now she

>   resides in the *mandala* of the rising sun
>   with face full as the forest lotus . . .
>   with a gait graceful as a young swan
>   breasts high, rounded and mature
>   wearing a garland of lotus blossoms
>   book in hand
>   clad in yellow garments

Now she

>   devours the mover of the entire universe
>   like limp *darbha* grass
>   holding the bodies of eternally dark Vishnu and Shiva . . .
>   standing upon a corpse

And now

>   her lotus eyes quiver through drinking wine . . .
>   seated upon a lion
>   with ten arms

In paintings of this series, very often a caption naming the form of the Goddess appears on a margin. But the devotee, who one can imagine looking at the image, must almost certainly have known the *shloka* by heart: for him word and image come together, inextricably bound, expanding outward from within.

As Kripal—he is almost certainly the main painter of this dazzling series—renders them, the forms of the goddesses throb with energy: eyes large, gaze firm, face radiant. Regardless of whether her aspect is benign or fierce, she is always dressed in great finery and appears magnificently bejewelled: diadem, strands of pearls adorning forehead and temples, many-stringed necklaces, armlets with pompoms, wide bracelets, girdles at the waist, anklets, toe-rings. Topping everything is the crown that she so often wears, pointed and bedecked with lotus buds. But, a truly glowing detail, sprinkled throughout on this elaborate jewellery are little pieces of iridescent beetle-wing cases, stuck on so as to simulate the flashing appearance of emeralds. Each time the Goddess appears as a vision, truly the one 'with whose closing and opening of eyes universes are dissolved and created', these 'emeralds' glisten with an unearthly light.

The Goddess, whom we see here riding in state on a chariot drawn by two fierce-looking tigers, is unnamed, but one can see that she is here in her *rajasic* (dynamic) form, with the powers of darkness—*tamasic* (dark and inert) in appearance—riding behind her or walking ahead. She herself—like Tripurasundari, 'the most beauteous one in all the three worlds'—is golden of complexion, and accoutred with weapons: *khadga*, bow, arrow and drum. She looks straight ahead while a dark-bodied, four-armed attendant waves a *chamara*-fly-whisk over her head. Another *tamasic* figure, also four-armed, leads the chariot forward, *trishula* in one hand, drum and *khadga* and *khappar*-bowl in the others.

There is majesty here, but also a rare combination of grace and power. One can almost hear the slow motion of the heavy wheels, feel the heat of the breath emanating from the snarling mouths of the two tigers, but also get transfixed by the beauty of the Goddess's form.

SHIVA, EVER SOLICITOUS OF HIS OTHER HALF

Folio from a *Rasamanjari* series
Opaque watercolour and gold on paper
Pahari, from the family workshop of Kripal–Devidasa of Nurpur;
c. 1694–95
17.4 cm × 28.5 cm
San Diego Museum of Art, Edwin Binney Collection

This startlingly bold image may well reflect a partial misunderstanding of the text on which it is based, but it makes a powerful impression.

The classical fifteenth-century Sanskrit text the *Rasamanjari* by Bhanudatta Mishra occasioned a long and great series of paintings that Devidasa, son of Kripal of Nurpur, painted for a royal patron in the nearby state of Basohli in the hills. The work deals with the classical theme of *nayak*s and *nayika*s— heroes and heroines—and is distinctly erotic in texture and feeling.

It opens with an invocatory verse—the one on which this painting is based— in which the author pays homage to his *ishta* (cherished) deity, Shiva. The structure of the verse is somewhat complex and the Hindi translation of the Sanskrit verse, inscribed at the back of this folio, reads thus: 'He [Shiva] looks at the uneven ground, first hesitates, [then] extends his foot. Roaming about in the forest, he plucks wild flowers with his raised right hand. Relaxed in comfort on his bed [covered with] a tiger's pelt, he presses his beloved to his body's side. In this manner does Shiva fully experience the pleasure and causes Parvati's side to gracefully tremble.'

The Hindi text departs somewhat from the original Sanskrit verse. The antelope skin of the original is replaced here by a tiger's pelt, for instance. But even more striking is the manner in which the painter seems to interpret, visually, the image that the author may have had in his mind.

Without saying so specifically, Bhanudatta was almost certainly envisioning Shiva as Ardhanarishwara, the 'Lord Whose Other Half Is Woman', his androgynous aspect. In this form, Shiva's left half is female, as he has subsumed Parvati, his consort, within himself, thus becoming *purusha* and *prakriti* conjoined in one.

It is for this reason that Shiva is using the right side of his body, thus sparing Parvati from doing anything that might cause her fatigue. And so Shiva's right foot is extended, he plucks wild flowers with his right hand, and he sleeps with the weight of the body on the right side. In this manner does he cause his left half, Parvati, to 'gracefully tremble' with delight at the care that her Lord shows.

The painter, however, shows Shiva and Parvati as separate figures. We see the divine couple twice. To the left of the painting, Shiva entwines his arm caressingly around Parvati, and plucks a flower from a blossoming tree. This tree divides the painting virtually into two halves. In the right half, we see the couple again, lying on the tiger skin. They are awake, enjoying each other's company. Shiva's legs are almost wholly stretched out, Parvati's slightly bent and close together.

The 'bed' is brilliantly rendered. It is a tiger skin, seen as if from above, its fierce, symmetrically drawn claws, the finely delineated head, the regular stripes, and the curling tail making for a remarkable pattern. The entire scene is set against a rich, red ground which leaves just enough room at the top for a strip of sky to show. At the bottom of the drawing we can see flowers and grass painted in a stylized fashion.

The figures are relatively short but are rendered with a singularly firm line. Shiva is depicted as the perfect recluse, with matted locks, his body clad only in a leopard skin, a serpent entwined around his neck and shoulders. But the third eye on the forehead and the crescent moon in the locks leave no doubt that this is no ordinary ascetic. Parvati, on the other hand, is like any graceful *nayika*, elegantly dressed, bejewelled, wearing a soft expression.

There is some awkwardness—deliberate ambiguity?—in the manner in which Shiva's form is rendered as he walks. It is his back, not his chest, that we see, and the arm around Parvati's head is his left arm; the leg that almost touches Parvati's is his left leg.

We also see a frontal view of Shiva as he lies down, revealing new details: the third eye in the midst of the *tilaka* marks on the forehead and the string with a *nada*-whistle attached to it. While lying down, Shiva's thighs are covered not by the leopard skin he wore while standing but by one end of Parvati's striped red wrap.

It is a stridently bold image, sparse but wonderfully decorative, the couple's almost unapproachable majesty suddenly softened and tempered by human warmth.

———————

Devidasa, the greatly gifted son of Kripal of Nurpur, is one of the few painters whose name can be firmly associated with a series of paintings from the hills, in this case the Rasamanjari. *The last folio of that series bears a colophon which states in a chronogram that the work was completed in the year equivalent to 1694–95* CE *at Basohli for the raja Kripal Pal.*

SHIVA AND PARVATI AMONG THE CLOUDS

Isolated folio
Ink and colour on paper
Pahari, Basohli school, by Devidasa of Nurpur; c. 1675–80
23.5 cm × 16.2 cm
Cleveland Museum of Art, Edward L. Whittemore Fund

It is not easy to tell whether this painting—soaring, mysterious, incomprehensible in many ways—comes from a series that we do not know anything about, or whether it was made as a single, individual creation. Almost naturally—unless the painter was rendering a private vision that he had had—one assumes that it was made at the command of a patron, for that was the normal way in which things worked at nearly all Rajput courts. And if it *was* the patron who commissioned it, what might have occasioned it: a dream, a new *dhyana shloka* that he might have come upon, the envisioning of a different setting in which he wanted to see his *ishta* deity? One can only speculate.

Here, Lord Shiva, whom one sees so often in Pahari painting, is rendered occupying a different space than Kailash, the mountain peak he usually inhabits. With his divine consort, Parvati, resting in his lap, he is far above the earthly sphere, among the clouds, seated on an elephant skin that lies underneath the couple like a flying carpet. All around him are swirling banks of clouds, some rolled up into bales, others twisting around, some mere wisps. Against the clouds, the heron-like birds flying about look up towards the couple. Down on the earth, far, far below, a sparse row of brilliantly coloured trees appears, growing in a band of dark brown soil which in turn rests upon another band, bare and much lighter in colour.

What worlds are these, what spheres, one wonders, before one's eye is drawn back to the Lord, seated up there in all his majesty, in his four-armed form.

Parvati, richly bejewelled, clad in a red sari and blouse, sits with one leg tucked under and the other raised but bent at the knee, looking up at him—hands folded, a look of devotion in her eyes. Shiva is bare-bodied, his only garment an animal skin round his loins—the tail of the beast clearly visible, draped over one knee—and sits with legs crossed so as to form the lap in which his consort is seated.

All the iconographic details are in place: the third eye on the forehead—and the head not in true profile but slightly turned for the third eye to show

clearly; three horizontal *tilaka* marks, the *tripundra*, following closely the shape of his curved eyebrows; the snake coiled round the neck, gazing at Parvati; the matted hair piled up in a knot on the head; the three sandal-paste-yellow parallel marks seen all over the body: neck, forearms, legs. What stands out as different, however, are the *ayudha*s the Lord carries: the familiar drum in the upper left hand apart, in the upper right hand is a long double-edged sword held aloft, in the lower hands a *mala* of prayer beads, and a *khappar*-like bowl, hinting at other aspects of divinity such as Brahma. Who knows where these come from: the painter's imagination or from the text of some obscure *dhyana shloka*?

The elephant hide on which the divine couple is seated is evidently a reference to the aspect of Shiva as *gajasura-vadha murti*, when he took the hide off the elephant demon with the nail of a single finger. It makes one wonder if the scene the painter renders here has something to do with the Lord leaping up into the skies after that victory over the demon. Whatever the case, visually the image is stunning: consider the loving figures of the divine couple, the swirl of the clouds, the superb colouring both in the sky and on earth, the forms of the trees. It is as if one is being made witness to a vision: rarefied and intimate at the same time.

———————

It is more than likely that the work is in the hand of Devidasa of Nurpur: some folios from his own Rasamanjari, *like the one with Shiva and Parvati playing a game of* chaupar, *now in the Metropolitan Museum of Art, New York, come to mind; so do the trees from the* Rasamanjari *painted by his father, Kripal.*

INDRA DANCING

Detail from a Jain *Panchakalyanaka pata*
Pigments on cloth
Possibly Aurangabad, Maharashtra; c. 1700
1220 cm × 80 cm (entire *pata*)
Sena Gana Mandir, Karanja in Vidarbha, Maharashtra

Unlikely as it might seem, Indra, the Vedic god who figures so prominently in Hindu myths (he is also known by the name Shakra), appears occasionally in Jain texts too. When he does feature, it is not in his role as the god of rain, thunder and lightning. In the Jain texts, he keeps an eye on the future, descends to the earth on occasion, and participates in significant rituals.

When a Brahmani conceives the future saviour of mankind, it is Indra who arranges for the foetus to be transferred to the womb of a Kshatriya princess; when a *tirthankara* is born, Indra descends with his consort, Shachi, riding their mount, the great elephant Airavata, to celebrate the event; when a *tirthankara* plucks out all the hair on his head in a grand gesture of renunciation and detachment, it is Indra who receives, most reverently, that hair in the palms of his own hands.

There are no independent shrines dedicated to him in Jainism, but in Jain paintings he is seen now instructing Harinegameshi to effect the transfer of the divine foetus from one womb to another; now performing *snatra puja* in which he performs the *abhishek* (ceremonial bath) of the newborn, taking him to the Sumeru mountains; now standing before the *tirthankara*, bowing low to receive the plucked hair in his hands. Here, in this detail of a *pata*, we see him dancing with devotion and abandon.

In Hindu iconography, especially in paintings from Rajasthan and the Pahari areas, Indra usually appears with his entire body covered with countless eyes—there is a story connected with that in which a curse figures prominently. In this painting he is portrayed as a normal figure endowed with divinity—handsome and youthful.

The detail here is from a sixteen-panel-long *Panchakalyanaka pata*, relating to the first of the twenty-four *tirthankaras*, Rishabhanath. Like all standard *Panchakalyanaka* renderings, detailing the five most auspicious events in the life of a *tirthankara*—*garbha* (conception), *janma* (birth), *diksha* (attainment of knowledge), *kaivalya* (detachment) and *moksha* (release from the cycles of rebirth)—this *pata* also goes into the celebrations at the time of the birth of the *tirthankara*.

Indra, who in the Digambara Jain tradition is named Saudharma Indra, leads the other gods in these celebrations. His court in the heavens is filled with great musicians and dancers, and when we see him descending from the heavens and taking part in the celebrations at the birth of the *tirthankara*, he takes on the role of a divine dancer himself. 'Dancing Indra' is a recurring theme in Jain belief and practice—for instance, in an early rendering one sees him in a fifteenth-century painting in a temple, Tirupparuttikuam, on the outskirts of Kanchipuram in Tamil Nadu. Even today, in a re-enactment of the gods' celebration of the birth of a *tirthankara*, a layman takes on the role of Indra as he dances, and his wife that of his consort, Shachi.

In this superb rendering, Indra wears a beautifully crafted golden crown, and profuse jewellery on the body; his torso is flexed, head gently bent towards the right, upper part of the body bare except for a long scarf with broad end-panels in gold draped round the shoulders, lower part of the body in a blue dhoti with a pattern of stylized golden flowers secured with a short *patka* tied at the waist; and his legs are placed as though he is about to break into a slow dance.

But what draws instant attention to itself is the fact that he has multiple arms, as many as twenty on either side, which fan out to form a moving circular pattern. In some of the hands he holds blooming lotus flowers, but in more than half of them, resting on the palm, stand diminutive little figures of young women—Indra's *apsaras*—some of them dancing, others holding musical instruments or clapping. They all look towards their Lord but he does not spare a glance for them, his face, instead, full of concentration.

Dwarfed by this large, beautifully painted figure, stand other figures—men with musical instruments in their hands: a *sitar*-like instrument, a *dafli*-drum, *veena*, *dholak*-drum, cymbals, and so on. All these figures are set against a plain scarlet-red monochrome background. There are other panels in the *pata*, of course, 'documenting', as it were, the various episodes—birth, renunciation, lustration, delivering the great sermon, among others. Panel after panel succeeds the one above in rich succession.

Various styles seem to be at work here, names like Bikaner, Bundi, Golconda and Aurangabad come to mind. The art historian Saryu Doshi, who drew attention to this brilliantly conceived and painted *pata*, speculated about its stylistic affiliations—'Rajasthani palette with a Deccani slant, the Deccani treatment of landscape, the compositional elements from Bikaner as well as Golconda'—leading to the suggestion that it was probably painted for some Jain family of Rajasthani origin which came later to settle for whatever reasons in Karanja, and invited artists from the Deccan to execute this complex but dazzling work.

———

Two things about the figure of dancing Indra are striking. One, the manner in which the arms are fashioned, all emerging from the elbows rather than, as generally seen, from the shoulder. This is a treatment that is far more commonly seen in Kashmiri painting than in Rajasthan. At the same time, there is nothing else in the painting to suggest any connection with Kashmir. Second, to the left leg is attached a right foot, a confusion often seen, but generally in folkish rather than classical work. Both features leave one a bit puzzled.

MERU, THE GOLDEN MOUNTAIN

Folio from a manuscript of the *Anadi Patan*
Assam, north-eastern India; late seventeenth or early eighteenth century
14 cm × 32 cm
Kamarupa Anusandhan Samiti, Guwahati

'O great king!' the sage Sukadeva says to Parikshit in the *Bhagavata Purana*,
'No human being, even if he be blessed with the longevity of the gods,
can adequately comprehend by mind or express by speech the extent of
the Lord's creation . . .' The sage then names countless 'island-continents',
among them Jambudvipa, the continent we live on, which forms the central
layer of this 'lotus-like earth'.

At the very centre of Jambudvipa stands the 'all-gold Mount Meru, the king
of all mountains . . . It is as high as the extent of the continent itself; it forms
the pericarp of the lotus in the form of the earth. It is thirty-two thousand
*yojana*s in extent at the top, and sixteen thousand yojanas at its foot, and its
root lies as deep under the earth's surface. . . .' Then follows a description
of the various mountains which rise on Mount Meru's four sides as its
supports—the mountains Suparshva, Kumud, Mandara and Merumandara,
'each of them ten thousand yojanas in length and height'. On these four
mountain ranges stand four great trees—the mango, the *jambu*, the *kadamba*
and the banyan, as if they were their flags.

The painter of this extraordinary leaf sets out here to visualize Mount Meru,
in the *Anadi Patan*, revered in the north-eastern region of India and written by
Sankaradeva (1449–1568), the most famous of all Vaishnava saints active in
that area. Sankaradeva was a great devotee of the *Bhagavata Purana* and the
Anadi Patan can be seen to be an Assamese version of the *Bhagavata Purana*.

The mountain has been described in a whole range of early texts, but no two descriptions agree. In any case, one can see that the painter was on his own, considering that 'no human being can adequately comprehend' this creation, as the *Bhagavata Purana* declared. He therefore sets off unfettered, letting his imagination soar.

At the heart of the leaf is the great mountain itself, bathed in gold, rising in tiers from the bottom to the top, one inverted-cone shape topping another. These gold cones are contained in a stepped pyramid, painted in red ochre. They look as if they were vessels, on whose top rim curving handles are attached. Are these there for the gods to lift them with?

Each of the cones is larger and more decorative than the one below it. On either side of this glistening structure are two curved forms filled with colourful stripes, leaning away from Meru, yet supporting it. These, of course, are the four mountains that the text mentions, their names inscribed at the bottom of the page, just below the image: Suparshva and Kumud on the left, and Mandara and Merumandara to the right.

On the tip of these mountains one can see vegetal forms—part leaf or bud, part stem—that resemble nothing recognizable but stand here for the four trees that the text mentions. There are other forms or shapes, also unrecognizable. Thus, at the bottom, we can see seven stripes on either end—seven layers of the earth perhaps?

Remarkably little is known about painting in the north-eastern region of India in general, and it seldom enters any discussions or accounts of Indian painting. But here is a work—untutored perhaps but remarkably sophisticated—that forces itself on our attention. Where it was done—possibly at one of the *satra* monasteries of the kind that Sankaradeva founded—or by whom remains unknown. There is no date, no colophon.

———————

Meru, the golden mountain, figures prominently in a range of myths and texts, and it is visualized differently almost each time by different painters in different lands. The manuscript of the Anadi Patan *to which this leaf belongs is sometimes ascribed to 'the Darrang style', after a district of Assam by that name. In quality this manuscript stands close to another text, the* Tirtha Kaumudi, *which has been assigned by one scholar to the last quarter of the seventeenth century.*

VASUDEVA TAKES THE INFANT KRISHNA ACROSS THE YAMUNA RIVER

Folio from a *Bhagavata Purana* series
Opaque watercolour on paper
Pahari, by the Mankot master; c. 1700
17.5 cm × 28.1 cm
Government Museum and Art Gallery, Chandigarh

From the workshop of painters active in the very small principality of Mankot seem to have come some remarkable paintings—portraits, court scenes, *Ragamala* leaves, above all, a *Bhagavata Purana* series—that take one's breath away by their boldness and by the passion with which they are painted. Colours glow and crisply drawn figures stay etched against large, flat areas in monochrome; action is compacted, all redundant details firmly eschewed; and emotional responses are evoked with the barest of details. Clearly, the master painter of this *Bhagavata Purana* series proceeds on the assumption that everyone knows the sacred and stirring tale; he is only retelling it in the manner that he knows best: in images.

He did paint some stunning portraits at the same time that he did this series, but here he comes into his own at a very different level. He approaches the text—even if he was not a devout Vaishnava himself—with the deepest reverence and conviction. Through him, one sees the world of the gods and their wondrous deeds, different as it is from the world of men, and he persuades us to believe that this is the only way that things must have happened in the days that now lie buried in the past. When Krishna, before being born, gave *darshan* to his parents who were in prison, he must have taken the very four-armed aspect that the painter shows us in one of the folios; when Kamsa is pulled down from his throne, this must have been the way in which he, taking his last breath, reached out to touch Krishna's feet in the hope of salvation. And so on. We are not only told the tale but also, ever so gently, the higher meaning that lies embedded in it.

Here, the newborn Krishna is being taken to safety by his father, Vasudeva. The guards posted outside the prison had all gone to sleep, all the beasts had fallen quiet; and this was the moment for Vasudeva to slip out and take the newborn across the river and exchange him with a newborn girl, the Goddess in another form, as divinely ordained (see p. 190). But the skies are violent at this moment, and rain pours down ceaselessly. Vasudeva, taking the infant in his arms, has to wade through the river. The river, the text says, was 'covered with foam created by waves raised by the velocity of the swiftly moving waters and that made for hundreds of fearful whirlpools'. But this did not deter Vasudeva. Following him, however, and 'warding off the rainwater with his hoods spread over Vasudeva's head, like an umbrella' was none other than the serpent Shesha, Vishnu's gentle couch in the myths. At Krishna's approach, the tale goes, the Yamuna began slowly to recede, for she was waiting for the days when Krishna would sport on her bank and bless her by his very presence.

In the painting, everything follows the text closely: the clouds and lightning in the sky, the pouring rain, the many-hooded Shesha, the 'hundreds of fearful whirlpools in the waters'. But the magnificent tiger we see on the nearer bank of the river is sprung upon us by the painter as a surprise, as if asking us to figure out the reason for his presence. We might see him as symbolizing the many dangers that surround Vasudeva and Krishna—terrified father and innocent son. At the same time we might also wonder if the painter has brought the beast in as a symbol of the presence of the Goddess, whose vehicle the tiger is and who has been born as a daughter in the household of Nanda and Yashoda, the very infant who is to be brought back in exchange for Krishna.

There is marked simplicity in the rendering but also deep understanding and feeling. The streams of raindrops are carefully discontinued where there is a shelter, under the sole tree at left and under the body of the serpent, even in the little space formed by the curve of its body on the outer side. The river is a magnificent presence, the painter using a dark chocolate-brown ground on which swirling waters make countless whirlpools and eddies. Nothing is quite as it would appear to the naked eye, and yet everything is how it was once—so the painter seems to assert.

The present painting bears the number '3' on the top register where is also inscribed, in Takri characters, a brief caption describing the scene. The series might not have been very extensive, but it is difficult to judge its extent considering that the folios are now dispersed, the largest group now being in the Government Museum and Art Gallery at Chandigarh. It is of interest to note that another series based on the same text, and using much the same compositions, although in the vertical format, was also painted in the same workshop, a little later, perhaps, and certainly not marked by the same refinement as this one.

THE GREAT GODDESS BATTLES THE DEMONS

Folio from a dispersed manuscript of the *Devi Mahatmya*
Opaque watercolour and slight gold on paper
Rajasthan, from a Sirohi workshop, painted at Balotra; 1703
14.8 cm × 19.5 cm (outer)
14 cm × 16.8 cm (inner)
Private Collection

In the war between gods and demons—symbolizing the eternal conflict between the forces of good and evil—the Great Goddess, implored by the gods to help them, goes out to endless battle. The Goddess's task is never complete for evil never ceases to be. Thus, if one demon is subdued, another takes his place.

With the annihilation of one of the most powerful of demons, Mahishasura—he with the head of a great buffalo—for instance, other threats make their appearance. She has to take on Chanda and Munda now, Dhumralochana or Raktabija at another time, and Shumbha and Nishumbha who seem never to give up. The story is told at great length in the *Devi Mahatmya*—literally, 'Glory of the Great Goddess', also referred to as the *Durga Saptashati* or the *Chandi Path*—an almost independent text embedded inside the *Markandeya Purana*.

Traditionally, the *Devi Mahatmya* has been regarded as a 'potent', greatly efficacious, text, invoked and recited in times of great stress or calamity. There are many stories of how it came to the aid of those in distress. In the hill state of Chamba, for instance, in the eighteenth century, a great event was once organized at which, it is said, there was a recitation of the text 100,000 times by a gathering of priests when the ruler had been imprisoned by Mughal authorities. In fact, there still exists a palace there, called the Akhand-chandi—'uninterrupted recitation of the Chandi text'—in commemoration of the event.

Throughout the Rajput world—in Rajasthan and the Pahari area—manuscripts of the *Devi Mahatmya* were repeatedly scripted and painted. From the relatively small state of Sirohi itself, in south-western Rajasthan, has emerged more than one manuscript of the text, including of course this one.

The page is packed with furious action. In the top-left corner, the Goddess appears, riding her ferocious-looking tiger who leaps forward as if to pounce upon the horse of the chariot on which his mistress's adversary is seated. The Goddess, youthful-looking, crowned and dressed in a brief *choli*-bodice and skirt, sits calmly on her tiger-*vahana* and hurls weapons—*khadga*, dagger, lance, *trishula*—at the demon with all her four hands.

The six-armed demon facing her, seated on a chariot, is also seen discharging one arrow after another at her, but it would seem as if they have gone singing past her. Nothing, miraculously, has done her any harm; they have, in fact, not even touched her. On the ground lies a dying warrior, about to be trampled upon by the demon's horse but still extending one hand to touch the feet of the Goddess, as if in a gesture of seeking her blessings and asking her forgiveness.

While wild action occupies the top half of the painting, the lower half is marked by seven figures. They are all warriors, four at right, on the side of the demon, advancing towards the three at left who are marching towards them. A clash is in the offing, for every soldier is heavily armed—helmets on heads, quivers filled with arrows tied to waists, mace, staff, bow and muskets held threateningly. These figures do not appear as engaged in the battle—some of them can be seen, in fact, with faces turned towards the viewer, but there can be little doubt that on the succeeding folio of this manuscript, these men would have sprung into resolute action too.

There is something 'folkish' about the rendering; the refined lines and exquisitely smooth finish one sees in countless Rajasthani works are missing here. But the artless manner in which the painter takes us into the heart of the battle, crowding the entire page with figures battling or dying, makes a distinct impression. At the same time some things, clearly worked out by the painter, demand close attention. The demons—the principal adversary can unfortunately not be named for want of a caption—do not have the aspect of demons that we ordinarily see in Indian paintings—nearly naked, beast heads grafted on to scaly human bodies, bloodshot eyes, thick hides bristling with coarse hair and, frequently, bird toes.

Here they seem to have been modelled upon real enemies—invading Muslim hordes perhaps?—looking very human, fully clothed, with large turbans on their heads. They seem familiar. Another thing worthy of notice is the fact that the entire background is a rich blue, as against the conventional red appropriate to the scene of bloody encounters on the field of battle. It is entirely possible that the painter had conceived this page differently, suggesting that the entire action is taking place in the sky, as it does in the text, for everyone could leap and fling himself into the air in the heat of battle. Soon, however, with all the demons subdued and slain, things will return to normalcy. For, as the text says, then 'the winds began to blow calmly' and sacrificial fires 'burst into flames once again'.

The colophon page of this particular manuscript has survived and it states that the work was painted at Balotra, within the Sirohi domains, in vs 1760, that is, 1703 CE. No royal patron is mentioned.

RASAMANDALA
THE ETERNAL DANCE

Folio from a dispersed *Bhagavata Purana* series
Opaque watercolour and gold on paper
Central India, from a Malwa workshop; first quarter of the eighteenth century
20.3 cm × 37 cm
San Diego Museum of Art, Edwin Binney Collection

The setting, the occasion, and the bliss of this scene do not have to be established for true devotees of Krishna: they know them only too well. It was on the full-moon night of 'the blessed month of Karttika', as the text of the *Bhagavata Purana* tells it, that Krishna danced this eternal dance with his countless beloveds. 'Exceedingly beautiful shone the glorious Lord, the son of Devaki, in the midst of those pairs of damsels like a priceless sapphire strung between a pair of gold beads.' The series of intense, emotional events leading to this moment—this eternity of experience—are behind everyone by now. Hearkening to the call of his flute, the *gopis* had all gathered in the fragrant grove where he stood: beauteous, blue-bodied, clad in yellow. After making the motions of persuading the *gopis* to go back to their own homes, he sported with them in the waters of the Yamuna. Then, sensing that they were beginning to take his presence for granted, he suddenly disappeared from their midst. This caused great consternation and grief among the damsels, who began to look everywhere for him, full of remorse, their pride appropriately humbled. At which, after a while, the Lord reappeared, the text says, and decided to begin his *rasa-krida*—sportive play—with them.

A great *mandala*-circle was formed. Everyone began to dance, and there are impassioned descriptions of measured steps and sinuous movement, knowing smiles, bending waists and heaving breasts, fluttering garments, dangling earrings, beads of perspiration and loosened braids of hair. In the centre of the circle formed by dancing and clapping pairs of *gopis*, Krishna

229

placed himself and his companion, the 'favoured one'. This, however, gave rise to a wave of jealousy among the throng of *gopi*s: why is he dancing with her alone? Sensing this, and knowing that each *gopi* wished to be close to him, Krishna, by his illusory, yogic powers, multiplied himself countless times, placing himself between every pair of *gopi*s in this circular dance. No one felt abandoned, all traces of jealousy vanished. And there they were: 'sapphire strung between a pair of gold beads'.

As many as five chapters of the *Bhagavata Purana* are devoted to this episode, the celebrated *Rasa Panchadhyayi* as it is called. The chapters are regarded as the 'crest-jewel' of the sacred text. In these everything comes together: the promise, the pain, the ultimate bliss. Inspired by the ancient Sanskrit text, later poets and commentators have created their own versions of that miraculous, magical night. Watching this divine spectacle, one text says, 'celestial damsels were themselves smitten with passion, and the moon-god stood motionless in the skies, forgetting his course through the skies'. 'Two and two the cowherdesses joined hands,' another text says,

> between each two was Hari the companion:
> Each thinks that he is at her side, and does not recognize another of his illusions;
> Cowherdess and Nanda's son, alternately, like a dense cloud and lightning all round.

Seeing this sight,

> Brahma, Rudra, Indra, and all the other gods,
> And *gandharva*s each with his wife, seated in aerial cars,
> Looking on at the joys of the dancing circle with delight were raining down flowers
> And the wives gazing on that joyous spectacle, enviously were saying,
> 'Had we been born in Vraja, we too would have danced and sported with Hari.'

But this night was no ordinary night, and this no ordinary spectacle.

> This night advanced; then six months had passed away
> And no one was aware of it.
> From that time,
> The name of that night has been
> The Night of Brahma.

Considering the centrality of this theme in the painters' and devotees' scheme of things, it must have been challenging in the extreme to visually render it, to capture its essence. A large number of paintings of uneven merit were made. This work, folkish as it might seem to begin with, is distinguished by—in addition to the richness of its colouring and the emphatic abstractions that one associates with Malwa workshops—the painter's soaring conception.

The draughtsmanship may be a little coarse, but the painter creates two highly imaginative circles, or *rasamandalas*. In the circle at left, Krishna is seen with one maiden at the centre, and all the other *gopi*s form a ring around the divine pair. But, this not being enough, in the circle at right the artist places the same pair at the centre, and in the outer circle, Krishna is multiplied countless times, standing next to each *gopi*. It is in the placing of the two circles, however, that magic lies. For, after a while, the two identically sized circles begin to appear as if they were two giant, cosmic wheels of the chariot of Time, the 'still point of the turning world'. Meanwhile, above in the skies, the aerial vehicles of the gods have come to a stop, and heavenly nymphs break into a dance of their own.

The range of work that was turned out in the workshops of the Malwa region was enormous, varying from the folkish to the highly sophisticated and precise. Bold abstractions, however, mark Malwa work throughout, as does rich, intense colouring.

THE HOUSE OF THE PANDAVAS IS SET ON FIRE

Folio from a *Bhagavata Purana* series
Opaque watercolour and gold on paper
Pahari, by a member of the Manaku–Nainsukh family; c. 1765
29.5 cm × 41 cm (outer)
26 cm × 37 cm (inner)
Museum Rietberg, Zürich, Eberhard and Barbara Fischer Collection

The central theme of the great epic, the Mahabharata, the rivalry between the Kauravas and their cousins the Pandavas, figures also in the *Bhagavata Purana*, even if sporadically. The episode where the Pandavas are sought to be destroyed by deceit must have been one that especially stirred the painter's imagination, and in this leaf he responds brilliantly to its dramatic visual possibilities.

But first one must explain briefly the context of this painting. After the kingdom that the blind Dhritarashtra ruled over was divided between the cousins, the Pandavas had to leave Hastinapura and move to the city of Varanavartha. But that was not enough for the eldest Kaurava, Duryodhana, who had a diabolical plan up his sleeve. The wise Vidura warned the Pandava brothers to beware of the perils of fire, quoting a proverb: 'The conflagration that devastates a forest cannot hurt a rat which shelters itself in a hole or a porcupine which burrows in the earth.'

Meanwhile, Duryodhana, ostensibly as a gesture of goodwill, sent a confidant to build for the Pandava brothers and their mother, Kunti, a 'commodious new dwelling' which was raised with great speed. However, it was a *lakshagraha*, a 'house of lac', built of combustible material: hemp and resin packed in the walls and between the floors, and plastered over with mortar well mixed with pitch and clarified butter. The Pandavas lived in the house for some time but slowly grew suspicious of Duryodhana's motives. When an emissary of

Vidura arrived to warn them again, they were convinced that a plot had been hatched. They therefore had a secret passage dug that would allow them to escape quickly from the house.

On a very dark night, a great windstorm arose. Bhima, one of the Pandavas, decided this was the moment for him, his brothers and their mother to escape, and while fleeing he set the house on fire. It burnt 'fiercely and speedily'. However, a Bhil woman and her five drunken sons, related to Duryodhana's agent, had stayed on in the house and they were charred in the fire, and so the word went around that it was the Pandavas who had perished. There was a show of sorrow on the part of the Kauravas, but inwardly they rejoiced. Much else was to follow, of course.

The *lakshagraha* on fire is what the painter, with great elan, renders here. There is fire, fierce and speedy, everywhere, from end to end on this page.

The flames rise and jump and lick everything in sight. At the back, dimly seen, are the remains of some structures; above, stars shine lustreless in the sky; in the dark, through spiralling banks of smoke, some figures lying on the ground can be vaguely discerned. But it is the fire that holds one in thrall, for it is treated with remarkable flair.

Sprouting from a myriad roots as it were, the flames have a life of their own. One can almost feel the heat and smell the smoke. The impression that all fire is orange in colour vanishes swiftly when one sees the leaf from close and with care. A range of colours reveals itself then: red and yellow of different intensities, black and grey, even white. It is as if the painter was aware that in the tradition, fire—Agni—is not simply fire: it has several 'tongues', each bearing a different name: *svaha, svadha, sudhumravarna, sphulingini, pradipta, saptajihva, saptaidha* and *saptavahana,* each denoting a different hue, type, intensity and purpose. All these thoughts must have been swirling in his head as he worked.

———————

The treatment of fire is so varied in the hands of Indian painters that one marvels at their inventiveness. When Krishna drinks the forest fire in one painting, for example—the davanala achamana *episode in the* Bhagavata Purana—*it is of one kind; in another painter's hand it takes on a different form and a different hue. But in the hands of the members of this celebrated family of painters, the treatment of fire remains almost uniform. When the Prachetasas, in a painting from an earlier episode in the* Bhagavata Purana, *burn a forest down with their breath, the fire is exactly the same as in this painting. Some things last, and their glow never diminishes.*

THE EMERGENCE OF VARAHA
BOAR INCARNATION OF VISHNU

Folio from a *Bhagavata Purana* series
Opaque watercolour and gold on paper
Pahari, attributed to Manaku of Guler; c. 1740
21.8 cm × 32.2 cm (outer)
17.6 cm × 28 cm (inner)
Government Museum and Art Gallery, Chandigarh

The Puranas speak, again and again, of momentous events, threatening the very existence of mankind, upsetting the balance in which the elements are held, endangering the future of the earth. But each time the earth is saved and mankind is liberated from oppression, all due to divine intervention, as the texts keep repeating. In the *Bhagavata Purana*, among the most revered of texts, it is the great god Vishnu who incarnates himself, descending to the earth in one form or another to battle and destroy the forces of evil. The stories are complex—narratives interspersed with philosophical musings and discourses—but told in stirring, gripping detail.

There were times, the text says, when the earth was subjected to untold hardships, for it was completely taken over by *asuric* forces (forces opposed to the benign deities). Hiranyakashipu and Hiranyaksha—the latter meaning 'the one with the golden eye'—were two *daityas* (malign beings), sons of Diti, who unleashed unprecedented terror. Hiranyaksha, in fact, seized the earth and took it down with himself into the womb of the waters. Till, of course, persuaded by a host of gods, the great Vishnu decided to descend to earth. It was the form of Varaha—the Primal Boar—that Vishnu took when he challenged the demon Hiranyaksha, all-powerful, and unbearably arrogant in his defiance of the forces of good.

A great battle ensued, and more than one chapter in the Third Book of the

Bhagavata Purana is devoted to describing it. Spiteful words were exchanged between the adversaries, who hurled weapons at each other and engaged in physical combat. Blows were struck with maces and javelins and discuses. In the midst of all this, the demon suddenly summoned up his powers of black magic, his *asuric maya*. What followed was cataclysmic. As the text says, 'all creatures got panicky and thought that the end of the world was imminent'; 'terrible stormy winds began to blow and spread the darkness of dust . . . ; volleys of stones fell from all quarters as if discharged from slings . . . the sky, being covered with clouds accompanied by lightning flashes, and thundering and pouring pus, hair, blood, excretion, urine and bones, seemed devoid of luminaries . . . the mountains appeared to shower various weapons, and naked rakshasas with their hair let loose appeared with spears'. In the midst of all this, however, the Lord stood firm, not moving even slightly 'as if he were an elephant struck by a garland'.

This is the scene that the painter Manaku envisions here. Having finished the *Gita Govinda* in 1730, he had embarked on a singularly ambitious project: painting a series based on the *Bhagavata Purana*. The work was never completed. For reasons unknown, it was brought up to a point in the form of finished paintings and continued in the form of drawings: first flushes of thought rendered into compositions. One does not know the extent of the entire work, but apparently hundreds of drawings, works of great brilliance, were made by him, aided perhaps by sons or assistants.

The paintings themselves, of which more than a hundred have survived, are breathtaking in their range and energy. Manaku, one knows, was fond of dense narration: the episode, for instance, of the battle between Vishnu as Varaha and the demon Hiranyaksha runs into several folios, each move, each parry and thrust being documented in detail as the combat continues, filling in the pages from end to end. The temper of these works is so different from what one sees in his 1730 *Gita Govinda*.

Here, the painter captures with breathtaking imagination the scene of the *asuric maya* that Hiranyaksha creates. One can almost sense the very heavens shake and tremble with sounds that fill all quarters, and a shower of weapons falls from the sky; snakes hiss about in the air; rocks fall and scatter; bones and pieces of flesh fly about. The moment is such that all beings—*rishis* and *siddhas*, demons and spirits, *gandharvas* and *vidyadharas*—flee in sheer terror. All this while, Varaha stands firm, feet solidly planted on earth, hands holding on to weapons, head held aloft, the all-knowing eye unwavering, the flaming, golden discus whirling at dizzying speed on an upraised finger. Stillness in the midst of commotion, the good standing firm against evil.

In Manaku's incomparable hand, in other leaves of this *Bhagavata Purana* series, the king Prithu ensnares the earth-cow and brings her to his quarters to yield all that she can; the Prachetasas clear the earth by burning forests down; the boy Dhruva stands firm and immovable for years as he meditates upon Vishnu. An entire world—different time, different space—unfolds before our very eyes.

———

This Bhagavata Purana *series has no colophon—apparently because it was never finished. In any case, we do not have a closing leaf, and the date that we assign to it—1740—is notional. The work must have taken Manaku years to complete, although one does get the feeling that he worked with considerable speed. Manaku was left-handed, it appears, judging from the manner in which he renders many of his figures, including Krishna in the* Gita Govinda, *favouring the left hand.*

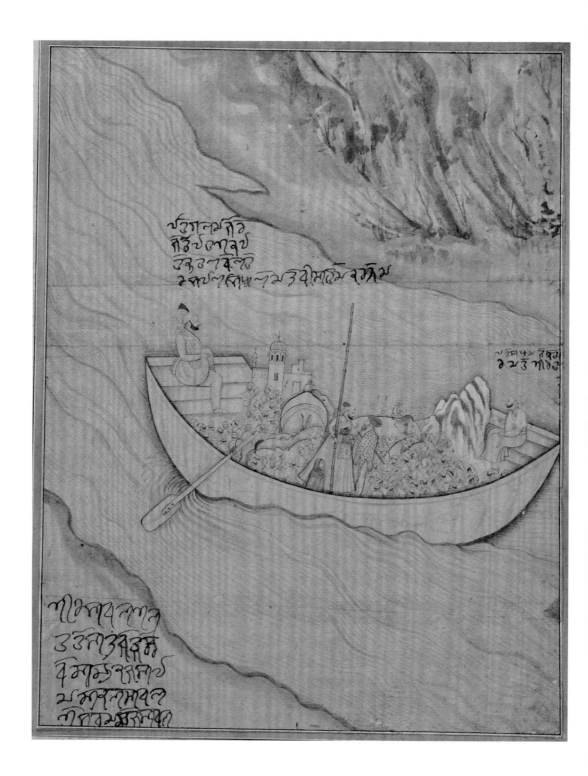

A BOAT ADRIFT ON A RIVER

Leaf illustrating a folk legend
Tinted brush drawing on paper
Pahari, by Nainsukh; c. 1765–75
36 cm × 28.5 cm
Bharat Kala Bhavan, Varanasi

It is not always easy to get the full measure of what Nainsukh, that highly gifted painter from the small state of Guler, put into some of his works. Over a tinted drawing like this—'unparalleled in the whole of Pahari painting', as the art historian W.G. Archer put it—a sense of mystery and drama has hung for several decades. There have been different interpretations of what it is all about—it was once called 'An Allegory of Disaster', which almost certainly it is not—and it remains shadowed in enigma.

But clearly, some cataclysmic situation is depicted: on a steeply angled hill torrent is afloat a massive boat, carrying virtually a whole kingdom. On the farther bank of the rushing river, a blazing fire rages, consuming, 'like a thousand hungry moths', all that comes in its way. The middle of the barge is densely packed with a crowd of men, many wearing Gaddi caps—native to the Pahari area—and animals and objects, even a mountainous rock and a segment of a palatial building. But at either end of the boat sits an isolated figure: at the stern a youthful-looking prince, with a plume prominently stuck in his turban; at the prow a somewhat heavier and older man, burdened, it seems, with the weight of cares. At the dead centre of the crowded boat stands a tall man wearing a Muslim-style *jama* tied under the right arm and holding in his right hand a very long pole; by his side stands a diminutive figure, a young woman, her whole form draped in a veil with only the face visible. The tall man is conversing with a *sannyasi*, a holy man with long, matted hair and beard, clothed in leopard skin, with a rod tucked under his arm.

The ground is plain, the river uncoloured save for light grey streaks that mark the wavy surface; the banks are touched by a light wash in greyish green; the splendidly rendered fire raging on the farther bank is lightly tinted in orange and grey. Whatever colour there is, is applied thin. A little white and grey define the contours of the mountainous rock—a suggestion possibly of snow on the high peaks, habitat of the Gaddi hillmen. The *sannyasi*'s matted hair is coloured rust-brown. But what stands out is the smooth ecru of the uncoloured paper, adding to the suggestion of a vast uncharted expanse, evoking feelings of vague unease.

Archer's discussion of this drawing—it was he who saw it as 'An Allegory of Disaster'—is filled with great feeling. Speculating, he sees the work as summing up events in the life of Balwant Singh—Nainsukh's patron—whose last years were very troubled, in his view. Some disaster had struck the prince, he says, leading to great destruction, and the work is thus an allegory: the left half showing Balwant Singh as he was, and the right the hard, harsh state to which he was reduced, like the wandering *sannyasi*. In this catastrophe, his former life was swept away, 'as if by a raging torrent'.

Poetic and persuasive as this interpretation is, it poses problems. For one thing, the two halves of the painting are not as neatly differentiated from each other: the right half too is filled with many signs of state with horses, elephants and the like. More than this, it is the information that the inscribed notes on the drawing itself provide—given up as indecipherable at one time—which goes against Archer's interpretation. The two men at the stern and the prow, according to the inscription, are musing about the foolishness of the man with the pole in the middle, identified as the 'Mir' who, at this critical point, is more interested in marrying and learning the secrets of making a *rasayan*-potion from the *sannyasi* than in saving the boat. The perilous position of the boat is referred to again in the inscription at bottom-left, a Persian saying being cited to say that in such circumstances only disaster can lie ahead.

This is admittedly a prosaic reading of this painting compared to the 'Allegory of Disaster' interpretation, but it is based on what the information on, and inside, the work points to. In any case, where one differs with Archer's view of the work more strongly is when he says it is lacking in Nainsukh's 'normal verve', adding that perhaps the painter was 'unnerved by the disaster and for the time being forfeited his mastery'. These are unjust words. For this painting has the clear stamp of the master on it, filled with great energy and inventive power, combining grandeur with fine detail, evoking an enduring sense of wonder and mystery.

———————

The inscriptions—all in Takri, that hard-to-read script native to the hills—are spread over three places in the drawing. In the one at the top, the seated man at the stern wonders about the foolishness of the man who is thinking of marrying at this critical time; the one at right similarly wonders about what kind of a stupid 'Mir' this is; and the five lines at bottom-left contain a saying in Persian that speaks of the dangers of a foolish man being at the helm.

THE DEVI DIAGRAM

Isolated folio
Thinly laid opaque watercolour on paper
Pahari, from the family workshop of Nainsukh of Guler; c. 1780
51.5 cm × 60 mm
Present whereabouts unknown

On an uncommonly large sheet of uncoloured paper stands a Devi, unusual of form but with a riveting presence. Naked but for the brief loincloth around her middle; all weight resting on her lone leg; fifteen spindly arms, unevenly spread out—nine at left and six at right; hair matted and dishevelled; hypnotic look in the eyes; teeth partially bared and clenched; a frenetically energetic (*ugra*) expression on her face—an image of sheer power. No inscription identifies her; no one knows her name for she does not fall into any iconographic scheme. But the family of painters—descendants of Nainsukh in the branch of one of his sons, Nikka, in whose collection this unique object was first seen—certainly knew her and her power: she was the one who moved them to paint, who looked after their well-being, nurtured their talent, and kept them utterly focused. She was the anima of their work; possibly, the *siddhi* that must have been, in days gone by, the personal deity of members of the family.

The fifteen arms that she is shown with—weaving a spidery web?—all have their meaning, for where most of them end are inscribed, close to her open hands, some names enclosed within roughly drawn circles. Nearly all the names are those of hill states, some of them very small principalities: thus, Chamba, Qila Kangra, Mandi, Suket, Kahlur, Kangra Nadaun, Jaswan, Siba, Datarpur, Sujanpur, Mankot, Jammu, Shahpur, Nurpur, Jasrota and Basohli. At the same time, however, there are names of three persons as well, all Sikh chieftains: Shri Jai Singh, Shri Gurbakhsh Singh (his son) and Ramgarhia Jassa Singh. These were men who were heads of Sikh *misls*, who had carved

245

out by force small domains for themselves, when this part of the Punjab—
in the plains but very close to the hills—was almost up for the taking, the
binding authority of the Mughals having declined by then, and a state of
chaos generally prevailed.

What could have brought the names of the Pahari states and these three Sikh
chieftains together in this 'diagram'? The family did not offer any insight.
One is speculating here, but there is every likelihood that they are all there,

together, because members of this painter family had worked in, or for,
them. Interestingly, names within some circles seem to have been effaced
with white pigment, and some added, beyond the reach of the arms. In any
case, it is a record of sorts: a mapping as it were of the spread of the painter
family throughout this region.

The most significant inscription on this diagram, however, is 'Shri Guler',
both because it occurs in the centre of the picture directly above the head of
the deity and because it has the honorific 'Shri' before the name of the state.
This in so many ways is wholly appropriate because this family of artists, now
resident at Rajaul, is known to have belonged originally to the state of Guler.

Thus, for Guler to have been singled out for the honour is understandable. One can sense a clear process of thinking in the making of this diagram: one notices, for instance, that the words 'Shri Guler' were inscribed first in a large circle under the foot of the Goddess, and then, on second thoughts or under advice, effaced from there and taken to the top, directly above the Goddess's head.

In significant ways, the diagram is related to the deeply religious outlook that so many painters brought to their work. The artist in the hills was frequently a devotee, a personal follower of an intensely personal deity whom he called his *ishta*. Nobody speaks of the *ishta* too willingly, or openly, for it is strictly a private matter. But it is not hard to guess that as portrayed here this goddess was held up as *ishta*; she stood perhaps for painting itself as practised in this family.

It is not only for the information it yields that this singular work—without a parallel in Indian art history—is significant: it is a work of art of great power in its own right. The mysterious way in which inspiration descends from somewhere and enters the mind and through it the brush of the painter is somewhere revealed in this image. The *ugra* expression on the Goddess's face, the set of her jaws, the abandon with which her hair flies about, are there to speak of something that is at once inscrutable, enigmatic, impenetrable, perhaps even defiant.

RAMA, SITA AND LAKSHMANA CROSS THE GANGA

Folio from a Ramayana series
Opaque watercolour on paper
Pahari, from the first generation after Nainsukh of Guler; c. 1775–80
24.5 cm × 35 cm (outer)
19.6 cm × 30.4 cm (inner)
Museum Rietberg, Zürich, Barbara and Eberhard Fischer Loan

The Ramayana—that great epic, and one of the most revered texts of India—is filled with passages of tremendous power and beauty, which imprint themselves indelibly on the heart of the reader or listener. When Rama prepares to go into exile for fourteen years, firm in his resolve to honour the commitment his father, Dasharatha, had made in a moment of weakness to one of his three wives, Kaikeyi, every effort is made to dissuade him from leaving Ayodhya. But Rama does not waver. '*Praan jaaye par vachan na jaaye*'—'A word once given cannot be retracted, even if it means giving up one's life'—is what he declares in Tulasidas's Hindi adaptation of Valmiki's great text. Rama's utterance has turned into a saying that one continues to hear till today. Episodes from the epic are remembered, and its values continue to be cited, even in our mundane daily lives. In countless ways, the text lives on.

Everyone—each reader, each devotee, each painter—naturally brings their own understanding, their own *utsaha*, or energy, to the text. There are a series of paintings devoted to the Ramayana in all kinds of styles: Rajasthani, Pahari, Mysore, even Mughal. And what the painters do with it is a subject of great fascination: how and why each of them focuses on specific episodes, interprets situations, penetrates characters or empathizes with them. For the painter of this extraordinary series—someone in the first generation after Nainsukh, in the Pahari area—the episode he renders here must have had a special meaning.

It shows the princely exiles—Rama and Sita and Lakshmana—crossing the river Ganga in a ferry, having left Ayodhya behind. There is nothing especially dramatic in this moment. But the painter must clearly have had something in view while ruminating over the text. His mind made up—so one imagines—he fills nearly the entire page with a breathtaking rendering of the downward rushing river: swirling, vast, almost ocean-like in its expanse, with just the green edge of a bank let into the page at either corner. On that river, high up on the page is a sliver of a long boat in which figures can be seen riding—the three royal exiles, two ferrymen, a couple of horses—but painted on so minuscule a scale as to be barely discernible. Why, one wonders, would the painter be so intent upon rendering it thus: with all that concentration on the river, and the hero of the story almost finessed out?

It is hard to be certain but something tells one that in the very next folio, which is now lost, the painter would have given visual form to that portion of the text where the boatman, having successfully taken Rama and his companions across the river, has a brief conversation with Rama. In exile now, all that Rama could offer the boatman in return for the service he has rendered them was the ring he was wearing. But the boatman declines to accept anything. When Rama asks him why, the boatman simply falls at the Lord's feet and says: 'What I have done is very little, just taken you across these waters; but you are the one who is going to eventually take us across the *bhavasagara*: the ocean of sorrow that is this world.' In his own fashion the painter is coalescing the river of his experience with the uncharted ocean of sorrows.

What is of interest is the fact that in Valmiki's Ramayana, upon which this great series draws, there is no exchange of this nature between the boatman and Rama. But in the popular imagination it exists. A widely repeated and oft-recited text in vernacular verse, a very abbreviated version of the epic, brings the episode in. *'Tum aaye ham ghaat utaare'*, it runs, *'ham aayenge ghaat tumhare / tab tum paar utaaro Ram.'* Meaning: 'When you came, we took you across these banks. The day will come when we will be at your shore, Rama. That will be the time for you to deliver us to the other shore, we hope.'

The painter was undoubtedly aware of this text, or something like it.

———————

The series in which this folio is found is generally referred to as the 'Bharany Ramayana', on account of it once having been in the possession of the art dealer, Bharany. The entire series, now widely dispersed, bears no text or inscription, or captions. It is as if the painter/s felt these were not necessary; the viewer would have known each episode intimately.

KING DASHARATHA'S CREMATION

Folio from a Ramayana series
Opaque watercolour on paper
Pahari, from the first generation after Nainsukh of Guler; c. 1775–80
25 cm × 35.5 cm (outer)
20.7 cm × 31 cm (inner)
Fondation Custodia, Paris, Frits Lugt Collection

King Dasharatha's death, as envisaged in Valmiki's Ramayana, is an event fraught with different emotions. To the profound sadness in his son Prince Bharata's heart is joined raging anger. Having arrived from his maternal grandfather's home, he learns of the sequence of events that had transpired in his absence: his own mother's machinations that led to Rama's exile, and then his father dying of grief.

But first, the king has to be cremated with due honour and ceremony. Bharata consults with the family's guru, the sage Vasishtha, and preparations are made. The prince, as the text says, raised the body from where it had been kept and 'placed it in a magnificent couch, adorned with every kind of precious stone' before taking it to the banks of the Sarayu river. Fires were lit, 'according to the rules of the funeral rites', to the accompaniment of 'rituals of the priests and the sacrificial attendants'. And then when the funeral procession set off from the palace for the river, everyone—the entire population of the city—followed, 'choked with tears in their throats, and disconsolate in their mind'.

The text continues: 'The people went along the path, scattering silver, gold and various kinds of clothes in front of the king. In the same manner, some others brought sandalwood, sweet aloes, different fragrant essences, with heaps of *sarala*, *padmaka* and *devadaru* woods and many other kinds of fragrant substances', all meant for the funeral pyre. At that time, 'the crying sounds of thousands of women, pitiably weeping with agony, were heard like the sounds of female curlew birds'.

The painter turns out a magnificent page, building upon some of the details that the text provides, but also adding to the scene what must have been within his own experience of seeing a royal funeral in the Pahari setting. The bier—called a *vimana* in the local language, an aerial chariot as it were—is richly festooned here with flower garlands and streamers as it is carried on a number of shoulders and begins to move out of the palace. There is an odd mix of grief and celebratory rituals that one sees in this rendering, the latter generally observed when a person who has had a long life passes away. The 'celebration' here is ceremonial, with some persons in the surging crowd blowing on conches, striking brass gongs, playing on stringed instruments.

But the grief too is all too real: as in the Pahari tradition, the entire male population of the city or the state gets their heads shaved—a sign of mourning—and moves with leaden feet ahead of the funeral procession. There is an enormous crowd, row upon row of persons—old and young, strong and infirm, householders and recluses, saints and sinners—emerging from the palace, spreading out on to the barren plain, grief written on every face, some covering their faces to hide their tears, others stepping out of the phalanx of mourners as if unable to move any further. One sees a *sannyasi* and a *kanphata jogi*, a man completely bent with age, and another totally blind with his eyes bound.

At one spot the royal ensigns are gathered—caparisoned elephants and horses, flags and other royal standards. As the crowd moves it begins to get thinner towards the bank where, in faint outline and not without colour, smaller groups of the privileged—members of the royal family, advisers and elders, a few chosen courtiers—stand around the pyre which is enveloped in flames, thick billows of smoke rising from it. A little further, their figures drawn so small that it is hardly possible to see them with any clarity, some persons—the princes Bharata and Shatrughana included, of course—have entered the waters of the Sarayu, performing rituals that purify, while retainers stand on the bank, towels in hand, ready for use. The observation is remarkable and the rendering shot with deep feeling. A deep pall of gloom has come to settle over the page.

Compositionally, the scene is brilliantly set up: the tilted angle at which the outer walls of the palace are seen, the impression of physical descent in the crowd of pall-bearers, the bare plain that takes on the contours of a peak as it rises upward, the sandy nature of the bank, the steep fall in the course of the river. It is all very carefully thought out, and the impact it makes is rich and instant.

———————

Unfortunately, it has not been possible thus far to determine the painter in whose hand this remarkable series is. To attribute it to a member of the first generation after Nainsukh—one of his four sons or either of his two nephews—is all that can broadly be done. One thing is certain, however: this painter comes very close to Nainsukh in the light ease with which he draws and the sympathy with which he views individual figures.

SHIVA AND HIS FAMILY

Isolated leaf
Opaque watercolour and gold on paper
Pahari, from the Seu–Nainsukh family workshop; c. 1800
31 cm × 23.5 cm (outer)
27 cm × 19 cm (inner)
Private Collection

It is a quiet evening. With the sun about to set, the sky is tinged with streaks of red. There is a nip in the air, judging from the small log-fire in the middle distance. A river descending from the mountains flows gently by. And on its grassy bank Shiva, having left his lofty abode in Kailash behind, has decided to settle for the night. His small family is with him, and their few belongings are all at hand. He might be Trilokinath—literally, 'Lord of the Three Worlds'—but this is all he needs. In this quiet corner of the lower hills, he seems to be completely content.

There is an aura of utter calm around him. If fact seldom, if ever, has one seen Shiva as relaxed as he appears here. He stands bare-bodied but for a lilac-coloured cloth wrapped round the waist, weight resting on one leg, the other lightly crossed against it, leaning against his great *vahana*: the Nandi bull. His tall *trishula* is held almost casually in one hand, his arms snuggle against Nandi's back, both elbows hidden. But the hands, with exquisitely tapering fingers, are fully visible, the one with the trident resting over Nandi's hump, and the other disposed as if he were gently stroking the smooth, dark body of his beloved bull: a gesture of affection, for the bull needs no hand to steady him, standing as firm and relaxed as his master.

Shiva's form is slim and athletic—firm, long torso, narrow waist, glowing skin. His hair, held by a narrow headband, falls loose down his back; his head is slightly inclined to one side, gaze gently fixed on his family. As he

257

appears here Shiva could be, the painter suggests, just a simple grazier—except that we know who he is. Majesty never leaves him: the trident apart, a thin crescent moon rests on his locks, and a snake loops itself lazily around his middle, like a favourite waistband.

The eye now follows Shiva's gaze to the bottom-right corner of the painting where Parvati crouches by the riverside, filling water in a gourd-vessel for household use. She, a figure of utter charm—chiselled features with translucent, porcelain-like beauty; long, languid eyes; dark, flowing hair—is, unlike her husband, most elegantly dressed. Even in this near wilderness, she wears a gold striped skirt with a matching *choli*, and a veil to go with this ensemble. She is at the centre of an enchanting cameo, with the divine couple's two naked little boys playfully trying to divert her attention. Karttikeya, as many as three heads clearly visible, clings to her back and reaches for her veil while Ganesha, seated to her right, one foot idly dipped in water, wraps his little trunk round her right arm, pulling her in his direction. Face beaming with a mother's delight, she looks on.

It is an idyllic scene, with the father, Shiva, watching from a slight distance, bemused by what he sees, and Parvati, the mother, completely absorbed in her children's playful antics. It is as if the painter were transferring what he might have experienced in his own life to the life of the divine couple. What makes it all very special is the belief that folks in the Pahari area still entertain: that each year, Shiva leaves his Kailash home and descends to lower climes to keep an eye on his 'subjects', to live with them, and like them.

The leaf is dazzlingly coloured and the attention to detail is astonishing. One needs to notice, for instance, the little spot in the middle of the painting, under the shade of two trees, where the 'homestead' of the family is: things lie around casually—a calabash, a rod, an upturned vessel. Above them, draped on a makeshift clothes stand, hang the couple's 'garments', left there to dry after washing: Shiva's leopard skin and Parvati's patchwork wrap. On the ground is spread, carpet-like, the large skin that once was of Gajasura, the elephant demon, whom Shiva flayed alive with just the nail of his little finger. Parvati's *vahana*, the tiger, crouches there as if keeping watch.

Stray clouds hang in the sky even as the orange of dusk forms a streaky bank below them. The forms of the mountain rocks on the other side of the river reflect faintly in the water, and where the river negotiates a bend, at the bottom of this leaf, the flow suddenly picks up and streaky waves form on the surface of the water. Nandi, the noble bull, is a sight in himself: dappled black, grey and white, wavy black dewlap spotted with white, alert of eye but placid of aspect.

There is brilliance in the detail but what one experiences above all else is the serene, supremely becalming air in which the entire scene is wrapped. Unlike Shiva's abode on Kailash, no cedar trees here are drenched by rushing waters; there is no odour of musk nor music of the *kinnaras* here, as the poets imagined on those high mountains. All that reigns in this corner of the hills is peace.

———————

A detail demanding attention is the broad margin which surrounds the principal scene. It is easy to see it as extraneous to the painting but it is not: for it is made up, if one looks closely, of gently moulded mountain peaks, piled one on top of the other. These, modelled upon how Manaku rendered some high mountaintops in his own paintings, are possibly the painter's suggestion of the high terrain that Shiva has left at least temporarily, in favour of the lower hills with their grassy slopes and lush trees.

VISHVARUPA
THE COSMIC FORM OF KRISHNA

Rajasthan, possibly Marwar; mid-nineteenth century
33.5 cm × 33.5 cm
Sven Gahlin Collection, London

Arjuna asks Krishna many questions on the battlefield of Kurukshetra. In response, the Lord decides to reveal to him his cosmic form and Arjuna is able to see a sight that no mortal had seen before. There he stood, the Bhagavad Gita says, 'sore, amazed, thrilled, o'erfilled, dazzled, dazed', trying to absorb that marvellous form filling all space. Krishna then speaks to Arjuna about the form he has taken and his words are some of the most eloquent, impassioned descriptions of divinity ever to be written.

Everything is contained in the Lord, all Time, all Space. In that form dwell all gods, all creatures of the earth; whole worlds are generated and then destroyed. 'I am Time grown Old,' Krishna says to Arjuna, and the warrior prince sees Time's deadly destructiveness even as he takes in 'an explosion of countless eyes, bellies, mouths, ornaments, and weapons, gleaming like the fiery sun that illumines the world'. 'Not through sacred lore, penances, charity, or sacrificial rites, can I be seen in the form that you see me,' Krishna says.

And yet, generation after generation, and in region after region in India, artists have been attempting to capture that very form in their work. It is a daunting task, for the vision is at once grand and terrifying and wondrous. The brilliance of the words of the eleventh chapter of the text is not easy to match, and to compress everything into one soaring image is near impossible.

For how does one capture everything: the 'fiery rays of crown and mace and discus', 'brushing the clouds with flames of countless colours'; 'roiling

261

river waters streaming headlong towards the sea' like 'moths in the frenzy of destruction flying into a blazing mouth'; the 'many mouths and eyes and thighs and feet and bellies and fangs seeing which the worlds tremble'; the 'throngs of gods entering the great form—howling storm gods, sun gods, bright gods, and gods of ritual, gods of the universe, twin gods of dawn, wind gods, vapour-drinking ghosts, crowds of celestial musicians, demigods, demons and saints'; a form that has 'no beginning, or middle, or end'?

This Rajasthani artist grapples with the task and creates a dazzling image which one has to read slowly and carefully. For there is much to discover in it, filled as the work is from top to bottom with details, references, allusions. First, one must take in the flaming ground that might well consist of countless warriors ranged on the field, and the dark clouds that fill the sky above, with the hint of a rainbow beginning to form.

Then one can begin to find faces lightly hidden in the white aura around the divine head, and discover that what looks like a crown from a distance is in fact the golden *vaikuntha* that devotees aspire to attain; while what looked like a *tilaka* mark on the forehead is actually Brahma. The eyes are no ordinary eyes, but the sun and the moon; and from the nostrils emerge winged angels.

Flanking the waist and defining it are concentric arcs that might stand for the strata of the earth. Warriors move within the giant figure; rulers are carried in palanquins; pilgrims gather before temples; snakes station themselves around sacred icons. And so on.

The eye can barely take in all the details that the painter has packed into the image here. Unlike many other painters who visualized, with great effect it needs to be added, the Vishvarupa with rows of heads, and arms and legs, the painter of this image simply shows Krishna in his Krishna-Vishnu form—a single head, two legs, and four arms, with the hands bearing the four familiar *ayudha*s: the conch shell, the discus, the mace and the lotus.

Notwithstanding all the turmoil that the destructiveness of Time brings, there is something peaceful about this image. One is reminded of the words of Ralph Emerson and Henry Thoreau in the context of the Bhagavad Gita. They said it was as if 'an empire were speaking to us, nothing small or unworthy, but large, serene, consistent'.

KRISHNA STORMS THE CITADEL OF NARAKASURA

Double page from a manuscript of the *Bhagavata Purana*
Opaque watercolour and gold on paper
South India, from a Mysore workshop; c. 1840
25 cm × 36.84 cm (full spread)
21.2 cm × 30.5 cm (single page)
San Diego Museum of Art, Edwin Binney Collection

On this double page from a manuscript of the sacred *Purana*, rich saturated colours invade the senses; streaks of gold shimmer and gleam; tiny little figures bustle about, moving, embracing, combating; seas surge, clouds rumble, elephants move with dignity.

The manuscript is remarkable for the visual excitement that it offers but it also comes as somewhat of a surprise because it comes from south India, from Mysore. Even if it bears no date and no names of painters, it has two slivers of internal evidence: it is written and painted on European paper with the watermark 'Gior Magnani', and on the flyleaf it bears the impression of an embossed oval seal with the words 'High Highness, Rajah of Mysore' in English characters.

We now know that the patron of this and other works (that have recently surfaced) was that enlightened ruler of Mysore, Krishnaraja Wodeyar III (ruled 1799 to 1868, though virtually deposed by the British in 1831), whose name as a patron of the arts is a legend in that region. Personally gifted—a scholar of Kannada and Sanskrit, a writer to whom as many as forty works are attributed, greatly interested in astrology and *mantrashastra*, a composer of music—he is said to have commissioned a vast range of works among which, evidently, was this copy of the *Bhagavata Purana*.

In the course of the telling of the tales—the second half of the great text is the one that this copy treats—wondrous things happen and are illustrated: the Gomanta mountain is set on fire; Arjuna's swift arrows form a canopy over a burning forest to keep rain from dousing it; the entire city of Dwarka is thrown into the sea. Here, on this double page that all but bursts with energy and animation, a great battle rages between Krishna and the demon-king Naraka, perpetrator of untold atrocities.

Naraka had, as the text says, secured himself in his own city of Pragjyotishpura, well protected as it was with 'inaccessible hilly fortifications and mounted missiles and weaponry', and made unapproachable with 'moats of water and fire and belts of stormy winds'. But nothing was going to get in the way of the Lord as, mounted on the sun-bird Garuda, he winged his way to Naraka's citadel, shattering hill and plain with the loud blast of his conch. A fierce contest ensued but eventually, the demon was vanquished and beheaded. And Krishna was received with all honour by the slain demon's own mother, the Earth Goddess.

The page is magnificently conceived. The island city is placed in the midst of waters plied by ships with tall masts. The fortifications with their mounted missiles and weaponry, moats of water and fire, and belts of stormy winds are constructed with elaborate care; and the action is laid out in great, fierce detail.

Krishna on Garuda appears over and over again, in every corner of the painting, till he enters the very heart of the fortress, going past the massive gateway with mountainous elephants standing guard in the portals. It is a bewildering field where arrows fly over heads, scimitars flash in hands, and elephants charge their way in, trumpeting and crushing everyone under their feet. The din and the noise of the battle is captured with extraordinary elan by the painter as he takes the viewer into the very vortex of the action. Even the gods come rushing to see this divine drama, stationed in their aerial chariots in the sky.

Nothing, no detail, is eschewed, whether it is the lustre of the body of the five-headed Mura, the richly caparisoned elephants carrying Naraka's generals into battle, or all the gifts that the Earth Goddess offers to Krishna as he enters.

———————

There are several other illustrated manuscripts which belong to the stylistic complex of which this Bhagavata Purana *manuscript is a product. Among them: the* Sri Tattva Nidhi, *which is a virtual pictorial encyclopedia of iconography with close to a thousand paintings; a* Devi Mahatmya *extolling the exploits of the Great Goddess; a now dispersed Ramayana in several volumes, within which are estimated to have been close to two thousand paintings. What else was there, one will never know.*

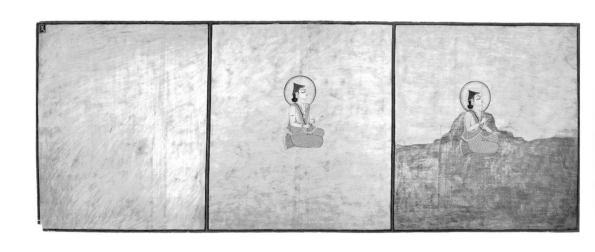

THREE ASPECTS OF THE ABSOLUTE

Folio from a manuscript of the *Shri Nath Charit*
Opaque watercolour and gold on paper
Rajasthan, from a Jodhpur workshop, by Bulaki; 1823
47 cm × 123 cm
Mehrangarh Museum Trust, Jodhpur

The painter of this stunningly daring work seems to have gone where not many had gone before him. For he wants to paint the origin of all existence. In the Nath religious tradition, which had become dominant in the brief period that Maharaja Man Singh was on the throne of Jodhpur (1803–43), it was the *mahasiddhas*, great perfected beings, who had addressed themselves to this subtlest of all matters.

The Absolute—known, in the Indian philosophical tradition, by different names like Brahman, Tat—was at the core of their teaching. This they conceived as that 'supreme, transcendent and immeasurable' essence, as the scholar Debra Diamond put it, that coexists with all creation. The doctrine of the Absolute, so central to the Nath sectarian tradition, figured predominantly in the text called *Shri Nath Charit*, the sacred account of the Naths.

When it was decided to have the *Shri Nath Charit* illustrated by painters, the challenge must have been seen as nothing less than daunting. For how does one represent nothingness, and how does one move beyond it?

This painting, and others like it, arose from that challenge. The scale on which the painters chose to paint was large, most unlike the miniatures that one ordinarily sees. Horizontal in format, each folio measured 47 cm × 123 cm. No person could hold it in one hand—it had the dimensions of, perhaps even the intention of being seen as, a panel from a mural.

Bulaki, the painter of this folio, made a triptych, as it were, of one folio, dividing the surface into three equal squares. The first square, beginning from the left, is absolutely blank. It is just flat shimmering gold. This, as he conceived it, is the formless, the eternal, self-luminous essence. In the square that follows one sees a human form, that of a *siddha* Nath (a perfected being), seemingly floating in air. This was the first manifestation of the cosmos in subtle form.

In the third square, a *siddha*, silvery light emanating from his body, brings into being cosmic matter and, with it, consciousness. In the painting of this folio one can see that great subtlety and imagination have been at work. Here Absolute reality 'is defined by what it is not (without form, without origin, without colour, etc.) by employing undifferentiated fields of gold pigment'.

The Nath *siddha*, nimbus surrounding the head, whom we see in this painting—ash-besmeared body, a conical cap on the head, large rings in the ears like those of the *kanphata* sect of *jogis*—is a figure similar to those that appear in other manuscripts. This was the standard rendering for *siddhas* of that order and one sees the figure, with very minor variations, in large manuscript after manuscript of this period from Jodhpur—the *Nath Purana*, for instance, the *Shiva Rahasya*, the *Shiva Purana*.

What is striking about these images is their abstraction: the blank gold spaces, waves in the primal ocean painted as endlessly stretching concentric arcs, each of the same colour, the stem and leaves of the cosmic lotus emerging from Vishnu's navel. Seeing them in folio after folio is to be transported into an astounding, surrealistic world of thought.

———————

Painting in the Jodhpur workshops did not consist only of large works or series such as the ones mentioned here. There were portraits, durbar scenes, depiction of moments of celebration and worldly joys. But these Shri Nath Charit *paintings, virtually unpublished till they were displayed in a major exhibition some five years ago, added a new and important dimension to our understanding of the work from that state and the related kingdom of Nagaur. A large number of painters are listed as having been involved in these great enterprises. All of them bear Hindu names save Bulaki, the Muslim painter of this folio. He must have stood out from the group for in one inscription he is simply referred to as the 'Mussalman* chitara'.

Observation

A CHAMELEON

Leaf, now in an unbound album
Opaque watercolour on paper
Mughal, Jahangir period, by Mansur; c. 1600
11 cm × 13.7 cm
Royal Library, Windsor Castle

That distinguished connoisseur, Jahangir, was never short of words when it came to praising the great masters who were attached to his court. 'Ustad Mansur Naqqash,' he wrote in his memoirs, the *Tuzuk*, 'who has been honoured with the title of Nadir-al 'Asr, and in the art of painting [*naqqashi*] is unique in his age . . . In the time of my father's [Akbar's] reign and my own, these two [Abu'l Hasan and Mansur] have had no third.'

Mansur, about whose antecedents one knows virtually nothing, was truly a man of extraordinary talents. When he was painting in the Akbari atelier, we see him frequently described as a *naqqash*, a word which could mean both painter and illuminator. In many leaves of the imperial manuscripts on which he worked, he is mentioned *after* the master artist who drew and composed the page—his name follows that of Kanha, for instance, or of Basawan—and he is named as the '*naqqash*'. This would suggest that his position was somewhat subordinate to that of the master artist.

But soon—and he seems to have entered the Jahangiri atelier noiselessly, almost as a matter of course—he finds mention as 'Ustad Mansur', a master in his own right. And when this is followed by the majestic-sounding title that the emperor conferred upon him—Nadir-al 'Asr, meaning the Rarity of the Times—one knows that he had reached the peak of his skills, and of fame. On a given number of paintings, some of them inscribed in the hand of the emperor himself, his name is followed prominently by this title. Perhaps no one could have asked for more in terms of appreciation.

275

The painter's range of work is extraordinary—from historical scenes recorded in chronicles to illuminations, from individual portraits to renderings of groups. But it is as a painter of flora and fauna that Mansur was without a rival. A wonderful range of flowering plants apart, paintings of falcons and hawks, partridges and cranes, floricans and barbets, hornbills and pheasants and peafowls bear his name. Each is a masterly study. If a zebra was brought in from Abyssinia, it was Mansur who was called upon to draw a 'portrait' of the uncommon beast; if a turkey cock was brought in by a noble from Goa,

and the emperor went into a paroxysm of delight at the sight of this 'strange and wonderful' bird, 'such as I had never seen', it was Mansur once again who was asked to paint it 'so that the amazement that arose from hearing of [the likes of them] might be increased'. Clearly, it was this master painter's uncanny powers of observation and his mastery of brush and palette that made him the emperor's first choice.

As Mansur renders it, this chameleon, having jumped up to perch on the branch of a sparsely leaved tree, is evidently eyeing some insect, perhaps even a butterfly. It has already changed its colour to the green that matches the leaves around him, but it is the coiled-spring-like tension in the body, claws firmly latched on to the branch, the tail curling up and, above all, the look in its sly eye—alert and all-knowing—which compels attention.

The skin of the lizard is brilliantly rendered—'exactingly, tactilely dotted all over with shaded green spots, and its spine . . . saw-toothed from neck to tail with perfect points of colour', as Cary Welch noted. Mansur's observation is remarkable and Welch, in his colourful description, envisions the painter 'on all fours, inching his way through a thicket towards its prey, cunning and silent as a cat'. If a twig had snapped, he adds, 'the chameleon would have fled, and this miraculous picture would not exist!'

It is difficult to date this painting and judgements range from 1595 to 1615. The likelihood of its having been made in the Jahangir period is greater. There is, as the scholar Asok Das has observed, the faint trace of an inscription, possibly in the emperor's hand, placed along the vertical edge at extreme right. However, there is another inscription—a credible attribution but not a signature—on the body of the page itself, reading 'Ustad Mansur'. The general impression is that Mansur's work ceased after Jahangir, no work of his associated with the Shahjahan period having come to light.

LEARNED DISPUTATIONS BETWEEN JAIN MONKS

Pigments on wood (front and back)
Gujarat; second quarter of the twelfth century
8.2 cm × 77.5 cm
The Goenka Collection, Mumbai

There are very few works among 'Jain' or western Indian painting that centre on a 'historical' event, but this wooden *patli*—book covers between which loose folios were placed—clearly makes a reference to one: a celebrated learned disputation that took place between the Shvetambara monk Devasuri and his Digambara rival Kumudchandra. For all their other-worldliness of outlook, the Jains recorded things temporal too with great care, but not always in visual form. This *patli* therefore truly stands out.

This event, especially well remembered among those of the Shvetambara—literally, 'clad in white'—persuasion, figures in a full-length text, the *Prabandhachintamani*. It records the triumph of their monk Devasuri who defeated his Digambara—literally, 'clad in space', meaning wearing nothing—rival on points of philosophy and doctrine. The event is said to have taken place at Patan, at the court of the twelfth-century Solanki king Siddharaja Jayasimha. The disputation itself does not figure on this half of the *patli*, but the events that build up to the disputation form the theme here.

The series of scenes are meticulously set out and, in a remarkable departure from the stereotypical renderings of canonical texts such as the *Kalpasutra*, the painter makes us witness to what must at that time have been stirring events in Gujarat, certainly within the close-knit Jain community.

On the obverse side of the *patli*, which features a delicate frieze of *hamsa* birds along narrow margins on its tapered ends, we are afforded views of the two rival groups, as it were. A Jina shrine appears at the extreme left, and a gateway. This is followed by a vignette within an enclosure where the Shvetambara Devasuri is in conversation with someone identified as P(andit) Manikya, while a group of men sits listening to the discourse.

The Digambara monk Kumudchandra is also seen conversing with his followers. Similar settings continue on this face of the *patli*, from left to right: one sees a nun or *sadhavi*, dressed in white raiment, dancing before Kumudchandra but being turned away. Then she is seen speaking of this to the Shvetambara monk. Here, a delightful view is brought in also of a small

market with vendors and buyers. But the more dramatic scenes are at the back of the *patli*—the inner side, in other words.

Here one sees Devasuri setting off towards Patan along with his followers, for the *shastrartha* (religious or philosophical debate) has been announced. Two attendants hold a *chhatra* over the pontiff's head, some lay devotees precede him, and a wonderfully animated group of musicians leads in front. The chariot they see coming in from the opposite direction is clearly meant to be an auspicious omen. All is going to go well, they must be saying to themselves.

At a remove from them is the entourage of Kumudchandra, who sits in a palanquin with some lay followers in front. What they see across a stream, at the foot of a tree, is a serpent: evidently a bad omen. At the extreme right we see this monk also being turned away from the gate of the queen's palace: another bad beginning. There are no rigid divisions of space. Everything flows like a continuous stream and it is the viewer who must separate sequences and differentiate between locations.

In one sense, the entire rendering uses well-established conventions: the familiar red ground; the formulae for the rendering of figures, including three-quarter profiles and the projecting-further eye; the complete lack of interest in depth; the standard manner of depicting things like water, foliage, architecture.

But, within these constraints, there is great liveliness in the scene. The painter evidently delighted in the opportunity to go beyond his framework, and brings in, at each step, vignettes of life and details of objects that he must seldom have got the occasion to explore. At the same time, there is wonderful rhythm in his work: the sinuously rendered bodies, the alertness that informs the frames, the sweep and flutter of scarves and loincloths, the gauze-like lightness of some of the textiles. It is as if, like a devoted Shvetambara, the painter were celebrating both the historical occasion and his own good fortune.

Inscribed on both surfaces of this wooden patli *are brief captions in Sanskrit, in old Devanagari characters, descriptive of situations and characters. The town is named, so is the Jina shrine, as of course are the two principal monks. Even the omens the two rivals see on their way are identified through inscriptions.*

1

PORTRAIT OF THE EMPEROR AKBAR

Leaf from an artist's sketchbook
Mughal; c. 1600
22.4 cm × 16 cm (outer)
13.3 cm × 13 cm (inner)
India Office, London

'In his august personal appearance he [Akbar] was of middle height, but inclining to be tall,' wrote the emperor's son Jahangir, recalling his father in his memoirs, the *Tuzuk*.

> He was of the hue of wheat; his eyes and eyebrows were black, and his complexion dark than fair; he was lion-bodied, with a broad chest, and his hands and arms long. On the left side of his nose he had a fleshy mole, very agreeable in appearance, of the size of half a pea. Those skilled in the science of physiognomy considered this mole a sign of great prosperity and exceeding good fortune. His august voice was very loud and in speaking and explaining had a peculiar richness. In his actions and movements he was not like the people of the world, and the glory of God manifested in him.

This account draws in part upon what are conventionally taken to be signs of a great leader, and one discerns too a recalcitrant son's late tribute to his father in the passage. This kind of description is, however, rare in the literature of the period. One has only to turn to the account of Abu'l Fazl who had been commissioned to 'write with the pen of sincerity the account of the glorious events and of our dominion-increasing victories' to gain some idea of the way the emperor was usually seen.

Royalty, 'that light emanating from God, and a ray from the sun', sat naturally on him, and the qualities that should mark a great king—'a paternal love towards the subjects', 'a large heart', 'a daily increasing trust in God' and 'prayer and devotion'—were all his. In chapter after chapter, dealing even with the relatively dry accounts of administrative matters, the chronicler cannot help opening his account without saying something about the emperor's brilliance of mind and about his vision for the land. But we cannot construct a physical picture of him from such accounts.

The emperor is of course seen in countless paintings made during his own reign and that of his successors. In the illustrated manuscript of the *Akbarnama* alone, he is at the centre of the scene in folio after folio. This portrait, however, just an informal sketch, brings us closer to the man than almost any of his formal portraits. In commissioned 'illustrations', he might be seen recklessly pursuing a rogue elephant, having a mystical experience during a hunt, unhesitatingly ordering that a rebel be thrown down a parapet in punishment, or offering worship to the sun. But there would always be an official aura about him.

In this sketch, the emperor is divested of all signs of royalty, all the glamour that goes with power. We see instead a simple man: casually dressed with an *atpati* turban on his head, lost in thought, gaze directed downwards, eyes almost closed. It is a noble head, moving because of the honesty with which it is rendered.

The qualities of a great king that Abu'l Fazl had listed—'a paternal love towards the subjects', 'a large heart', 'a daily increasing trust in God' and 'prayer and devotion'—are all here, one senses. This is a man to whom the humblest of men could have related.

Was this portrait commissioned? Did the emperor sit for it, if he truly sat for any portrait of his at all? It is most unlikely. Painters of great talent, and certainly among them those high in favour at the court, must have had the opportunity to see the emperor from close, but it is not easily conceivable

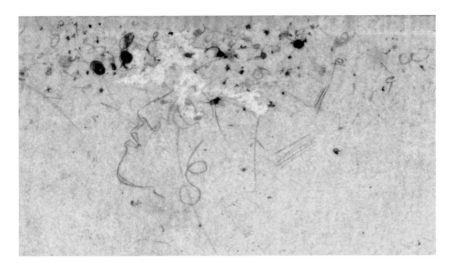

that any portrait sessions were held, with the emperor sitting for the painter. Almost certainly, the painter of this affecting portrait must have seen the emperor several times, but here he is recollecting, not constructing, an image.

―――――――――

This portrait of the emperor has sometimes been published but almost always been excerpted from the page on which it is found. On the original, uncoloured page that must have come from the sketchbook of an artist, the emperor is undoubtedly the principal figure, but he appears in the bottom left-hand corner. At the very top is an unfinished tilted head of a lady and at some distance from it a decorative lozenge-shaped panel. There are signs of rubbing and damage at the very top of the page.

285

A YOUNG SCHOLAR

Mounted on a page from an album
Opaque watercolour, gold and ink on paper
Mughal, by Mir Sayyid Ali; c. 1555
31.6 cm × 20 cm (outer)
19 cm × 10.5 cm (inner)
Los Angeles County Museum of Art, Edwin Binney Bequest

This enchanting study of a young man, barely past his youth, seated on a carpet, legs tucked under, leaning slightly forward as if to read from a book, has been differently described by art historians: 'A Young Scholar' by some, and 'A Self-Portrait' of the master painter Mir Sayyid Ali by others.

That it is a young scholar is indicated by the book placed on the *rehal* (bookrest) in front of him; the suggestion that this could be a self-portrait of the painter comes from the tablet that lies at an angle at one end of the carpet. On the top is inscribed a couplet in Persian, and at the bottom what might be seen as a signature. These read:

Bar sar-e lauh-e u nawishta ba-zar
Jor-e ustaad beh ki mehr-e pidar

The sternness of the master is [must be seen as] far above the affection of a father.

And at the very bottom:

surat-e sayyid ali nadir-al mulk humayun shahi

The work of Sayyid Ali, Rarity of the Realm, Humayun-Shahi [owing his allegiance to the king Humayun].

287

The meaning of the first word in this line—*surat*—remains ambiguous, for it could stand either for 'an image of' or 'an image by'.

A pen case—it could also be a brush case—and an inkwell lie close by on the grassy patch on which the carpet is placed. A curled-up scroll of paper— the form suggests a European inspiration or influence—lies casually at one side. These are clues that point to the young man being a writer/calligrapher or a painter.

Concluding from the manner in which the name of Sayyid Ali appears here—the honorific 'Mir' is omitted, but the title conferred upon him by his patron, Humayun, stays—some scholars have argued that this must be a self-portrait of the painter, and that the work must have been done close to 1555, when the painter had moved to India with Humayun who had returned by this time from Kabul.

The charm of the image remains unaffected by these questions. The look of untouched innocence and curiosity on the face of the young man is moving, as is his gentle yet eager stance.

The facial features are reminiscent of Central Asia: flat cheeks, small eyes, arched eyebrows, thin lips, quite like those seen in many an Iranian painting of this period. But in the form and its rendering there is great delicacy: the long torso, the slim waist, the thin, tapering fingers; and, of course, the elegantly patterned *jama* around which a diaphanous piece of white muslin is wrapped with stylish casualness. Tied discreetly to the bright-red narrow waistcloth is a small dagger, a common accessory of the time.

The dress has turned more or less Mughal-Indian but the turban with a gold band tied around it bespeaks a different source: Iranian or, in some manner, Deccani. Different elements come together but the impression that the whole ensemble makes is one of sumptuousness and refinement.

Meanwhile, the lilac-mauve rocks that rise in the background and the lone tree with its sparse leaves and gently twisting and turning trunk and branches allude to the tasteful Iranian works of the period.

———————

That this is a self-portrait of the master painter Sayyid Ali is a suggestion that was forcefully made by A.S. Melikian-Chirvani, as against the general view that this is a generic painting of a handsome youth in the Iranian tradition. There is also the suggestion that there might be a reference here to the training of the painter by his father, Mir Musavvir, whom we see in a painting holding a long petition addressed to his patron, now in the Musée Guimet. At the edge of the carpet on which the young man sits are cartouches inscribed with lines of Persian verse but they are either rubbed or partially obscured by the knees; had they been possible to read, one might have had a better clue to 'understanding' the image.

TWO CAMELS FIGHTING

Single leaf with panels of text in four lines at top
Opaque watercolour on paper
Mughal, Akbar period, by 'Abd-al Samad; c. 1590
18.8 cm × 22.4 cm
Private Collection

In the early years of the sixteenth century, the great Persian master Bihzad—whose name is still a legend in the Islamic world—had painted a picture of two fighting dromedaries with such a dazzling display of brushwork that it was to linger long in the memory of painters. Some Mughal versions of his work were made, among them this superbly painted one by Khwaja 'Abd-al Samad. The Khwaja, one knows, was one of the most gifted painters of Humayun's and Akbar's courts.

He was already a celebrity at the Persian court, and when the emperor-in-exile returned to India in 1555, he was accompanied by the famous *ustad*. Originally a painter in the Persian style, he was one of the founders of the synthesized 'Mughal' style, going on to head the Akbari atelier and nurture young talents like Daswant.

Humayun's admiration for 'Abd-al Samad was great. He referred to him as *farid al-dahr*, meaning 'the unique one of the time', in the gifts he sent to Rashid Khan, the ruler of Kashghar, among which was a grain of rice on which 'Abd-al Samad had painted 'a large field on which a group is playing polo'. All the Mughal rulers retained their interest in, and respect for, fine workmanship. A master painter like 'Abd-al Samad must therefore have been keen always for a work like this to be held up to his peers as proof of his incomparable skills.

These fighting camels are of exceptional interest, especially in this context, for 'Abd-al Samad painted them when he was eighty-five years of age. We know this because the painter has written four sentences at the top of the page. This is both rare and poignant: 'At the age of eighty-five,' the lines read,

> when my powers have dwindled, my brush has slowed down, and my remarkable sight has grown dim, I painted this with my enfeebled brush for Sharif Khan (may his life be long!), my felicitous and mature son, who occupies a high position in the domain of knowledge, who understands subtleties and is aware of all things, and who is deserving of the mercy of the All Merciful.

These words, written in bold *nastaliq* characters, are followed by a signature in a very tiny hand, just below the fourth line: 'painted by 'Abd-al Samad'.

When 'Abd-al Samad painted this, following in Bihzad's distinguished footsteps, he took the old master's composition but for some reason reversed it, possibly to avoid it being seen as an exact copy. The execution is entirely his own, displaying breathtaking virtuosity. The rocky landscape with trees, gnarled with age and swiftly being denuded of leaves, is impressive enough, but in the fighting dromedaries one sees that attention to detail and that combination of vigour and delicacy which was a painter's dream to achieve.

Observe the minutely twisted and braided robes and bands of the harnesses of the dromedaries; the bristly hair on their bodies, each singly painted; the light foam at their mouths as they snarl and bite; the hairless patches on their thigh and knee joints; the knitted brows of the keepers who are busy trying to bring the fighting beasts within control; the motionless spindle of the old man at top-right observing this fight from a distance; the knots of the ropes which the keepers pull at; and the stricken look in the eye of the darker, hairier dromedary who is having the worst of the fight.

Seeing the quality of this exquisitely painted work in the hand of the master even at that old age—Shirin Qalam was the sobriquet he had earned from Humayun, meaning 'Of the Sweet Pen/Brush'—one almost begins to believe in the rice grains on which polo games were painted and whole couplets in Persian inscribed. His mastery of detail even on the most minuscule scale is evident in another work in 'Abd-al Samad's hand, now in the Gulshan Palace Library in Tehran. It shows the young Akbar holding a small painting in his hand, 'in which the entire scene depicted in the painting is repeated'.

———————

Khwaja 'Abd-al Samad, apart from being a master painter, was appointed to high administrative positions too. He was director of the royal mint at Fatehpur Sikri and for some time he was made supervisor for the production of leather articles. His last appointment was as diwan *of the city of Multan. The better part of the great* Hamzanama *series was produced under his vigilant and visionary eye.*

'WHEN THE LAMP OF LIFE IS EXTINGUISHED'

Leaf, possibly detached from an illustrated manuscript
Opaque watercolour on paper
Mughal, Akbar period; c. 1585–90
29 cm × 20.5 cm
Bernisches Historisches Museum, Bern

Inside a chamber set in the midst of the courtyard of a house, a man has hanged himself with a rope tied to the ceiling. There is hushed silence in the scene—no one else seems to be inside the house; there is no other sign of human life. There is only the body of the man dangling from the rope, his hair dishevelled, turban loosened and slipping from his head, his *jama* flung open, revealing the *paijama*-trousers underneath and the bare chest.

The head tilts to the side, the mouth is slightly open. A small wooden stool lies toppled on the floor of the octagonal chamber. It is at a very slight remove from the body, to suggest that the man used it to raise himself to the noose and then, at the last fateful moment, pushed it away. Careful preparation for the act is thus established. But we have no clue to the circumstances leading to this tragic act that has 'extinguished the lamp of life' of this man.

There may have been a clue in the two lines of text that appear at the bottom of the page, but these are now so rubbed off as to make the words completely illegible. All we are left with is the image of the hanging man. It is possible that poverty led him to this tragic decision. There is some suggestion of this in the fact that the house—typically Akbari in its architecture—is singularly bare, devoid of all appointments. There is no indication of any affluence on the man's person, no ornaments, no jewellery; the clothes that he wears are barely adequate. It is as if from a once-comfortable state he had sunk into straitened circumstances. But this can remain only a guess.

The scene is superbly conceived, and executed with thoughtful, painstaking attention to detail. The manner in which the head is treated, for instance, or the falling turban rendered, speaks of a masterly hand at work. One also notices from the disposition of the limbs that the suicide is recent, as if the body were still possessed of warmth. The introduction of the finely detailed trees behind the back wall of the house, the flowering plants in front and the presence of the peacock on the roof of the chamber, seem to be more than mere decorative additions. Through them, the painter seems to suggest that while this man's life has come to an end, the world goes on as usual and remains full of beauty.

The colouring of the work is delicate, with a marked preference for lilacs and mauves, apart from the brown and red sandstone of the walls and the fine, tiled pattern in jade green on the floor. The painter has obvious problems with perspective but nothing stands out as being truly awkward. Nothing, in any case, interferes with the powerful feeling in the painting.

The manner in which an atmosphere of utter silence is built up, bit by bit; the fine detail, for instance, of the water pitcher in the courtyard on a wooden

stand turned upside down to suggest that it is completely emptied—all these speak for the intense manner in which the painter appears to have entered into the spirit of the painting.

Suicide is not a common theme in Indian painting even if tales in old texts, both Persian and Indian, speak of it from time to time. One cannot escape the feeling that, just possibly, it was an incident that the painter knew of from his own experience, one that had made a deep, searing impression on his mind.

———————

One is reminded by this painting of the fact that one of the most brilliant painters at the Akbari court, Daswant, is known to have taken his own life. As Abu'l Fazl tells us: 'Daswanth. He is the son of a palkee-bearer. He devoted his whole life to the art, and used, from love of his profession, to draw and paint figures even on walls. One day, the eye of His Majesty fell on him; his talent was discovered, and he himself handed him over to the [Khwaja 'Abd-al Samad]. In a short time he surpassed all painters, and became the first master of the age. Unfortunately, the light of his talents was dimmed by the shadow of madness. He committed suicide.'

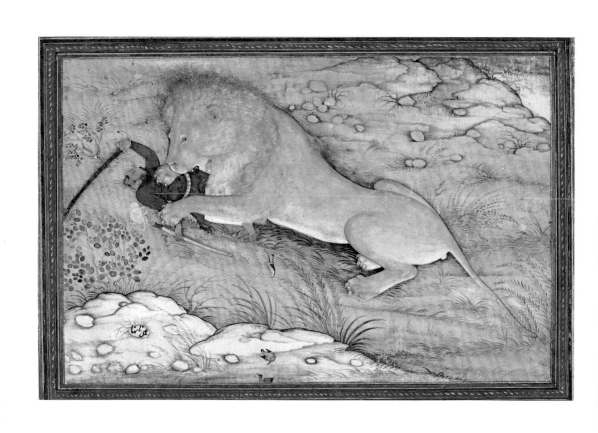

PERILS OF THE HUNT

Opaque watercolour on cloth
Mughal, by Nanha; c. 1615
24.5 cm × 37.2 cm
Free Library of Philadelphia, John Frederick Lewis Collection

Among the large number of Indian paintings featuring hunting scenes are several that show a lion or a tiger being slain. It was, evidently, a favoured theme, a celebration of valour and of the excitement of the chase. Akbar on horseback, sabre in hand, engages in the spectacular *qamargha* hunt; Jahangir strikes down with his sword a lion attacking his elephant; Nur Jahan takes aim at lions with her matchlock; Rai Anup Singh of Bikaner slays a beast in the presence of the emperor; Maharana Sangram Singh tracks down a tiger and shoots it; different rulers of Kota go out in dense forests to hunt lions; Balwant Singh of Jasrota strikes with a bared sword a tiger that had pounced upon an attendant of his.

Nor is there any dearth of accounts—including a long one by Jahangir—of these noble animals being hunted. But each time, it is man that triumphs. The beast might have made the first strike but it is always struck down. Here, however, is a painting that reverses the situation—a lion that has pounced upon a hunter and overpowered him, with no hope left for the man.

This, however, is not the only reason why this extraordinary painting stands out. It bears a painter's name—Nanha—discreetly inscribed in Persian characters on a small rock in the bottom of the painting. We know something—from inscriptions and credible attributions—about Nanha from a number of other paintings belonging to the Akbari and the Jahangiri courts, but he is most often associated with portraiture.

One knows him to have rendered the likenesses of the emperors Babur and

299

Akbar and Jahangir, Rajput princes like Suraj Mal and Bhim Singh, Mughal nobles such as Zulfiqar Khan and Saif Khan. An indication of his special status in portraiture is to be found through the inscriptions in the paintings. The composition may be attributed to one painter, some faces might be in the hand of another painter, but the most important face in the image, the *chehra-i naami* as it was called, is often attributed to Nanha.

It is unusual for him, then, a specialist in portraiture, to have turned to depicting this magnificent beast. The work is also made on cloth and not many paintings on cloth from the Mughal workshops are known. Why, then, would this surface be picked for this work by the painter, or the patron? Was there a particular reason? Is it a fragment of a larger painting? One does not know.

It is clear though that gifted painters like Nanha could turn their hand in any given direction, almost at will. This is a painting by a master painter:

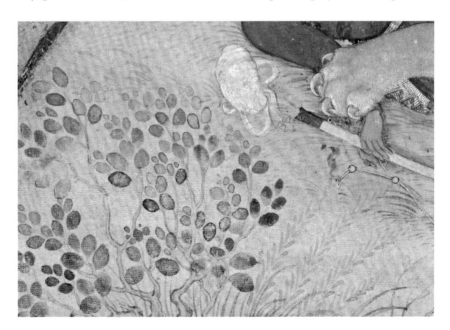

the extremely subtle, sharply observed, gradations in the colouring of the lion's coat; the sinuous outline of its form; the sly look in the beast's eye, part triumph, part anger; every bristle in the lion's mane articulated even as it merges with the shoots of grass.

The hapless man, a hunter turned prey now, is also a remarkable study of fear. The sword he has bared, useless now, is still held in the right hand, while the scabbard lies close to the other arm which is pinned under the lion's claws. The turban has slipped off on to the ground; and a lone slip-on shoe lies flung away.

What would this man have been doing in this almost barren, rocky tract of land? He could not possibly have been looking for a lion to combat. The sword is likely to have been a weapon he, like most men in those times, would have been carrying as a matter of course. Who is he then? The painter provides us with a hint: a dead bird lies on the ground not far from where the action is. Was the man a bird catcher, an ordinary hunter in the wilds?

———————

We know very little about Nanha, the painter. His name figures in some of the inscriptions on portraits, possibly in the hand of Jahangir himself. He seems to have worked both in the Akbari and the Jahangiri ateliers, but it is doubtful if he lived on to work for Shahjahan. From a laconic note on a painting we know that another great painter, Bishan Das, who was commissioned by Jahangir to travel to Persia for bringing back likenesses, was his nephew.

A MINE EXPLODES DURING THE SIEGE OF CHITTOR, RAJASTHAN

Folio from an illustrated manuscript of the *Akbarnama*
Mughal, composition by Miskin, painting by Bhura; 1586–87
33 cm × 19.1 cm
Victoria and Albert Museum, London

The fight was going to be fierce. The emperor Akbar had decided to lay siege to Chittor, an almost impregnable fort built atop a steep rock and a source of great pride for the Sisodia rulers of Mewar, as a step towards subduing Rajasthan.

The then Rana of Mewar, Udai Singh, not a figure much admired in Rajput annals, had retreated tactically to the countryside on hearing of the advance of the Mughals, and the invading armies saw this as an advantage to be seized. But the garrison inside the sprawling fort-city was determined to defend it.

The year was 1567. The siege of Chittor is vividly recalled even today in Rajasthan, for there were many Rajput heroes who figured in it. On their part, Mughal chroniclers wrote with passion—and in dense detail—about this battle, as it was personally directed by the emperor and ended in victory.

This painting, from the imperial copy of the *Akbarnama*, is relevant because it shows that under the emperor's guidance, two mines close to each other were laid at the wall of the fort and filled with large quantities of gunpowder. They were both meant to explode at the same time but this did not happen. At first, only one part of the bastion was blown up; when the second blew up shortly after, the damage inflicted was not only upon the defenders but also the attacking forces. This is the moment that the painters—Miskin and Bhura—set out to capture in this vivid, if gory, scene.

303

The painters were of course not personally witnesses to the action, something that holds true of countless paintings said to be a 'record' of things as they happened. They were reconstructing the event based on hearsay and on accounts oral or written. Military history, of which a great deal has been written—for the siege of Chittor was a signal event—was not their concern; the siege lasted some four months, from which they picked one highly dramatic incident. The intent here is to capture the tumult of the action: bravery, tragedy, planning, foresight, confusion, all coming together.

The emperor stands at the bottom of the page, with the royal tents offering cover, hand extended, issuing instructions. Past the moat of water, and between the narrow passages of the rocks are horsemen and foot soldiers, carrying matchlocks, swords, lances, everything pell-mell. Above them rise the massive walls of the fort inside which—as if seen from above—we can see the brave soldiers of the garrison firing, shooting arrows, throwing down rocks; harried women in their chambers; people shouting instructions; some with pleading hands raised towards their shrines.

But what stands out in the scene, forcing the viewer's attention upon itself, is the explosion of the mine, and the carnage that it causes. The suddenness and the sheer force of the blast can almost be felt; and from the rain of fire and smoke bodies fall, reduced to cinders—footmen, soldiers on horseback, animals. The chill hand of death is everywhere.

The painting is the left half of a double page. On the right—also composed by the painter Miskin but painted by Sarwan—is another aspect of the same siege. In this painting, the royal tents are still in place, and soldiers are running about; tall walls are being raised on which more guns will be stationed, and *sabat* screens are being put up by masons and carpenters as part of the strategies of battle. Far in the distance inside the fort, one sees flames emerging from a building: a reference to the Rajput custom of *jauhar*, when women set themselves on fire rather than fall into the hands of the enemy. We are meant to see the raw, unvarnished face of war.

———————

Miskin, one of the most gifted painters working in the Akbari atelier, was the subject of a 1928 study by Wilhelm Staude, who attributed to him a large number of paintings and analysed his style. Since then other scholars have paid him close attention. As many as eighty-six paintings have been attributed to him so far, based purely on stylistic considerations, even though not a single one bears his signature or is dated.

IBRAHIM ADIL SHAH HAWKING

Leaf from the St Petersburg Album
Deccan, Bijapur, by Farrukh Beg; c. 1590–95
Opaque watercolour on paper
28.7 cm × 15.6 cm
Russian Academy of Sciences, Institute of Oriental Manuscripts

Celebrated as one of the most gifted of the Sultans of the Deccani kingdoms, Ibrahim Adil Shah had no dearth of men who sang his praises. The poet Zuhuri who had migrated to the Deccan from Iran sometime in the early eighties of the sixteenth century, and had taken employment under the Sultan, never tired of speaking of his 'munificence' and his 'excellences' in the most hyperbolic of terms. In a very early portrait of the Sultan in which he wears a typically tightly bound, gold-brocaded Deccani turban, are inscribed verses, not necessarily Zuhuri's, which laud him as the

> Khadiv of the world, the king of his age
> enthroned under an auspicious sign . . .
> light of the heart and of the eyes of the happy
> the benefactor of the soul of the generous . . .

The Sultan whom we see in this painting, riding, hawk on wrist, through an absolutely fantastic landscape, was nine years of age when he came to occupy the throne of Bijapur. He is just short of twenty years here and is identified through a minutely inscribed note towards the top.

It reads: *tasveer-i khaqan-i 'azam ibrahim adil shah*—'Portrait of the great *khaqan*, Ibrahim Adil Shah'. The title *khaqan* was traditionally reserved for the emperor of China or the rulers of Chinese Tartary (the Islamic khanates in western China), but also applied later, loosely, to any emperor. Ibrahim Adil Shah was neither the emperor of China nor any emperor, for the

307

Sultans of the Deccani kingdoms were not entitled to that status due to the overpowering presence of the Mughals in the north. If the inscription uses these lavish words for the Sultan then, in the manner of his poets, one understands that they are not speaking of the real world but one of dreams—much like the landscape through which the Sultan is seen riding here on his steed.

The young Sultan is elegantly dressed—his long *jama* in delicate pink tied low under the right arm, the flamboyant gold-brocaded Deccani *patka* tied at the waist, almost brushing the flank of the horse; the turban neatly tied with a golden cross-band. But it is the 'mysterious' landscape that truly seduces the eye in this work.

The landscape has Irani elements in it, signalling the artistic source of the Deccani style. But it also possesses closely observed, though poetically modified, flowering plants and trees of local origin. In the bluish rocks that seem to push their way through the vegetation towards the top lurk fantastic shapes as well as real animals and birds—jackals and pheasants and *saras* cranes. But all of this—the horizon, the golden haze in the atmosphere above—is dominated by the greenish black, somewhat rocky ground against which one sees countless plants and bushes, their outlines limned delicately in gold.

The lithe form of the galloping steed stands out against this dark backdrop as it heads towards the left, looking, like the hawk and the Sultan, at something it has spied in that direction. The horse cuts a magnificent figure with its legs dyed in pinkish red, wearing a harness glittering with gold and precious stones, and saddlery so delicately patterned that it reminds one of those illuminated *'unwan*s that adorn royal manuscripts. There is a keenness of observation here and a minute attention to detail that speak of a masterly hand at work.

An inscription, not relied on at first, identifies the portrait as being the work of that gifted painter Farrukh Beg who, while working in the Deccan after coming away from the Mughal court in the north, is generally referred to as Farrukh Hussain. The painting has been variously ascribed and dated, ranging from the early 1600s, as Milo Beach argues, to about 1590. The latter, it seems, is closer to the truth, for that is about the time when Farrukh Beg moved to Bijapur and this might well be among the earliest works he painted there.

───────────

While writing on this painting, the art historian Mark Zebrowski ascribed it to an artist whom he called the 'Leningrad Painter', evidently after the fact that the work belonged to what was also known as the 'Leningrad Album'. He saw that painter as working 'in a more Islamic mode', and someone who was 'particularly partial to gold arabesque, sweeping calligraphic contours and paradisical setting'. Whether the artist was Farrukh Beg, Zebrowski was uncertain, pointing out that the 'badly written attribution to Farrukh' is seen on the 'painting's eighteenth century mount'.

SULTAN IBRAHIM ADIL SHAH II

Opaque watercolour on paper
Deccan, from Bijapur; c. 1610–15
17 cm × 10.2 cm
The British Museum, London

Uncommonly gifted though he was—musician, poet, calligrapher, connoisseur
of the arts, reconciler of faiths—it takes effort to extricate Ibrahim Adil Shah,
Sultan of Bijapur, from under the encomia that his chroniclers and courtiers
heaped upon him. Zuhuri, the court poet, dedicated a whole treatise to him
in the form of three long essays. But it is in the Sultan's own work, the *Kitab-i
Nauras*—'Book of the Nine Sentiments'—that one comes closest to seeing him
for what he was.

Being a remarkably tolerant man, one who lived in two worlds (not unlike
Akbar), he saw himself both as a devout Muslim and a Hindu devotee. The
book opens with an invocation, in traditional Sanskritic or Hindu manner, to
Saraswati, the goddess of learning and of music. This is then followed with
words of praise for, and submission to, the Prophet Muhammad.

The language in which he wrote it—Dakhani Urdu, with a heady mixture of
Sanskrit words and Urdu usage—is in itself a mirror to the twin directions in
which his thoughts ran. Describing himself in the third person, he wrote as
though he were a Hindu deity:

> In one hand he has a musical instrument, in the other, a book which
> he reads and sings songs related to the Nauras. He is robed in a
> saffron-coloured dress, his teeth are black, the nails are . . . red and
> he loves all. Ibrahim, whose father is god Ganesh and . . . mother,
> pious Saraswati, has a rosary of crystal round his neck, a city like
> Vidyapur [Bijapur] and an elephant as his vehicle.

He had given a name to his favourite musical instrument—Moti Khan; and the elephant that he describes as his vehicle was the famous Atash Khan whom we see him riding in different paintings.

There is clearly a touch of the romantic fabulist in the Sultan's personality, and it is this quality that Ibrahim's painters evoked in their work. This portrait, which bears neither the name of the person portrayed nor of the artist who painted it, is legitimately seen as that of the Sultan himself. In it, he stands in the midst of a fanciful, black-green ground, relieved by superbly painted finger-like clusters from a nearby tree, and flowering shrubs and blooming lotuses on the ground.

He is most elegantly dressed: typically conical Deccani turban on his head, one hand holding a small handkerchief, the other a pair of *kartal*-clappers. The textile of which his *jama* is made—brushing the ground here with its hem—is gauze-thin with subtle stripes, and he wears it over a pink tight-fitting breeches-like *paijama*. But there are two things among the king's

apparel that really draw our eye: the gold brocaded *patka* which is tied at the waist, and the ample, shawl-like *uttariya*, also gold-brocaded and, like the *patka*, exquisitely patterned. Both are rendered with a wonderful sense of movement as if they are swaying, like the diaphanous *jama*, in a gentle breeze. Meanwhile, far at the back of the image, we can see a tall, multi-storeyed, palace-like structure.

There is elegance but above all great delicacy in the treatment of the figure. The image is one of quietude and poetry. The Sultan bears a gentle, tranquil expression, gaze directed slightly downwards, appearing to be lost in his thoughts. The kerchief and *kartal* he carries are both symbols—the kerchief that of aristocracy as in the Islamic world, and the *kartal*, an unusual percussion instrument, standing almost certainly for devotional singing, as in the Hindu tradition. Stuart Cary Welch wrote once that 'wherever Ibrahim stepped, flowers and leaves preened to the rhythms of his *kartal*-clapper'. But Zuhuri the poet went a step further and spoke of the Sultan in the context of his *Kitab-i Nauras*:

> The reason why the book is called by this name is that the Indians call a mixture of nine juices nauras . . . and if the Persians believe it to be the fresh fruit of the tree of his learning . . . it is appropriate; and in this sense also that this beloved of perfect beauty (*Ibrahim*) has newly appeared on the stage of existence from behind the curtain of invisibility . . .

This painting has recently been attributed to the painter Ali Riza. Sultan Ibrahim Adil Shah, scholars agree, remains a somewhat mysterious figure despite all the paintings we have of him and all that his court poets wrote. The image that emerges of him is that of a person 'intensely sensitive, creative and romantic, as well as probably impetuous, melancholy and somewhat unbalanced', in Mark Zebrowski's words.

313

AN OLD SUFI
(also published as DOLOR)

Leaf mounted as an album page
Opaque watercolour on paper
Mughal, Jahangir period, by Farrukh Beg; 1615
19.5 cm × 14 cm
Museum of Islamic Art, Doha

> Than his [Farrukh Hussain's] painting nothing better can be imagined.
> The expert painters take pride in being his pupils. . . . From the sight
> of his black pen blossoming, spring-like beauties have learnt wiles.
> The freshness of his painting has put the portrait of the beautiful to
> shame, and has thrown it into the whirlpool of the jealousy of his
> painting . . .

The words are those of a poet at the court of the highly cultivated Sultan of
Bijapur, Ibrahim Adil Shah II.

As mentioned earlier, the celebrated painter named in this passage goes
under the name of Farrukh Beg, but here he is called Farrukh Hussain; and
his strongest association is not with the Deccan but with the Mughal court
in the north where he worked first in the Akbari atelier and, several years
later, for Jahangir.

Scholars have worked hard to build a clearer history of this man and
finally, a picture of this restless soul seems to have emerged. He was a man
honoured by Jahangir in words approaching those he used for Abu'l Hasan
and Mansur; an artist who (to quote the scholar Milo Beach) 'to an unusual
extent seems to have been in charge of his own life.'

Farrukh Beg, born c. 1545, trained in the Khorasani style and, having worked

315

in Iran first, made some quick moves: from Iran to Kabul, then to the Mughal court at Lahore, from where, some time later, he moved to the Deccan, and then returned to Agra to work under Jahangir. The range of styles he worked in is equally astonishing, from purely Persian with all its elegant stylizations to the more urgent, vigorous style that we see in the *Akbarnama*, and then to images of Sufi mystics 'silently cocooned in their auras'. His approach has often been described as maverick and he seemed to decide on the spur of the moment to take off on a path that he had never trodden before.

Farrukh Beg clearly based this painting, a 'dramatically inventive, darkly glowing miniature', on a European engraving by Marten de Vos who, in turn, had interpreted an earlier work by Dürer. In that engraving, titled Dolor, recalling Melancholy, the page is divided into two almost equal parts. In the right half, an old man is seen slumped into a chair, almost unmoving, in a dark room with a large map tacked on to a wall at the back. All he is doing is staring at a kitchen cabinet where a cat is helping itself to some spilt milk while a dog quietly curls up at the feet of his master. In the left half of the engraving, in contrast, there is all light and activity. A woman is busy digging the earth with a spade, and in the background men and women of the village go busily about their work.

Taking off from that engraving, Farrukh Beg created what is seen as 'a psychic self-portrait'—he was seventy years of age at this time, according to the inscription on this work—in the garb perhaps of a grey-bearded, careworn Sufi. In the course of transforming the engraving, he excised the entire left half of the page, shifted the scene outdoors, brought in some sheep and another cat, but kept the kitchen cabinet, however contrived it might look.

But there are intriguing additions. The fantastic tree under which the old Sufi sits, for instance, the leaves of which, in Carey Welch's words, 'grow in unlikely red, green, and yellow cabbage shapes, so clustered as to seem an infinity of forests—the illumined thoughts of a mystic floating heavenwards'. Behind the seated man there is a table—another addition—on which rests a book and not one but two pairs of eyeglasses: one resting on the book and the other lying by its side, almost raising the suggestion that the world can be seen through two different spectacles.

Was this Farrukh Beg's final major production? We don't know, but it is arguably his purest achievement.

———————

The painting bears two inscriptions: one at the bottom saying that it is the work of 'Farrukh Beg', and the other written on the right margin, going up vertically, stating that 'this Wonder of the Age, Farrukh Beg, at the age of seventy' showed it to the emperor after he returned from his victory over the Rana in Ajmer in the regnal year 10, which is the equivalent of 1615 CE. On verso, there is a panel of exquisite calligraphy in nastaliq *in the hand of 'Ali. On both sides there are broad borders superbly painted with floral patterns that recall Shahjahani work. A small seal of Nand Ram Pandit appears on the border of the painting while on the border at the back there is the impression of a large dynastic seal of the emperor Jahangir.*

شبیه حضرت جهانگیر بادشاه که شبیه حضرت اکبر بادشاه را می بیند

JAHANGIR WITH A PORTRAIT OF AKBAR

Leaf mounted on an album page
Opaque watercolour on paper
Mughal, Jahangir period, by Abu'l Hasan and Hashim; c. 1610
29.7 cm × 24 cm (outer)
18.3 cm × 11.6 cm (inner)
Musée Guimet, Paris

There are not many portraits of this kind: an emperor holding in his two hands, almost reverently, a portrait of his own father. In Indian art, there are images of men, or women, looking at paintings: Jahangir himself with an image of the Virgin; princes casting fond looks at the likenesses of their beloveds; forlorn *nayika*s wistfully gazing at the faces of their lovers who are there somewhere, but far away. But there is nothing quite like this.

One begins to wonder what could have occasioned it, or who might have thought of it: patron or painter? The question is particularly important because of the relationship between father and son. That Akbar was inordinately fond of his son—he is known to have fasted and prayed and visited holy shrines, asking to be blessed with a son—is well known. What is also known is the differences and the tension that slowly grew between the two in later years, leading to Jahangir, then called only 'Shah Salim', setting up a parallel court at Allahabad, far from his father's capital city.

One possibility is that this painting was commissioned because Jahangir, once on the throne, was completely reconciled with his late father, and remembered him with filial fondness. In his memoirs, he frequently refers to Akbar, and always with great respect and affection.

Whatever the case, the work is highly accomplished, and in many ways affecting. The emperor's dress alone dazzles—gold-brocaded *jama* with floral patterning; an elegantly tied turban to match; strings of pearls with rubies and emeralds; a large studded pendant at the chest. A discreetly painted nimbus (symbolic of divine light) shines behind his head; the look in the eye is august but gentle. There is an aspect not only of majesty but also of nobility that marks his entire figure.

The emperor's gaze is directed towards the painted portrait of his father even if it is not directly on it. The great Akbar, also nimbate, his face seen in a three-quarter view, wears a gentle expression. Simply dressed in white as was his wont, he sits at a window, holding in his left hand with its almost outsized fingers an orb, symbol of world dominion, as if about to hand it to his son. Both men are seen sitting in a *jharokha*-window—a formal setting— the balustrade of which is covered with a piece of carpet, floral in the case of Akbar, figurative with Persian figures in the midst of floral or geometric patterns in the case of Jahangir. Despite the formal settings, a quiet exchange between father and son appears to be taking place in this painting.

There are different inscriptions on the work. In a late hand, at the bottom of the page, are written descriptive words in Persian to the effect that 'this is a portrait of His Majesty, Emperor Jahangir, looking at the portrait of His Majesty, Emperor Akbar'. But the other two inscriptions, one on the globe that Akbar holds and the other directly below his portrait, next to the carpet on Jahangir's window, hold greater meaning.

On the orb appear the words '*shabih-i hazrat 'Arsh Ashiyani, 'amal-i Nadir-uz Zaman*', meaning, 'The Portrait of 'Arsh-Ashiyani [literally, 'Nesting in Paradise', Akbar's posthumous title], the work of Nadir-uz Zaman [that is, Abu'l Hasan]'. The other inscription, not easy to read because it is partially rubbed off and against a very dark ground, says, '*shabih-i hazrat Jahangir Padshah ki dar . . . sinn-i si salagi sakhta, 'amal-i Hashim (?) was chihra name islah-i Nadair-uz Zaman*'. The translation is, 'The portrait of His Majesty, Emperor Jahangir, at the age of thirty years . . . painted by Hashim (?), the notable face improved by Nadir-uz Zaman'. The inscriptions raise questions, but there is little doubt that two painters appear to have collaborated on this image, with Abu'l Hasan playing the primary role.

———————

This is among the best-known, closely studied portraits of Jahangir, and has been interpreted by many scholars over the years. It was even suggested at one time that the portrait of Akbar was added later, replacing some other image that Jahangir originally held. The respective ages of Hashim, who was much the older of the two painters, and Abu'l Hasan who, though much younger, is here mentioned as having corrected or improved upon the portrait, creates further uncertainty. The portrait was dated by one scholar to c. 1595–1600, well before Jahangir came to sit on the throne, but this is now generally believed not to be the case. The mention of Abu'l Hasan's name with the title 'Nadir-uz Zaman' gives it a decidedly later date than 1600.

JAHANGIR PREFERRING A SUFI SHAIKH TO KINGS

Leaf from the 'Leningrad Album'
Opaque watercolour on paper
Mughal, Jahangir period, by Bichitr; c. 1615
25.3 cm × 18.1 cm
Freer Gallery of Art, Washington, Smithsonian Institution

> By the grace of God is he truly a king both in form and spirit: the
> Shah Nur-ud Din Jahangir, son of Padshah Akbar;

> To all appearances, even as kings and potentates stand in attendance
> upon him, his gaze falls, inwardly, ever upon holy dervishes.

The two Persian distichs that appear within cartouches above and below
this dazzling image are likely to have been composed and added later, but
they draw attention forcefully to themselves: not only because they describe
what the image 'contains', but also because they play skilfully upon two
words: *surat* and *maa'ni*—form and spirit, so to speak, but, in truth, outward
appearance and inner essence, a theme much favoured in Sufi discourse.

So many elements, visual and allegorical, come together in this quintessentially
Jahangiri painting, that one can turn breathless making full sense of them.
The emperor, magnificently bejewelled and wearing a *jama*, the upper muslin
jacket of which, thin as 'woven air', clings to his athletic form, is of course
Jahangir.

His head is surrounded by a glittering twin nimbus that combines the forms
of the moon and the sun; he is seated, legs tucked under, on a curiously
shaped and precious-stone-studded high throne with delicately carved legs,
and an hourglass-shaped pedestal of European design. Before him, in fact

beneath him, stand four men: a bearded Shaikh; a heavily turbaned Sultan; a European monarch; and a relatively young-looking man, wearing a Hindu-style *jama* tied under the left armpit, holding up a painting in his hand to catch the emperor's attention.

All the figures are, however, identifiable as they have been drawn from other images. The European figure is King James I of England, taken directly from an English work by John de Critz, which might have come with Sir Thomas Roe, the British ambassador to Jahangir's court. The Sultan can be identified as the Sultan of Turkey. The young man in the bottom-left corner is the painter Bichitr whose name appears on the footstool next to the throne, a contemporary attribution, if not a signature. But the most important figure in this group is the bearded Shaikh who is none other than Shaikh Hussain, descendant of the revered saint Khwaja Mu'in-ud-Din Chishti, to whose shrine in Ajmer the emperor Akbar, father of Jahangir, had turned once to ask for the boon of a son.

That son is the one who sits now on this resplendent throne. The Shaikh is important because it is upon him alone that the emperor's gaze rests, even as he offers him, as a mark of imperial favour, a beautifully bound and clasped volume. This is where the *maa'ni* of the couplets above resides. Setting all earthly grandeur aside, it is to the spirit that the emperor submits. The message is clear.

There are other things to turn to. The four putti, evidently derived from European works which were by this time a fairly familiar sight in Mughal India—having been brought in by missionaries and ambassadors and travellers—are spread over the page. Two of them are flying heavenwards—the arrows of one of them are broken and therefore useless, the other is hiding his face as if embarrassed by failure. The other two, at the bottom of the hourglass, are, however, busy gathering the sand that keeps falling. They seem to be trying to stop the flow of time that the hourglass symbolizes. Or perhaps it is they who have inscribed on the hourglass a verse in Persian that invokes the blessings of God upon the emperor and says: 'O Shah, may you live for a thousand years!' Could this work have been painted and presented to the emperor on the occasion of his birthday?

While magnificence is scattered all over the page, and symbols abound, one also needs to remember that Jahangir, for all his engagement with worldly pleasures and the pursuit of power, did reflect upon life and turn inwards from time to time. A short passage cited by Milo Beach from his memoirs, the *Tuzuk*, comes to mind:

> Although we have the business of kingship before us,
> Every moment we more and more think on the dervishes.
> If the heart of one Dervish be gladdened by us
> We count that to be the profit of our kingship.

———————

Bichitr, the painter of this sumptuous page, is known to have worked for both Jahangir and Shahjahan. This page, with a late, overwhelmingly ornate surround, was mounted for an album and figured in the famous 'Leningrad Album'. On its back is a calligraphic panel in the hand of 'Imad-al Hasani; the borders were made by the illuminator Hadi, and are dated AH 1169 (1755–56 CE).

JAHANGIR TAKES AIM AT POVERTY

Page, possibly for an album
Opaque watercolour, gold and ink on paper
Mughal, Jahangir period, attributed to Abu'l Hasan; c. 1620
36.8 cm × 24.6 cm (outer)
23.8 cm × 15.2 cm (inner)
Los Angeles County Museum of Art, Nasli and Alice Heeramaneck
Collection

This painting was meant to be seen as a political statement, as is evident from the two-line inscription in Persian etched in the sky directly above Emperor Jahangir's head. It reads: 'The auspicious portrait of His Exalted Majesty who, with the arrow of generosity, eradicated the trace of *daliddar* from the world and laid anew the foundation of a world marked by justice and munificence.' The word *daliddar*—from the Sanskrit *daridra*—is explained in a brief note written below it in a thin hand: 'in other words, the personification of poverty'.

It is easy to see that this remarkable work, like others from Jahangir's reign, is rich in allegory and intriguing in the symbols it uses. Jahangir delighted in having his painters create work with strong messages. In one work, one sees him sitting down for a repast with his contemporary, Shah Abbas, the ruler of Iran, even though the two monarchs had never met in life; in another, one sees him embracing the same monarch, Shah Abbas, the two standing respectively on a lion and a lamb that rest on the map of the world, drawn on a globe. Those from his court—princes and grandees and other noblemen—and others outside, including ambassadors and missionaries, must have been expected to see these images, and admire the political allegory.

Here the emperor stands, facing left, arms disposed so as to hold a bow at full stretch, taking aim and about to shoot an arrow at an emaciated figure, dark and bearded and unable to stand erect. This is poverty personified, as the inscription states. An arrow shot earlier has already met its mark, embedded as it is in the forehead of the poor figure, and another is about to hit. A rosy-cheeked putto, naked and winged, stands close by, holding up three more arrows for the emperor to shoot.

The emperor, bejewelled and beautifully dressed in a mauve-coloured *jama* tied at the waist with a colourful *patka*, cuts a handsome figure. To add to the majesty of his bearing is the nimbus that surrounds his head. He stands, as might have been expected, not on grassy ground but on a globe which encircles a lion and a lamb. Power and meekness coexist, 'drinking from the same stream' as it were. The globe in turn is supported by a bearded *sannyasi-* like figure who lies on the back of a large fish.

Almost certainly the painter had in his mind the Primal Fish, first incarnation of Vishnu, and the figure of Manu, here reading from a book, possibly a

Veda. This painting thus intriguingly takes one back to the Hindu myths of creation and to the age when life began to take form.

From here one moves to the European world of symbols, for up above, descending from the clouds are the figures of two putti, holding between them a large crown, meant to be placed on the head of the emperor. The iconography, as also the shape of the crown, is evidently of Christian origin, the painter taking his cue from the Polyglot Bible, or some other European work which might have come in the baggage of a missionary priest.

Between the putti and the person of poverty, where the earth begins to curve towards the horizon, is yet another surprising element, but of 'local' origin. Upon a low, glistening white grave-like structure stands a post to which is tied one end of a long, looping festoon, to which bells and little flags are attached; the other end is held by a putto in the clouds far above. It is possible this is intended to be a reference to the legendary chain of justice—the *zanjeer-e adal*. That chain, one knows, the emperor had installed outside his palace for the aggrieved to use to draw his personal attention. Justice and munificence, as the inscription states, come together.

Clearly, what one has here is a work that is brilliantly conceived and most skilfully executed. Each of the parts claims attention, but everything is held firmly together in the whole. It might be a 'message' painting, a political statement, but it refuses to be dismissed thus. For in it resides vision and great painterly quality.

———————

The work, judging from the uneven borders around it, must have been mounted in an album, although it now exists as an isolated leaf. Most scholars regard it as yet another great work by Abu'l Hasan, master as he was at rendering symbolic imagery. However, it bears no signature or contemporary attribution.

THE EMPEROR JAHANGIR GIVING AUDIENCE

Folio from a dispersed manuscript of the *Jahangirnama*, later mounted as an album page
Mughal, by Abu'l Hasan, Nadir-uz Zaman; c. 1620
31.5 cm × 20.5 cm
The Aga Khan Collection, Toronto

This work is an evocation of the grandeur of the Mughal court, its power and its authority, colour and variety, order and tumult.

Very few courts—except perhaps that of the Ottomans—were as immersed in rules of etiquette and governed by the strictest codes of conduct as the Mughal. These codes were laid down from the very start of the dynasty, in the reigns of Babur and Humayun, but information about the Akbari court, provided by the tireless Abu'l Fazl, is far fuller and richer in detail. Apart from pomp and ceremony, one gets from him a picture of the solid and dense administrative machinery, with procedures, rules and regulations at every level.

Of Akbar, he writes that His Majesty received his subjects twice in the course of the day. 'First, after performing his morning devotions, he is visible from outside the awning to people of all ranks. . . . This mode of showing himself is called, in the language of the country, *darshan* [viewing]; and it frequently happens that business is transacted at this time.' But the emperor also 'frequently appears at the window, which opens into the state hall, for the transaction of business; or he dispenses there justice calmly and serenely. . . every officer of government then presents various reports, or explains his several wants, and is instructed by His Majesty how to proceed.'

The custom of appearing at a window, giving a *darshan* from a *jharokha*, seems to have been adopted by Akbar from the Rajput princes. And it was a custom

wholeheartedly adopted by the emperor Jahangir, for in his memoirs he refers several times to *jharokha* appearances.

In this painting, Jahangir appears in a *jharokha* at the very top, a marble window above the easily recognizable red sandstone structure of the massive fort at Agra. At the level where the emperor sits and gazes down upon his nobles and subjects appear only two other heads, those of princes, visible in smaller windows on either side.

Below these, arranged precisely on the raised marble platform and then in the vast courtyard, one sees the rank and file of the Mughal empire gathered together to gain a 'sacred' view of the emperor and, hopefully, to have petitions heard. Prominently visible towards the left is the golden chain which had been installed at the emperor's orders: if grievances remained unattended to, the petitioner could pull on this chain with bells attached, and hope for the emperor's attention.

Here, beneath the imposing walls, men of high rank, grandees of the empire, stand in serried order, in the appropriate degree of proximity to the emperor. Most of them are identified through minute inscriptions that give their names, either on collars or girdles.

The scene below them is not orderly but infinitely more colourful, for here 'commoners' of every conceivable type and station have gathered. One sees Hindus and Muslims, Turks and Afghans, Persians and Abyssinians; petty officials and petitioners, minstrels and account-keepers, mahouts and plain onlookers. All of them are looking up except those who are being shooed away. Every single face is studied with care and rendered with intensity. The painter never loses contact with reality, even when, or especially when, he gets down to portraying lowly subjects, trumpet players and singers. In his own manner, he is presenting a microcosmic view of the great diversity of India.

———————

The painter also brings in, as if detached from all this bustle and activity around him, the lone figure of a venerable, bearded old man of God behind a door in the middle of the painting. Just below that door are inscribed, in faint letters, the words: 'aml-i kamtareen-i khana-zadan Abu'l Hasan': *the work of the lowliest of the low, Abu'l Hasan, born in the service (of the emperor).*

TWO TULIPS AND AN IRIS

Single leaf, probably intended to be mounted as an album page
Mughal; first quarter of the seventeenth century
32.1 cm × 20.1 cm (outer)
26.3 cm × 15.9 cm (inner)
The Aga Khan Collection, Toronto

> Tulips of many colours cover these foothills [around Kabul]; I once
> counted them up; it came out at 32 or 33 different sorts. We named
> one of them as the rose-scented, because its perfume was a little like
> that of the red rose; it grows by itself on Shaikh's plain, here and
> nowhere else. The hundred-leaved tulip is another . . .

Thus wrote Babur, the first of the great Mughals in India. His passion and his
sensitive eye were inherited by a whole line of kings, and with Jahangir and
Shahjahan became an obsession.

Sharp, precise observation had always marked the Mughals. One notices,
for instance, this description of an Indian flower, the *jasun*, once again in the
words of Babur:

> It is not a grass; its plant is in stems like the bush of the red rose.
> The flower of the *jasun* is fuller in colour than the pomegranate,
> and maybe of the size of the red rose, but the red rose, when its
> bud has grown, opens simply, whereas when the *jasun* bud opens, a
> stem on which other petals grow, it is seen like a heart amongst its
> expanded petals. Though the two are parts of the one flower, yet the
> outcome of the lengthening and thinning of that stem-like heart of
> the first opened petals gives the semblance of two flowers. It is not
> a common matter.

Babur's eye was clearly that of a miniaturist. The artists working for Jahangir and Shahjahan, possessed of the same keen eye, sometimes imparted to the flowers that they painted an unearthly air of lyricism, combining the natural and the ideal.

Jahangir found it hard to resist the beauty of flowers. When he was in Kashmir, and saw flowers blooming everywhere, he asked the great painter Mansur, who had travelled with him, to record them and the painter, in the emperor's own words, drew 'pictures of more than a hundred'. But Mansur did not merely record: he saw them with eyes of wonder. One can sense this in some of those signed studies.

The master painter whose work this is—Cary and Antony Welch have attributed it to the Shahjahani painter whom they designate only as the 'Master of the Borders'—wants us to see how finely he has observed these flowers: the erect stalk of the tulip in the centre undulating lightly, its single leaf of rich and subtly variegated green curving about the stalk and inclining its tip 'as if in a slow and measured dance around the centre'. The fine shading of the pinks and the streaks of yellow in the petals, the crispness with which they curve and, in the Welchs' words, 'open enough to reveal the depth of pink along their inner surfaces' are equally subtle and precise, as are the cupped petals of the iris, 'slightly parted to reveal pollen like the softest powder'. The other tulip to the left on this page, somewhat smaller, receives less attention.

It is the tulip under the name *lala*, after the rose, that figures most commonly in Persian and Urdu poetry. There are exquisitely poetic names for different kinds of tulips: the Tulip of the Desert, the Tulip with a Burnt Heart, the Tulip with a Head Bent in Sorrow, and the like.

These are descriptions that serve the poet's purpose well, for he likens the tulip often to the beauty of the face of the beloved. *Lala-rukh*—'with a face like a tulip'—is how the beauteous one is often described. The greatest of the poets writing in Urdu, Ghalib, once used the rose and the tulip in a different context when he said:

> *sab kahaan, kuchh lala-o gul mein numaayaan ho gayeen*
> *khaak mein kya suratein hongi jo pinhaan ho gayeen*

Meaning, roughly:

> Not all, just a few of them have taken the form of these tulips and these roses;
> who knows what beauteous faces, and how many, must be lying hidden under the cover of this dust.

———————

Very often, flowers as painted by Mughal masters show an exquisitely coloured and patterned butterfly hovering above them. One of the more famous of these studies bears the name of Ustad Mansur, and is now in the Maulana Azad Library in the Aligarh Muslim University.

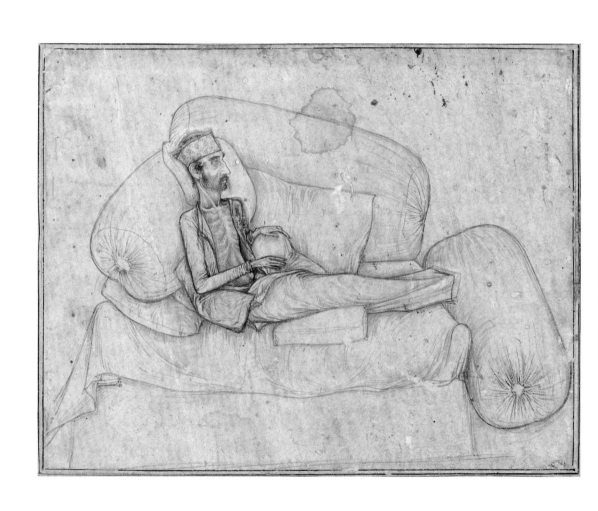

THE DYING MAN: INAYAT KHAN

Leaf, possibly from an artist's sketchbook
Ink and light wash on paper
Mughal, Jahangir period, attributed to Balchand; 1618
10.5 cm × 13.3 cm
Museum of Fine Arts, Boston

The year was 1618. Early in October that year, 'news came of the death of Inayat Khan', the emperor Jahangir recorded in his memoir, the *Tuzuk*. Before speaking of this work—which, in the eyes of Coomaraswamy, remains 'one of the supreme achievements of Mughal painting'—let us return to Jahangir's words even if the passage that follows has been cited all too often: 'He was one of my closest servants and subjects,' the emperor writes.

> In addition to eating opium he also drank wine when he had the chance. Little by little he became obsessed with wine, and since he had a weak frame, he drank more than his body could tolerate. . . . Finally he developed cachexia and dropsy and grew terribly thin and weak.

> Several days prior to this he requested that he be taken ahead to Agra. I ordered him brought to me to be given leave to depart. He was put in a palanquin and brought. He looked incredibly weak and thin. 'Skin stretched over bone.' Even his bones had begun to disintegrate. Though painters have striven much in drawing an emaciated face, yet I have never seen anything like this, or even approaching it. Good God! Can a son of man come to such a shape and fashion? The following two lines of poetry are appropriate to the situation. 'If my shadow doesn't hold my leg, I won't be able to stand until Doomsday. / My sigh sees my heart so weak that it rests awhile on my lip.'

Finding the sight so strange I ordered the artists to draw his likeness. At any rate, I found him so changed that I said: 'At this time you mustn't draw a single breath without remembrance of God, and don't despair of His graciousness'. . . . Since his distress had been reported to me, I gave him a thousand rupees for travelling expenses and gave him leave to depart. (But) the next day he travelled the road of non-existence.

With stark honesty, the painter of this swift but intense study captures what might be close to the last moments of Inayat Khan, who once occupied the position of a *bakhshi* at the court, and whose portrait as a handsome young man has also survived. Propped up by cushions of all kinds, covered by a sheet, he lies, legs stretched out, but with the torso more or less upright, leaning against a bolster because he is not able to support himself.

The clothing he wears is minimal: a *topi*-cap on his head, a long-sleeved jacket that flies open at the chest to reveal the ribcage, an arrangement as it were of 'dissolving' bones. Thin hands with spindle-like fingers rest on a cushion. But it is the glazed look in the eye that catches our attention most of all—staring dimly at the nothingness that lies ahead.

The effect is tremendously moving, the sense of desolation emphasized by the bareness of the room and the lack of colour in the work.

Intriguingly, there is another remarkably close version of the work. It is a fully painted work—everything other than the white sheets and the platform-like bed is painted in rich colours—now in the Bodleian Library at Oxford. The dying man's stance in both paintings is nearly identical but in the Bodleian painting there are other additions in the scene: part of a decorative carpet, a narrow door at the back, and niches in which thin-necked bottles stand. Whether these changes add to the work or diminish it in some manner by taking away from the 'aesthetic shock' that the brush drawing produces will always remain a question.

————————

Jahangir mentions 'artists' who were ordered to draw the likeness of Inayat Khan, but if there were other studies of Inayat Khan as a dying man in other hands, they are now lost. The drawing bears no artist's name. However, on the painting two inscriptions, nearly completely effaced, have lately been read: on the left corner of the sheet, the words in Persian, reading 'amal-i Balchand, banda-yi dargah' *('the work of Balchand, servant of the court'), and at upper-right, simply 'Balchand'.*

JAHANGIR RECEIVES PRINCE KHURRAM

Folio from the *Padshahnama*
Opaque watercolour on paper
Mughal, Shahjahan period; c. 1635
35.8 cm × 24.2 cm
The Royal Library, Windsor Castle

> *Shahjehan-Nama*
> *The History of the reign of the emperor Shahjehan—Son of Jihanghuir, &*
> *Father of Aurangzebe.*

> This is the most splendid Persian Manuscript I ever saw. Many of the
> faces are very well painted & some of them are portraits. The first is
> the portrait of Timur or Tamerlane, & the second that of Shahjehan.
> This was the book which was shown to me at Lucknow, & I was
> there informed that the deceased Nabob Asophuddoulah purchased
> it for 12000 Rupees, or about pounds 1500.

So wrote the Governor-General of India, Lord Teignmouth, in 1799 when he
presented this manuscript—one of the most sumptuous works ever produced
for the great Mughals—to his sovereign, George III, upon his return to
England. He had received this 'Chronicle of the King of the World' from the
Nawab of Lucknow as a gift to take back home. Exchange of gifts between
courts was customary. The emperor whose chronicle this was—Shahjahan—
had himself sent, in 1638, an illustrated manuscript 'as a gift to the glorious
and exalted King of England'. The gift for Lord Teignmouth was received
with much appreciation. This manuscript—the *Padshahnama*, the name by
which the official chronicle of the reign of Shahjahan, *Shahjahannama*, is more
commonly known—has remained in the Royal Collection ever since.

Shahjahan, in his own eyes and those of the world, was no ordinary king.

How self-consciously he styled himself—'Illustrious heir of *Jannat Makani*, the Emperor Nur-ud Din Muhammad Jahangir, son of *Arsh Ashiyani*, the Emperor Jalal-ud Din Muhammad Akbar, son of *Jannat Ashiyani*, the Emperor Nasir-ud Din Muhammad Humayun . . . (descended from the founder of the Mughal dynasty), the Great Lord and Universal Conqueror, the Pillar of the World and Religion, Emperor Amir Timur Gurgan, the first *Sahib-i-Qiran*, Lord of the Auspicious Planetary Conjunction'—tells one something about how the official chroniclers at his court, and his painters, might have been expected to portray him.

The *Padshahnama*, both in words and images, had to reflect all the glory and all the magnificence of his court and present him in the brightest light possible. Consequently, the work—the manuscript of the *Padshahnama* in the Royal Library at Windsor Castle is a fragment, containing only forty-four illustrations, covering the first ten years of his reign—is filled with the most opulent imaginable images of durbars and processions, battles and sieges, acts of valour and necessary cruelty, and an occasional private moment.

The most gifted painters attached to the imperial atelier—Abid, Balchand, Bichitr, Bishan Das, Payag, Daulat, Bulaki, Bhola, Murar, among them—were entrusted with the task. At the head of all the images—as appropriate to an imperial manuscript—was a pair of *shamsa*s, magnificently painted sunbursts symbolic of divine light. A double page showed on its right half the founder of the dynasty, Amir Timur, seated and holding a crown in his hands, which he seemed to be offering to his descendant, Shahjahan, seen seated on the left half. Everywhere there are symbols and metaphors.

While most images in the *Padshahnama* reflect events that were relevant to the emperor's own reign, there are some that are in the nature of 'flashbacks'. On this leaf, for instance—relatively less crowded and even somewhat serene—Shahjahan is looking back upon himself when he was still a prince, known as Khurram, and his father Jahangir was the emperor. There is some uncertainty about the exact occasion, but it possibly relates to the moment after the prince had presented his father a rare ruby-and-pearl armlet which he had brought with him after a successful campaign in Rajasthan.

The prince, with a prominent nimbus round his head, stands to the left, his right hand raised in greeting and obeisance, and the emperor, his father, sits his right hand raised to touch his chest in a gesture of acknowledgement. An attendant stands at the back. Below them stand nobles of the realm, each a superbly observed portrait, many of them wearing medallions with the emperor's effigy round their necks or on their turbans.

Further down, at the bottom of the page stands another group: eight men, each wearing a different turban to establish their different origins. But the eye travels quickly, as it is meant to, towards the central panel just beneath the emperor's throne, where in grisaille a venerable Shaikh is portrayed holding a globe to signify 'world dominion', while two angels hover above. The symmetry of the arrangement of figures is broken, but with a clear purpose.

———————

Not all the paintings in the Padshahnama *are signed or carry attributions. But this leaf, though unsigned, has been attributed to the painter Abid, son of Aqa Riza and thus brother of the gifted Abu'l Hasan.*

THE CAPTURE AND DEATH OF KHAN JAHAN LODI

Folio from the *Padshahnama*
Opaque watercolour on paper
Mughal, Shahjahan period, by Abid; c. 1633
35.8 cm × 24.2 cm
The Royal Library, Windsor Castle

The scene is gruesome. Successions in Mughal India were often disputed or contested and rebellions against the new monarch were not uncommon. When Shahjahan ascended the throne, the Afghan Khan Jahan Lodi, once high in favour at the Jahangiri court, did not pledge unquestioning loyalty to the new monarch. In fact, as the official chronicle puts it, 'his brainless head had become a nest of false and demonic hopes and vain fantasies'. Open defiance marked his conduct, and the imperial forces were ordered by the emperor to hunt him down. Khan Jahan was pursued, captured and killed. His severed head along with those of his sons and some of his followers were despatched from the battlefield to the emperor as trophies of war. Shahjahan was then in Burhanpur, in the southern parts of his empire, and the chronicle states that he had Khan Jahan's head mounted on the gate of his palace as a warning to others with rebellious thoughts.

What the highly gifted painter Abid 'records' here is, however, not a true record. He is reconstructing the event, possibly in the light either of how it was narrated to him or how he was instructed. Khan Jahan Lodi had already been killed in battle and his beheading did not take place in the almost ceremonial manner that this painting shows, as one learns from contemporary sources. Here, the triumphant Mughal generals and soldiers surround the man in the lower half of the painting, proud banners and pennants flying in the background.

One highly placed warrior forces the rebel to his knees and holds his head while another begins to cut it off slowly with a knife; the rebel's eyes are still open and staring ahead. Other men, armed to the teeth and wearing steel armour and helmets, stand around the scene or converse with one another. Two generals stand slightly above, their horses facing each other, but they do not even spare a glance for the beheading 'ceremony'. Some heads, dark and unkempt, severed from their bodies with flies swarming above them, are strewn on the ground; other soldiers stand holding severed heads firmly in their hands. Among the crowd one can also see the Rajput chief Madho Singh, dressed in saffron clothing, whose lance had in fact earlier killed Khan Jahan; here he simply stands and looks on, like the others.

It is the uncompromising, if reconstructed, reality of the battlefield that Abid presents here—a gory scene of retribution, execution and decay. Who was present on this occasion, or how events had unfolded, seems to have been a matter of no concern to him. But he composes the scene with brilliance. Unmindful of the landscape in which the event actually took place—it was near Kalinjar in present-day Uttar Pradesh—he creates his own, an Iranate plain with flowers blooming on the ground and stylized rocks rising almost vertically at the back.

A lone, beautifully painted plane tree dominates the upper half of the page, softening the impact of the grisly scene below.

The scaling of the figures is entirely arbitrary. Four or five soldiers on the other side of a rise in the ground, with only their heads showing, are painted on the same scale as those far closer in the lower part of the page. Far above, at the very top of the painting beyond the hill, one can see other soldiers, the plumes on their helmets moving in the breeze. They appear to be like members of a theatrical chorus—in fact, playing something like 'the role of choral commentation', as the scholars Milo Beach and Ebba Koch have suggested. But their heads are small in scale. Memories of similar compositions—a row of curious heads peeping over the hill—seen in Iranian works must have lingered on in the Mughal artistic imagination.

———————

On the leaf, several inscriptions in Persian can be seen, even if they are difficult to read in reproductions. At the bottom in the centre is the most important of these, recording that this is 'amal-i-banda-i dargah 'Abid', meaning 'the work of the slave of the court, 'Abid'. The word 'Shahjahani' that appears on the sleeve of one of the executioners does not identify that man. It needs to be read with the inscription that speaks of 'Abid, for it is he who is 'Shahjahani', meaning owing his allegiance to the emperor Shahjahan. Other inscriptions invoke blessings on the emperor or identify some relatively minor figures.

AN ENCAMPMENT IN THE HILLS

Opaque watercolour on paper
Kutch, Gujarat; c. 1800
32.5 cm × 52.5 cm
Heidelberg Museum, Juergen and Barbara Lutt Collection

Kutch, with its Rann—'a space without a counterpart in the globe' in the words of the celebrated British explorer and soldier Sir Alexander Burnes—likened in appearance to a tortoise, *kachhapa*, by others, and described in the Mahabharata as a 'cardamom-like island', has rarely been associated with painting of any sort. And yet, sometime in the eighteenth century, from it sprang what is possibly the only true school of landscape painting in India.

The story is long and complicated but in it figure at least two uncommon men: Rao Lakhpatji, who ruled Kutch from 1741 to 1760, had a marked taste for the exotic and a great sense of curiosity about the outside world; and Ram Singh Malam, a local sailor who reached the shores of Europe as a shipwrecked young boy, stayed there for close to eleven years, learnt different skills and returned to his native land, loaded with exotica of all kinds including European engravings of city views.

There are serious gaps in our information but it would seem that the Rao took immediately to this ingenious sailor-craftsman and entrusted him with various tasks, including building the great Aina Mahal, or the Hall of Mirrors, filled with curiosities of all kinds—Venetian glass, celestial globes, mechanical toys, Chinese tiles, rare silks, a dancing fountain, and the like—in his capital city, Bhuj.

But there were also those engravings which Ram Singh Malam brought back: views of the 'Piazza San Marco' and the 'Grand Canal of Venice', of Rome with the 'Piazza del Popolo', of the 'Palace of Count Dhaun' at Vienna, of English cities and buildings including 'the Cathedral Church of York', the 'Chapel of the Holy Trinity in the Cathedral of Canterbury', the 'Grove of the Ball Hall', the 'Royal Palace of Windsor'. Intrigued with these, and with their outlandish features of receding lines, perspective, shading, hatchings, and so on, the Rao appears to have asked his own painters, the Kamangars of Kutch, to produce copies of these.

The result? One engraving with four or five copies of it, each by a different painter; each copy a valiant struggle to understand and to come to terms with a new medium, a new way of seeing. This went on for a while and clearly some local painters were cleverer than others. Then it appears to have occurred to them, or to their patron, to abandon the copying of European engravings and to begin looking at their own surroundings to produce 'views'.

A large number of views of Kutch emerged from the brush of these artists—paintings, not engravings—of places that were easy to relate to. There were views of the Bhujia Hill that dominates the landscape of Bhuj, the lake of Desal Sar, the *dargah* of Pir Haji Kirmani, the town of Anjar seen from different angles, the towns of Mandvi and Bhuchau and Mundra, and so on.

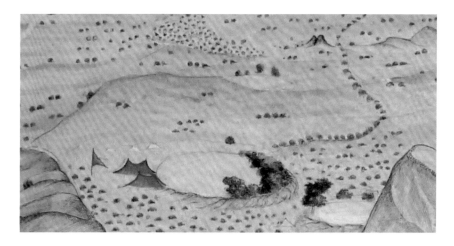

And through this experimentation, a remarkable body of work was created. Standing out in that group is this view of an encampment in the hills. A vast space is seen, as if from a considerable height, bare and uninhabited, with rocky blue hills in the foreground and in the far distance. There are no signs of life, and only a few features can be clearly distinguished: a path, a nearly dry riverbed, but, more prominently, an encampment of red—royal?—tents by the side of a small pool of water in the heart of this vast expanse.

Everything is brown and barren but for the little dots that mark stray bushes, and the hills which are a light but shimmering blue. There is a remarkable stillness about the work. The air feels thin and dry and, like it, nothing seems to move in this vast terrain. An eerie majesty presides over the scene. One notices that here the unnamed Kutch painter relies on nothing that he has seen before in a painting: everything comes from his own observation. The landscape is invested with a feeling that no outsider could have brought to it.

————————

A number of European engravings bore labels at the bottom which were translated roughly into Kutchi and inscribed at the back. This suggests that someone who knew those engravings was translating them for the local painters. Many of the observed landscapes of Kutch towns and surroundings also carry long inscriptions specifying the point from which they were observed, and so on. The Kamangar painters of Kutch were earlier used to painting portraits of rulers and nobility, or views of durbars, in a style that is reminiscent of work done in Jodhpur and Nagaur.

THE RAO OF KUTCH'S PROCESSION OUTSIDE ANJAR

Opaque watercolour on paper
Kutch; third quarter of the eighteenth century
25 cm × 45.5 cm
Private Collection

Among the surprising group of paintings from Kutch that emerged—suddenly—from a gallery owner's holdings in Heidelberg some years ago was this astounding view that is as much one of a landscape as of a procession. The receding view of the landscape is evident; the procession, however, can only be seen with some effort for even though the scene teems with people, they are painted on so small a scale that they are completely dwarfed by the land and the sky between which, ant-like, they spread out row after row.

The painting is meant to record a specific occasion: the visit of the ruler—he remains unnamed but it is just possibly that great enthusiast and patron, Rao Lakhpatji—to the important town of Anjar in his domains. An inscription in Kutchi-Gujarati appears at the back of the painting, which can be roughly translated as 'The noble Raoji had come to [the town of] Anjar. At the time that he departed from Anjar for the auspicious city of Bhuj, the crowds of people who gathered to see him on the Savasar side, and the procession of the noble Raoji, appeared like this. This [painted] leaf represents that occasion.'

The unnamed Kamangar painter of Kutch—having seen a whole range of European engravings of landscapes and city views (see previous painting)—sets out here to paint what can only be called an 'atmospheric picture'. The elements he draws upon for doing this are the rumbling grey clouds in the sky, the walled town of Anjar in the far distance, the procession of the Rao, the retinue that spills over the paths and the fields, and the green expanse of land all around. He invests the scene with a distinct sense of place and of occasion, but the emphasis is clearly on creating an atmosphere. Few works, apart from those that deal with the explicit poetry around the Ragas (musical modes) or Baramasa (the seasons) in Rajput painting, come close to the mood that is evoked here.

One can sense at once the stirring of a gentle breeze, the sounds in the sky merging with those made by the musicians, the murmur of excitement in the crowds, the vivid spectacle. But slowly one takes in the astonishing amount of detail with which the picture is packed: the colourful elephant carrying the Rao; others following it at a respectful distance; the countless soldiers and retainers walking ahead; and, in between, the rows of gaily attired people who stand neatly along hedges to see the procession make its slow, majestic way.

One notices that the painter brings in as many women as men in the crowds, all of them dressed in a colourful red, the ample turbans of the men often matching them in intensity. The tall tower that rises on an eminence within the walled city, the tiled sloping roofs of countless houses, the *shikhara*s of temples with flags fluttering from them are all carefully

introduced. And then of course there is the expanse of land, the cultivated fields close to the city walls taking over where the brown, fallow land in the foreground ends. It is all, in its own way, a poetic celebration of this fertile tract of land.

———————

The narrow black borders that surround this work are markedly rubbed, much like one sees on so many other paintings from Kutch. This rubbing comes possibly from its having been stuck inside a frame. The European engravings which came into Kutch with Ram Singh Malam, the sailor (see previous painting, p. 351), all had black borders too.

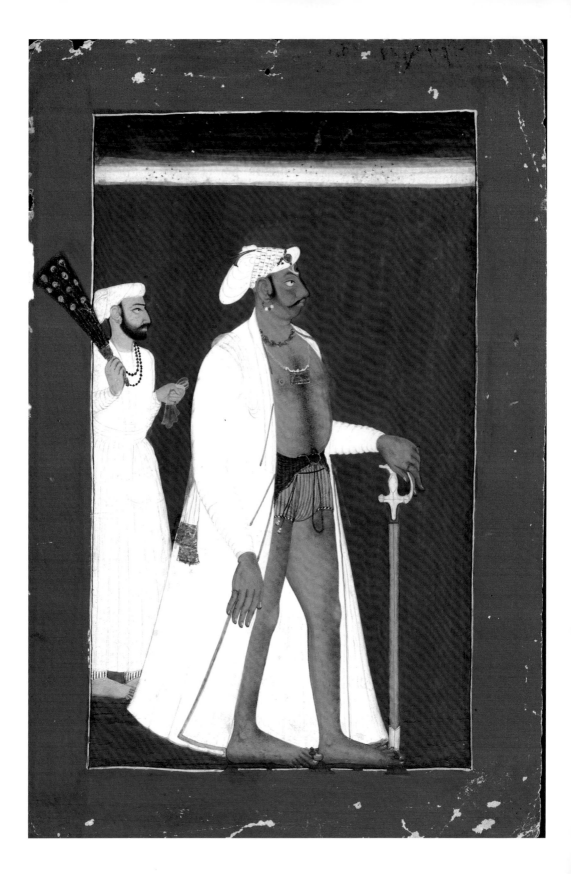

RAJA SIDH SEN OF MANDI: AN INFORMAL PORTRAIT

Isolated folio
Opaque watercolour on paper
Pahari, from a Mandi workshop, possibly by Khinnu; c. 1700
30.5 cm × 20.4 (outer)
24.8 cm × 14.7 cm (inner)
Government Museum and Art Gallery, Chandigarh

There are not many portraits like this that one can think of from the range of Indian art. The first impression that this painting makes is one of some coarseness: the pigments are rather roughly applied, the page does not have that attractive glaze which one sees so often in the work of other masters from the Pahari area, and the bodily details are too strong, too earthy. But, seen from another viewpoint, in this extraordinary portrait the painter achieves the nearly impossible: he combines an extreme informality of appearance with great majesty of bearing.

Sidh Sen was no ordinary man, and even in his own lifetime the state over which he held complete sway—Mandi—is said to have reverberated with stories of his uncommon prowess and personal strength. It was widely believed that he could take a coconut and crush it in the palm of his left hand, or rub the legend off a coin simply by pressing it between his thumb and forefinger. His devotion to Shiva and his consort was exemplary, and as a Tantric, he is believed to have acquired magical powers. It was said that a *gutka*, or magic amulet, which he wore around his neck, enabled him to fly each morning to the source of the river Ganga from Mandi and return in time to attend to affairs of state.

Tall of build and possessed of a massive frame, the raja towered over everyone else in sight, whether seated or standing. His painters represented him over and over again: standing with a curved sword held aggressively in both hands; stepping out with implements of worship to offer puja at a shrine; seated smoking a *huqqa*, telling *rudraksha* beads, his head bare except for a topknot in which a flower of the *dhatura* plant, so beloved of his deity, Shiva, is stuck; supervising a military campaign with his commanders who stand by his side, taking orders.

Each time, however, the painters seem to have decided, while portraying their patron, to turn to iconic formulae that lay embedded in their consciousness: the world of *lakshana*s. If we see him standing, right arm falling straight along his side, the fingers of his hand reach well below the knee: a reference clearly to one of the *lakshana*s—attributes by which he can be recognized—of a *mahapurusha*, a great or suprahuman man. When they show him sitting with one knee brought up, his thigh is too massive to be embraced fully by one of the court maidens. The chest is lion-like, a forehead full and wide 'beyond even Meru's flank', as the texts said. On the many occasions when we see his body bare, it is marked all over by meticulously rendered hair, most prominently in a furry vertical line that runs from chest to navel, similar to Shiva's as conceived by the master painter active at Mandi then.

Ancient descriptions of a Chakravartin come to mind:

> One should know that the King of Men should be represented with the gait of the King of Elephants, the leader of the herd, with the gait of the Wild Goose . . . He has the rank and the great power of the King of Elephants, the sharpness of mind of the Leader of Bulls, the strength of a King of Lions, the majesty of a King of Wild Geese: such is the outward appearance of the Master of Men.

It is by borrowing broadly from these descriptions that the painter shows Sidh Sen here, striding forth, left hand firmly placed on the hilt of a long sword, great floor-length white robe flying open to reveal a pair of striped drawers, pillar-like legs, and feet clad in giant wooden sandals. The set of the mouth is firm and the gaze unblinking. References to the raja's personal faith are brought in: the *dhatura* flower stuck in the cross-band of the turban, the prominent *shakta tilaka* mark, a small whistle attached to a string, commonly worn by *jogi*s, and an amulet dangling against his hairy chest. There are subtle references here but, in the final analysis, the image is earthy, weighed down with sheer energy.

There are some touches of delicacy too, like the gossamer-thin handkerchief held by the attendant, the golden edge of the raja's scarf barely visible on the other side of his chest, the fineness with which the enamelled necklace of beads is rendered. The background is a flat bluish grey, ending at the top in a straight line above which, suddenly, the white-and-blue horizon begins, marked by tiny speck-like birds flying against it.

———————

Paintings in the style of this portrait are visibly and remarkably different from the refined, precise style in which the large-sized leaves of the Bhagavata Purana, *or the* Ramayana *were painted at Mandi not long before this. The circumstance can only be explained by the fact that the family working at Mandi earlier died out completely, or that another family of painters started working in a style that they found more appropriate to the earthy nature of themes—like this portrait—that they were handling.*

361

RAJA BALWANT SINGH EXAMINING
A PAINTING WITH NAINSUKH

Isolated folio
Opaque watercolour and gold on paper
Pahari, by Nainsukh of Guler; c. 1745–50
21 cm × 30 cm
Museum Rietberg, Zürich, Barbara and Eberhard Fischer Collection

Had it not been for the presence of the now celebrated painter Nainsukh himself in this painting, one might have liked to begin describing it from the bottom-left corner. There sits a *dholak* player, an exquisite study of this simple, unidentified musician: dark of complexion, wearing a loosely tied turban and simple white clothing, his *dholak* resting at a slight angle in his lap, delicate fingers poised to strike, eager expression on the face.

But then attention has to shift quickly to the right half of the page, for there—an uncommon occurrence in Indian painting—one sees patron and painter together, not only in close proximity to each other but looking at the same painting: the prince, Balwant Singh of Jasrota, seated on his elegant throne and his favoured painter standing directly behind him, body bent forward at the waist, hands folded in an attitude of submission and respect. An exchange seems to be taking place: the prince making a comment perhaps on the work he holds in one hand, and the painter straining forward to hear it.

No particular event that we know of is being recorded here. It is a quiet afternoon: the sun is peeping from just below one of the rolled-up curtains in the middle of the painting, and the time is devoted entirely to savouring some of the joys of life. The prince smokes a *huqqa*, a painting is being discussed, musicians sing and play. A view of the kind of leisured life some princes in peaceful corners of the Pahari region led is all that Nainsukh seems to be intent on capturing.

But there is so much to see and savour in this work, for the painter invests every detail with feeling and elegance. The cool expanse of the marble terrace, the pale-yellow flooring of the *baradari*, the salmon-pink edge of the fronting wall, the carved wooden balustrade at the far back, the outlines of slender pillars, the cloth screens in white edged with gold, the golden throne with its decoration so reminiscent of the herbal borders on Mughal *patka*s, the *huqqa* surprisingly encased in a floral fabric cover, the loops and curls—Nainsukh's favourites—of the *huqqa* pipe: it is all executed with both precision and delicacy.

At the same time, however, the accent is on simplicity. The striped pattern of Balwant Singh's turban, the gold edging of Nainsukh's own *patka*, or the thin band of gold in the standing courtier's turban are all understated. The plain white clothes and the fine outlines of the figures merge seamlessly with the marble floor, as though not to draw attention to themselves. He has made the entire scene appear as though seen through a sheet of diaphanous gauze. There is, too, that distinctive sense of space, that airy openness, which Nainsukh so loved to evoke.

Also, the painter brings us very close to the characters seen: the tall, ageing man seated with his shoulders slightly hunched and hands respectfully laced in his lap; the standing courtier-like figure with slightly straggly hair tucked under his turban and a case with a pair of scissors protruding in his waistband; the dark-skinned musician playing on the *morchang* or Jew's harp, both hands raised to his mouth; the singer with the *tanpura* and the extended arm, and of course the *dholak* player. Nainsukh observed these 'ordinary' men with remarkable keenness. And when he paints his own likeness, he does so with no attempt to disguise a feature like his slightly protruding teeth or his middle-aged heaviness of girth. Things are stated with moving honesty.

And yet, some things in this painting—which had dropped out of sight for long years and then suddenly re-emerged—remain closed to us. Who, one wonders, is the tall man seated facing the prince? Is he the one who has brought this painting to the patron's notice? Who is the man standing behind him with the telltale pair of scissors tucked in his waistband? And the painting with the speckled-yellow borders in the prince's hand—almost certainly the figure on it is Krishna and, judging from its style, it is not Nainsukh's work— is the prince seeking his painter's comments on it?

Questions like these arise, of course, but none of them succeeds in disturbing the air of serenity and elegance that the work breathes. One just settles down and savours it.

———————

There has been some discussion and disagreement among scholars, especially concerning the evidence it yields about the relative ages of Nainsukh and Balwant Singh. While W.G. Archer maintained that Nainsukh was of the same age as his patron, and that this work represents an occasion in which Nainsukh, seeking employment under this patron, is inviting him to approve a sample of his work, there is the other view that Nainsukh was decidedly older than his patron and that he had entered the prince's service at least ten years before the date of this work. Issues like these are debated because the highly gifted Nainsukh is possibly the only Pahari painter whose life and work we can reconstruct with some confidence.

VILLAGERS AROUND A FIRE

Isolated folio
Opaque watercolour on paper
Pahari, by Nainsukh; c. 1765–75
20.8 cm × 16.5 cm (outer)
15 cm × 11 cm (inner)
Indian Museum, Kolkata

This painting is in many ways the most dramatic of Nainsukh's works. In it, he sets out to explore the world of light and dark around a crackling wood-fire burning in the centre. Figures are placed boldly against the darkness of the night, shadows flicker, walls emerge gradually, leaves glisten in the light, and half the people seated round the fire are silhouetted against the flames. A velvety darkness surrounds the group, and in the intensely black sky stars glow like scattered embers. The effect is vivid and the work technically very daring in the context of Indian painting in general.

Art historian E.B. Havell, writing in the early years of the twentieth century, saw it as a painting 'done with the simplicity and directness of a true genius', the painter, in his view, 'probably a descendant of the painter of the Bagh frescoes who in a different milieu recorded his impression of Indian life as faithfully as his ancestor did in the old Buddhist *vihara*'.

Earlier in his career, Nainsukh might have played with some of the elements we see in this startling painting. But here he seems to have decided to test himself, pressing against established limits, breaking out of the safe circle of convention. Here the night is not, as was usual, suggested merely by torches and candles burning under elegant glass cases; the light does not glow on its own, casting no shadows, with every object perfectly lit. We do not know what led Nainsukh to depart from convention: competition, the patron's fancy, a challenge posed by a work brought in from outside or simply the wish to break free, do something truly different. What is certain is that, judging from what has survived of his oeuvre, this painting stands out as a tour de force, an experiment that was not followed up. His interest in this kind of work does not completely die out, but by and large there is a quiet return to his own world where imagination takes precedence over simple observation, and another kind of poetry fills the air.

As almost always, Nainsukh invests the painting with great human interest and warmth. The setting has a rustic charm. Seated around the fire on this wintry night are fifteen persons of varying ages, while from the nearby house

a young woman, draped in a long veil and perfectly framed against a lit doorway, turns gently to look at the company. The wall of another house with a sloping roof rises at left, and two trees spread their branches over the group, some finely articulated leaves yellowed by the light they catch.

At the centre of the semicircle of men sits a bearded man, face seen frontally, shoulders slightly hunched on account of the cold, body draped in a double-sided green-and-mauve shawl. He smokes a simple villager's *huqqa*, its stiff, curved stem held in the right hand. Not everyone pays him attention, although the old man next to him, holding a child in his lap, and the other man flanking him turn earnestly towards him, as if listening. Of the other men who sit about, some are grave and self-absorbed, some look back towards a companion who is holding forth, one turns aside to smoke a small *gurguri-huqqa*, and so on.

The types, the individual characters, are established by Nainsukh with remarkable assurance and immediacy. These were perhaps the very kind of persons he felt most comfortable with in life: the village headman, the local *vaidya*-physician, the goldsmith, the petty shopkeeper, and the like. Deftly, and with a few strokes, Nainsukh whittles down the distance between them and the viewer. The night prevails, but so does human warmth.

———————

It has been suggested that the bearded man in the centre might be none other than Nainsukh's patron, Balwant Singh. While there is some general resemblance, there are things that argue against this identification. The man, for instance, is without any mark of rank or status; in the company that he is in, there is no indication of any deference being accorded to him. Above all, there are many in this group who smoke the huqqa, *something that would be unthinkable in the prince's presence unless the other smokers were peers, which they clearly are not. It would seem that in bringing in this face, Nainsukh was simply depicting a type that he knew well, rather than inducting his patron surreptitiously into this villagers' gathering.*

THE KRISHNA STORY ENACTED: THE RASALILA CONTINUES IN THE MEWAR ROYAL PALACE

Folio from a series depicting the *rasalila*
Inscribed on verso with six lines of text in Rajasthani Hindi
Opaque watercolour and gold on paper
Rajasthan, Mewar, attributed to Jairam of Udaipur; 1736
67 cm × 48.5 cm
San Diego Museum of Art, Edwin Binney Collection

The range of activities recorded by the painters of Mewar for their patrons, the rulers of this princely state, is extraordinary. There are scenes of royal hunts, battles and processions; rulers in moments of intimacy with their consorts; performing puja inside family shrines; entertaining royal guests; paying homage to holy men; sitting in consultation with their confidants, and so on. Here one sees the Maharana, Jagat Singh, seated watching a visiting group of actors perform scenes from the *lila* of Krishna. The text on verso, translated, begins:

> Om Shri Maharajadhiraja Maharana Shri Jagat Singh had this rasa(lila) of (by a performing troupe from) Vraja performed on the 15th day of the bright half of the auspicious month of Karttika of the (Vikrama) year 1793.

This is not the only folio devoted to the *rasa* theme at Mewar: a whole series appears to have been painted, beginning with a scene in which, as the Maharana and his intimate circle sit watching, someone dressed as Ganesha comes into the court, and receives royal homage, for he is 'the Lord who removes all obstacles'. As many as ten, perhaps even eleven, folios followed, each showing the same inner courtyard, the same *qanat*-cloth-screen enclosure, the same staircase leading to the top floor, the same outer 'garden' courtyard

371

where minor characters rest and entertain themselves while waiting for the performance inside to end. The scenes being performed inside naturally keep changing, as does a part of the audience, but the setting remains unaltered, essentially with a view to maintaining continuity.

Here in this folio one sees the same marble palace setting, the same unusual perspective, the night sky, the crowded group, with only minor changes made. The pleasure-loving Maharana (Jagat Singh II) is of course there, presiding over the scene. Col James Tod, chronicler of princely Rajasthan, wrote of his 'determination to be happy amidst calamity' and 'addiction to festivals devoted to idleness and dissipation'. The rendering of the *rasalila*—the enactment of the miraculous deeds of Krishna—must have had a special place in the ruler's heart. This painting may have been the record of a particularly great performance.

Mathura, that city on the Yamuna perennially associated with Krishna, is where performances of the great *rasalila* seem to have originated. From there, troupes of remarkably skilled professional performers used to fan out and perform in different places in the country. Their performances enacted different episodes from the Krishna story, from his childhood onward, culminating with Krishna's 'erotic/mystical' circular *rasa* dance with the *gopis* on the full-moon night of the month of Karttika—the month in which this painting series is dated.

In this episode, while musicians play, Krishna is seen first speaking to the *gopi*s who have left their hearth and home to join him on this full-moon night, and then dancing with them. Reminders of episodes that have already been performed are placed far at the back, such as the stage prop of the Mount Govardhan, which Krishna had once lifted to protect his kinsmen from incessant rain, and a canopy with its exquisitely painted roof showing Indra in the midst of the very clouds that he commands to unleash their fury upon Vrindavan (see p. 197, 'Krishna Lifting the Mount Govardhan'). Apart from the Maharana himself, others in the audience are undoubtedly princes of the royal blood, chiefs and others of high rank, holding their hands in gestures of wonder, or talking to one another as though discussing the finer points of the performance.

There is a great deal of colour in the painting—the gold of the textiles, the rich red of the royal cloth screens, the blue of Krishna and the clouds, among other things. But the overwhelming impression is of the scene being bathed in moonlight. The reference to the full-moon night of Karttika in the inscription on verso becomes meaningful. And, appropriate to the theme being enacted, there is animation on the part of the performers, but on the part of the audience a gravity that borders on reverence.

A ROYAL TIGER HUNT

Inscribed on verso with seven lines of text in Rajasthani Hindi
Opaque watercolour and gold on paper
Rajasthan, Mewar, by Jiva; 1749
86.4 cm × 51.6 cm
San Diego Museum of Art, Edwin Binney Collection

Together with sedate scenes of quiet devotion—waving *arati* lamps in front
of skilled performers of *rasalila*, sitting at prayer in his personal shrine—
Maharana Jagat Singh's painters also created for him a world of great
animation: the world of the hunt and the chase. They could not, of course,
produce an exact record of such events, as they did of religious ceremonies
and performances, for the nature and the pace of the action during a hunt
did not allow this. But they did aim for a reconstruction and seem to have
set about the task with verve and enthusiasm. We see him hawking, hunting
boars, shooting tigers, exercising his favourite elephants. There is in these
scenes a vigour that is in sharp contrast to the quieter paintings set within
the palace walls.

The long inscription on verso sets the scene. Translated, it begins:

> Shri Maharajadhiraja Maharana Shri Jagat Singh killed a tiger; the
> bullet was fired by the (maharana's own) auspicious hand.

In the painting, the Maharana appears together with many companions
and followers, at the edge of a swampy jungle where tigers roam. The bustle
and noisy activity that are the essence of such shikar expeditions have been
rendered ingeniously by the gifted Jiva together, possibly, with his son, Jugarsi.

It is not easy to see how the action proceeds. Therefore one has to weave
one's way through this large leaf slowly. The Maharana and his close

companions have evidently arrived in two boats, seen tied at the very bottom of the folio, at the edge of the swampy lake where royal servants sit waiting. The Maharana himself, seated along with four companions behind a tall bamboo hunting blind, then takes aim and fires with his matchlock in the north-westerly direction. The hide, or hunting blind, is at the lower edge of a clearing in the jungle where a nervous, raging bull is tied to a tether, with what appears to be a whole pride of tigers circling around him.

Only gradually does one realize that we are meant to see this as a single snarling tiger who moves about, circles, tears the bull apart and scatters his limbs around, is then hit by the Maharana's bullet, falls to the ground, rolls about, and makes his wounded way up through the thicket, where we see him at least three times again before he is surrounded by a host of beaters and footmen and firecracker experts.

This is by no means the only painting of a hunting scene in which the same animal appears more than once—appearing from behind a bush, leaping into the air, and then falling to the ground after being shot—with the painter availing himself of the old Indian device of continuous pictorial representation. But in this painting, the painters seem almost to go over the top, representing the same tiger fifteen times within the same frame, at first whole and unwounded, and then hit, blood flowing from its shoulders. It is confusing at times, but there is also excitement in the effort to capture the whole sequence of action, even if not everything falls into place.

It is difficult to make out, for instance, the sequence of events in the middle of the painting where the Maharana appears again, twice: once carried in a palanquin, and then on horseback as he makes his way through the forest terrain. The very last time we see him is when he seems to be quitting the painting frame on horseback at right, behind an elephant carrying the carcass of the shot tiger. The hunt has come to an end. But the continuity is broken at places: although the figure of the Maharana, nimbate and magnificently attired, is brought in three times, it is not easy to explain or understand the fact that he has changed his dress—he wears a green *jama* when seen shooting from the gun at the bottom, and an orange-red one when he is in the palanquin or on horseback—unless of course different hunting expeditions are being suggested by the painter.

So absorbing is the course of events in this painting that one almost neglects to pay attention to the superb detailing in the work—the variegated foliage, the liveliness of the tiger, the powerless rage of the bull—and to the inventive 'stippled' effect that one sees in the bushes or in the patterns made by firecrackers. Jiva brings in some extraordinary vignettes: the ghostly light that falls on the stunted bushes and trees as the firecrackers explode above them, the two small hunting lodges that are almost lost in the landscape, the well that occupies one obscure corner of this remarkable painting.

———————

As is common with long, detailed inscriptions on Rajasthani paintings, the names of many persons who were present on the occasion are listed, as if to document and authenticate the occasion. Here, for instance, Nathji, the thakur Sirdar Singh, the babu Bharat Singh, are mentioned, among others, as part of the group.

RAO RAM SINGH I OF KOTA PURSUING A RHINOCEROS

Opaque watercolour and gold on paper
Rajasthan, from a Kota workshop; c. 1700
32.1 cm × 47.6 cm
Private Collection

The elephant has lassoed the neck of the rhinoceros with his long trunk. We do not get to see how the hunt ended, but despite the damage to this leaf, the viewer becomes a virtual witness to this stirring scene. In the words of art historian Cary Welch, this painting makes us 'feel the thud of feet and the lashing of ropes, and hear the clang of bells'.

The prince riding the elephant and embedding his long lance in the hide of the rhinoceros is Rao Ram Singh of Kota—the state which had been carved out of the larger territory of Bundi by the emperor Shahjahan in 1631. He was evidently fond of hunting and we see him several times in the midst of dense forests and surrealistic rocky terrain, shooting tigers, cutting down wild boars. His painter/s created for him records of these hunts while being equally interested in capturing the powerful force of elephants: now charging at great speed as in this work, now combating other elephants, now tugging at the great iron chains meant to restrain them in royal settings. In Bundi or Kota we seldom see an elephant at rest, posing, as it were, for the painter. And it is not easy to think of another region or style in which this great animal, this 'ancient life force, delicate and mighty, awesome and enchanted', with his 'masked gray visage', as Peter Matthiessen put it, has been rendered with greater flair or sharper understanding.

To one's regret, remarkably little is known about the painters who worked for the Kota court. Not more than one or two names have survived: Niju who painted for Rao Durjan Sal, or Sheikh Taju, whose name surfaces in some inscriptions. The scholar Milo Beach identifies one distinct, unnamed hand, which he has named as that of the 'Hada Master' (the Bundi–Kota region being known as Hadaoti, or land of the Hada clan).

Of interest is the fact that while battle scenes and elephant fights might have begun to be painted in Bundi—the mother state, so to speak, of the Hada clan of Rajputs—with the founding of the breakaway state of Kota, the painters who were responsible for these works moved to that new state, giving Kota work a distinct 'artistic identity'. It is as if hunting scenes and elephant combats, observes Beach, became a hallmark of Kota, among the earliest hunting scenes done there being the one in which Rao Ram Singh features again, seen hunting at Mukundgarh. In contrast, painters who remained and continued to work at Bundi concentrated on 'more traditional literary and religious subjects', turning out some exquisite works in those genres.

The sheer dexterity with which this hunting scene is painted and the bounding energy of which it is possessed take one's breath away. The painter seems to have turned the enormous bulk of the elephant almost to weightlessness, its massive legs moving light-footedly here, like those of a galloping horse. The remarkable assurance of line, the refined tonal modelling, the soft delineation of hair and wrinkles, the agitation in the flapping fan-like ears, and, above all, the knowing look of concentration bordering on triumph come clearly from the brush of a great master. The rhinoceros—a surprising presence in a hunting scene, considering how rare that animal might have been in these parts—is also treated with deft ease, its dark, thick hide contrasting with the skin of the elephant, and its panic-stricken movement coming across so convincingly.

In contrast with these beasts, the two men on elephant back appear pale despite their energetic involvement in this spirited engagement. One notices that there is little colour in the painting save on the caparisoning of the royal elephant, but one also notices the remarkable attention to detail in the rendering of the rope-harnesses, the soft texture of the textile twisted like a rope around the neck of the elephant, the bells and other accessories attached to the ropes, the patterning on the saddlery. The background is bare of vegetation save for some sparse grass on the ground. Clearly the chase is not, unlike in so many hunting scenes from Kota, in the thick of a jungle.

The beginning of painting at Kota and Bundi, and the course it then took, has been a subject of debate among eminent scholars such as W.G. Archer, Pramod Chandra and Stuart Carey Welch, among others, and their opinions analysed and evaluated by Milo Beach. In his most recent essay, 'Masters of Early Kota Painting', Beach has, instead of isolating master painters at Kota, introduced the idea of 'master styles'. Acknowledging that there are no sources giving documented historical information about painters or paintings at Kota, he has attributed important paintings to three painters that he has identified simply as A, B and C.

RAWAT GOKUL DAS OF DEOGARH AT SINGH SAGAR

Inscribed on verso in Rajasthani Hindi in Devanagari characters
Opaque watercolour and gold on paper
Rajasthan, Deogarh, by Bagta; 1806
54 cm × 79 cm
The Ashmolean Museum, Oxford, Howard Hodgkin Collection

This action-laden but at the same time strangely quiet painting bears an inscription which helps the viewer to 'place it'. It says that it bears the likeness of 'Maharawat Sri Gokul Das', whom one knows to have ruled over the small *thikana* (principality) of Deogarh, owing allegiance to the much larger kingdom of Mewar. The place, the inscription records, is the 'Sig [Singh?] Sagar', a lake within the domains of the Maharawat. It adds that by the side of the ruler at this time were his 'uncle Rawat Gyan Singh and Amarji'; and that it was painted by the artist Bagta who presented it 'in the pavilion on Monday, the 12th of the dark half of the month of Sravan in the Vikrami year 1863 [1806 CE]'.

Rawat Gokul Das—a man described by the British resident James Tod as 'one of the finest men I ever beheld in feature and person . . . about six feet six, perfectly erect, and a Hercules in bulk'—was evidently fond of hunting. We see him, as painted by his favourite—perhaps his only—artist, the highly gifted Bagta, seated, holding a rifle in his hands; hunting a boar on horseback; enjoying a feast at the end of the hunt; and so on. But in this work, hunting is only one of the activities that Bagta brings in. There is so much else crowding the page. In fact, it seems to be a record of an entire expedition.

The Rawat must have chosen to move to his private summer pavilion situated in the midst of a lake—the Singh Sagar—approached by a bridge from land. An entire retinue seems also to have followed him: elephants

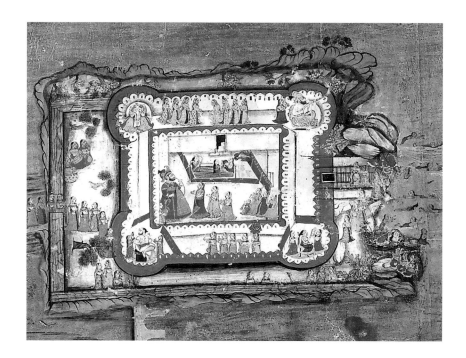

and camels and horses; carriages drawn by oxen on which the ladies of his harem must have ridden; and several servants. Of course the Maharawat is there too, indulging in his favourite sport. In the lower part of the painting towards the right we see him outside the pavilion, standing on a rock, shooting at fowl in the lake, his close companions by his side. He appears again shooting from a turret, his gun directed towards the thickets in the distance. But we also see him inside the pavilion having his hair trimmed, watching ladies bathing in the central courtyard. The intention of the work, painted 'with a verve that is almost unique in Rajput art' as Milo Beach has observed, is 'not to show a single moment of action, but all those events which together define this relaxing expedition, as well as the activities that animate this particular site'.

When one sees the painting from close—and there is no other way in which it deserves to be seen—one realizes how much Bagta has packed into it, and with what flair. If there are horses in the work, one sees them from the front, the rear, the side; they appear to stand or move at a dignified pace or even enter the waters of the lake. The lone royal elephant that has obviously brought the Rawat to this spot stands at majestic ease; the oxen keep their positions by the side of the chariot-like *palki*s (palanquins) in which the women of the royal household have travelled. Men bearing royal standards occupy one spot on the land, and those busy preparing food another; footmen and retainers crowd almost all available level spaces.

And then, suddenly, the landscape takes over. Large rocks, bold and brooding and almost hiding monster forms, stand at the lower end of the page. A well-laid-out garden intervenes at one point. The bridge leading to the pavilion is seen from the side as if lying flat on the surface of the water. And along the irregular rim of the lake, rocks and fowl and vegetation stay in constant negotiation, as it were. Nothing quite like this almost surreal landscape seems to have been painted by Bagta again, for his time and attention were concentrated on individual portraits and groups of men, something in which he excelled, and towards which he bent his exuberant energy.

———

The careers of Bagta and his talented son, Chokha, have been possible to trace through the information that inscriptions have yielded and through a reconstruction of their styles, as Milo Beach has done. Bagta appears to have begun his career at the Mewar court but then moved by 1769 to Deogarh where, away from the established tradition and/or competition that the Mewar ateliers posed, he could move into a different groove, freer and bolder and more flamboyant.

TWO PORTRAITS OF KALA, THE SEPOY

Pages taken from an album
Watercolour on paper
Delhi, from the family workshop of Ghulam Ali Khan; c. 1815
39.7 cm × 25.4 cm
37.9 cm × 24.9 cm
The David Collection, Copenhagen

'This is quite a life to my liking. I am deep in Politics and War. The country is beautiful, and the climate superior to anything I ever saw.' The words are those of William Fraser, from a letter written by him to a relation back home in Scotland. He does not mention, however, that he was also 'deep in painting'. Today his name is inextricably associated with a great album of paintings and sketches—among the finest work of its kind—done for him and his older brother, James, by Indian painters who were shared between the two and Colonel James Skinner of the famous Skinner's Horse.

Before he left Scotland at the age of eighteen, William had been cautioned by his mother to stay away from 'the dissipation and corruption' of India, so as not to lay 'a foundation for future remorse and misery'. Her worries turned out to be unfounded—her son immersed himself in India in a very different way. He learnt Indian languages, from Persian to Bengali, set about obtaining a 'knowledge of Eastern manners and literature', was keen on 'a personal intercourse with natives of all denominations and castes' with a view 'to acquire idiom, dialect, manner, characters, prejudice, religion, internal arrangement, ancient hereditary habits and distinguishing characteristics'. These commissioned studies of the people amidst whom he lived and with whom he worked are part of this earnest desire to learn more about India.

The two Frasers, William and James, have, sadly, not left much by way of information about the Indian artists who worked for them and for

Colonel Skinner. The name of Ghulam Ali Khan of Delhi surfaces, but only briefly. However, they did help bring into being an extraordinary gallery of characters. Anyone could be a subject—a 'munshi', a 'deewan', a 'zumeendar', a 'chuprassee'. There are studies of 'Oojala jath of Bulluh vill(age), district Kurnal' and 'Ghureeb of Baanuh Lakhoo district Soneeput'; of 'Beeroo, a goorung of Goorkha' and 'Koolub-u-Deen, Chukatta Mohgul, native of Sirhind'. In the correspondence between the two brothers, there is mention of 'a Portfolio of native Drawings, some old and valuable as being illustrative of native costume and feature groups of Goorkhas, Sikhs, Patans, and Affghans, Bhuttees, Mewattees, Jats, and Googers'.

Among the most telling, and in a sense, most moving, of these studies are these two images of one man, named Kala. Some documentation has come down about him. He was one of the favoured soldiers in Colonel Skinner's regiment but he also appears to have served as an orderly to the Fraser brothers, a duty in the course of which he had, showing extraordinary courage, saved William's life by taking on an attacking tiger and cutting it down with his sword. The event took place in 1810, according to a note, and five or six years later, William had his artist make a portrait of Kala, based on his description.

So here Kala stands, bare of body except for a brief dhoti round his loins, feet slightly apart, right arm stretched and in his hand a bared sword. In the other hand is a scabbard and belt. Kala—almost certainly a nickname on account of his dark complexion; his real name was 'Dhurum Chund'—as he appears here, is a picture of fierce self-awareness. He is filled with energy and confidence, and there lurks a determined expression on his unkempt, bearded face. The event this study refers to might have taken place five years earlier, but the look on the face, and the stance, both brilliantly captured, suggest that he has just emerged from that fierce encounter with the wild beast.

Interestingly, however, Kala is portrayed in another guise—as a uniformed sepoy of Skinner's Horse, one of the Colonel's 'Yellow Boys'. Here he stands, in the scholar Rosemary Crill's description, dressed in 'a black jacket with red frogging and a tall shako, and wearing a red and saffron cummerbund, but without the yellow surcoat'. His bearing has the same erect self-assurance that one saw in the other portrait, his eyes the same expression. But there is also a sense of discipline—enforced by the splendid uniform—so far removed from the air of wild, untamed nature that marks the other portrait.

Mildred Archer is right when she says that 'technically these drawings—[Kala's obviously included]—surpass all other known Company pictures'. But they are more than that, for they seem to be only a hair's breadth away from providing us with an understanding of these men's true character.

———————

There are no substantive accounts of the painters who worked for the Fraser brothers or for Colonel Skinner. Some names appear tangentially—Lallji and Hulas, for instance—but one wishes there were more. Two manuscripts that were prepared for Skinner—the Tashrih al-Aqwam *(an account of the origins and occupations of some of the sects, castes and tribes of India) written at Hansi in 1825 with 110 miniatures, and the* Tazkirat-al Umara *(historical notices of some princely families of Rajasthan and the Punjab) written in 1830, and illustrated with thirty-eight portraits—are known, but the names of the artists are not.*

MAHARAJA NARINDER SINGH OF PATIALA IN PROCESSION

Isolated folio
Opaque watercolour and gold on paper
Punjab, Patiala; c. 1850
70.5 cm × 89 cm
Sheesh Mahal Museum, Patiala

One could easily get lost in all the glitter that saturates the eye on this page. But then we would miss the point that the painter and/or the patron sets out to make here. The maharaja whom we see here—Narinder Singh (ruled 1842–62), one of the most notable of the rulers who sat on the throne of Patiala—presided over a resplendent court and surrounded himself with all pomp and circumstance. Durbars, processions, parades seem to have been a routine.

Here, however, in this uncommon painting—truly large for a miniature—what one sees is not the procession *of* the maharaja, but the maharaja *in* procession. An enormous, dense phalanx of men—riders on horseback, accoutred soldiers, footmen in neat European-style uniforms—moves in slow, measured steps from right to left, keeping pace with a group of magnificently decorated elephants ridden by princes and men of rank.

The dark, smoky forms of the elephants, barely relieved by gold-worked caparison, rise like a cloud till the eye reaches the pre-eminent elephant, supporting a scalloped howdah in which appears the figure of the maharaja himself—nimbate, grave and dignified, and seemingly oblivious of the panoply of power that surrounds him. A rank of men wearing blazing-red turbans walks very close to the royal mount, the most trusted royal protectors keeping a vigilant eye on a virtual forest of vertically held lances. Insignia of royalty held aloft by another group of unseen soldiers creates one more

shield for the ruler. The entourage is extremely detailed: the serried ranks, the individuated faces of men in the crowd, the glitter of the uniforms, the minutiae of weapons and saddles and fly whisks. The procession, though, is not the maharaja's. For here he is a follower.

Well ahead of him and his immediate companions on elephant back—among them his brother, the Kunwar Sahib—is yet another file of elephants. On the back of one of these, also under a domed howdah, as if riding in state, is the sacred scripture, the Guru Granth Sahib, neatly covered with a cloth, a devout attendant waving a *chauri*—fly whisk over it.

It is the Holy Book that is being taken around: *this* is the master, then, that the maharaja is following. The painter wishes us to see that despite all the panoply of regalia, the ruler too is a devotee. The point made is sharp and the impact stunning.

There is much else to divert the eye in this exquisitely crafted and thoughtful painting: the walled city in the distance; the file of men along a ridge, some

of them with falcons on their wrists; the range of carriages that move along—
elegantly carved state chairs and horse-driven phaetons and palanquins
borne on shoulders. Equally finely articulated are the characters of the men
who form the maharaja's immediate entourage. Almost certainly, many of
the persons one sees here could have been identified at sight by those who
knew them, for each one of them is closely studied. The portraits were not
only of men of rank but even of the lesser persons, reminding one of the
studies of common men that one knows were done in such large numbers
at Patiala.

---

*We do not know the name of the painter, but almost certainly it is in the hand of
someone who owed allegiance to the Jaipur–Alwar style while being aware
of the work of the Pahari painters who were also active at Patiala. It is of
interest to recall that a great many craftsmen whose descendants still work in
Patiala actually came from Alwar and nearby areas in Rajasthan, just south of
the Punjab. The studies of common characters—pandits and peons, peasants and
small shopkeepers, and the like—that the Patiala collections were rich in, often
carry identifying inscriptions, something that makes them singularly valuable.*

PORTRAIT OF A PRIESTLY FIGURE

Isolated folio
Opaque watercolour on paper
Rajasthan, from Nathdwara, by Ghasiram; c. 1910
24 cm × 17 cm
Private Collection

Somewhere in the space between a photograph and a painting stands this striking image of a priestly figure, posing. The surprise is that it comes from one of the most conservative centres of painting in Rajasthan—Nathdwara, literally, 'Portal of the Lord', not far from Udaipur—where all art seemed to revolve around the intensely loved figure of Krishna as 'Shrinathji', and the traditions associated with his worship. At that place, and around it, there were sudden stirrings of change in the second half of the nineteenth century. A new artistic world was opening up for the burgeoning painter community there: photography had started coming in, and European prints had entered the awareness of many artists.

Substantively involved in the change that came in with them was a young painter, Ghasiram. The times were in many ways heady: an enlightened and generous patron of art, the Tilakayat Govardhanlalji, was the head priest of the flourishing establishment; from nearby Udaipur the ruler, Maharana Fateh Singh, had picked a gifted painter, Kundan Lal, and sent him to the Slade School of Art in London; some court painters began handling the camera, among them Mohan Lal; Raja Ravi Varma of Kerala who pioneered the style that is now named after him, was a guest of the Maharana's. It is in this milieu that the young Ghasiram grew up. Soon he was to become someone 'against whom all others of his period are inevitably measured', as Tryna Lyons, a scholar of Rajasthani painting, put it. Ghasiram's father, Hardev, was a painter, and he had thus grown up in the tradition. But gifted as he undoubtedly was, and very curious, Ghasiram was intrigued

by European imagery, seduced by the new art of photography, eager to experiment with new techniques, and ready to absorb.

Ghasiram's sketches, both in brush and pencil, are witness to his remarkable skills as a draughtsman, and in them he stayed for the most part with the tradition. With time he rose to become the *mukhia*—chief—of the painters' atelier attached to the great shrine at Nathdwara, and is credited with having painted an extensive series of close to a thousand leaves based on the *Bhagavata Purana*. But in his heart he also wanted to keep experimenting, both with photography and with a new style inspired by, or close to, it. A photograph of him holding in his hand an album of photographs has survived; he also began to dress on occasion in a European-style jacket and waistcoat, much like Kundan Lal, the 'England-returned' artist, used to do sometimes. And he began to sign his paintings, in English characters, the name at bottom-right varying from 'Hardev Ghasiram' to 'Chitrakara Ghasiram' to 'Painter Ghasiram, Nathdwara'.

The elegantly dressed person, all in pristine white—long kurta, dhoti, wrap-around shawl—whom we see in this portrait remains unidentified but, clearly, he belongs to the priestly class at Nathdwara, and Ghasiram—he has signed the portrait in English as 'H[ardev] Ghasiram, Nathdwara'—has made him pose in the same manner in which we see countless men posing in those early photographs from India: princely figures or members of the nobility. Against a plain blue wall, he stands barefoot—appropriate for a priestly figure—but all around him are the 'properties' of a studio picture: a European-style chair; a European-style table covered with cloth on which are placed two books, one lying flat, the other open; one wooden shelf at extreme left, and another at right, the latter featuring more books, piled up or arranged. Evidently, a gentleman interested in reading, perhaps even greatly learned. Considering other 'studio photographs' of its kind, all that is missing is a partially seen hanging curtain and a flower vase on the table.

Clearly, Ghasiram had a photographic image inmind, and the degree of observation he brings to his task as a painter is quite remarkable. The image is sympathetic and very human; the treatment of the face, the hands held against the stomach, lightly crossed, the feet, is singularly skilled, the modelling delicate and the line nearly perfect. The work does remind one very strongly of a photograph, but that all of it is painted by hand is amply clear.

Ghasiram was deeply admired during his own lifetime, both at Nathdwara and outside. And he is remembered—he died in 1931 at the age of sixty-two—with affection. Besides having created some fine paintings and given a different turn to the tradition of painting at Nathdwara, he did two things: one, he helped raise the social and economic status of traditional painters through being what he was; and, two, he lowered 'communal barriers' in that very rigidly organized society by taking and training apprentices from different castes.

A LADY OF RANK

Isolated folio
Opaque watercolour on paper
Delhi, 'Company' style; c. 1875
17.5 cm × 13.5 cm
Private Collection

The times had changed. European tastes and the advent of photography in India had brought about many transformations by the time the second half of the nineteenth century set in. The painter's view of his own vocation underwent a change, it seems, as much as the patron's way of seeing himself/herself. Portraiture was not unknown in Indian art—it was, in fact, not only valued but had touched great heights in some periods—but the portraits one begins to see from this point onward are of a different kind.

Photographers took portraits, most of them *en face*: princes posed for them as much as those who were appreciably lower in the social order. And then, sometimes, these photographs were coloured by hand, to simulate paintings. But things moved in another direction too, for portraits were also made by painters in simulation of photographs.

While portraits of women, certainly of high-born women—real, observed portraits as distinguished from idealized images—were virtually unknown earlier, they began to be painted now, though these women were not yet ready to pose for photographers. On the other hand, women who belonged to the world of performance—courtesans, nautch girls, acrobats, among them—posed readily for photographs, as much out of self-awareness as for advertising their wares or skills.

But only the affluent could afford paintings; and, quite suddenly, high-born women began to allow themselves to be seen by painters and to be portrayed,

many of them stepping out of the purdah for the first time. The chronology of these changes has not been fully documented, but one knows that this was happening—and the circle kept widening—from the second half of the nineteenth century onward.

This portrait, like many others of its kind, arises out of that context. The names of the lady and the painter are not known; nor is there any clear indication of the region from which this painting comes, although one can guess at Rajasthan or Haryana. Clearly, the setting the painter had in mind was what he had seen in so many photographs: a heavy curtain drawn theatrically to the side; globular glass lanterns housing candles hanging from the ceiling; a table on which rests a selection of small objects; sometimes a chair over which a shawl is draped; a couple of neatly bound books; and so on.

The lady here stands in that kind of setting: the obligatory curtain is a dark green; the table is covered with a pink cloth that hangs down to the carpeted floor; on the table is a small tilting mirror, a couple of hairbrushes, and a platter with a wine flask and a cup; the wall at the back is painted a greyish blue against which the three glass lanterns hanging from the ceiling stand out nicely; resting on a base nailed to the wall is a small hurricane lantern.

But what sets the image apart is the wonderful apparel that the young lady wears. It is a riot of colours and patterns: a beautifully embroidered short-sleeved *choli* that comes right down to the waist; a multicoloured skirt with a pattern of small embroidered squares; a light veil that partially covers the head and hangs in front covering the chest and a part of the skirt.

The young woman is decked in jewellery, around the neck, on the head, round the wrists and ankles. But she—neither a princess nor a courtesan but perhaps someone of some rank—is not weighed down by the finery. She looks straight ahead, boldly. There is no delicacy either in the features or in the expression, but there is clearly an air of authority. Our gaze too remains with her.

––––––––––

The thought of this painting coming either from some place in Rajasthan or in Haryana stems chiefly from the impression that the young woman's dress makes. Long waist-length cholis were also worn in Gujarat, but the whole ensemble resembles those commonly seen in the northern rather than in the western parts of India.

401

A GROUP OF COURTESANS

Opaque watercolour and gold on paper
Northern India, 'Company' style; first quarter of the ninetenth century
26 cm × 31.2 cm
San Diego Museum of Art, Edwin Binney Collection

Not many names of the artists who turned out such arresting work as this have survived. One knows about the late-Mughal, Company-school painters such as Ghulam Ali Khan, and Ghulam Murtaza Khan, a little even about Lallji, but few works are signed or clearly attributed. Who then painted this remarkable group of courtesans? The artist is possibly from Delhi—it may well be Ghulam Ali, for he had, as displayed in this painting, a deeply honest and evocative style, often moving in its humanity.

In this remarkable group of six women, there is an unfamiliar air of abandon and self-assurance, for they are very different from all those delicate princesses and *nayika*s that one sees in Indian paintings. Clearly, they are courtesans—*tawaif*s as they would be called—known to be women of pleasure, but of the class of singers and dancers that occupied a distinct, even high, place in the society of the times.

In Delhi and Lucknow, as much as in Hyderabad and Lahore, these are the kind of women who would have been known, perhaps even celebrated, by their individual names, and whose company would have been sought by a high-ranking nawab or *ra'is*. Umrao Jan Ada, a Lucknow courtesan and poetess of distinction, and subject of one of the few Urdu biographies that has survived, would have belonged to company such as this.

Here the painter, who must have known the world of these women well, brings in a whole establishment, allowing us to recognize rank and nature clearly. The cool white interior, with elegant niches set in walls and rolled-up split-bamboo screens, is not ostentatious in its appointments, but there are signs of comfort and elegance: the spotless white sheet that covers the entire floor, the embroidered cushions and bolsters, the large cloth fan that hangs from the ceiling, every fold and hook clearly articulated.

The two young women who occupy the centre of the painting, seductively dressed and free of all coyness, are clearly the central figures—perhaps the most sought after, and certainly commanding the greatest attention here. But the others, 'as usual in scanty attire', appear equally at ease. The tall young

woman who stands on the extreme right—she might well be Piari Jan, a *tawaif* who appears to have been the subject of more than one portrait— strikes an indolent pose, wearing the briefest of *cholis*, an ample *ghaghra*, hand almost insolently on hip.

The curly-haired, petulant-looking girl smoking the elaborate *huqqa*, and the one wearing a yellow skirt are a notch lower than the two main figures, but seem to have minds of their own. Keeping everyone company and serving them with the customary *paan* is the older woman occupying the left corner of the painting.

There is undoubted charm in the work, and considerable sophistication. Notice the studied sense of space, the delicate colouring, the careful distinction between skin complexions, the fine attention to detail in the elegant objects that lie about the scene—*huqqa* and *paandaan*s and *peekdaan*s and *supari*-boxes—and, above all, the air of ease about the figures.

One of the most interesting things about this work is that one sees in it women who are true to life, portrayed as observed by the painter, and not, as is all too often the case, as imagined or idealized, or belonging to given types.

This work is produced very close to the era of early photography in which, as far as women are concerned, it was the performers—dancing girls, singers, and the like—who posed for photographers, striking coquettish, seductive stances. That those photographs served as advertisements of themselves or cartes de visite is abundantly clear.

Passion

AN ELOPEMENT

Folio from a *Laur Chanda* manuscript
Pre-Mughal, Jainesque; middle of the fifteenth century
18.2 cm × 10.5 cm
Bharat Kala Bhavan, Varanasi

As night descends, a drama begins to unfold. The lover, Lorik—hero of Mulla Daud's celebrated Avadhi romance in verse, *Chandayana*, more popularly known as *Laur Chanda*—arrives at the palace of his beloved, Chanda, in the middle of the night. His entry is unnoticed, for the sleepy guard at the gate of the palace has almost dozed off. Lorik throws a rope for his lover waiting in the upper storey so she can slide down. Chanda advances eagerly to catch the end of the rope while a palace lady attempts in vain to stop her. Lorik stands below, looking above, his body tense.

There is lyricism in Mulla Daud's words, but even more so perhaps in the manner in which the unnamed painter renders them here. With a sense of remarkable freedom, he creates a world of his own in which there are no correspondences to reality. The royal palace is stripped down to a bare skeleton, with no walls, doors or windows. Only a flattened angular dome and slender pillars provide a hint of opulence.

The inky-blue night sky seems to have descended to the earth, consuming the background with countless stars. All the figures remain clearly etched in perfect light, although the lone hanging lamp tells the viewer that the day is long gone and night has fallen. With great forethought, some areas are left uncoloured, exposing the white sheet on which it is painted. Notice the space enclosed within the billowing veils of the two young women, or the outline of Chanda's long, trailing braid. The snaky rope that Lorik has thrown up remains suspended in the air on its own, defiantly, and decoratively, without having reached Chanda's hands.

The forms of the figures are all remarkably stylized. While the athletic-looking Lorik has the torso of a lion—broad chest, narrow waist—and holds his hands in studied gestures, Chanda and her companion are slim of build. Chanda's waist is so slender that it is almost at the point of disappearance. The eye travels to Chanda's uncommonly small breasts too, for the painter wishes us to notice that she is barely a woman.

The faces, seen in true profile, are sharply chiselled. But it is the eyes of all the four figures that compel attention. They are heavily elongated under those fine wavy lines that mark the eyebrows. While one eye seen in profile extends virtually to the ear, the other eye is suspended in the air, just outside the contours of the face. This points clearly to the work's 'Jain' ancestry where one sees a similar treatment. Though there is not much attention to the articulation of the hands and feet which remain awkwardly inelegant, one can see the remarkable sophistication of other aspects of this folio.

The dispersed manuscript to which this startlingly bold leaf belongs bears no date, does not have the name of any artist or scribe, and contains no mention of the place where it might have been produced. One is reduced therefore to making guesses, and in that state one wonders if it does not come from some place in Uttar Pradesh where Avadhi, the dialect of Hindi in which Laur Chanda *is composed, must have been understood. Stylistically, it bears the clear impress of the Jain or western Indian group of works, but one knows that those works did not all come from Gujarat or Rajasthan and were not all Jain in content.*

तमहिकिमनमथ्यब्धएद्गद्गुणदिद्गडइवरदाराबालाकिनयाकडाघलानाक
रच्चीनलीआराघपत्तालिदलंकांग्नकप्रद्धालविद्ध्रामयंतीसुतनुकराच्छीरराड
कर्मानिविसपिच्क्लुघाघाालएदक्धानचकटाद्वबालाग्गाख्या।।छाश्रीा।।छाश्रीाछ

सीमंतसीद्धरिद्धिद्धूरीअत्पूरीआमातीत्रचंगाराघछडीजडीश्रकिमालिकिजालिकि
फलिमलिग्गोद्धाश्याद्धापितद्धिकमितांब्जमध्याग्गोरंगारावचनातिलकग्गांकुर
तिकादरांद्धिघ्मदालसविघ्रमिमनग्द्धघ्रेंकांनसुखंपथिमयासदगछनीवा।।६७॥

LONGING AND UNION

Panel from the *Vasanta Vilasa* scroll
Pigments on cloth
Gujarat; 1451
1100 cm × 23.5 cm
Freer Gallery of Art, Washington, Smithsonian Institution

Clearly, the magic of spring—the season that 'lets itself loose / like a cunning and brazen courtesan / trying its best to sell its charm and splendour'—is not lost upon poets or painters. Kalidasa, the great fourth-century Sanskrit poet, evoked it as the season in which 'Fine woven silks dyed scarlet with mallow juice / swathe round hips; delicate silks saffron-dyed, / shining pale gold, veil the perfect orbs of breasts', and women 'dress with light-hearted elegance'. Several centuries later, a Gujarati poet described a beautiful woman in springtime thus: 'Her eyebrows seem like Manmatha's bow, the lovely woman's necklace the bowstring, her glance the arrow, which with its brilliance dazzles the whole world.'

The *Vasanta Vilasa*, a celebrated lyrical poem in the *phagu* genre—poetry, often sensuous and erotic, that centres on the beauties of the spring month of Phalguna in the Indian calendar—seems to have been composed in the middle of the fourteenth century. But the long cloth scroll—nearly eleven metres in length—now in the Freer Gallery, consisting of the entire text, possibly even expanded from the original, with brilliantly designed painted panels, was produced only in 1451, nearly a century later.

We know this from a colophon which appears at the bottom of the scroll, for it mentions not only the exact date but also that it was scripted in the Sultanate city of Ahmedabad by the scribe Ratnagara who considered himself an *acharya*, or teacher, for 'the delight of his patron', Shah Shri Chandrapala.

413

In many ways the scroll—apart from its uncommon length and its format—comes as a complete surprise. For the style in which it is painted is rooted in the 'Jain' tradition with which one ordinarily associates canonical or hieratical texts like the *Kalpasutra*, the *Kalakacharya Katha*, the *Parshvanatha Charita* and others. Even if the surprise is lessened a little when one remembers that many *phagu*s were written by Jain sadhus—the *Sthulibhadra Phagu*, the *Neminatha Phagu*, for instance, filled with sensual descriptions only to emphasize the need to eschew the bodily temptations that the spring season offers—no other poem of this genre appears to have been illustrated.

Here, however, the painter identifies himself completely with the erotic sentiments that the text and the season evoke. There is uncommon frankness in the rendering of some of the scenes—the pining, the long, passionate embraces, even couples locked with complete abandon in the sexual act—which take one instantly away from the world of *tirthankara*s and revered ascetics seated in meditation or mortifying their flesh. Clearly, the so-called 'Jain' style was not confined to Jain themes. A great many of the paintings in this scroll are now almost erased, making it difficult even to reconstruct the figures in them. But one can see almost everywhere that there is wonderful liveliness in the renderings.

The standard Jain or western Indian conventions are of course present and one recognizes the figural types, both of men and women—the lithe poses

and angular lines, the pert faces, the daringly shown further eye hanging in the air—but also the treatment of objects and motifs that almost frame the personae: the stylized trees, cushions and *chhatra*s floating about in the air, the textiles with their superb *hamsa* figures or scrolling vines, the wisps of clouds that peep

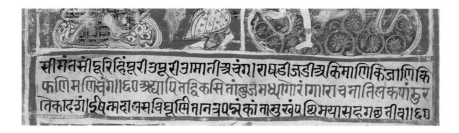

even into interiors, and so on. In the *Rajatarangini*, as Coomaraswamy once pointed out, there is a description of women's eyes whose corners 'appeared to play the part of the stem to the ruby-lotuses of their ear-ornaments'. One sees them here in this lush fifteenth-century scroll.

———————

The Vasanta Vilasa *scroll is a rarity in Indian painting. It was owned by the scholar Nanalal Chamanlal Mehta at one time but is now in the Freer Gallery of Art, Washington. Mehta and Norman Brown wrote in great detail about the work, evaluating, appraising, making sense of the relationship between the text and the paintings and even of the text itself, since it freely mixes Old Gujarati with standard Sanskrit. Nachiket Chanchani, who has studied the scroll with care, points out how Ratnagara, the scribe, takes on the role of the composer/creator of the* phagu *at places rather than remaining only a copyist. Sadly, both the original author of the poem and the painter of the scroll have remained unnamed.*

॥अद्यापितांविरहवह्नि
निपीडितांगीतन्वींकुरंगनयनांसुरतैकपात्रीं।नाना।
कृतमंडनमावहंतीं।
तांराजहंसगमनांसुद
तींस्मरामि॥१९
चंपा
१८

REMEMBERING THAT FAWN-EYED BEAUTY

Folio from a *Chaurapanchasika* manuscript
Opaque watercolour on paper
Possibly early Rajasthani or from the Mathura–Agra region; second quarter of the sixteenth century
17.5 cm × 22.5 cm
L.D. Museum of Indology, Ahmedabad, N.C. Mehta Collection

> Even now,
> I remember her,
> that fragile fawn-eyed girl,
> her body burning with fires of parted love,
> ready for my passion—
> a beauty moving like a wild goose,
> bringing me rich ornaments.

This is how the Sanskrit text inscribed on the top margin of the painting reads, leading one gently but surely into a highly sensuous world of word and image. The words are those of the eleventh-century Kashmiri poet Bilhana, and come from his celebrated classic, the *Chaurapanchasika*, literally, 'Fifty Stanzas of the Love Thief'.

According to the legend that has grown around this elegant poem, the poet was sentenced to death by the father of the princess Champavati, with whom he fell in love and whom he secretly used to visit. The daring of the poet and the impudence of his act deserved that punishment, in the raja's judgement. However, as the poet was being led to the gallows, on the way he composed these verses and recited them aloud one by one. The raja was so moved by the words, it is said, that he granted pardon to the poet. All was forgiven.

On Bilhana's verses are based the series of paintings—among the most inventive and the most challenging in Indian art—from which this folio comes. In many ways the *Chaurapanchasika* is spoken of as a seminal series, for it was the first among several other series or manuscripts painted in the same or closely related style: among them, the dispersed *Bhagavata Purana*; the *Aranyaka Parvan* in the Asiatic Society of Bombay; the *Devi Mahatmya* in the Himachal Pradesh State Museum, Shimla; the *Laur Chanda* series divided between Lahore and Chandigarh. One of these bears the date equivalent to 1516 CE, another 1552, and so on. The place of execution varies but is never securely established. Where this almost defiantly bold style originated remains a question.

Nothing in this richly coloured painting, or in so many others of this series or style, obeys ordinary laws. Flowers placed on cushions and bolsters stay suspended in the air; daytime scenes showing open lotus blossoms also have part of the background painted like a star-studded night sky; water cisterns are 'opened up' frontally for stylized basket-weave water to be seen in them. The figures are conceived with singular elan: women with impossibly large bosoms, ample hips, and waists so slim as to be on the point of disappearance. But everyone moves with lithe ease. Large lotus eyes, sharp noses, and small, pert mouths mark faces. The textiles are almost weightless: ends of diaphanous veils stay stretched in the air, the tassels attached to them failing to weigh them down. There is a profusion of jewellery with large black tassels attached, as we see in this painting, to wristlets, ends of plaits, anklets. But none of this jars—it all blends into a harmonious whole as one moves from one folio to the next.

Champavati, the princess whom Bilhana speaks of, that 'fragile fawn-eyed girl', moves here light-footedly, with the grace of a 'wild goose'—*raj hamsa* is the expression used in the Sanskrit text—from her decorated but forlorn chamber to reach a water cistern. It is to pluck those cooling lotuses perhaps, in her state of 'burning with fires of parted love'. But the painter wishes us especially to see the large black bumblebees—*bhramaras*—that are beginning to hover around her face in a circle as if unable to decide whether to stay close to her lotus face or to move towards the lotuses in the pond. Interestingly, there is no reference to these bumblebees in the text: the painter has clearly taken off, as he often does, entirely on his own, matching poetic flight with visual daring.

———————

Nothing is known about the painter of this series even though, speaking of the Chaurapanchasika *group of works, two names appear repeatedly on some* Bhagavata Purana *folios—Mitha and Nana—which have been interpreted by some scholars as those of the two painters involved. But this remains a question. In no other series does any name appear. Only a fragment of the* Chaurapanchasika *series has survived—eighteen folios in all—but one can be almost certain that originally there must have been fifty leaves, one folio for each stanza of Bilhana's poem.*

पंतीश्रवणेवत्सनाअंकुरकोकिळनादहृष्टा शामामधूरस्वात्नघूर्णेनेत्रागो
अका किळकोहृळन॥तरुणारुणसंकाशेदसनाचित्रकंचुका॥सहकारव
रूयीनःक्रीडंतीरूचसखवीयुला॥१५॥

THE MUSICAL MODE GAUDI RAGINI

Leaf from a *Ragamala* series
Opaque watercolour and gold on paper
Deccan, possibly Ahmednagar; last quarter of the sixteenth century
20.32 cm × 17.78 cm
Los Angeles County Museum of Art, Bequest of Edwin Binney

Ragamala poetry and paintings give expression in words and images to musical modes. The text inscribed on this painting, in two and a half lines of Sanskrit written in the Devanagari script, describes the Ragini Gaudi. She, it says, is a beautiful young maiden, dressed in a dazzling costume the colour of the rising sun. Her eyes are swimming from drinking wine, and she frolics with her companions in the grove of mangoes where the cuckoo sings a song of loneliness. This is not how Gaudi might be described in another text, but here, relying implicitly upon it, the painter envisions her standing in the centre of the page, touching her forehead with a single flower—reminiscent of someone?—surrounded by beautiful trees and flanked by two other maidens.

The one at left carries a *veena* that rests on her shoulder, and the other, at right, holds up a cup of wine. The dress that the Ragini wears, especially the skirt over which an ample *orhani*-veil is thrown and tied at the waist, does have the colour of the rising sun, a flamboyant orange; her companion wearing a yellow skirt is indeed holding a cup of wine, and there is some similarity between the leaves of the tree in the centre with those of the mango.

But here the correspondence with the text seems to end. Other trees take over the scene—an opulent palm with a thin, serrated trunk and dazzlingly rendered fronds stands at left; another bursting with exquisite flowers rises at right; one can see, too, trees that resemble a banyan and a pipal. No cuckoo bird is to be seen here.

It is the painter's flights of fancy and his departures from the text that really make the painting so striking. The three maidens, stately of build with narrow waists, long torsos and ample hips, stand—or are they floating?—on a wonderfully decorative bluish ground dotted with blades of grass limned in gold. It feels more like a luxuriant carpet than earth. The glimpse of sky at the top is in gold. But we see the artist's poetic imagination most in play in the way he has turned the rocky terrain at the bottom of the painting into soft, moulded, wine-coloured cloud-like shapes. What exactly are these, one wonders. That a peacock struts across them, gaze turned upwards as if to look at the Ragini and her lovely companions, assures one that this is firm ground, but what kind of ground?

Ragamala leaves from this group, with Sanskrit texts inscribed in the top register—no complete series has survived even though many are likely to have been painted—remain a subject of discussion among scholars,

because no one has been able to precisely date or place them. Most would agree that they are from the Deccan region, but where exactly from is the question. Opinions vary: from Ahmednagar to Bijapur to somewhere in the northern part of the Deccan, between Malwa and Aurangabad. Some similarities between the style in which they are painted and that of an early manuscript from Ahmednagar, the famous *Tarif-i Hussain Shahi*, can be seen. But these leaves display other stylistic elements too, some of them of extreme visual sophistication, that make it difficult to ascribe them with certainty to Ahmednagar.

———————

Some of the Deccani Ragamala *paintings, including this one and the Kamodi Ragini reproduced by Stella Kramrisch, appear to have belonged once to the royal collection of Bikaner that was housed in the Lallgarh Palace. Another leaf from this series, envisioning the Ragini Trivani—interestingly with very similar cloud-like formations at the bottom—is now in the collection of the Bharat Kala Bhavan, Varanasi.*

मार्हदानानब नुयलतालिभिनात जोबनिकानुरमोनारमञ्जकटेनररचयेने भुमिद्रो
निरम्या॥कारमीरेनुद्रयनरससुलिकु शीगानराले कोडजुनमदनफलयालिभिगितर्णहे
वसन्धा॥रमलुयमरेगनालिडेजर्वदलेन रत्न प्रकरर्चितोगोडेयगोतेतराशिराराहदये
तियलावाकनसकोयुककालियुवलिसिरिबसोंरसि्यमानुचरमनन्तलेलिलनिदिदजावन
तिमधुरतकालिकामसलूमसमे्ददकुलल्लतानायनयोनेसम्मतभूतिलन्तगुएलिला्मचाडिय
मानज्वारोजानाब्वामाउरारसिंयीघिनालतेनमैर्जोजिनकानक्ररणजुकर्वबानगेदियनरकममजाल॥६॥
म

RAGA VASANTA

Leaf from a *Ragamala* series
Opaque watercolour on paper
Deccan, possibly Ahmednagar; c. 1600
24.5 cm × 18.7 cm
National Museum, New Delhi

> A restlessness stirs in these illuminations. A flicker pervades them, is
> caught within the outlines of the figures and is also shot forth from
> there. On this sputtering level nets are cast by will itself, and the
> figures caught within their meshes so tightly that their traits conform
> with them. It is not their own will and they act by compulsion to such
> an extent that they have become the very shape of that compulsion.

The words are those of the great scholar Stella Kramrisch about a different
group of paintings from the Deccan—illustrations to the *Nujum-al Ulum*
manuscript.

But they also seem to catch the spirit of some of the early *Ragamala* paintings
from that region. There is an air of abandon in many of them, but also that
of restlessness. The joyous celebration one senses in these paintings perhaps
comes from the fact of their being rooted in music, a world, in the words of
the poet Zuhuri, 'saturated with melody'.

Unlike most paintings from the Deccan which carry inscriptions, these
Ragamala series feature long texts in Sanskrit, not in Persian or Dakhani.
At places the Raga, named and described at length in the Sanskrit text,
is translated into Persian, serving as a title for the painting. Sometimes the
essence of the mood that the Raga evokes is given in Persian too. But it is
clear that these series were made for patrons who knew and read Sanskrit,

who were perhaps outside the circle of patronage which the Sultans of the Deccan ordinarily offered.

The long text in Sanskrit—six lines, closely spaced and unattractively written—in the top register of this painting speaks of the 'glorious and irresistible season' of spring, with soft, warm textiles being discarded, forests waking up to the sounds of birds, young maidens whetting the minds of suitors with the coloured water they throw at them. But the verses do not identify the Raga to which they are related.

The word *vasanta* makes its appearance in the text which suggests that the Raga the painting depicts is Vasanta Raga. Yet the luxurious swing suggests that the painting might be of Raga Hindola (meaning swing), also associated with spring. In any case, the painting leads one to precisely those charms of the season—that fragrance in the air, and the beauty of the beloved—which one reads of in the text.

In the painting the two lovers sit in luxuriant ease, his leg lazily dangling from the throne-like swing, and she of the lissom body resting demurely in his lap, head slightly bent, one hand raised as if in acknowledgement. Or is she perhaps trying to protect her face?

Two leafy trees bend over them, leaning as if about to touch each other, while three maidens stand flanking the swing. The one on the left plays on her *veena* while the other two, at the other end of the swing, are sprinkling coloured water over the lovers with their *pichkari* jet-syringes. Close to them is a large golden bucket-like vessel in which stand two other *pichkari*s, ready to be used. There is an air of merriment in the maidens' uninhibited stances, one of them even bold enough to raise a leg high at a provocative angle.

Everything is blossoming: the flowering shrubs in the background, creepers twining around trees like lovers in embrace; birds winging their way against the gold in the sky. A neatly laid water channel with a fountain cistern in the centre of it flows quietly below, at once offering a soothing sound and serving as a source of water for the two Holi-playing maidens. Sadly, we cannot fully see the eager duck making its way to the water channel as much of it seems to have been rubbed off the page.

The apparel is as rich and exquisite. The lover on the swing is dressed in a beautifully patterned orange-red *jama* with pointed ends and a short turban with colours to match. The veils of the maidens, especially the one worn by the musician, are again delicate of pattern, and the skirt worn by one of the maidens at right is marked by broad, graceful stripes of different colours. The figural types, especially those of the maidens, are recognizably Deccani: broad-hipped, tall and well built, with relatively small heads. But the charm of this brilliantly conceived work transcends boundaries of region and style.

———————

This Ragamala *leaf is very close in composition to another of the Vasanta Raga in the Edwin Binney Collection in the San Diego Museum of Art. The Sanskrit text on that painting, a* dhyana *of the Raga, is identical to the one here, and is followed by the words 'Vasant Raga' in Persian characters, leaving one in little doubt that it is Vasanta and not Hindola that is the Raga treated of here. Unfortunately, it has not been possible so far to locate the source from which the text comes.*

भारागनट ॥ जालतुंमारीछुरलीनिकबजाऊं ॥ जेतीतांनुंमाावतकैपिया ॥ तितीटूंउपजाऊं ॥ तिहोरेत्रारस
॥ नहुपतिसुपीया ॥ अर्पनेतुमहि प रहिराऊं ॥ कुंसहिमानतीहोहयेबेविहो ॥ ईरूपर्याचालमिमनाऊं ॥ उंमजायदुरो
॥ कुंजकुटीमैं किंटपकरगहिल्याे ॥ घूंघुरघोलजधानप्यारीकौ ॥ गरैबाहुलगाऊं ॥ तुंराधधईंमाखोहि मासेबि
पेरीतगतनउपजाऊं ॥ तिहारिसीसपेंबैनीगूंथू ॥ हमसिरमुकुटधराऊं ॥ सरदासप्रभु हीतरराधका राक्षनदरैंने
कहाऊं ॥ ७ ॥

RADHA AND KRISHNA EXCHANGING ROLES

Folio from a *Sur Sagar* series
Opaque watercolour on light board with added coloured board borders
Rajasthan, Mewar; c. 1700–25
39.5 cm × 28.6 cm
National Gallery of Canada, Ottawa, Gift of Max Tanenbaum

There is a well-known saying about the relative esteem in which great poets writing in Hindi were held. It opens: '*Sur soor Tulasi sasi, udugan Kesavadasa . . .*'— meaning, among the poets, 'Sur (Surdas) is the sun, Tulasi (Tulasidas) is the moon, and Kesava (Keshavadasa) is like a star'. The rest, the saying continues, are like fireflies that give out but an occasional glow. The pre-eminence of Surdas (1474–1581?), blind poet of Mathura, passionate devotee of Krishna, is seldom questioned.

Among the stories told of his life is one which speaks of an encounter between the poet and Vallabhacharya, the great philosopher and founder of the Krishna-centred Vallabha *sampradaya* (religious tradition). As a simple singer of devotional songs, Surdas used to chant *bhajan*s in honour of Krishna, sitting each evening on the banks of the Yamuna. His moving, melodious music began to attract widespread notice, and Vallabhacharya himself once came to listen to him. When Surdas learnt that the great Vallabha was in the audience, he approached the great teacher with folded hands and asked if he had liked what he had heard. He had indeed, said Vallabha, but then asked Sur why he was constantly begging Krishna for his favours, beseeching Him to take him across the ocean of sorrows. 'Why do you not simply celebrate Krishna, sing of his glory: his beauty, his childhood, his loves, his *lila*?' 'But I am blind,' said Surdas; 'I have never "seen" him' is what he meant. At this, Vallabha whispered a mantra into the poet's ears, as a guru does, and said, 'Go, from now on you will be able to see him, but *only* him.'

From then on, the legend goes, Surdas's compositions took on another 'colour', as it were. And in *pada* after *pada* that he composed, he celebrated Krishna, and all his *lila*, his descriptions shot with uncommon vividness and intensity. It was as if he was actually *seeing* his *ishta* with his own eyes. The legend acquires a special poignancy in the context of painting. For in each series of *Sur Sagar* paintings—and there were more than one—Surdas is brought in: always present in some corner of the page, seated with legs tucked under, playing a pair of cymbals, singing. The suggestion clearly is that, blind as the great poet was, the painting represents how he must have envisioned Krishna and his glorious deeds.

Here, on this folio, we are left in no doubt, for in the top register the text of his *pada* is inscribed. The composition is in Raga Nata, and begins thus: '*Laal, tumhari murali nekey bajaaoon / jaun taan tum gaavat ho piay, tey hi taan banaaon . . .*' The words are Radha's, and she addresses Krishna: 'Let us exchange roles, my love. Whatever melody you are playing on your flute, let me strike it first.' And then the poem goes on to detail each reversal of role: 'Let me do your hair, and let me wear your peacock crown, with me wearing your jewellery, and you wearing mine,' she says. 'You turn into the proud and offended beloved, and let me sit, appeasingly, at your feet; you cover your face with a veil, as I did, and let me take the veil off you with love.' And so it goes on. The sport generally goes under the name *viparita rati*, meaning love with the roles reversed, quite beautifully stated in verse.

The unnamed Mewar painter visualizes the scene/s brilliantly. Beginning with the top-left, Krishna and Radha are in their normal *rupa*, so to speak: Krishna playing his flute, and Radha listening enraptured. But then, in vignette after vignette, the roles change: Krishna, instantly recognizable on account of his dark complexion, turns into a woman, and Radha takes on the role of her lover. Krishna has his hair done by Radha; they exchange clothes and jewellery; they walk about in the forest, she leading him; there is mock anger and appeasement; the lovers bend in an erotic embrace but the roles stay reversed. Finally, after the eye has travelled over the page and traced their movements, in the bottom register—Radha playing the flute and Krishna listening—they stand, unmoving in time, as it were, very close to where Surdas is seated, singing.

There are the usual visual conventions that one associates with Mewar painting at this point of time: rich and luscious groves of trees, spreading their leafy crowns like a peacock's plumage; the bold red ovoid shapes against which the figures are etched; lotuses blooming in ponds; cows grazing and calves frisking about. But here, the effect is overpowering. One can almost smell the fragrance, and hear the melodies fill the air.

———————

The induction of the author or poet in each painted folio based on his composition is known from other series—the poet Daud in the Laur Chanda *series, for instance. There is more than one series of* Sur Sagar *paintings, but so much is now dispersed. A leaf very close to the present one in theme and treatment is in the Los Angeles County Museum of Art, although the painter/s remain unknown. There is a somewhat faded folio of the* Sur Sagar *in the collection of the Gujari Mahal museum at Gwalior which seems to carry a name: possibly, Manohar. But the folio needs to be seen from close, not as it is now—framed in glass and displayed at an inconvenient height—before one can be certain of this reading.*

GAZING FONDLY INTO THE MIRROR

Isolated folio
Opaque watercolour and gold on paper
Rajasthan, from a Bikaner workshop, by Nathu; 1665
15.9 cm × 11.8 cm
San Diego Museum of Art, Edwin Binney Collection

On the verso of this painting is, surprisingly—surprising because for a painting from Bikaner, this is a rare occurrence—an inscription in Sanskrit. It is of one and a half lines and begins with the words: *'kachita sundari ekantasya . . .'* (a beauty [seated] by herself in a quiet corner, with her maids). The inscription does not quite do justice to the crisp elegance of this delicately coloured image.

On a terrace set in the midst of a garden this *sundari*—beautiful young woman—sits, attended upon by two maids. One of them, *chauri* in hand, stands behind the high-backed chair in which the aristocratic young woman sits, her lithe body strikingly alert; the other, her form inclined slightly forward, holds up a mirror in which the young woman is regarding herself. No exchange seems to take place; there is no indication of elaborate preparation on the 'princess's' part; no hint of a lover or hero approaching.

Who *is* she? Does she represent the musical mode Vilavala, which is often represented by the Ragini gazing at herself in a mirror while adjusting some piece of jewellery? A *nayika* waiting for her lover and doing a final check on her appearance? Or is the painter, based in the Rajasthani state of Bikaner, conjuring up the glamorous image of some distant beauty, inspired either by some Mughal painting or by accounts that must have trickled into the Rajput courts—in Rajasthan as much as in the Pahari region—of the beauty of the women in the imperial courts, and the luxury with which they surrounded themselves?

433

All that one can be sure of is that this is no true portrait, for portraits of high-born women were almost never painted. There is something vaguely Mughal or Deccani about the finish of the work, and the figures and their attire; in fact, even about the setting. The tall cap worn by the maid with the fly whisk; the princess's diaphanous *peshwaz*-gown—so gossamer-like that her nipples are clearly visible through it—that falls open just below the *choli* area, revealing delicate skin; even the high-backed chair are all indicators. The Sanskrit inscription offers no help for it simply states that this beauty is seated in a secluded place, alone. It is the style alone, not even the name of the painter, which tells us that the work is from a Bikaner workshop.

Longing fills the page. There is an umistakable expression of quiet eagerness on the face of the princess and in her stance: not leaning against the richly cushioned back of the chair but sitting up straight. Again, the manner in which she steadies the mirror with one hand and the fact that she has taken one foot out of a shoe are meant to be read with care. The tree under which she sits, laden with ripened mango fruits—symbols of passion—and the cypresses at the extreme right, suggestive of elegance and of lithe frames, are also not without meaning.

The soft expressions on the three faces are immediately striking. A clear mood is reflected in this work, aided by the remarkable refinement of workmanship. Notice, for instance, the minuteness with which the textiles, the garments, the foliage of the tree, the patterning on the carpet, even the studding of the arms and legs of the chair, are rendered. The textile patterns—those delicate sprigs of flowers one sees on the princess's *paijama*, or on the *phenta*-waistbands that the two maids wear—are strongly reminiscent of Shahjahani patterns. But then those royal 'Mughal' designs had travelled rather quickly to other courts, both in Rajasthan and in the Pahari region.

———————

Many ateliers flourished at Bikaner and names of great 'Usta' painters, all Muslims—Rukn-ud-din, Sahib Din/Shah Din, Qasim, among them—circulated widely in the region. It is clear, however, that by the middle of the seventeenth century, work at Bikaner had moved away from the earlier 'Rajput' manner and had begun to lean heavily towards the naturalistic Mughal style, reflecting the politics of the times and the close relationship that had developed over the years between the Rajput rulers of Bikaner and their Mughal overlords.

THE LONGINGS OF LOVE

Folio, possibly from a *nayika* series
Opaque watercolour and gold on paper
Rajasthan, from a Bundi workshop; c. 1770
24.3 cm × 15.8 cm
Harvard Art Museums/Arthur M. Sackler Museum

Clearly, the young lady is a *virahini*: in love but separated from her lover; 'burning in the fire of separation', as so many descriptions of this particular state express it in Sanskrit and Hindi rhetorical poetry. *Nayak*s and *nayikas*— 'heroes' and 'heroines'—their love in separation and their love in union: these are favourite themes in such works. And when painters turn to these works for inspiration, some of the most moving renderings are those that depict love in separation.

To take an example: when one sees a maiden rushing indoors as dark clouds gather in the sky and a strong wind begins to blow, one knows that she is unable to bear the sight, for everything reminds her of him who is not by her side. *'Dhurvaa hohi naa ali uthai dhuvaan dharani chahun kod / jaarat aavat jagat ko paavas pratham payod'*, the seventeenth-century poet Bihari says in one of his *doha*s in his *Satsai*. 'This is not the misty cloud of the rainy season,' the *nayika* says to herself, or as though to a confidante; 'this is the cloud of smoke that is rising from the fire of separation and, having consumed the rest of the world, it is advancing towards me now.' Delicately, a state of mind is brought to life both by the poet and the painter; an intense world of suggestion is opened up.

One does not know if this painting is based on a specific verse, but a closely related work has a distich in Hindi written on verso: *'Yaad aavai jab piyu ki, viraha uthai man jag / jyun chooney ki kaankari, jab chhirako tab aag'*. In translation: 'The moment I think of my lover, this desperate feeling of separation returns;

it is as if my heart were a clod of burnt lime: each time even a drop of water falls on it, it begins to sizzle, for there is nothing but heat locked inside.'

It is a hot night and the *nayika* here has chosen to cool herself by lying in the open, on a couch placed on a marble terrace. She has removed all clothing from the upper part of her body, save for a diaphanous veil which covers virtually nothing of her nakedness. In this state she lies, gazing at the full moon in the sky, lost in thoughts of her lover, yearning for him to be by her side. The cooling moonbeams offer no solace; nor does the sight of a pair of birds flying together far above her. A maid stands at the head of her couch, hands folded, body slightly bent forward as if waiting for a command. But the *nayika* keeps staring vacantly, her thoughts elsewhere.

There is great refinement in the rendering, so typical of the work that emanated from workshops active at Bundi in the eighteenth century. Piece by piece, the painter wants us to take in each detail. The bareness of the marble terrace; the sinuous disposition of the *nayika*'s body, not a straight line in sight; the manner in which she fingers a pearl on her necklace, as if keeping count of something; her eyes taking in the pair of birds, one eagerly

pursuing the other; the full moon now tarnished; the suggestive forms of the perfumed water containers by the side of the couch. Note, too, with what fineness the painter has rendered the *nayika*'s hair, the golden gathered ends of her transparent veil, the pulsating rhythms of her lower garment that somehow catch the agitation of her mind.

———————

It is difficult to determine whether this folio comes from a series: most likely it does. One can be certain, however, that it is a moment, or state of mind, that the painter is rendering here and not the portrait of a specific person. A nayika *is a* nayika, *standing for countless others of her kind. Almost certainly, some verse must have risen instantly to the mind of the discerning aesthete while holding this painting in his hand.*

DISTRAUGHT KRISHNA

Folio from a *Rasikapriya* series
Opaque watercolour and gold on paper
Pahari, from the workshop of Purkhu of Kangra; c. 1780
30 cm × 22 cm (outer)
28.5 cm × 18.5 cm (inner)
Private Collection

In sixteen sections—*prabhava*s is what they are called—and close to 400 verses, the poet Keshavadasa of Orchha created what is regarded as a classic in its genre: the *Rasikapriya*. The title is difficult to translate in one word, as is all of the Braj Bhasha text, for it is replete with words and expressions, similes and metaphors, which can only be savoured in their rich cultural context. One thing is certain though: the work, completed by Keshavadasa towards the very end of the sixteenth century for his patron, Rao Indrajit, has stayed as a benchmark in what is called *ritikala* poetry—poetry of the age of tradition. It is all about love: that of the *nayak* for the *nayika*, and hers for him.

Krishna becomes for the poet the ideal *nayak*, and Radha the archetypal beloved. Through them, and occasionally through a *sakhi*-friend, intense love is expressed, experienced, celebrated. The beauty of the *nayika*, from toes to tresses—*nakha-shikha* in classical terms—is described in the most elegant terms. The descriptions of the eight principal types of *nayika*s are of course followed by subcategories (see also pp. 457–58, 'To Set Out with Eagerness'). Love is expressed or remains discreetly hidden. Lovers' emotions—excitement, confusion, despair, embarrassment, stupor—are examined. Excuses for secret meetings are sought, invented, discovered. And all this in sonorous verses. Witty and lilting, sensuous and subtle, the *Rasikapriya* is a breviary of delights, to be savoured by the connoisseur of poetry as much as by the devotee of Krishna and Radha.

The fame and popularity of Keshavadasa's *Rasikapriya* came to be reflected in the fact that entire series of paintings were based on it, at court after court, soon after the work was completed. In what is called the 'popular Mughal style', an illustrated text was produced as early as the second quarter of the seventeenth century. Illustrated texts were also made at other centres—Malwa, Mewar, Bikaner, Bundi, Kota, among them. From the Pahari area, apart from isolated folios availing of the text, at least two extensive sets are known to have survived, the paintings all within oval frames with the spandrels in the corners decorated with elegant arabesque patterns. Above the speckled top margin a caption appears, often accompanied by a number, indicating the verse it illustrates. In this work, the caption says '*Shri Krishna ki prachhanna cheshta*', meaning the 'secret fluster of Krishna'. The verse it seeks to illustrate is number 22 in the fifth *prabhava* of the *Rasikapriya*.

It is a delightful vignette. Krishna is tying his yellow turban, but his gaze is not directed at the mirror that lies on the carpet before him: it has strayed to the beauty who sits framed in a window in the house facing his. The *sakhi* who stands by his side, holding a garland of flowers, speaks to him tartly. 'You are wandering in your thoughts,' she says, 'gazing at the beauty across at the window while thinking at the same time of the one with whom you sported earlier. You are remembering how you tickled her, sang to her, placed a garland round her neck. Was she the one with whom you spent the night? Is that why you yawn from time to time and are all distracted?' She does not get any answer, of course, for Krishna's wayward eyes and thoughts are all on the beauteous one he now gazes at.

It is all elegantly laid out by the painter. The frozen action of Krishna's hands as he tries to tie his turban; the gesture of wonder that the *sakhi* makes; the feigned disinterest in the eyes of the beauty across from Krishna's richly decorated home; the peacock that makes a sudden appearance in the tree; and the blossoming shrub: everything is brought in with clear intent. The colouring is discreet, and of course the slightly lost look on Krishna's face adds to the enchantment. The lilt of Keshavadasa's verse—'*chhori chhori baandhi paag, aaras saun aarsi lai*' (What ails you today that you keep tying and retying your turban?)—is all, or nearly all, there.

Purkhu of Kangra is associated with very colourful procession scenes, and with a series of somewhat dry portraits, but this work appears to pre-date him slightly and is possibly in the hand of a senior member of the same family. The other, closely related series of Rasikapriya *paintings, again from the Kangra region, but with broader, somewhat flattened oval frames, is also finely handled. There is little doubt that the Nainsukh family's style had begun to penetrate the work of members of other painters' families at this time.*

A GLIMPSE OF THE LOVED ONE

Folio possibly from a *Rasikapriya* series
Opaque watercolour and gold on paper
Rajasthan, from a Bundi workshop; mid-eighteenth century
24.1 cm × 15 cm
San Diego Museum of Art, Edwin Binney Collection

Almost certainly it is the first meeting of the eyes—*purva raga*—that the painter makes us a witness to here. The suggestion seems to be that the *nayika* has just finished her bath—the lotus pond at the bottom of the painting and the vessels lying on the floor close to the throne-like *chauki* indicate this—and is dressing up. She has first put on her *ghaghra*, but has not as yet donned her *choli*.

At that moment, a light wind begins to blow, displacing the curtain over a window of the house next door and revealing a young man who peers out. His face is reflected in the mirror that the *nayika* is looking into. Caught completely by surprise, and greatly flustered, she gathers her legs up and covers her bare torso as best as she can. But, while doing this, she keeps that mirror, and that reflected face, firmly within her gaze. Things, it would seem, are beginning to happen.

Situations such as this have been envisioned by poets, bards and painters again and again. Poets and painters add a new twist in each rendition to add to their audience's delight. In another painting from Mewar, for example, one sees a *nayika* who, having prepared herself to meet her lover with the help of her friends, goes out alone in her garden, waiting for him. Checking her appearance one last time in the mirror held in her hand, she suddenly sees reflected in it not just her face but that of the lover too. Without her noticing, he has slipped in from the back and now stands quietly behind her.

The two faces in the mirror seem to puzzle her greatly and the verse inscribed on that painting says: 'Have I gone mad? Is he so much in my thoughts that I am no longer able to see myself alone in the mirror?' These are lovers' games, or the poets' and the painters'. There are other enchanting renderings on the same theme—a bare-bodied *nayika* standing upon a *chauki* in her courtyard, reaching out for something, or looking at herself in a mirror while a *nayak* peers down at the scene from a nearby balcony.

In this painting we see another variation—the blowing of the wind of love, as it were, with the evocative cloud formations providing a firm indication of this. The *nayika*'s awkward but charming manner of sitting—all huddled up, knees pressing against her bare chest, the downward glance, the mixture of abashment and interest—tells its own story. But it is all subtly said. '*Woh*

ek din to meri kaayenaat hai jis mein,' an Urdu poet wrote, *'teri hayaaon sey uljha tha mera zauq-i nazar.'* (Can I ever forget that day—the day that means the world to me—when the eagerness of my eyes and your abashment met for the first time and became locked together forever?)

There is in this work that refinement and delicacy of feeling which one associates almost naturally with the ateliers of Bundi. The theme might be well worn, but the painter brings to it remarkable freshness. The hand is well practised but not tired. The great elegance of the forms—whether of the *nayika* in this tremulous moment or of her maid who holds the mirror for her to look into, the refined colouring, the crisp detail seen in the treatment of the hair or in the shading on the faces, the straight lines of the architecture offset by the lush vegetation at the back, the freedom with which those golden clouds are handled—everything makes for delightful viewing. There are no loud notes here, only whispers. The painter knew how to coin new and poetic phrases.

THE BOWER OF QUIET PASSION

Folio, possibly from a series based on Nagaridasa's poems
Opaque watercolour and gold on paper
Rajasthan, from a Kishangarh workshop, possibly in the hand of Nihal
Chand; c. 1750
22.9 cm × 31.8 cm
San Diego Museum of Art, Edwin Binney Collection

The lovers, the poet says—the text is inscribed at the back of the page—
spent the night in quiet rapture, lost to the world, apparently unaware of the
passage of time. In the morning, not finding them back in their homes, their
friends hastened to the bower only to find them still fast asleep. They had
to be woken up, but gently: one of the beauties took up her stringed *veena*,
another her *pakhawaj*-drum, and suddenly the sound of music filled the air.
Notes of the Raga Vibhasa reverberated in the forest; birds broke into song;
and the morning breeze, laden with the fragrance of lotuses, began gently
to blow.

This is all the verses say; the lovers are not named, the bower remains
unidentified, the companions' reason for hastening there on not finding the
lovers in their homes is not explained. But the poet knows nothing more
needs to be stated. For it should be clear to everyone that the lovers are none
other than Radha and Krishna; they have sneaked away from their village
homes to spend the night in the forest; their companions are concerned that
the village should not find out about their 'secret' love.

It is the quiet passion of the divine lovers that the poet celebrates in this
picture, and this he does with great, subtle care: the twosome, still peacefully
asleep on that cooling bed of lotus blossoms, eyes closed but arms lazily
draped around each other; the companion *sakhis* crowding each other in
the rich, dense forest; the lotus lake, astir with blossoms now that day has

dawned, and towards which one *sakhi* bends to pick a flower; the luxurious expanse of foliage rendered in exquisite shades of green. It is a romantic but imagined moment, and the painter captures it as elegantly as the poet whose verses are penned in nine lines of Hindi text at the back.

The painting has been attributed to Nihal Chand, the most celebrated of all Kishangarh painters, and the verses are by his chief patron, Sawant Singh, ruler of that state, a devout Krishna worshipper who wrote under the pen name of Nagaridasa ('Radha's slave'). *Nikunj lila*—'love play in the bower'— was a favourite theme of both the poet and the painter, it would seem. The word *nikunj* in itself carries undertones of secret passion, and in Sawant Singh's poetry it stands for an idyllic and private place, completely hidden

from the eyes of a prying world. Nihal Chand, perhaps an equally fervent devotee of Krishna, seems in his own fashion to peer into that *kunj* and delight in it. Here, the dreamlike setting, the fine detailing, the highly stylized figures—tall, slim frames, delicate skin, sharp features, long, dreamy eyes, flowing hair—all seem to point to the hand of this master painter, even if his name does not appear anywhere on it. The fact that the leaf bears the number '3' at the back suggests that the work might have belonged to a series celebrating the love of Radha and Krishna at different moments. Other images such as the two bearing garlands in their hands and standing in a forest bower, riding in a boat on a lake with *sakhi*s playing music, or

swimming towards each other—works attributed to Nihal Chand—come instantly to mind. The magic is common to all of them.

There are other versions of this painting, but they are clearly in emulation of it. There is also a drawing—a preliminary one?—closely related to this work, now in a private collection in Switzerland. The forest setting, the figures of the two lovers asleep on a couch of lotuses, the morning hour, are almost exactly the same as those in this finished painting. There is very little colour in the drawing, however: only the yellow of Krishna's garment and the pink tips of lotuses. And in the drawing, there is only one *sakhi*, named Lalita in the verses inscribed at the back, playing her *veena* to wake up the lovers.

———————

Apart from visualizing his royal patron's verses on Radha and Krishna, Nihal Chand (c. 1710–82) also painted portraits of rulers, a hunting scene and a fine portrait of a Shaivite sadhu. What accounts for his wide fame, however, is what is believed to be his finest creation: a highly stylized beauty with impossibly long, dreamy eyes, and fine chiselled features, who is often regarded as Radha.

THE BOAT OF LOVE

Isolated folio
Opaque watercolour and gold on paper
Rajasthan, Kishangarh, by Nihal Chand; c. 1735
40.6 cm × 30.5 cm
National Museum, New Delhi

If a gossamer-thin veil of almost unearthly romance is what we see covering virtually everything in this painting, it comes from at least two different sources, if not three. The inspiration appears to have come from the verses of the poet-king Sawant Singh, who was the ruler of Kishangarh, but whose heart was in far-off Vrindavan, the land where the object of his adoration, Krishna, had once sported. There, in Vrindavan, he was Nagaridasa, the pen name he took, meaning 'the humble servant of Radha'. 'The wind had pity on me and unveiled her face / And the lightning lit up her fair countenance,' he wrote once, not about Radha but about a young girl who, according to legend, he had fallen in love with and had become his muse: Bani Thani.

Bani Thani was not her real name but a reference to her delicate form: tall and svelte, and fair of complexion. There has been much difference of opinion about her role, even about whether a person like her existed at all, but her name comes up each time that one speaks of Kishangarh painting. That aquiline nose, the thrust-out chin, the thin lips, the high-arched eyebrows; but, above all, those lotus-bud-like eyes that sweep across the face: starting from near the ridge of the nose, they take an upward curve, and end up almost close to the ear. These marked the courtesan's face as much as Radha's whenever we see her in the paintings of this period from Kishangarh.

The other source to which the delicate, sensuous paintings of this kind can be traced is the painter Nihal Chand who more or less invented the delicately limbed, porcelain-faced female figures one encounters in these works. The painter is believed to have come from a family of standing, for his great-grandfather Surdhaj Mulraj is said to have served as a minister under a former ruler of Kishangarh, Man Singh. Not much more is known about Nihal Chand, except that he was a frequent visitor to his royal patron when he started living in Vrindavan; and that he sometimes signed his name— when he did—in the Persian script. The present painting is 'signed' across the top with *'aml-i Nihal Chand'*: in the hand of Nihal Chand.

It is not hard to tell the time of day during which the 'Boat of Love' is afloat. The sun is about to set, a band of brilliant orange-red marking the sky far in the distance even as darker streaks brush across the space above it, indicating the slow arrival of darkness. Small hilly mounds appear at the back, some structures glistening atop them even in this light. Towards the middle of the painting is a whole series of buildings in white marble and red sandstone: palaces, pavilions, places of worship from which wide flights of steps lead down to the lake.

On the lake, gliding through a whole bank of blooming lotuses, is a sleek boat with figures seated in it. The two divine lovers, Krishna and Radha, cutting delicate but majestic figures, sit facing right, their heads surrounded by nimbuses, while a group of young women—*sakhis*—station themselves in front of and behind them. The scene depicts *jala-vihar*: taking your leisure on the waters amidst quiet and stillness.

It is in the lower part of the painting, however, that a kind of drama unfolds. Screened by dense, almost forest-like foliage—dark-crowned trees and whole banks of elegant plantains—we see the lovers again, standing flanking a tree, Krishna holding up one arm, a garland dangling from his hand, while Radha, facing him, looks up at him: love in her eyes, one hand held up in wonder or as if about to speak. The twosome are all by themselves, thoughts of gentle passion, the joy of togetherness swirling in the air around them.

It is up to us to read the painting, the moments it contains, as we will. Does the action move from the bottom upwards: the lovers having met and spent time on their own away from everyone's eyes, and then moved up to enter the boat of love; or is it that the lovers have got off the boat at the end of the ride, and moved down to that fragrant grove to be by themselves? Who knows? Does it really matter?

———

The painter Nihal Chand enjoys, in the context of Kishangarh painting, an iconic status. Countless paintings are attributed to him, some on less-than-convincing grounds. But there is a stamp of unquestionable quality on works signed by him, or wherever the 'signatures' seem to be credible. There were others who preceded him at Kishangarh, and those who succeeded him. But in the eyes of connoisseurs, he stands alone, all by himself.

TO SET OUT WITH EAGERNESS
THE ABHISARIKA HEROINE

Folio from a *Rasamanjari* series
Opaque watercolour and gold on paper
Pahari, attributed to Kripal of Nurpur; c. 1660–70
23.2 cm × 32.4 cm (outer)
17.8 cm × 26.4 cm (inner)
Dogra Art Gallery, Jammu

The *Rasamanjari*—roughly, 'a bouquet of delights'—may have been written by the poet Bhanudatta in the fifteenth century in far-off Bihar, but to find its finest expression in visual form, the text had to travel a very long distance and across two centuries. It was in the Pahari region, and by the hands of a master painter who belonged to Nurpur, that the Sanskrit verses of the original text, with 'its abundant flow of honey', became as celebrated as the text had been.

Nearly each one of the 138 verses of the *Rasamanjari* is a celebration of love, finding its form in the *nayika*s and *nayak*s who experience it, explore its countless facets, and live its nuances, with an intensity that is rare. The theme is age-old. Even the broad classification of types into which the heroines are cast is not new, for as early a text as the 1500-year-old *Natyashastra* of Bharata speaks of them: the young women who wait with eagerness, prepare dainty beds, keep their tryst despite nights turning rough and stormy, or feel dejected, complain about their lovers setting off on journeys in the season of love, turn bitter and angry, are struck by remorse over having made unjust accusations, and so on.

Once heroines were described as falling only into eight principal categories—*ashta-nayika bheda*—but, over time, and certainly in the hands of a poet like Bhanudatta, the categories kept multiplying: heroines young or mature;

'one's own' or 'another's'; committed or uncertain; newly married or experienced in the arts of love, and so on. The stirrings of passion took on an incredible range of hues. Other poets, most of them writing in Hindi, were also to explore the theme, but Bhanudatta's text remained a classic. As Coomaraswamy observed: 'One is amazed at the combination of such intimate knowledge of the passions of body and soul with the will to codify and classify.'

Kripal, the painter, appears to have felt the passion that inhered in those verses and responded to them with an intensity that matched it. Knowing that it was not individuals but types who were being spoken of, he created an ideal form for the *nayika*: tall and lissom, large-eyed, slender-waisted, broad-hipped, covered elegantly from head to toe in finery and ornaments. She moves with the grace of a swan, bends like the willow, looks with eyes that move, dart,

458

play, send out signals, all in a trice, like an accomplished dancer. As to the *nayak*, he chose to cast him as Krishna—the eternal, archetypal lover.

However, while depicting the verses, Kripal seems to have been aware of the hazards of being too literal or realistic. Therefore, he kept evolving his paintings in the direction of abstraction: simplifying compositions without losing their richness, playing around with architectural details, placing them at startling angles, relying on symbols. The backgrounds change at will, raindrops fall in one part of the painting and not in the other, trees rise tall or sink low as he commands them. Somehow, in his hands all the elements work together: the bounding character of the line, the sumptuousness of decoration, forms impinging upon borders, the perilous tilt of beds, the garlands that lie curling on them. And, over all this, the pieces of beetle-wing cases that he uses to enrich jewellery, diadems, even textiles at times, cast an iridescent glow.

In this painting the young *nayika*, an *abhisarika*—of the type who 'belongs to another'—steps resolutely out of her home to meet her lover, even though the night has turned stormy and clouds loom threateningly in the sky. Like one possessed, she moves on, unmindful of all dangers. When her *sakhi* tries to argue with her, she looks back haughtily, saying that when one is eager, 'even the clouds are like the sun, the night as day, darkness as light, the forest as a home . . .'

And so the *nayika* presses on through the menacing darkness, towards the cluster of trees, artfully lowered at left to reveal the lover who sits there, waiting. What, unfortunately, is difficult to see in this reproduction is the tiny specks of beetle-wing cases which the painter has strewn all over the dark background behind the *nayika*. But when one moves the painting in one's hand even slightly, they jump to life, glowing like a myriad fireflies in the night. That small effort the viewer must make to discover all the magic that this painting has to offer.

'UNENDING PASSION'
THE RATIPRIYA HEROINE

Folio from the *Rasamanjari* series
Opaque watercolour and gold on paper
Pahari, attributed to Kripal of Nurpur; c. 1660–70
23.8 cm × 33.4 cm (outer)
19 cm × 27.3 cm (inner)
Dogra Art Gallery, Jammu

Aspects of love, the games lovers play, the range of emotions they go through, are all there in Bhanudatta's rich text, the *Rasamanjari*.

Here, the *nayika* is *ratipriya*—'one who is soaked in passions'—and the situation that the poet envisages has an enchanting twist to it. As the lovers lie together in 'never-ending passion' on a bed inside a richly decorated chamber, limbs entwined, eyes locked, passion unsatiated and still mounting, the *nayika* shows remarkable presence of mind and sly wit, for she is the 'mature one who delights in lovemaking'. The rites of love have gone on endlessly, and the lover has lost track of how far the night is gone. Suddenly, he becomes concerned about time and asks the *nayika* if dawn has broken. The *nayika*, afraid that their lovemaking will come to an end if he realizes that daybreak is indeed at hand—for strict codes prohibit lovemaking in daytime—quickly thinks up a ruse.

As the poet says:

> The swift-footed night flees as the lover eagerly consummates one love rite after another—now sucking her nether lip red like the bimba fruit, now caressing her bosom, now hugging with passion her neck, loosening her braid of hair and removing the last vestige of garments from her body. Suddenly he is curious to know if the

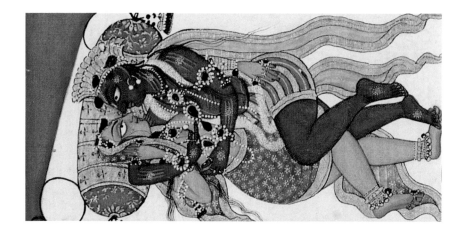

sun has arisen. At this the nayika, not wanting this lovemaking of theirs to end, swiftly covers the lotus buds that she had decked her ears with, using the end of her garments, lest their opening with the sunrise should betray to him the fact that the day has dawned.

In the light of what the poet describes, the eye quite obviously darts first towards the *nayika*'s gesture as she brings her hands to her ears to keep her lover from seeing the opening lotus buds. Her passion at least matches his, and she is as reluctant, if not more, to leave the bed of love.

Other things add to the mood: the swaying rhythm of the lovers' forms; the lamps with their dying flames seen in a last flicker, the birds that twitter in the branches of the trees outside, the little pool of water that has come alive with life at dawn, and the watchman at the gate outside stirring back to wakefulness as the night ends. The sky is a very light blue, with tiny specks like vanishing stars; and in the far-right corner the inconspicuous form of the dying crescent moon appears.

As in the rest of this visually stirring series, the painter has little use for the usual kind of perspective or rendering of depth. Only when absolutely necessary—as in the little grove at the extreme right of the page—does he betray an interest in receding planes and in establishing any kind of sense of distance. Objects are tilted, shifted about, enlarged or abbreviated, expanded or narrowed down, for his aim is to choose whatever view or scale is appropriate to the statement being made. The scarves, his and hers, as they trail their courses across the bed, the legs all but entwined, the tassels that seem to vibrate with movement, all have rhythms of their own. What truly interests the painter is the essence of the situation.

The colours that he plays with enhance the mood he has created: the brilliant saturated reds on the flat expanse of the wall, in the beloved's sari, as well as on one of the cushions on the bed; the greys and blues that define Krishna's form and the second bolster; the black openings of the doorways, the muted and sharp greens in the fringe of the bedcover and in the little outdoor area. Everything explodes with an intensity which echoes the passion of the lovers.

———————

Kripal's son, Devidasa, also painted a Rasamanjari *series which bears the date 1694–95 and was painted for a ruler of Basohli, Kripal Pal, just across the river Ravi from Nurpur. Devidasa stuck broadly with his father's vision of the text, but also made some changes, prominent among them the replacing of Krishna as the* nayak *with a mortal figure. Most engagingly, there was a third* Rasamanjari, *painted by Golu, son of Devidasa. It is as if each generation of this family of painters was keen on producing its own take on Bhanudatta's text.*

'AS DESIRE RISES'

Folio from a *Gita Govinda* series
Opaque watercolour and gold on paper
Pahari, by Manaku of Guler; 1730
20.5 cm × 30.7 cm (outer)
15.2 cm × 25.5 cm (inner)
Government Museum and Art Gallery, Chandigarh

> If remembering Hari enriches your heart,
> If his arts of seduction arouse you,
> Listen to Jayadeva's speech
> In these sweet soft lyrical songs.

These are among the opening words of the poet Jayadeva's classic work in Sanskrit, the *Gita Govinda*, 'Love Song of the Dark Lord'. Nearly eight hundred years have passed, and yet Jayadeva's words about Hari—Krishna by yet another of his many names—that are sweet, soft and lyrical, and filled with seduction, continue to enrich the heart of the devotee and the *rasika* (discerning aesthete) alike. They also pose a challenge to the painter who takes it upon himself to give them visual form. For in Jayadeva's words are hidden, as the art historian Barbara Miller observes, 'a wealth of meaning embedded in structurally intricate forms and concepts drawn from various leaves of Indian literary tradition'. One of the earliest painters to venture into that territory, at least in the Pahari region, and rise to the challenge was the greatly gifted Manaku, who came from the little principality of Guler.

The year was 1730. The young painter had assisted his father, Pandit Seu, who had been working on a series based on the Ramayana, and took upon himself the task of rendering, on a large and ambitious scale, the last part of the great epic, creating what is now known as the 'Siege of Lanka' series.

But, quite possibly, the first entirely independent, stand-alone, project he embarked upon was the painting of the *Gita Govinda* of which this is a folio.

Manaku must have been familiar with the story of Krishna and seen images of the deity at his own home, in the village and in the neighbourhood. But the Krishna of the *Gita Govinda* was different: neither static nor constant, deity and lover at the same time, a beguiling figure 'dark as a cloud', wearing his favourite yellow garment and a garland of wild flowers, richly bejewelled, decked in a crown topped by lotus buds and peacock feathers, his body anointed with caste marks, his eyes 'flirting like blue night lilies in the wind'. He would now 'dance to delight the heart of the *gopi*s', now seduce them, make passionate love, take Radha tenderly in his arms, or fall on the ground while pining away in separation from his beloved.

Manaku seems to have decided to render him essentially as Madhava, both 'honey-sweet' and a 'subduer of foes': a wayward but passionate lover in the context of Jayadeva's lyric poem but also as divinity itself. Or else why would he show him, from time to time, as four-armed even in the midst of his love play with the *gopi*s in this series?

When he finished his *Gita Govinda* series, the last folio was inscribed, not by him in his own hand but by someone else, a pandit perhaps, with a colophon in verse form. That colophon was once the subject of sharp, even acrid, controversy among scholars: the date in it, couched as a chronogram, was generally accepted: vs 1787, that is, 1730 CE. But whether Manaku, mentioned in the verse by name, was a painter or a patron, and whether Malini, also mentioned in the verse, was a princess or a metre, were things debated about with passion. It would seem now that there is wide acceptance of the fact that Manaku was indeed the painter of that great series. We also know from other sources that he was the son of Pandit Seu, and the elder brother of Nainsukh, the great and celebrated painter.

What concerns one, however, is the magic that Manaku wrought while working on this magnificent series. That he was a very sharp observer is clear, but here he set out to create a different world: idealized, lyrical, soaked in real passion but in so many ways other-worldly at the same time. Intense colours mark his work but they do not dominate, for the eye keeps landing upon Krishna and Radha and the *gopis* who flit in and out of his leaves as they do in Jayadeva's. His choice of beetle-wing cases, which he uses on ornaments and textiles with stunning effect, looks entirely appropriate to the theme at hand.

There is great precision in the way he draws; but with the same precision he plays around with forms, foliage in particular. Trees and leaves in his hand take on a life of their own, some of them suddenly shooting forth branches where one least expected them, sometimes taking on a partly golden aspect that sets off the rich, sage green of the rest of the page, or as if mirroring the presence of the dark body of Krishna and the fair golden form of Radha. The foliage serves now to shield the lovers from public gaze, now to separate episodes, now to merge with the lovers' bodies or to pick up their various hues. Above all, however, it is the effulgent vision that he created of Krishna and of Radha which works its magic upon the viewer.

One has to read his work with care, however, for one could get it wrong. Here, 'lovers meeting in darkness / embrace and kiss / and claw as desire rises / to dizzying heights of love'. But one needs to understand that it is the inconstancy of Krishna that the poet and the painter are speaking of. It is not the same damsel whom one sees three times in the mode of continuous narration: the one he embraces is different from the one he makes passionate love to, who again is different from the one he is about to kiss. A web is being woven, a story created. And surely some confidante of Radha's is going to report all this to her whose body continues to 'bristle with longing', whose 'breath will suck in words of confusion' and 'whose voice will crack in deep cold fear' of abandonment.

'ABASHED AT HER DELIGHT; OF HER DEEP JOY AFRAID'

Folio from a *Gita Govinda* series
Opaque watercolour and gold on paper
Pahari, by a member of the first generation after Nainsukh; c. 1775–80
15.2 cm × 25.1 cm
The Kronos Collections, New York

It may not be easy for everyone to absorb the combination of eroticism and devotion that Jayadeva's great lyric poem contains, especially considering that the work is regarded as almost sacred. But the reader of the work or the viewer of the paintings that visualize the *Gita Govinda* ignores almost as a matter of course the contradiction, and proceeds to read and see. When he does, sheer poetic delight can wash over him.

The lyric opens with the promise of a dramatic narrative, for the very first words of the opening stanza are placed in the mouth of Nanda, Krishna's foster-father, chief of the herdsmen of Vraja who is out in the fields, grazing cows along with others. Suddenly, seeing a storm brewing in the skies, he addresses Radha, who is often thought of as being a little older than the adolescent Krishna, and asks her to take Krishna home. 'Clouds thicken the sky,' he says; '*Tamala* trees darken the forest, / the night frightens him. / Radha, you take him home.' The painter of this magnificent series renders this verse in another leaf, showing Nanda issuing the orders and, as Radha and Krishna begin to walk homeward, depicting the approaching darkness of the night, the thickness of the forest behind them. But in this series of paintings, as in the poem, this is the last we see or hear of Nanda and his companions. Here, in this leaf, in any case, strange and beautiful things happen in the forest on the way. As the poet says: 'They leave at Nanda's order, / passing trees in thickets on the way, / until secret passions of Radha and Madhava / triumph on the Yamuna riverbank.'

This is how the painter visualizes the scene of 'the secret passion of Radha and Madhava' as it unfolds on the Yamuna riverbank. The lovers stand close to each other, Krishna throwing his left arm around Radha's shoulder and gently reaching out to touch her breasts with his right hand. Radha makes futile gestures, restraining his left hand, and pointing with her own right hand to the path they must take, following Nanda's orders. But there is no conviction in her resistance, for she turns back and gazes lovingly into Krishna's eyes, standing like an elegant dancer, left leg lightly crossed against the right, her toes touching the earth. Behind them, the dark forms of trees loom, the *tamala* grove dotted with a few palm trees. Further behind, almost invisibly and noiselessly, the river flows. At the further end of the river, small hills rise, and stars are already beginning to appear in the darkening night sky.

From a purely narrative point of view, the painter's decision to devote a whole folio to this quiet, tender moment, just before energetic, frenetic passion takes over, speaks of consummate intelligence. Soon, there is going to be talk of the *tamala* trees' 'fresh leaves absorbing strong scents of deer musk', of 'gleaming saffron flower pistils' turning into 'golden sceptres of love', of 'budding mango trees' trembling from 'the embrace of rising vines', 'yellow silk and wild flower garlands' and 'suggestive smiles'. The 'wondrous mystery of Krishna's play in Vrindavan forest' is going to be unveiled.

But, for the moment, there is quietude and a discreet expression of rising passion. The way in which the trees in the background are depicted—two of them with split trunks, another two in which the trunks come closer together, and those behind the two lovers embracing, one of them dark, the other lighter in colour—are not without meaning. The stillness of the night in the painting is strangely affecting, the rising trees tall and dark, the river in the background in quiet flow, the fronds of the tall palms motionless. Against this setting, the lovers' forms, exquisitely drawn, stand as if in a masque, dazzlingly lit.

The unfailing sense of colour, the incredibly fine, fluent line, the working out of details and atmospheric effects show up in folio after folio of this series. The relative looseness of brushwork in the rendering of the trees here is, however, unusual as is the flat, almost unobtrusive treatment of the river in the background. The same river is going to behave differently in other folios: now taking a zigzag route, now letting another stream merge with it, now breaking its banks and rising in spate. It is all so carefully, exquisitely worked out.

––––––––––

The first generation after Nainsukh—his four sons and two nephews—was responsible for some of the most brilliant series ever painted in India: this Gita Govinda, *a* Bhagavata Purana, *a* Ramayana, *a* Nala–Damayanti *series. Unfortunately, however, till now it has not been possible to isolate the hands of these gifted painters and attribute a series to one particular individual. But that it was this gifted group which created this collective effulgence is amply clear.*

THE PAVILION OF LOVE

Isolated folio
Opaque watercolour and gold on paper
Pahari, by a member of the first generation after Nainsukh; c. 1775
28.3 cm × 19.7 cm
National Museum, New Delhi

One cannot be certain whether this wonderfully delicate and sensitive folio comes from a series of paintings based on a text—the *Rasikapriya* of Keshavadasa, for instance, or the *Satsai* of Bihari—in which *shringara* (love) is the leitmotif, the predominant theme. This painting too is all about love. The painter leads us here to witness a moment of great tenderness while imparting to it at the same time an air of universality, of being beyond time. The setting for the tryst might be specific—'*phool mahal mein baithey dono, neel kamala aur peet chameli*', as one verse says: 'In the pavilion of flowers, we find the two sitting together: blue lotus and yellow jasmine.' But the reference clearly is neither to space nor to time. If the two here are Radha and Krishna, as they certainly are, their love is not of this world, the painter seems to be certain.

The reticence with which this is stated is remarkable. The lovers are completely naked, with not a stitch of clothing on them, and yet there is nothing carnal about the scene, no suggestion of lust. Radha did have, earlier, a thin veil wrapped around her body, perhaps, but it is now completely off her shimmering form: there is just the barest suggestion of it clinging as a diaphanous presence to Krishna's back. Krishna of course is without any clothing. All that can be seen on the two lovers is jewellery: pearl necklaces, gold wristlets or armlets, gold and pearl earrings. These the painter brings in with great daintiness.

As Krishna holds Radha in a light embrace, right hand supporting her head from the back while caressing her flowing hair, with his left he reaches out

473

to touch her breasts. And as he does that Radha, eyes slightly downcast, extends her right arm to the cushions behind her as if to steady herself for the quiet surges of passion. The way one leg of each of them, raised and bent at the knee, is disposed keeps one from seeing any more of their nudity. The eyes of the lovers are locked, but one can be certain that not a word is being spoken. Quietly, almost too quietly, one can see 'blue lotus and yellow jasmine' simply shine in a subdued, tremulous light.

The setting is almost other-worldly. A golden pavilion open on all sides—pillars studded with precious stones, a gold-and-scarlet cloth screen jauntily tied up and raised, the roof almost completely covered with flowering creepers and branches of flanking trees, mango at right and plantains at left—is set in the open, with a small flight of steps leading up to it. In the distance faint outlines of tree trunks can be seen and nearby a creeper wraps itself round the trunk of another tree. While the bed, also of gold, its sides decorated with an elegant design of sprigs of flowers, and furnished with beautifully patterned cushions, draws attention to itself on account of its refinement, the painter simply fills the page with the kind of suggestions that

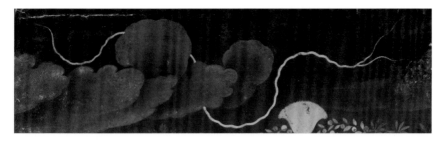

love poetry in India is so rich in. The season portrayed is that of the rains when irresistible longings rise in lovers' hearts and the sights of the season are meant to be delighted in to the full.

The clouds and lightning that fill the sky mark the rainy season, of course, but they are also clear references to the forms of the two lovers: he dark like the cloud, and she of fair complexion; he patient and 'deep', she impetuous and brilliant, like lightning. Up there, close to the sloping tiled roof of the pavilion, one can see a bird—the *chatak* of Indian poetry that has waited all year for drops of rain to fall—with its neck raised towards the skies. Also present, although barely visible because of the prevailing dark in the atmosphere, is a peacock, at extreme right between branches, its long neck rising, like that of the *chatak* bird, and looking up. Meanwhile, appropriate to the season of rains, the mango tree is lush with fruit in all its colours— saffron, orange, yellow, green.

There is no text that accompanies this work. But in this fragrant composition, all that needed to be said has been stated perfectly by the painter.

RE-ENACTING KRISHNA'S MARVELLOUS DEEDS

Folio from a *Bhagavata Purana* series
Opaque watercolour and gold on paper
Pahari, first generation after Nainsukh of Guler; c. 1780
27.7 cm × 35 cm
Museum Rietberg, Zürich, Barbara and Eberhard Fischer Loan

Five chapters in the Tenth Book of the *Bhagavata Purana*, called the *Rasa Panchadhyayi*, have passages that speak movingly of the love of the *gopi*s for Krishna. One of these passages is depicted in this exquisite work. It is a night of joyous celebration. Everyone is gathered together: the *gopi*s like a cluster of stars and Krishna as *chandra*, their moon. But suddenly, from their midst, Krishna disappears, leaving everyone bewildered. It is as though he wanted them to experience the pain of separation. The *gopi*s are disconsolate. Was this glorious night meant to end like this? The autumn moon that shed a cool light over everything when they were all together in this forest now burns everyone with its 'heat'. The trees no longer appear as lush or perfumed as they did when Krishna was with them. No one—the deer, the trees, the creepers—can give them a clue as to where Krishna has gone.

Then one of the *gopi*s comes up with an idea: while we wait for him, and to lessen the pain of his absence, why don't we emulate 'the divine sports of the lord', re-enact his deeds? And so the *gopi*s take on different roles as they re-enact Krishna killing Putana, his being tied to a mortar by his mother in chastisement, his lifting the Mount Govardhan, his subduing the serpent Kaliya, his magical flute-playing.

The painting appears at first glance to feature this group of beautiful women—each resembling the other—going about doing strange things. But as soon as one realizes that the entire scene is an enactment of Krishna's life, things begin to fall in place. With a dazzling leap, the painter—sadly, still unnamed, but surely a follower of Nainsukh's, a son or a nephew perhaps—lands us into the heart of the action.

It is all broken up into recognizable segments. Beginning from the left, in the upper arc, one sees a *gopi* act out Krishna's part as she bends forward and sucks at the breast of another, who raises her hand to her head as if dying while her breath is sucked away: surely Putana, the demoness. Watching all this is a group of *gopi*s who, like the women of Gokula, cannot bear the sight of the infant Krishna in this dire situation, while 'Yashoda' holds out her veil in a gesture of pleading, or as if she were removing the evil eye from her child. Close by, as one moves right, a *gopi* turns into the mortar to which 'Krishna' is tied with a cloth band, while 'Yashoda' stands holding a chastising rod in her hand. A *gopi* 'lifts' the Mount Govardhan—her *dupatta*, nothing else—on her raised hand while others seek protection. 'Krishna' plays his flute and the *gopi*s sing and dance and come crawling towards where he is, even as some others are dragged away by angry mothers-in-law. Close to the foot of the tree at bottom-right, two *gopi*s think they have seen on the ground the footprints that Krishna had left. But perhaps the most magnificent cameo among all these is the one where a *gopi* throws her blue garment edged with gold on the ground: it falls, taking the form of the many-hooded serpent, Kaliya, and upon it she stands and dances. She has turned into Krishna, who else?

The level of skill and refinement and imagination in the entire *Bhagavata Purana* series by this generation of painters from Nainsukh's family is remarkably high. But even in that brilliant group, this folio stands out and shines.

Sanskrit verses relating to this theme, from chapter thirteen of the Tenth Book of the Bhagavata Purana, *are inscribed at the back of this folio: there is thus no uncertainty about what the painter is visualizing here. The number '79' is also noted both in Devanagari and Persian numerals. This 'enactment' is seen in other* Bhagavata Purana *series as well, some from Rajasthan, and at least one in the pre-Mughal style. But none of them comes close to this one in feeling and refinement. An uncoloured drawing of this theme and composition is in the Victoria and Albert Museum, London.*

NALA ENTERS DAMAYANTI'S APARTMENTS

Folio from a *Nala–Damayanti* series
Opaque watercolour and gold on paper
Pahari, by a member of the first generation after Nainsukh; c. 1790
28.2 cm × 39.1 cm (outer)
22.6 cm × 33.5 cm (inner)
The Amar Mahal Museum, Jammu, Dr Karan Singh's Collection

The delicacy of feeling that one sees in series after series painted by members of the first generation after Nainsukh of Guler—the *Bhagavata Purana*, the *Gita Govinda*, the Ramayana, the *Satsai*, among them—one comes upon again in the rendering of the ancient love tale of Nala and Damayanti. The story, which occurs in various forms and versions in different texts including the Mahabharata, is well known: The handsome king of Nishadha, Nala, and the princess Damayanti of Vidarbha fell desperately in love without ever having met—it was a *hamsa* bird that was the messenger of love, recounting their beauties to each other. Damayanti's father announced a *swayamvara* at which she could select her husband and all the princes, including four gods, descended from the heavens to take part in that ceremony. Finally the gods, knowing full well Nala's love for Damayanti, tricked him into undertaking the task of pleading their case with her.

While preparations for the *swayamvara* were on, and every male was in any case forbidden from approaching the women's inner apartments, the gods made it possible for Nala to gain access to them by granting him, temporarily, the boon of invisibility. Nala made bold and entered the apartments only to fail in his mission for the gods, for Damayanti would not hear of choosing anyone but Nala as her husband. The story goes on from here.

The early part of this tale of love and longing, and eventually of tribulations, is told sonorously and with relish in a twelfth-century Sanskrit classic, the

481

Naishadhacharita of Sriharsha, and it is this text that the painter/s of this series leaned on. For whatever reasons, the entire story could not be fully completed: it was brought up to a point—the very beginning of the *swayamvara* ceremony—in the form of paintings, forty-seven of them. The rest of the story was continued as drawings, some of the most refined in the entire range of Pahari art.

In this work the painter takes us, together with the invisible Nala, into the very heart of the women's apartments in Damayanti's palatial home. The text of this part of the narrative emphasizes Nala's noble character. The young prince, it says, was in his imagination already delivering the message of the gods to Damayanti when he was woken from his reverie by the shouts of the girls of the palace—they were frightened by his voice, coming as it was for them from an invisible source. On his part, entering the apartments, he saw a young woman who had 'uncovered her thighs to paint them, and jostled another startled maid who was passing by'. Then, 'seeing first the root of the arms of a girl who was binding her hair, then the breasts of another as she was painting them, and then the navel as her clothing got loose, he closed his eyes', apparently out of decency.

But for us the painting is remarkable for two reasons: for the exquisite skill with which the invisible form of Nala is drawn, and for the series of little vignettes of life in the women's apartments that are all brought together here. One cannot visualize a better way in which an invisible presence could have been rendered. In the most delicate manner possible, the painter draws just the outline of Nala's form so that even the viewer has to strain a little to detect it. But that done, it is not difficult to imagine the commotion inside the apartments at the touch of an unseen body or the hearing of a disembodied voice. In some ways the viewer, knowing the secret of Nala's invisibility, becomes identified with him and then sees and understands the startled reactions all around.

For the most part, normal activity goes on in the palace and, unmindful of the presence of the 'intruder', the maidens are seen whiling away time by playing a game of ball-throwing or adorning themselves or simply conversing. Some of the subjects are familiar: a young girl who is having her hair combed as she sees herself in a mirror; a maiden taking a bath in the courtyard; a girl rearranging her veil; another archly lifting her right arm and then flexing it at the elbow to play with her hair; a maid preparing *paan* for her mistress. But there are also here two details that one does not see often: a maid carrying a large dish covered with an embroidered coverlet, and another, sitting in the bottom-right-hand corner actually embroidering, a round box with a domed lid lying next to her, possibly containing skeins of silken threads. A 'Chamba *rumal*' in the making?

From the point of view of understanding processes, it is of interest that a complete set of 110 closely related preliminary brush drawings in sanguine compositions, quickly dashed off as if to work out later, were first made, covering the whole story that the Naishadhacharita *tells. However, on those drawings—all of them now in the National Museum in New Delhi—there are occasional notes in the margins, made either by a senior in the family or by a pandit familiar with the text, pointing out the changes that need to be carried out for getting the sense of the text right.*

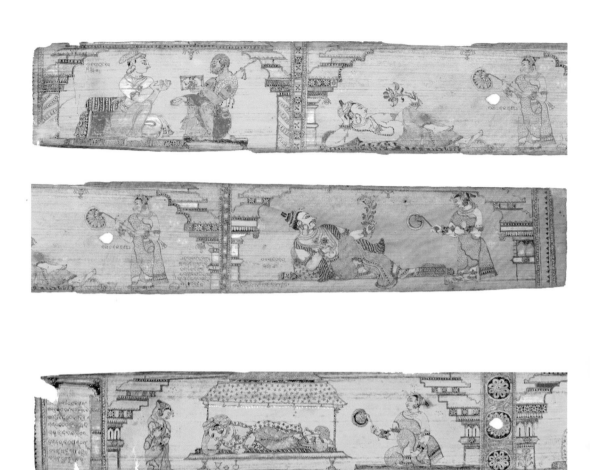

GLIMPSING THE BELOVED AND PINING FOR HER
PRINCES LONG FOR THE BEAUTEOUS LAVANYAVATI

Double-sided folio from a dispersed manuscript of the *Lavanyavati*
Opaque watercolour and lamp-black on palm-leaf
Eastern India, from an Orissa workshop; eighteenth century
4.9 cm × 41.1 cm
San Diego Museum of Art, Edwin Binney Collection

Astonishingly, one of the earliest techniques used for manuscript writing in India, going back to the tenth century if not earlier, continues to survive in the land till today: that of writing on palm-leaf with a stylus. Considering that it was in use long before paper was introduced in India, it might have stood in danger of being completely abandoned after paper became a common commodity in the land, and the preferred surface to write on. But palm-leaf manuscripts did not disappear, and continued to survive in small pockets. There, in those pockets it would seem, palm-leaf manuscripts were synonymous with learning, and learning with sacredness. Texts written and painted on palm-leaf were in the eyes of many surviving signs of a tradition in which texts were sacred. That is how from as late as the eighteenth century one keeps coming upon palm-leaf manuscripts, both written and illustrated, some of them of exquisite quality.

Lavanyavati is one of these illustrated manuscripts from Orissa, brilliantly conceived and executed, to have come down to us. The text is not sacred in itself: it is a romance, written by Upendra Bhanja, and still widely read and recited in the Orissan region. It tells the story of the love of Chandrabhanu, prince of Karnataka, and Lavanyavati, princess of the fabled land of Simhala. In the beginning things proceed as they often do in the early love tales of India: the hero or the heroine sees a painted portrait and falls passionately in love with its subject. In this work, a wandering sadhu shows the portrait of the beauteous Lavanyavati to Prince Chandrabhanu. The sadhu has been carrying the portrait about with him from court to court at the request of his patron, the king of Simhala. Predictably, the prince finds the beauty of the princess irresistible. But in this he is not alone, for every prince who sees her portrait is smitten.

This folio is from among the most sumptuous of illustrated Oriya manuscripts, one that was referred to as 'a touchstone for quality in Orissan palm-leaf illustration' by the scholar Joanna Williams. As the painter sets it up, in the panel at extreme left, one of the princes, elegantly dressed and seated in a formal court setting, is being shown the portrait by the sadhu. We are barely able to see the prince—the scale of the work being what it is—but, judging from the way he spreads his hands out in a gesture of amazement, the prince is visibly moved. In the adjacent panel, also in an architectural setting, complete with decorative columns and cornices, the ruling prince of Nepal is seen lazily reclining on the floor and lost in a reverie, large floral sprig in hand, but mind clearly wandering towards the vision of the princess that he has just seen. A woman attendant stands close by, fanning the prince. It is an image of luxury and opulence that the painter succeeds in creating with the barest of means. More princes figure in other segments of the folio: the painter makes each one look different, but they all appear in a distracted state, lost in thoughts of the enchanting Lavanyavati.

There is a languid elegance in the rendering. Everything—mood, setting, status—is established without crowding the page, the uncoloured ground and empty spaces adding to the effect of sparseness. At the same time, the detailing and the precision remain remarkable. The great variety of architectural ornamentation, the patterning on the textiles, the apparel of the wandering sadhu down to the *rudraksha* beads he wears, the colours and lushness of the floral sprigs, the majestic bearing of the female attendant—who stands as if her centre of gravity were different from that of the others—all convey an air of opulence and rising passion, and command instant respect for the skill of the painter.

———————

The 'terse assertions' that the painters of this, and similar, manuscripts are able to make puts this group of works in a class apart. A few other illustrated manuscripts too—for instance a Gita Govinda, *a* Rasika Haravali—*are marvels of compactness, and yet they capture every nuance that the poets of those works must have had in their minds. Between the two sides of this folio, there is no privileging of one over the other, the same level of feeling and skill being sustained throughout.*

TWO LOVERS

Folio from a *Ragamala* album
Pigments on cloth
Orissa; mid-nineteenth century
16 cm × 12 cm
Private Collection

Rhythms of the mind and body is what this painting is about. Two lovers sit on a low couch under a scalloped, cusped arch, he with legs crossed, naked to the waist, body arched, the fingers of one hand held in a gesture of admiration as he gazes at his beloved who sits in his lap, looking back at him. The lovers are profusely bejewelled. He wears a series of necklaces with pendants, armlets, bangles, large earrings, *kardhani*-belt, all of pure gold, it seems. His most unusual ornament is on his head where, attached to a narrow golden band that follows his high hairline, is a crown-like tiered piece of jewellery that ends in a sharply pointed finial. Streaming behind, and interwoven with his long plait of hair that snakes its way downward following the curve of his back, are strings of flowers of different colours, some of them woven into the hair on his head. The whole aspect is that of a dancer or a stage actor striking a studied stance.

The beloved, her entire body of golden hue, clad in a rich blue sari with a Sambalpuri-*ikat* end panel which flutters behind her, sits elegantly erect, one hand resting on her thigh. She too is bedecked with jewellery: choker-necklets, large circular earrings, armlets, broad bangles, a large nose-ring, though no crown-like object on her head. At the back of her head too are strings of flowers topped by something that looks like a large bun made up of blossoms. About both the figures there is an air of happy animation, a celebration of togetherness.

The eyes say it all too: hers with a *meenakshi*—fish-shaped—profile, and his

eye wide open, lotus-bud-like, filled with amazement at her beauty. So does the manner in which the bodies are disposed, his left hand going behind her so as to hold her in an embrace and then play at the same time with her lovely hair.

In another setting, this could have been a scene from Jayadeva's *Gita Govinda*—Radha and Krishna clinging to each other—but one knows that the panel is from a *Ragamala* series, illustrating musical modes. It is not an independent panel, for it forms part of an accordion-like album, if one can call it that, on which are featured twenty-eight panels—fourteen double-sided folios, one panel on each side—all within now slightly worn plain wooden covers. Every single panel 'illustrates' a Raga or a Ragini—musical modes—and some of them are even inscribed in a crude, late hand with captions, mostly in the Oriya script, identifying the mode: thus, Malava, Dhanashri,

Ramakari, Gujjari, Shavari, Gandhara, Karnata, Kakubha, Abhiri, Gaudi and the like.

The paintings have all been done not on paper but directly on very coarse cloth, using thick pigments which can be seen now as filled with cracks, in the technique closely resembling that used in Orissan *pata-chitra*s. Surprisingly, no pigment has suffered with time for they glow with the same intensity which must have been theirs when painted; all the damage that one sees on the album is in the form of abrasion, flaking. But nothing takes away from the elegant rhythms that invest each rendering. Here, women bend their lissom forms to pluck flowers, play with snakes emerging from lobed mounds, point towards gathering clouds, roam forests and groves, cling to their lovers, even as men gaze at them with eyes of passion, stand erect as if waiting for instructions, or sit sometimes in quiet meditation. What precise relationship these personifications bear to the musical modes themselves remains a teasing question, here as elsewhere, but the leaves breathe and pulsate with life.

There are 'iconographic uncertainties' in the renderings, as Joanna Williams pointed out in her study of this album, and one cannot be certain of the text that the painter here was following while envisioning these modes. It could perhaps be the *Sangita Damodara*, a text widely known in the Orissan region, but not everything sits squarely even then. The present panel is perhaps meant to illustrate Kodaba, a Raga not widely known. It is not unlikely that influences from other regions, especially neighbouring Andhra, had seeped into the Orissan *Ragamala* tradition. But the rhythms in these paintings, one can be certain, are all Orissan.

IN THE ROLE OF KRISHNA

Isolated folio
Opaque watercolour on paper
Rajasthan, from a Jaipur workshop, attributed to Sahib Ram; c. 1780–1800
69.2 cm × 47 cm
The Metropolitan Museum of Art, New York

Ananda Coomaraswamy once said of some Rajput drawings, 'This art . . . depends for its utterance on fundamental forms, upon significant relations of space and mass, upon whatever in life is universal, and it makes no study of transient expressions and individual peculiarities.' This is an observation of great value even if not applicable to all the work done at Rajput courts.

Coomaraswamy's immediate frame of reference was some drawings from Jaipur that he had acquired from descendants of the eighteenth-century painter Sahib Ram. These he saw as 'cartoons'—full-scale designs meant to be transferred to another surface like a wall or a tapestry—for two very large panels that hung in the palace library of the Maharaja of Jaipur. The panels depicted Radha and Krishna dancing, flanked by *gopis* singing, clapping or playing musical instruments.

Many of the drawings that Coomaraswamy had acquired, or had reproduced, were in fact pounces—delicately pricked along the lines with very tiny holes—from which traces for making copies could be obtained using extremely fine ash-dust. This drawing, however, is not a pounce though it is remarkably close to the one from the Coomaraswamy Collection in the Museum of Fine Arts at Boston.

The relationship of this and other drawings of the group to Jaipur is not hard to establish, for it was for the ruler of Jaipur—Maharaja Sawai Pratap Singh, many of whose portraits in a closely related hand have survived—that they appear to have been made. Sawai Pratap Singh was a man of great taste, and a Vaishnava by belief, who wrote poetry in Braj Bhasha–Hindi about the love of Radha and Krishna.

At his court, it is recorded, performances of the *rasalila*—the everlasting circular dance that Krishna danced with the *gopi*s on the full-moon night of the month of Karttika—were staged. The panels related to this drawing might well have provided the setting, paintings on the same theme surrounding the performers, perhaps even serving them as inspiration.

The figure that we see—unfortunately somewhat damaged at the edges and now only a fragment—was once described by Coomaraswamy as that of Krishna dancing. It is more than likely, however, as has recently been argued, that what we have here is in fact a woman dressed in Krishna's clothing, impersonating him. Such impersonations—playful exchanging of roles, imitating the Lord in his sudden absence, and so on—were not uncommon, being a part of the love play; and have been sung about by poets and rendered by painters who were devotees of the Vaishnava tradition (see p. 429, 'Radha and Krishna Exchanging Roles').

The distinctly rounded bust—the tightly worn *choli* barely able to contain the fullness of her breasts—the long hair snaking its way down along the temples, and the entire feminine attire, are all strongly suggestive of this being in fact a female figure. There is something utterly enticing about the face and the stance. The 'poetic curve' of the eye alone—reminding one, but not imitative of, the eye we see from Kishangarh where another ruler, Sawant Singh, wrote poetry revolving round the figures of Radha and Krishna (see p. 453, 'The Boat of Love')—is arresting in itself. It has been variously described as 'an iteration of the Indic lotus eye' and a 'gorgeous indication of a return to Sankritic aesthetic values'.

The look on the face, alternating between shyness and seduction, is soft, the slightly open mouth adding to the impact. Everything else—the superbly crafted turban with a pearl and emerald diadem topping it, a band of emeralds securing the turban at the lower end; rows and strings of glistening pearls; the gold-and-ruby necklace; the *karnaphul*-earrings; the feathery plume inclining downward—adds to the lustre of the image. As does, of course, the extended right arm, suggesting a movement in dance. The figure looks as if she is going to break into action, her arms gracefully moving, a cadenced step already taken.

What is central to drawings like this, the scholar Molly Aitken observes, 'is the unique balance . . . a perfect equality between Mughal sobriety and Rajput visual poetics'. Whatever the case, there is little doubt that at the Jaipur court, especially under Pratap Singh, there appears to have been a seamless blending of Mughal and Rajput elements. One look at an entry in the *roznamcha* diary kept at the Jaipur court would be enough to convince one of that: the private routine of the maharaja, with elaborate Hindu rituals of a devoted Vaishnava early in the morning, suddenly yielding ground, in the course of the same day, to courtly observances that seem to have been taken almost directly from the etiquette that marked the Mughal court.

Contemplation

INTIMATIONS OF MORTALITY

Leaf, possibly from an album
Opaque watercolour on paper
Mughal, Jahangir period, by Abu'l Hasan; c. 1618–20
11.1 cm × 6.5 cm
The Aga Khan Collection, Toronto

One can only repeat what has been said about this image in the essay at the beginning of this book. It is profoundly moving, its tone hushed and one almost falls silent looking at the lone, hesitantly moving figure who occupies the page. The man—an old pilgrim perhaps or, possibly, a mendicant who had seen better days—stands barefoot, leaning on a thin long staff as he struggles to move forward.

The body bears witness to the ravages of time: the bent back, the stooped shoulder, the snow-white beard, the lean, desiccated frame. But one can see, from the look in the eyes, that the mind is still keen and the bent of mind religious—he holds prominently a rosary of beads in his bony right hand and wears one round his neck. There are signs of indigence everywhere: the lower part of the body is bare, the feet are unshod, and the coarse apparel he wears consists mostly of a rough cloak used as a wrap, a folded shawl-like sheet thrown over the left shoulder, and an unadorned tightly bound turban.

Technically, the work is brilliant: one notices the roughness of the skin at the knees, the thinness of the fingers of the hands, the rendering of the beads in the rosary, each shrivelled and varying in size; above all, the virtuoso treatment of the face with its sage lines of age and experience.

The man remains unnamed, but did the painter know him? It is most unlikely that the painting was done for the subject, but then—accustomed as he must have been to royal commissions and grandiose themes—why did

Abu'l Hasan pick him? Was it simply a portrait that he was painting, or was he addressing a theme? Whatever the case, he seems here to embed into this isolated figure of an unknown man a universality of feeling.

Across centuries, and everywhere, poets have spoken of old age: the time when the meaning of things begins dimly to unfold, when the hollowness of it all makes itself manifest. For the man of God, there comes a time when one has to sit out and wait with patience and dignity, with submission and resignation rather than regret or defiance, for as the great Kabir said, this edifice of life is 'built on walls that are but sand and rests on pillars fickle as the wind'. Is this Abu'l Hasan's statement on the same theme, a painter's reference to intimations of mortality?

At the same time, as far as we are concerned, does the work resonate within us? Does it give rise to thoughts in our own minds, perhaps even remind us of parallels, of something we had once read and were moved by? Ali Sardar Ja'afri's long poem, *Mera Safar*—the 'Journey of Life'—perhaps? *'Phir ik din aisaa aayega / aankhon ke diye bujh jaayengey / haathon ke kamal kumhalaayengey'* (And

then the day will come / when the lamps of my eyes will grow dim / and the lotuses of my hand will begin to wilt). *'Aur barg-e zubaan sey nutq-o sadaa ki har titli ur jaayegi'* (And from the branch that is my tongue / all butterflies of speech and articulation will fly away / one by one). But then the poet goes on to write of returning to this earth, to another life, when he will be there to see 'seeds sprout in the soil / and little shoots begin to caress the surface of the earth / with their tiny fingers', opening his eyes to 'a world afresh / through each leaf, each bud that blossoms'. Is there something of this thought in Abu'l Hasan's painting: in the midst of the encircling gloom that the dark moss-green background represents, does that lone flowering plant close to the feet of the old pilgrim bring the promise of return, when he will see 'seeds sprout in the soil / and little shoots begin to caress the surface of the earth / with their tiny fingers'? One cannot know for certain, but the thought lingers in the mind.

———————

There is a faint inscription on the edge of the man's wrap which reads: 'amal-i Nadir-al Zaman, *the title with which Abu'l Hasan had been honoured by Jahangir. It reminds one of the similarly obscure placing of Abu'l Hasan's name in the painting 'The Emperor Jahangir Giving Audience'. One sees them as attributions rather than as signatures, for they are not in the hand of the painter, even if the painting is.*

FIVE HOLY MEN

Leaf from the St Petersburg Album
Opaque watercolour on paper
Mughal, Jahangir period, attributed to Govardhan; c. 1625–30
24.1 cm × 15.2 cm
Private Collection

Govardhan was the son of the painter Bhawani Das. That is why he is referred to in some inscriptions as *khanazad*, meaning 'born in the (royal) household', a painter in the second generation, in other words who, like his father, worked first in the Akbari atelier and then in that of his son, Jahangir.

Govardhan's early work might not have attracted much attention, for he finds no mention in Abu'l Fazl's select list of Akbari painters, but he must have kept growing in stature for, as time passed, he was apparently entrusted with a range of work—illustrations in the narrative mode in manuscripts like the *Akbarnama*, the *Dastan-i Masih*, the *Khamsa* of Mir Ali Shir Nawa'i; a book translated from the original Sanskrit into Persian on the philosophy and practice of yoga under the title *Bahr-i Hayat*, the 'Ocean of Immortality'; figures painted on the margins of pages of calligraphy; a few portraits.

The painter's own interest might, however, have been in painting images of men who were withdrawn, reclusive, keener on turning their sights inwards rather than looking at the world around them. Whether this came from a natural inclination or from his having worked on the 'yoga book' and thus becoming drawn towards that life cannot be known. But in his hand have survived some works that have been described as among the 'most emotionally penetrating' of all Mughal paintings.

The five *sannyasi*s whom we see in this remarkable painting remain unidentified. Each is a sharply observed portrait, but the figures bear no names, not even any sectarian marks on their foreheads which might have helped in identifying their persuasion. The smoke rising from the two piles of smouldering ashes, one at the front-right and the other at the back, suggest their being Shaivites—Shaiva *jogi*s often light small fires, or *dhuni*s as they are called, around themselves—but one cannot be certain. Could it be that these *sannyasi*s are in Srinagar in Kashmir? The shrine that one sees towards the right resembles the famous Shankaracharya shrine on a hilltop there. But one must now leave speculations such as these, and turn one's thoughts to the remarkable group that Govardhan has painted.

The five men here clearly form a 'group' even if in the painting no one is engaging with, not even looking at, anyone else. They are all virtually naked, only the barest of wraps covering them. All of them are ash-besmeared, their skins appearing an icy grey-blue. All of them, bar the one who lies with his back towards us, have long *jatas*—matted wild hair of sun-ripened brown colour—and the three whose faces we clearly see are immersed in their own thoughts, though not in meditation.

The *sannyasi* on the extreme left, with his beard reaching down to his navel and his face turned nearly full towards us, has a *mala*-rosary in his hand. The one directly under the tree sits on a deer skin, cross-legged. His matted hair is so long and rich as to form an almost shawl-like cover for his back, and he has allowed his nails to grow into curving claws. The oldest among these *sannyasi*s, a thin and bearded Methuselah-like figure, sits with eyes gazing beyond, his knees hunched up. One of the group of five lies stretched out at the back, face covered with an arm, apparently asleep. We can only see the back of the fifth. He is the youngest of the group, naked down to the thighs, with cropped, almost curly—and oddly—blonde hair, upper body slightly raised and lying on a bed of ashes.

A few objects are scattered about—dry sticks to keep the fire going, a ritual vessel, a conch shell. The atmosphere created by the painter is eloquent. An air of rich bareness pervades the scene.

———————

It is not difficult to see that European influences lurk somewhere in this painting. In fact, apart from the renaissance face of the old sannyasi, *the supine young figure has been tracked down to a specific European engraving. But Govardhan had so deeply absorbed and assimilated these influences that there is a completely Indian feeling in his work. This painting was once mounted in an imperial Persian album known as the St Petersburg Album which was later dispersed. On the reverse, as is common in rich albums such as these, is a page of calligraphy. The gold illumination on the blue borders on the verso bears the signature of Muhammad Hadi, and is dated* AH *1172, that is, 1758–89* CE.

A GATHERING OF SUFIS

Isolated folio
Opaque watercolour and gold on paper
Mughal; mid-seventeenth century
38 cm × 26.5 cm (outer)
35 cm × 24 cm (inner)
Private Collection

The Sufi masters, wrote Syed Hussain Nasr, 'are the princes of the spiritual world. In their hands the desert blooms into a garden, base metal is turned into gold, and the chaotic state of the soul is crystallized into a pattern of beauty reflecting the perfume of Unity (*al-tawhid*).'

We know that this painting is of an assembly of Sufis or Sheikhs. But what is the gathering for and where is it taking place? What *ahwal* or *maqamat*—the temporary states of consciousness or stations in Sufi philosophy—is the learned assembly experiencing? We can only guess. Since there are no musical instruments in sight, it is likely that the gathering is for a recitation of *anashid* or *naat*—hymns in praise of God, unaccompanied by musical instruments. What one can be sure of, however, is that the scene includes men here who have already entered the state of *wajd*, or ecstasy—'that bliss which is the opening for all inspirations and powers'.

In the group on the right, one can see an old bearded man throwing up his hands in the air in a state of inebriety at the top end. And in the same group, at the bottom, close to the finely crafted balustrade, another man has thrown his left arm up in the air while with the other he holds a younger man in embrace. One can see heads turning as if to share their appreciation with others, glances being exchanged, complete absorption on most faces. Many in the audience seem to be expressing delight, extending their hands in praise.

507

Clearly, it is a celebratory occasion. The royal-looking setting makes for a gorgeous spectacle—a great carpet spread under a gold-and-scarlet awning that reminds one of some Shahjahani paintings; a row of chandeliers suspended from its edges; golden candle stands and candles burning inside glass-cases placed all over the floor; a row of retainers standing at the foot of the raised platform, each bearing a tray of delicacies.

A sumptuous impression is made by all the men in both groups—are they from different Sufi orders, one might wonder?—each dressed with great refinement in long silken robes, plain or striped, covering their forms and elegantly tied turbans on their heads. The impression made, however, is one of noble gravity not of extravagance, and it comes not only from the finely groomed beards that they wear, but from the stances and the bearing of these sharply studied men.

It is striking, too, that there is no royal figure in sight in this *majlis*—one thinks of those fine paintings of Jahangir with Sufis and Sheikhs, of Dara Shukoh in conversation with men of learning. Here, everyone is of the same

rank; no one presides. But considering its quality, one presumes that the work must have been commissioned by some princely patron, and emanated from a royal atelier.

There are a number of paintings of Sufi saints from the Mughal period—men of learning and insight seated together, most often in a small circle with a little wooden *chauki* at its heart, on which some books are piled. Most often, these men are of different orders, belonging to different periods of time separated from each other not by years but centuries, and drawn from places that have nothing to do with each other. One can tell because often the men are named.

The intention of these paintings seems to be to pay homage to great men. This present work, however, does not seem to fall into that category. It has an air of immediacy, of being a record of a real occasion. What that occasion might have been eludes us though, for the work bears no inscription, and no figures are named.

Looming, too, over the scene, in the background, is a series of religious structures—marble domes and slim minarets glistening in moonlight—but they are merely elegant backdrop. None can be identified; they are not even meant to be specific. What are they hinting at then—timelessness? Other-worldliness?

MEDITATING DERVISH

Isolated folio
Opaque watercolour and gold on paper
Deccan, from a Bijapur workshop; c. 1650
16.5 cm × 12 cm
San Diego Museum of Art, Edwin Binney Collection

The eye travels first to the 'textile' in which this Sufi saint sits wrapped. That it is no real textile becomes clear on examination—it is, in fact, marbled paper. One does not know the exact term by which the technique was known in the Deccan—where it is seen used more often than anywhere else in India—but the paper was generally known here by the name of 'abri', from *'abr*, meaning cloud.

The technique of marbling is widely believed to have originated in the East; Turkey, where it is called 'ebru', is often thought of as its home. In Europe, marbled paper was referred to as 'Turkish paper', the Venetians having taken it there. In 1627, Lord Bacon described it in his *Sylva Sylvarum*:

> The Turks . . . have a pretty art of chamoletting of paper, which is not with us in use. They take divers oyled colours and put them severally (in drops) upon water; and stirre the water lightly, and then wet thin paper with it, and the paper will be waved, and veined, like chamolet or marble.

But attention must shift to the saintly figure who this work is about. The man depicted is a dervish, perhaps even a Sufi, seated in contemplation. There is a moving simplicity in the rendering. On uncoloured paper, and swiftly perhaps, the painter has portrayed the bearded man, cross-legged—or is he sitting huddled up, knees pressed against the chest?—head slightly inclined,

511

open hair streaming down his shoulders, hands seemingly joined but covered now by the simple 'marble' wrap.

The many-coloured swirling 'textile' made up by marbling is meant possibly to represent a faqir's patchwork wrap—a *gudri*—even if its folds here are accented with gold. A water bowl, suggestive possibly of the dervish's only possession, lies by his side. In the midst of all this simplicity, however, what catches the eye is the gentle expression on the face, reflecting the richness of his mind.

There is no inscription, not even a visual clue offered in the painting about the religion or following of this deeply reflective man. He is very likely a Muslim, like so many of the saintly figures portrayed by the painters of the Deccani Sultanates. But that is not a question that might have engaged the artist at all. What the emperor Jahangir recorded in his memoirs after meeting an ascetic comes to mind:

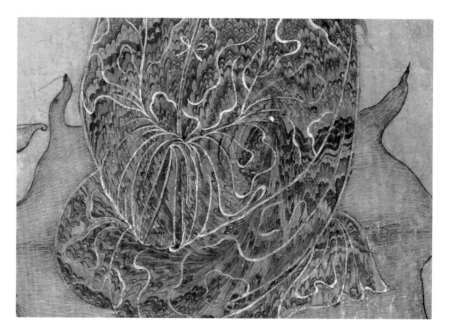

Luqman had a narrow hut
Like the hollow of a flute or the bosom of a harp
A rake put the question to him:
What is this house—two feet and a span?
Hotly and with tears the sage replied:
Ample for him who has to die.

The painter, one senses, has retained a deliberate sense of coarseness in the work—the unkempt state of the dervish, the manner in which the animal skin remains undefined and one end of it curls as if not properly cured, the fact that it is on a rough sheet of paper with uneven edges.

The emphasis is meant to be on the inward. There is about the figure an air of calm withdrawal and inner peace. Aware of this, the painter chooses the colours of the marbling with evident care, for they are soft and gentle, so as not to draw undue attention to themselves or to distract from the serenity of the figure. It is as if the artist had to quietly approach this man of God even in his painting.

The dervish remains, like so many other mystics and ascetics, unnamed. In the top-left corner there is an inscription identifying the figure as 'Hafiz Shirazi', but it is in a late hand and is clearly apocryphal.

A YOGINI

Leaf, possibly from a now dispersed album
Opaque watercolour on paper
Deccani; early seventeenth century
32 cm × 22.5 cm
Chester Beatty Library, Dublin

The word *yogini* is often somewhat loosely applied, for in different contexts it stands for different figures, though all of them are female. Literally, *yogini* is the feminine form of a *yogi*, a 'practitioner of yoga'; but she could be in the Buddhist world, from the world of Hindu Tantric practice or from ordinary life. Some of them are described as dedicated to the quiet pursuit of spiritual knowledge and mystical insight; others are ferocious semi-divines who assist in the processes of destruction and regeneration; still others are seen simply as casters of spells. The description of this mysterious creature thus extends from the 'devotional to the demure', from the 'passionate to the turbulent'.

In the context of the art of the Deccan, however, where one meets them more often than elsewhere, the term describes only such women as have left their homes and wander about, most often alone and most often carrying a stringed instrument. Occasionally, one might see them approaching a faqir or a *darwesh*, but there is no suggestion of permanent attachment, or of belonging to a group. They seem to be free spirits, presumably of religious inclination, but in essence free. One could perhaps call them *sannyasins* too, but these maidens, as *yoginis*, seem to have a different aura.

Often, even though there are signs of their having abandoned the world, with no maids or companions by them, they bear the aspect of princesses: an aloof bearing, finery on the body, aigrette in the hair. When we see one carrying a stringed instrument we wonder if she is strumming to herself, wandering about through hill and dale, making sad music. Could she be someone who was once in love but is now disconsolate and seeking to free herself from the snares of passion?

Folk songs often sing of women unrequited in love 'taking *jog*', turning to yoga in other words, and it is this state perhaps that the painters allude to when they envision *yoginis*. It is not easy to reconcile the outer and inner aspects but perhaps this is how the painter sees them—belonging to an aristocracy of the mind and hence their princess-like appearance.

The *yogini* in this image, one of the most famous *yoginis* in art, is truly intriguing. For she appears at once as an ascetic—ash-coloured skin, coarse hair tied in a topknot—and a siren. There are opposing moods, conflicting aspects in her svelte form. As Cary Welch put it, 'like many ascetics, she suffers worldliness'.

The golden *dupatta*, the elegantly cut *peshwaz* with pointed ends, the extraordinary profusion of jewellery on her form, the elaborate golden pin that holds her topknot together, all suggest that she comes from a princely setting. Even the palace-like structure far in the distance implies that she has turned away from all that was hers. But then the ash-besmeared body, the dreamy look in the eye take us in another direction. The pet mynah on her finger, who flirtatiously gazes at her ruby-red lips, perhaps alone knows something of the secret of her mysterious smile.

Adding to the enigma are elaborate poetic texts that surround the painting. Verse after verse speaks of the beauty of a maiden. Thus, for instance, 'the beloved's curly black hair, dishevelled by the morning breeze, is like hyacinths that perfume the air while, because tangled, it lends confusion'.

It is possible that the verses, taken from some poetic anthology and imported here, have nothing to do with the painting. Or do they hold a clue? For one of them reads: 'Those of spiritual insight dream of drinking from the fountain

of the beloved's lips; and the ailing heart of the lover is never without the (Persian) letters *alif* and *daal*, because the beloved's stature is straight as the former, her tresses curved like the latter.'

There are signs of artistic motifs having been drawn from a variety of sources in this superbly painted work: the rising swirling forms of the bare rocks at the back, contrasting with the lushness of the vegetation all around her. The numerous verses that appear on the surrounds and the borders of the painting are all written in a neat, although not a particularly elegant, hand in nastaliq *characters. They are full of descriptions of the beauty of the beloved and the distracted state in which it leaves the lover's mind.*

SAPTARISHI
THE SEVEN SAGES

Isolated folio
Opaque watercolour on paper
Pahari, from a Bandralta–Mankot workshop; c. 1700
21.1 cm × 20.7 cm (outer)
18.9 cm × 19 cm (inner)
Government Museum and Art Gallery, Chandigarh

This intriguing, visually exciting image takes one back in thought almost to Vedic times. For here, seated against a flat dark green background, one finds seven great sages, the Saptarishi, who find mention in age after age, in text after text: all assembled together, each doing his own thing—meditating, telling beads, performing yogic exercises, undergoing penance.

These men are seers, the embodiment of purity and sacredness, the mere mention of whose names elicits the greatest reverence. They were the holders and interpreters of eternal laws. To them the greatest of the land turned for counsel, the most powerful submitted. They were not all contemporaries, but it is as if by bringing them together in this manner, the painter was invoking their collective blessings. There was a time when it was believed that even thinking about them and concentrating on their names made one rise to a higher level of awareness. For they were all *manas putra*s—'mind-born sons'— of the creator, Brahma, himself.

It is of interest that even though the term '*saptarishi*' remains constant, the names of the sages keep changing from one *manvantara*—period of astronomical time within an aeon—to another. The Brahmanas may have one list, the Upanishads another; they figure in the *Yajurveda* as they do in the Mahabharata. The seven sages seen here are all identified through clear inscriptions in Takri characters. Starting from top-left, and moving clockwise, they are Vishwamitra, Jamadagni, Gautama, Vasishtha, Atri, Bharadwaj and Kashyapa. This list tallies exactly with the seven sages who are listed in two highly authoritative texts, the *Brihadaranyaka Upanishad* and the *Shatapatha Brahmana*.

Of course, these are not actual portraits of the sages: none exist. And when any of them is represented in a series of paintings, he is bound to look entirely different from how he appears in another series or manuscript. But though these are imagined, idealized renderings, the painter is very likely to have modelled his figures upon the recluses, *sannyasis*, *yogis* and the like whom he might have personally met or seen. There is clear indication of this in a 'portrait' of a *sannyasi*, inscribed with the name 'Prem Gir', which comes from the same collection and is in the same hand. The painter must have personally known or encountered him, and he is shown with the same long, deeply curving nails that the sage Gautama has in this painting.

None of this, however, takes away from the wonderful range of faces and stances that we see here, each painted with a rare intensity: Vishwamitra with his *jata* tied in a bun, seated on a deer skin, mouth covered with a *mukh-patti*; Jamadagni, seated cross-legged, head turned skyward almost as if frozen at that angle, telling upon a *mala* of prayer beads; Gautama, nearly naked, long-bearded, dark-complexioned, coarse thatches of hair marking the armpits, both hands, with long nails, raised above the head and locked; Vasishtha, young-looking, the only one in this group not sporting a beard, wearing a yellow garment round his loins, one hand firmly grasping a sacred vessel; Atri, dark-skinned, staring intensely ahead of himself, one hand in a *gomukh*-glove, evidently telling beads; Bharadwaj in a yogic *asana*, upside down with the weight of the body borne by his head and two hands resting on the ground; and the dark-skinned Kashyapa, seated cross-legged but naked, his middle covered by a leopard skin draped across the lap, eyes closed while applying *bhasma* sacred ash with one hand to his forehead. Each one of these singularly grave-looking, inwardly turned men is completely absorbed in what he is doing. In the centre of the circle that they form, a pile of ashes silently smoulders: the traditional *dhuni* of *yogi*s. It is a still, quietly affecting image.

How did the painter think of making it, one wonders? Was there an occasion? The only possible clue lurks in the three sheets of paper that the sage Vishwamitra holds in his hands or in those that lie by his side. On them, in the same Takri script, native to the hills, are inscribed a few lines, some of them repeated. In those, the name of a prince, 'Shri Mian Kailash Dev', occurs. In one sheet the blessings of Shiva, and in another the blessings of Hari are invoked upon him. Not much is known about Kailash Dev, except that he succeeded to the throne of Bandralta in c. 1715. The fact, however, that he is here referred to as a Mian—a cadet of the royal family—suggests that the work dates back to when he was still a prince. C. 1700 perhaps, then?

———————

The royal house of Bandralta, a very small principality in the neighbourhood of Jammu, and Mankot, an equally small principality very close to it, appear to have been served by the same family of painters, given the similarity in the style of the work done for the two houses. It is not unlikely that some members of the family worked at Bandralta and others at Mankot.

MAHARAO KISHOR SINGH OF KOTA CELEBRATING A RELIGIOUS FESTIVAL

Opaque watercolour and gold on paper
Rajasthan, from a Kota workshop; c. 1831
25 cm × 20.2 cm
Rao Madho Singh Trust Museum, Fort Kota

At Nathdwara—'Portal of the Lord'—that great centre of Krishna worship not far from Udaipur, as well as throughout Rajasthan and in extended areas of Gujarat, Krishna's *lila* is played out in a very special manner, for he continues to be celebrated, adored, invoked in the form of Shrinathji, the 'original' icon of the Vallabha *sampradaya*. Not everywhere does the Lord appear as if holding the Mount Govardhan aloft on his raised left arm, nor is his form—*svarupa*—rendered on the same scale. He can be seen as nearly life size but also as a small idol that does not fully span the palm of one's hand. He can be seen with two arms or four; he can be made in metal or stone or wood. But the memory always goes back to Nathdwara and, through it, to the Vraja region where Vallabhacharya discovered and installed the original image. Significantly, however, memory also travels to the series of rituals of Krishna worship that were established long ago by Vallabha's gifted and aesthetically inclined son, Vitthalnath. Everywhere, at temples affiliated to the *sampradaya*, it would seem, the same rich, cyclical, year-long series of festivals, fasts, performances, puja is observed.

Painting after painting shows priests and rulers standing, paying homage to the idol installed in their favourite temple or even within their own premises. But nowhere perhaps does one see a ruler as regularly, and in as devoted a light, as Maharao Kishor Singh of Kota. For he appears in Kota paintings looking so much like a priest of a temple—bare of upper body, clad only in a pristine white dhoti, head completely shaven, a long vertical *tilaka* on the forehead—that one would have a hard time identifying him as the ruler of a powerful state. From one image to the next, one sees him performing *arati*, assisting a priest, bringing offerings to place before the image of the Lord. The Maharao was soaked in devotion to Krishna—whether in the diminutive form of Brijnathji, to whom the entire state of Kota was dedicated, or of his personal idol, Brijrajji—and was close to one of the most famous priests who ever served the Lord at the parent shrine of Nathdwara, Dauji II.

The Maharao seems to have been well versed in all the rituals. There is an inscription on the top border of this painting, in a late hand in Devanagari characters. Translated, it says: 'The Prabodhini festival; 11th day of the bright half of (the month of) Karttika.' And here we see the Maharao performing the ritual associated with the great festival of Prabodhini: literally, 'awakening', recalling the end of four months of Vishnu's slumber. On that occasion, Sanskrit mantras are recited and conches are blown, even as a small rock, representing the Mount Govardhan which Krishna had once lifted to save his kinsmen from the wrath of Indra (see p. 197), is bathed in *panchamrita*, the 'five nectars', in a sequence: milk, yogurt, clarified butter, honey and sugar.

The Maharao crouches here at right—his rich jewellery setting him apart from the priest at left—pouring milk slowly from a conch shell held reverently in both hands, over the sacred, *shaligrama* (ammonite)-like, symbolic *shila* (rock). On the glistening marble floor, placed on pedestals or receptacles, lie objects used in the ritual: five earthen lamps in the four corners, flasks, *paan* boxes, Yamuna water in ewers covered with red cloth. But in the very centre of the painting, resting on a beautifully decorated *simhasana* (throne) is placed the sacred image of the Lord, sporting a peacock-feather crown, his two consorts flanking him. And over it, made with sugar-cane stalks tied at the top, a brilliantly arched canopy looms, following prescribed ritual.

At the back, occupying nearly two-fifths of the space on the page, rise three rectangles of solid colours, blues flanking orange: apparently textiles tightly stretched.

The visual impact that the painting makes is stunning, crisp lines all over the page, and rich colours setting off the light grey of the marble flooring, and the glistening white of the apparel worn by the Maharao and the assisting priest. But, in the final analysis, everything is subordinated to the feeling of utter devotion with which the painter is able to invest the painting: the overpowering sense of occasion, the complete involvement in the ritual, the solemn gestures and stances.

———

How strands of history and devotion intertwine in Kota is a subject in itself. As a part of the war booty that the victorious Mughal armies took in 1720 was the gold image of the state deity, Brijnathji, which the Maharao of that time, Bhim Singh, had taken with him to the field of battle. It was recovered years later from Hyderabad, almost conferring the mantle of legitimacy on the prince who brought it back to Kota.

شاه شرف بو علی قلندر

THE SUFI SAINT SHAH SHARF 'BU ALI' QALANDAR

Isolated folio
Opaque watercolour on paper
Delhi or possibly Haryana; c. 1750
22 cm × 17.4 cm
The British Museum, London

Shola-e yaad-e rukh-e pur noor u
Bu Ali sham-o seher mi sozadam

The memory of the flaming sight of that resplendent face
Singes me all the time, day and night, says Bu Ali.

The words belong to that highly revered, but now little-remembered, Sufi saint, Shah Sharf Bu Ali, who lies buried at Panipat in the state of Haryana. The resplendent face he refers to here is that of God, of course, but in the approved Sufi tradition, using the language and imagery of this world: that of lovers and beloveds. After all, true love—*ishq-e haqiqi*—is so different from *ishq-e majaazi*, love that is transient, illusory.

The name of this saint, born to Sheikh Fakhr-ud-din, a renowned scholar of his times, was in fact Sharf-ud-din, but everyone, it seems, knew him by the pen name under which he wrote his poetry, 'Bu Ali'—the 'Fragrance of Ali', after the prophet whom he so revered. There is some uncertainty about his dates: some say he was born at Panipat in c. 1400, but there is credible evidence that he was in fact born at Ganja in Azerbaijan in 1209 and moved to India as a follower of the Chishti order of Sufis.

Legends of his powers continue to be told. One recounts how he was able to solve the mystery of a ruler of Delhi, a virile man ordinarily, who would lose his manly powers whenever he sought to be close to his newly acquired mistress. It was through the agency of a wandering dervish that Bu Ali came to know the answer: the new mistress was, unknown to anyone till then, a daughter of the ruler himself from a woman he had abandoned a long time ago. The woman had died leaving the upbringing of the girl to a poor man from whose house the ruler had, unknowingly, picked her when she grew up into a beauty.

The fact having been established, Sharf-ud-din went looking for that dervish. The dervish turned out to be none other than the Sufi saint Qutb-ud-din Bakhtiar Kaki, the spiritual master of another celebrated Sufi saint, Farid-ud-din Shakarganj. The young Sharf-ud-din, till then only a scholar of religious texts, knew then that he had found his *murshid* (spiritual guide), and his calling. He left everything and turned into a dervish himself: a real *qalandar*, free of all earthly possessions and concerns.

There is something quite moving about this image, inscribed on the bottom margin with the words 'Shah Sharaf Bu Ali Qalandar'. The painter—we know nothing about him or for whom he painted, unless of course he was personally a devotee of Bu Ali—sees and renders him as the simplest of beings. Dressed in a coarse woollen garment—*suf*, from which according to one theory, the term Sufi was derived—we see him seated under a roughly painted tree: an appropriate setting in the Indian tradition for men of learning and spiritual beings. Legs tucked under him, in the familiar *do-zanu* position, his hands rest on his knees. There is nothing else in sight. It is as if he is sitting in the wilderness, away from all habitation, in the midst of some rushes growing at the edge of a small waterbody. The Sufi has an unkempt air: coarse white hair on head and a rough beard. What strikes one the most, however, is the look in his eyes and the manner in which his head is turned to the right. At first one might think of this as not worthy of much attention—it could be he is simply turning his head as is often done during *namaz*. But there is, one feels, a different suggestion here: he is turning his head as if straining to hear a sound: an unuttered sound, perhaps, something coming from the Unknown. The look of concentration in the eyes, even puzzlement, certainly reinforces the suggestion.

There is possibly a reference here to a legend told about him: that he used to stand in water meditating for a long, long time until he heard a voice that told him his meditation and penance were over, and it was now time for him to come out of the water and carry a message to the world.

In any case, this is the world which great Sufis inhabited: seeing sights unseen, hearing inaudible sounds. From the intensity but also the sheer artlessness of this image, it would seem that Shah Sharf Bu Ali belonged to that world.

———————

Shah Sharf Bu Ali was a poet of no small merit. An entire dewan—*complete works in verse—in relatively simple Persian, is attributed to him. It was published by the Islamia Steam Press at Lahore in a lithographed edition, undated but possibly more than a hundred years ago.*

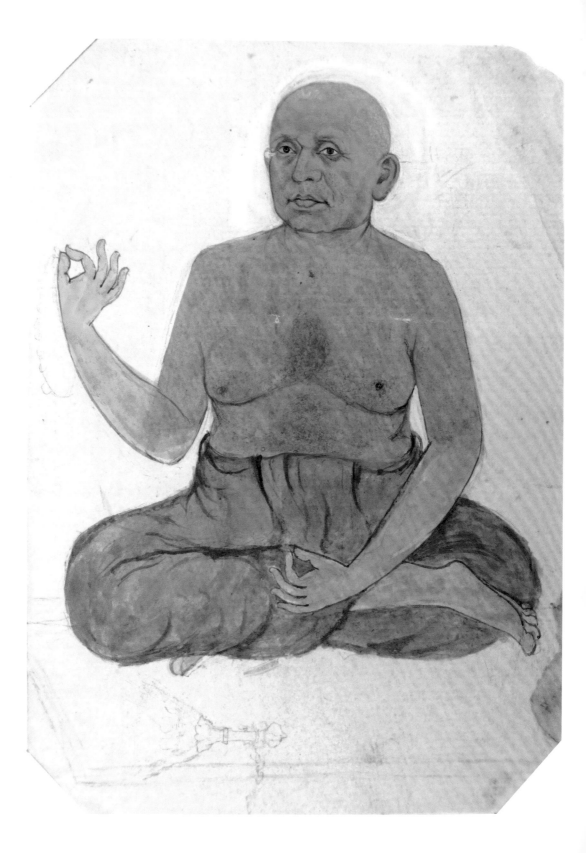

A PRIESTLY FIGURE SEATED

From a sheaf of portraits of individuals
Opaque watercolour on European paper
South India, possibly Tanjore, 'Company' style; c. 1850
16.5 cm × 13 cm
Private Collection

'Company' painting—the term is employed generally for work done by Indian painters for European patrons, mostly officers of the East India Company—can perhaps be seen to fall into two separate categories: work done, often using Western techniques, to suit European tastes or needs; and work done by Indian painters for Indian patrons, for 'internal use' so to speak, but availing of the same newly learnt techniques or ways of seeing. Company paintings were being done in different parts of the country, not just in the colonial centres mentioned in the introductory essay, 'A Layered World', but also in Lucknow and Kashmir, as well as the southern regions.

The quality of work varied of course—from natural history studies of the brilliance of Zain-al Din or Bhawani Das to those hastily produced, dreary sets made in large numbers by unrecorded painters simply documenting trades and professions, castes and carriages. European patrons often had reservations about the work done for them, but also expressed grudging admiration. Consider, for instance, what Captain Charles Gold, an Officer of the Royal Regiment of Artillery who took part in the siege of Seringapatam, and a painter himself, wrote in 1802 after he had acquired a study of a beggar and his wife by an Indian painter:

> The Moochys, or Artists of India, usually painting in the style represented in the present drawing, but in body colour and sometimes finish their pictures in the delicate and laboured manner of a miniature; though they are at the same time entirely devoid of

truth in colouring and perspective, and constantly err on the side of ornament and gaudiness of dress; except where the subject does not admit of much finery and decoration as with beggars; and then they possess considerable merit as to costume and character.

And then he writes of series of paintings of 'most ordinary castes and tribes', 'each picture representing a man and his wife, with the signs or marks of distinction on their foreheads, and not in their common but holiday clothes . . . These drawings do credit to the uninstructed authors of them.'

The 'Moochy', a term that Gold uses for 'all artists of India', was in fact a group that was active in the southern regions of India, the term meaning, oddly enough, leather workers, reminding one of similar appellations or derivations: thus, the painters of Kutch being referred to as of the Kamangar—makers of bows—community, or most Pahari painters belonging to the Tarkhan— carpenter—caste. He must have been using the term that had wide currency then, and was applied to painters in the Tanjore area which was always seen as a major centre of painting in the south.

In that pocket of Maratha power in the heart of Tamil territory, there were rulers of taste and discrimination, like Serfoji II who was portrayed again and again: by himself, with advisers and confidants, sitting in his durbar. We even get a couple of names of painters such as Ramaswami Maistry and Govindaswami Maistry 'of Tanjore'. In the second half of the eighteenth century, Tanjore was a centre of traditional Indian painting. But soon it was also to become the first region in the entire Madras Presidency (as it was then called) to produce 'Company' paintings. British taste had come in, and, increasingly, as the century advanced, more and more work started being made for East India Company patrons, catering to their tastes, using their watercolour technique and, later, availing of the newly arrived machine: the camera.

What is of great interest is the fact that there had always been an interest in portraying people, even ordinary people, at Tanjore—one refers here not to what is generally called 'Tanjore painting' today, shiny religious paintings on wood, with a great deal of impasto work, using gems and gold leaf. But most such work went unnoticed amidst the profusion of grand paintings of formal durbar scenes with crowds surrounding royalty. At some point, however, with the Maratha rulers virtually losing all power, and thus the power of patronage, that interest in portraying individuals of no special rank seems to have resurfaced. And some splendid work emerged from unknown ateliers.

This work comes from a large group: portraits of men and, surprisingly, women, mostly seated, seen frontally, looking directly at the viewer with no hesitation or self-awareness. It is not as if they are posing for the painter—the painter seems to have registered their appearances and captured them, later, in sketches, fully or partially coloured. There is a charming air of informality about these works.

There are portraits of pandits with caste marks on their foreheads, women holding prayer beads, shopkeepers with rolled-up umbrellas in their hands, and so on. Here, one sees a shaven-headed man, a priest perhaps, his face possessed of noble gravity, bare on the upper part of the body, flaccid-chested, dressed in a simple mauve dhoti, seated cross-legged. The face makes for a sharp, sympathetic study and every wrinkle and furrow has been brilliantly caught.

The man's hands are held in specific gestures, the left resting in the lap and the right raised to bring it up to shoulder level, the fingers disposed as if in *tarka mudra*—the gesture of holding forth or disputation. The fact that the painter has struggled with the fingers of the right hand—clearly no photograph was being copied here—adds charm to the study.

AUTHOR'S ACKNOWLEDGEMENTS

Some debts are a burden, and some a pleasure. Most of those that I owe are, fortunately, of the latter kind. To all those from whom I have learnt, or to whom I have been able to communicate something—there are far too many of them to be individually named—I remain grateful: family, friends, teachers, colleagues, students. In the course of working on this book, however, help has come especially in generous measure from many museum colleagues and collectors. Most of it must already have been acknowledged by the publishers, but I would personally like to recall the magnanimity and the warmth of some friends: Eberhard Fischer, Milo Beach, and Jorrit Britschgi; Caron Smith; Jas Grewal and Marika Sardar; Usha Bhatia, Saryu Doshi, Shailendra Hemchand and Poonam Khanna, among them.

To work with Chiki Sarkar, Nandini Mehta and Ambar Sahil Chatterjee at Penguin has been an unalloyed pleasure. Together we have made every effort to grind it all fine, as they say, while hammering this book into shape. I would like to offer them and the others mentioned above my gratitude.

Gar qabool uftad, zah-ey 'izz-o sharaf, is how they say it in Persian. 'Were you to accept what I offer, all the honour will be mine.'

PUBLISHER'S ACKNOWLEDGEMENTS

Generous grants from Jñāna-Pravāha, Varanasi, the Raza Foundation and IndiGo Airlines have made it possible to offer this book at a special price. Our special thanks to Suresh Kumar Neotia, Jñāna-Pravāha; Ashok Vajpeyi, Raza Foundation; and Aditya Ghosh, IndiGo Airlines.

Penguin Books India gratefully acknowledges, in addition, the help and generosity of the following institutions and individuals in the preparation of this book:

Dr Eberhard Fischer
Sir Howard Hodgkin
Sven Gahlin
Jürgen Lütt and Barbara Lütt
Mahrukh Tarapor
The Rietberg Museum, Zürich, and Jorrit Britschgi
The Museum of Islamic Art, Doha, and Leslee Katrina Michelsen and Marc Pelletreau
The Metropolitan Museum of Art, New York, and Navina Haidar, John Guy and Julie Zeftel
The Los Angeles County Museum of Art, and Stephen Markel and Piper Severance
The Fondation Custodia, Paris, and Mariska de Jonge

Publisher's Acknowledgements

The Cleveland Museum of Art, and Elizabeth Saluk

The Kronos Collections, New York, and Steven Kossak

The Nelson-Atkins Museum of Art, Kansas City, and Kimberly Masteller and Stacey Sherman

The National Museum, New Delhi, and Dr Venu Vasudevan and Dr V.K. Mathur

The Dogra Art Gallery, Jammu, and Kripal Singh

The Amar Mahal Museum, Jammu, and Jyoti Singh

The Mehrangarh Museum Trust, Jodhpur, and Karni Singh Jasol

The Sheesh Mahal, Patiala, and N.P.S. Randhawa

The Sena Gana Mandir, Karanja, and Dr Saryu Doshi

The Goenka Collection and Dr Usha Bhatia

The San Diego Museum of Art and Marika Sardar, Cory Woodall and James Gielow

The David Collection, Copenhagen, and Pernille Klemp

The Bernische Historische Museum, Berne, and Michèle Thüring and Angela Probst

The Ashmolean Museum, Oxford, and Andrew Topsfield and Hannah Kendall

COPYRIGHT CREDITS

GLOSSARY

abhisarika nayika	A heroine going to secretly meet her lover
acharya	A spiritual or scholarly teacher
Adbhuta	The Marvellous Sentiment, according to the classification of moods in the *Natyashastra*
AH	Anno Hegirae; the Hijri year; the numbering system used in the Islamic calendar
ahwal	A temporary state of consciousness, generally understood to be the product of a Sufi's spiritual practices
Ajanta	Rock-cut caves in Aurangabad, dating from the second century BCE to about 480 or 650 CE, famous for their murals
Akbarnama	A chronicle of the Mughal emperor Akbar's reign, written by his court historian Abu'l Fazl in the sixteenth century
Akhlaq-i Nasiri	'Ethics of Nasir', a philosophical treatise on ethics, social justice and politics by the thirteenth-century Persian philosopher and scientist Nasir al-Din Tusi
alif	A letter of the Persian alphabet
amal	Application of colours in Mughal painting
Anadi Patan	An illustrated manuscript, said to be the Assamese version of the *Bhagavata Purana*
ananda	The kind of bliss that can only be experienced by the spirit
Anvar-i Suhaili	'The Lights of Canopus', the Persian version of the Panchatantra fables.
Aranyaka Parvan	'The Forest Book', a section of the Mahabharata
arati	The ritual of making devotional offerings to a deity
Ardhanarishwara	The Lord Whose Other Half Is Woman—a composite

	androgynous form of the Hindu god Shiva and his consort, Parvati
artha	Worldly wealth or progress
Ashtasahasrika Prajnaparamita	A Buddhist text comprising 8000 verses on the 'Perfection of Wisdom'
asuric forces	Forces opposed to the benign deities
ayyaar	A class of wandering warriors in medieval Iran and Iraq
Baburnama	The memoirs of the founder of the Mughal empire, Zahir-ud Din Muhammad Babur (1483–1530)
Bagh	Rock-cut caves in Dhar district in Madhya Pradesh, dated between the fifth and sixth centuries, which once had famous murals that are now almost completely erased
bahi	The record books of family genealogies maintained at major Hindu pilgrimage centres
Bahr-i Hayat	The 'Ocean of Immortality', a book on the philosophy and practice of yoga, translated from Sanskrit into Persian
bakhshi	Title of a high official in the Mughal court
baradari	A pillared pavilion with twelve openings
Baramasa	Poems and paintings about the twelve months of the year
Basohli	A small principality in what is now Jammu and Kashmir, with a famous tradition of painting
Bhagavata Purana	Literally, 'Ancient Tales of the Lord'. As a Purana, it is one of the great texts of Hinduism, with its focus on devotion to the Supreme God Vishnu (Narayana). The story of Krishna, Vishnu's eighth incarnation, figures prominently in the text.
Bhagirath	A great king who brought the river Ganga to the earth from the heavens
bhajan	A devotional song
bhandar	A repository of ancient texts and other sacred objects
bhava	In the *rasa* theory, a 'mood' or 'emotional state'
bhavasagara	The ocean of sorrow that is this world
Bhayanaka	The Fearful Sentiment, according to the classification of moods in the *Natyashastra*
bhopa	A bard; a folk singer in Rajasthan who recites a chronicle
Bibhatsa	The Odious Sentiment, according to the classification of moods in the *Natyashastra*

Brihadaryanaka Upanishad	A primary Upanishad, widely known for its philosophical statements
Chakravartin	Literally, the Wheel-turning Master, a term used to describe a great man who influences destinies
chamatkara	A flash of lightning
Chamba	A principality in what is now Himachal Pradesh
Chamunda	A fearsome aspect of Devi, the Hindu Divine Mother Goddess. She is also one of the chief *yogini*s, a group of Tantric goddesses who are attendants of the warrior goddess Durga.
charana	Inferior demigods referred to in many Hindu dramas
charitas	Life stories focusing essentially on the most important events in the lives of the Jain *tirthankara*s
Chaurapanchasika	'Fifty Stanzas of the Love Thief', written by Bilhana, an eleventh-century Kashmiri poet
chehra	Putting in the details of a face in a painting
chehra-i naami	The principal or most important face in a painting
chhatra	A jewelled parasol, an auspicious symbol in Hindu and Buddhist traditions
Chingiznama	The illustrated history of Chingiz Khan composed by Rashid-ad-Din, commissioned by the Mughal emperor Akbar
chogha	A coat worn by men
daal	A letter of the Persian alphabet
Dakhani	A Muslim court language developed in the Deccan in the fourteenth century, similar to Urdu
daliddar	From the Sanskrit word *daridra*, or poverty-stricken
dana pushpikas	Colophons recording details of donation
darshan	Viewing, usually of a deity or revered person
darwesh	A Sufi dervish
Dastan-i Masih	'Story of the Messiah', a painting presented to Akbar by a nephew of St Francis Xavier
devaraja	A deified king
Devasano Pada Bhandar	A famous Jain library in Gujarat
Devi Mahatmya	A manuscript series in Sanskrit also known as *Chandi Saptashati*, literally, 'Glory of the Great Goddess'. It is embedded inside the *Markandeya Purana*, a Hindu religious text, composed during 400–500.
Devi	The Great Goddess in Hinduism, who has countless forms and names, such as Durga or Kali. In the eyes of her devotees she reigns supreme.
dharma	Right action, duty

Dhola Maru	A romantic tale of a couple, Dhola and Maru, deeply rooted in the folklore and oral traditions of Rajasthan
Dhrupad	An ancient form of Hindustani classical vocal music, usually spiritual in nature
dhuni	A small fire, often lit by the ascetic devotees of Shiva
dhyana shloka	A meditative, formulaic verse
dhyanas	Words to aid meditation upon a deity
Digambara	A Jain sect whose ascetic practitioners wear no garments
diksha	The attainment of knowledge
doha	In Hindi poetry, a couplet
durbar	A Persian term, meaning the ruler's noble court, or a formal meeting, where he holds all discussions on matters of state
farman	A royal decree, grant or permit
Futuhat-i Feroze Shahi	The autobiography of Feroze Shah Tughlaq, ruler of the Tughlaq dynasty and Sultan of Delhi during 1351–88.
gadaz	Persian; meaning, 'melting'
gajasura-vadha murti	A ferocious form of the god Shiva, which he assumed while killing a demon in the form of an elephant
gandharva	A term used for heavenly beings in Hinduism and Buddhism
Ganesha	The elephant-headed Hindu deity, worshipped as the god who removes all obstacles and ensures auspicious beginnings
Garuda	A large mythical bird that appears in both Hindu and Buddhist mythology
gharana	A system of social organization linking musicians or dancers by lineage or apprenticeship, and by adherence to a particular musical style
ghulam	A devotee or slave
Gilgit	A city in Baltistan in present-day Pakistan-occupied Kashmir
Gita Govinda	'Song of the Cowherd', a Sanskrit classic in verse by the poet Jayadeva, c. 1200. It celebrates the divine love of Krishna and Radha in intensely poetic words and images.
gopi	A 'milkmaid'; commonly refers to the group of cowherdesses celebrated in Vaishnava theology for their unconditional devotion to Krishna, as described in the stories of the *Bhagavata Purana*

Govardhan	The mountain Krishna lifted to protect his kinsmen from a deluge of rain
gudri	A quilted textile, commonly used as a shawl
Gulistan	'The Rose Garden', written in 1259; one of the two major works of the Persian poet Sa'di, considered one of the greatest medieval Persian poets
gurguri-huqqa	A hubble-bubble pipe
Guru Granth Sahib	The holy book of the Sikhs
gutka	An amulet or small satchel
hamsa	An aquatic bird, a goose or a swan; often used in Indian and South Asian art as a symbol
Hamzanama	An epic tale of adventure and sorcery, chivalry and magic, from the Islamic world. This work provided the theme for one of the greatest productions of the Mughal painting atelier under the emperor Akbar.
Hari	Another name for Vishnu; also for Krishna
Haridwar	An ancient city, now in Uttarakhand which, in Hindu eyes, is one of the holiest sites in India. The Ganga debouches from the hills to the plains at this spot.
Harivamsa	An important work of Sanskrit literature, containing 16,374 verses. This text is believed to be a *khila* (appendix or supplement) to the Mahabharata and is traditionally ascribed to Veda Vyasa.
Harshacharita	The biography of the Indian emperor Harsha by Banabhatta, also known as Bana, a Sanskrit writer of the seventh century
hashiya-kash	A margin maker in a Mughal atelier
Hasya	The Comic Sentiment, according to the classification of moods in the *Natyashastra*
howdah	A platform placed on the back of an elephant or a camel to carry wealthy people or for use in hunting or warfare
huqqa	A smoking pipe with a long tube passing through an urn of water that cools the smoke as it is drawn through
Indra	Vedic god of the heavens, weather and war
Inju	A community in Persia
ishta	A cherished or favoured deity, chosen by an individual, family or clan
Iskandarnama	One of the five poems in Firdausi's celebrated work, the *Khamsa*
jadwal-kash	A line drawer in a Mughal atelier

jagir	A feudal estate
jala-durga	A fort protected or surrounded by water
jala-vihar	The pastime of spending leisurely time on a boat
jama	An upper muslin jacket worn by men
jasun	The hibiscus, commonly known as the shoe flower
jata	Matted hair
Jataka	A voluminous body of literature concerning the previous births of the Buddha
jauhar	A Rajput custom whereby women immolate themselves to avoid falling into the hands of the enemy
Jayadeva	A great poet, who flourished c. 1200; author of the celebrated Sanskrit classic, the *Gita Govinda*
jharokha	A Hindi word for a window in a balcony
Jinacharita	One of the three sections of the venerated Jain canon, the *Kalpasutra*, which covers the lives of the four most prominent among the twenty-four *tirthankara*s—Mahavira, Parshvanatha, Neminatha and Rishabhanatha
Jog Bashisht	An illustrated manuscript from the Mughal period, based on a Hindu spiritual text written by the sage Valmiki
Jyeshtha	The first of the two hottest months in the Hindu calendar
Kailash	The sacred mountain peak that is the home of Shiva
kaivalya	Detachment
Kalachakra	The wheel of time
Kalighat	A distinct style of painting that originated in what is now West Bengal
Kalila wa Dimna	An Arabic translation of the Panchatantra fables
kalpa	An aeon; a very long period of time in Hindu and Buddhist thought
Kalpasutra	The most venerated of all canonical works of Jainism. It contains the biographies of the Jain *tirthankara*s, notably Parshvanatha and Mahavira.
kama	Passions of the body
Kamangar	Caste of bow makers
Kamsa	Brother of Devaki, Krishna's biological mother, and the tyrant ruler of Mathura. Kamsa was eventually killed by Krishna, as foretold in a prophecy.
kanphata jogi	An ascetic, belonging to a sect, who wears large earrings in the hollow of his ears
karkhana	A workshop or atelier

kartal	A handheld percussion instrument to accompany devotional songs and folk ballads
Karuna	The Sentiment of Compassion, according to the classification of moods in the *Natyashastra*
katib	A scribe in a Mughal atelier
Kauravas	The descendants of Kuru, one branch of the central royal family figuring in the Mahabharata
Kavipriya	An anthology of poems by the poet and scholar Keshavadasa written in 1601
khadga	A type of sword
khaqan	A title traditionally reserved for the emperor of China or the rulers of Chinese Tartary, loosely applied later to any emperor
khulai	Literally, 'opening up' a painting by giving it its final touches
khushnawis	A calligrapher in a Mughal atelier
Kitab-i Nauras	Ibrahim Adil Shah II, the Sultan of Bijapur, wrote this collection of fifty-nine poems and seventeen couplets to introduce the theory of the nine *rasa*s in the seventeenth century.
Krishna	An important and immensely popular deity in Hindu belief. He is variously celebrated as a God-child, a prankster, a model lover, a divine hero and the Supreme Being. He is an incarnation of Vishnu and is often depicted in paintings with a dark bluish complexion.
Krishnakarnamritam	A devotional text by Lilashuka, dating to the fourteenth century
Kubera	The god of wealth in Hinduism and Mahayana Buddhism
Kulliyat	The complete works of a poet
lakshagraha	A house built of lac that is highly flammable
lakshanas	Attributes by which a great personality can be recognized
Lakshmana	One of the younger brothers of Rama who, in the Ramayana, accompanied him into exile
Lakshmi	The Hindu Goddess of wealth and prosperity, both material and spiritual. She is the consort of Vishnu.
Lala-rukh	'With a face like a tulip'; a term used to describe a beautiful woman
Laur Chanda	A celebrated Avadhi romance in verse written by Mulla Daud in the fifteenth century

maa'ni	Spirit, inner essence
Madhu Malati	An Indian Sufi text, written in the sixteenth century by Mir Sayyid Manjhan Shattari Rajgiri
Mahabharata	One of the great Indian epics, believed to have been composed around the fifth century BCE. It chronicles the battle between the Kauravas and the Pandavas, two branches of the central royal family.
mahapurusha	A great or supra-human man
Mahashri Tara	A female Bodhisattva in Mahayana Buddhism. She is known as the 'mother of liberation', and represents the virtues of success in work and achievements.
mahasiddha	A great perfected being who has achieved the highest level of spiritual enlightenment
mahavihara	Pali for 'great monastery'
Mahishasura	One of the most powerful demons with the head of a buffalo
majlis	An Arabic term meaning 'a place of sitting', used in the context of 'council', to describe various types of special gatherings among common-interest groups for administrative, social or religious purposes
Mamluk	A soldier-slave of Turkish origin
Manaku	An eighteenth-century painter from a celebrated family of artists residing in the small Pahari principality of Guler
mandala	Literally, 'circle'; a spiritual and ritual symbol in Hinduism and Buddhism representing the Universe
Mandi	A small principality in what is now Himachal Pradesh, with a famous tradition of painting
Mankot	A small principality in what is now Jammu and Kashmir, with a famous tradition of painting
mantra	A sacred utterance or a syllable believed to have psychological and spiritual power
manvantara	A period of astronomical time within an aeon
maqamat	'Stations' in Arabic; a term that refers to the various stages a Sufi's soul must attain in its search for God
Maricha	In the Ramayana, a demon who, taking the form of a golden deer, lured Rama away, thus preparing the ground for the abduction of Sita
marut	Storm deities who are Indra's attendants
Matsya Purana	One of the oldest of the eighteen post-Vedic Hindu scriptures called the Puranas. Dated to 250–500, it narrates the story of Matsya, the first of the ten major

	avatars of Vishnu.
maya	A term used in Sanskrit and Pali literature meaning 'illusion'
meenakshi	Fish-shaped eyes
Meru	A sacred mountain in Hindu, Buddhist and Jain cosmology, considered to be the centre of all the physical, metaphysical and spiritual universes. It is also the abode of Lord Brahma and the demigods (*devas*).
moksha	Spiritual freedom
Muchalinda	A snake-deity who sheltered Gautam Buddha by spreading his hoods over him in inclement weather
mudhahhib	An illuminator in a Mughal atelier
mudra	A symbolic hand gesture in Hindu and Buddhist iconography
mujallad	A binder in a Mughal atelier
mukh-patti	A cloth used to cover the mouth
mullah	Generally used to refer to a Muslim man educated in Islamic theology and sacred law
muni	A revered monk, usually Jain
Mura	A five-headed demon guarding the palace of Naraka, the demon of the netherworld
Muraqqa-i Gulshan	An album in book form containing Islamic miniature paintings and specimens of Islamic calligraphy, normally from several different sources
musavvir	A painter in a Mughal atelier
Nadir-al 'Asr	Literally, 'Rarity of the Times', an honorific bestowed on the Mughal painter Ustad Mansur by the Mughal emperor Jahangir
naga	A snake; also, a group of serpent deities in Hindu and Buddhist mythology
Naishadhacharita	A twelfth-century Sanskrit classic by Sriharsha, chronicling the adventures of Nala Raja of Naishadha
Nala–Damayanti	A stirring story of a royal couple in Hindu mythology, which features in the Mahabharata, and which has inspired many paintings
Nalanda	An ancient institution of higher learning in Bihar, which flourished from the fifth century to 1197
naqqash	A word which can mean both painter and illuminator
naqqashi	The art of painting
Narada	A divine sage who plays a prominent role in a number of Hindu myths and texts
Narayana	A Hindu god, also known as Vishnu, venerated as the

	Supreme Being in Vaishnavism
nastaliq	A calligraphic script in Persian or Arabic
Natyashastra	An ancient Indian treatise on the performing arts, chiefly theatre, dance and music. Written between 200 BCE and 200 CE, it is attributed to the sage Bharata.
nawab	A title of nobility awarded as a personal distinction by the ruler
nayak/nayika	A romantic hero/heroine
Nayikabheda	A collective name for eight types of *nayika*s as classified in the *Natyashastra*
neerasa	Literally, devoid of delight
Ni'matnama	The 'Book of Delicacies', a treatise on the art of cooking, written for the Sultans of Mandu in 1500
nikunj lila	'Love play in the bower'; a favourite theme of poets and traditional painters
Oghaniryukti	A Jain philosophical text, bearing the date 1060
paan	A mouth-freshening wrap made of betel leaves
padmini	The 'lotus lady' referred to in Indian erotica and mythology as the highest form of beauty among female types
Padshahnama	The official chronicle of the reign of the Mughal emperor Shahjahan, illustrated by leading Mughal artists
Pahari painting	Generally seen as the northern branch of Rajput painting, it consists of the group of styles that flourished between the seventeenth and nineteenth centuries in the lower Himalayan states, with major centres at Basohli, Mankot, Nurpur, Jasrota, Kangra, Guler and Mandi.
palki	A palanquin
Panchakalyanaka	Considered to be the five chief auspicious events in the life of a Jain *tirthankara*
panchamrita	The 'five nectars': milk, yogurt, clarified butter, honey and sugar, used in a sequence in Hindu religious rituals
Pancharaksha	The five protector goddesses
pandas	Hindu priests
Pandavas	One branch of the central royal family figuring in the Mahabharata, they are the five sons of Pandu: Yudhisthira, Bhima, Arjuna, Nakula and Sahadeva. All five brothers were married to the same woman, Draupadi.
pardaz	Fine shading

Glossary

Parvati	Consort of the god Shiva
patka	A waistband worn by men
patli	Wooden book covers between which loose folios were placed
peri	A mythical being in Persian mythology, originally represented as evil but subsequently as a good or graceful genie or fairy
phada	A large painted textile from Rajasthan that tells a detailed and complex tale
phagu	Poetry, often sensuous and erotic, that centres upon the beauties of the spring month of Phalguna in the Indian calendar
pichkari	Jet-syringes, used to spray coloured water during the festival of Holi
pietra-dura	A technique of stone inlay work
pothi	A sacred book
pothikhana	A library
Prabandhachintamani	A semi-historical work composed by Merutunga Suri in 1304.
prabhava	In the context of this book, a section of a sacred text
Prajnaparamita	The Bodhisattva of Wisdom in Mahayana Buddhism, regarded as the spiritual mother of all Buddhas, having acquired the 'Perfection of Wisdom'
prayoga	Praxis
Puranic texts	Ancient Hindu texts, part philosophy, part myths
purdah	A religious and social practice of female seclusion
qalandar	A dervish, Sufi devotee, free of all earthly possessions and concerns
qamargha	A hunt
qazi	A judge ruling in accordance with Islamic religious law (the Sharia)
ra'is	A wealthy, high-ranking man
Radha	Krishna's cowherdess beloved who later attained the status of a goddess
Raga	A melodic mode used in Indian classical music
Ragamala	Poems and paintings expressing musical modes (Ragas) and the emotions they evoke
rajasic	Dynamic, responsible for motion, energy and preservation
Rajatarangini	A historical chronicle of the kings of Kashmir written in the twelfth century by Kalhana
Ramayana	One of the great Indian epics, it tells the story of

	Prince Rama, seventh incarnation of Vishnu, and the abduction of his wife, Sita, by the demon king of Lanka, Ravana. The epic emphasizes the victory of good over evil. As a text it figures in various versions, the oldest being that of the sage Valmiki.
Rasa Panchadhyayi	Five chapters in the Tenth Book of the *Bhagavata Purana* with passages that speak movingly of the love of the *gopi*s for Krishna
rasa	Literally, juice or extract. In Indian aesthetic theory, however, it stands for Flavour or Sentiment that a work of art produces in the viewer/listener/reader. Nine *rasa*s are spoken of in the theory.
rasalila	The enactment of the miraculous deeds of Krishna
rasamandala	The divine circular dance of Krishna and the *gopi*s, performed on the full-moon night of the month of Karttika
Rasamanjari	A fifteenth-century Sanskrit text dealing with the classical theme of *nayak*s and *nayika*s—'heroes and heroines'—distinctly erotic in texture and feeling. It was written by the poet Bhanudatta.
rasasvadana	The tasting of flavour
rasavanta	A work of art possessing *rasa*
rasayan	A term that in early Ayurvedic medicine means the science of lengthening lifespan
rasika	Literally, one who knows and is capable of tasting *rasa*; a connoisseur
Rasikapriya	A romantic work by Keshavadasa, a sixteenth-century Sanskrit scholar and Hindi poet, which inspired many painters to illustrate its episodes
ratipriya	One who is soaked in passions
Raudra	The Furious Sentiment, according to the classification of moods in the *Natyashastra*
Ravana	The demon king of Lanka and the primary antagonist in the Ramayana
Razmnama	The 'Book of War', the Persian translation of the Mahabharata, created for Mughal emperor Akbar in the seventeenth century
Rigveda	A sacred collection of Vedic Sanskrit hymns, counted among the four canonical sacred texts of Hinduism known as the Vedas
ritikala poetry	Poetry of the age of tradition

romaharsha	Horripilation; gooseflesh caused by experiencing sudden pleasure
rupa	Physical appearance or form
sabat	Stability, endurance, truth
sadhanas	Chants and invocations intended to protect the devotee, the chanter
sadhavi	Female ascetic or nun
sadrishya	In the context of 'Indian' portraiture, it indicates analogies and similes rather than verisimilitude in depicting a person
Sahib-i-Qiran	Lord of the Auspicious Planetary Conjunction, a common title for the emperor, Timur, in official and court chronicles of his times
Sahitya Darpana	A comprehensive treatise on aesthetics, written by Vishwanatha around the late fourteenth century
sakhi	A female companion
Samachari	The section of the *Kalpasutra* that contains the rules for monks
sampradaya	Religious tradition
samvartaka	A host of clouds that can bring about the destruction of the universe
Samvat	Denotes 'year' in the Hindu calendar
Sangita Damodara	A text on musical modes
sannyasi	A holy man
sarasa	Full of delight; suffused with *rasa*
Saraswati	The Hindu goddess of knowledge, music, arts and wisdom
Satsai	Literally, 'Seven Hundred Verses', a famous work of the early seventeenth century by the Hindi poet Bihari, in the Braj Bhasha dialect of Hindi
Shahnama	A great Persian epic written by Firdausi in the tenth century
Shaivite	A practitioner of the sect of Hinduism that regards Shiva as the Supreme Being
shaligrama	Ammonite, a fossil shell, associated with Vishnu
Shanta	The Quiescent Sentiment, according to the classification of moods in the *Natyashastra*
shastra	Theory, scripture
shastrartha	Religious or philosophical debate
Shatapatha Brahmana	Literally, a 'Brahmana of One Hundred Paths', one of the prose texts describing Vedic rituals

Shesha	In Hindu tradition, Shesha—also known as Sheshanaga or Adishesha—is the king of all Nagas (serpent deities), and one of the primal beings of creation. He is often identified with Balarama, Krishna's older brother.
shikargah	A place for hunting game
shila	A shortened word for shaligrama
Shiva	One of the three great deities of the Hindu triad. His role is that of the Transformer and the Destroyer.
shloka	A verse form in which the epics and many Sanskrit texts were composed
Shringara	The Erotic Sentiment, according to the classification of moods in the *Natyashastra*
Shvetambara	A Jain sect whose ascetic followers wear white clothes
siddha	A guru who initiates disciples into yoga; a liberated soul or an accomplished being
simhasana	A throne
Sohni Mahiwal	A tragic love story, popular as a folk tale in Sindh and Punjab
soz	Persian, meaning, 'burning'
Sthaviravali	The section of *Kalpasutra* containing the succession list of Jain pontiffs
Sudarshana chakra	A spinning disc-like weapon with serrated edges; also an emblem associated with the god Vishnu
suf	A coarse woollen garment said to be worn by Sufis
Sukadeva	The son of the sage Vyasa and the main narrator of the *Bhagavata Purana*
sundari	A beautiful young woman
Sur Sagar	A collection of devotional poems written by Surdas, the great blind poet of Mathura
surat	Form, outward appearance
Surdas	Blind saint, poet and musician, who lived in the fifteenth century, known for his devotional songs dedicated to Krishna
sutra	A collection of aphorisms in the form of a manual or a text in Hinduism and Buddhism. Literally, a thread or line that holds things together.
svabhava	Innate nature
Svayambhu	'Self-manifested' or 'that which is created by its own accord'
swayamvara	A practice of choosing a husband from among a list of suitors, by a girl of marriageable age

taaluqa	A subdivision of a district; a group of villages organized for revenue-collecting purposes
takhti	A small wooden tablet to write on
Takri	The script of the Western Himalayas
tamasic	Dark and inert
tambur	A fretted string instrument of Turkey and the former lands of the Ottoman Empire
Tantra	A discipline of meditation and ritual, centred on the theme of divine energy, which arose in India around the fifth century
tarah	A drawing in Mughal painting
Tarif-i Hussain Shahi	A Persian poem in eleven cantos, celebrating the reign of Husain Nizam Shah I (1565–69) of Ahmednagar
Tarikh-i Alfi	'History of the Millennium', written by Abd al-Qadir Bada'uni, commissioned by the Mughal emperor Akbar
tarka mudra	A hand gesture used during religious debates
Tarkhan	The carpenter caste
tawaifs	Courtesans, often singers and dancers who occupied a distinct, even high, place in late-Mughal society
Tawarikh-i Khandan-i Timuriya	The only extant copy of a manuscript richly illustrated, which deals with the history of Timur and his descendants in Iran and India, including the Mughal rulers Babur, Humayun and Akbar, compiled during 1577–78
thikana	A feudal estate
tilaka	A ritual mark worn on the forehead and other parts of the body by Hindus
tirthankaras	In Jainism, a *tirthankara* is a human being who helps others in achieving enlightenment and liberation of the soul
Trinavarta	A demon who takes the form of a whirlwind to kill the infant Krishna, at the behest of the evil Kamsa. This episode features in the *Bhagavata Purana*.
tripundra	Three horizontal tilaka marks across the forehead
trishula	A trident, usually carried by Shiva
Tutinama	Literally, 'Tales of a Parrot', a fourteenth-century Persian series of fifty-two stories. An illustrated version containing 250 miniature paintings was commissioned by the Mughal emperor Akbar in the later part of the sixteenth century.

Tuzuk-i-Jahangiri	Memoirs of the Mughal emperor Jahangir
Uddhava	A friend and counsellor of Krishna, who carries his message to the *gopi*s
ugra	Frenetically energetic
'unwans	The inscription in the beginning of a book, usually containing the subject of the work, the author's and publisher's names, the date, etc.
Upanishad	A collection of ancient Vedic texts which contain the earliest emergence of some of the central religious concepts of Hinduism, Buddhism and Jainism
ustad	An honorific title generally used for great teachers and artists
utsaha	Energy, enthusiasm, the excitement of anticipation
VS	Vikram Samvat: the Hindu calendar established by Vikramaditya, the emperor of Ujjain, starting in 57 BCE.
vahana	A vehicle
vaikuntha	The eternal abode of Vishnu
Vaishnavas	Followers of Vaishnavism, focused on the veneration of Vishnu
Varaha	The boar incarnation of Vishnu
Vardhamana Mahavira	The twenty-fourth and last *tirthankara* of Jainism (540–468 BCE)
Vasanta Vilasa	A celebrated lyrical poem in the *phagu* genre centring upon the beauties of the spring month of Phalguna in the Indian calendar. It was probably composed in the middle of the fourteenth century.
Vasuki	A Naga, one of the 'king' serpents of Hindu and Buddhist mythology
vidyadharas	Literally 'wisdom-holders', a group of supernatural beings in Hindu mythology. They possess magical powers and dwell in the Himalayas, attending to the god Shiva.
Vikramashila	One of the two most important centres of Buddhist learning in India during the Pala dynasty, along with Nalanda University
vimana	A chariot
viparita rati	Love play with the roles reversed, a woman playing the role of her male lover and vice versa
Vira	The Heroic Sentiment, according to the classification of moods in the *Natyashastra*

554

virahini	A young lady in love, but separated from her lover
Vishnu Purana	One of the eighteen Great Puranas, treating principally of Vishnu and Krishna
Vishnu	One of the three great deities of the Hindu triad. He is spoken of as the Preserver or Sustainer of life.
Vishvarupa	The cosmic form of Krishna
Vraja	A region in Uttar Pradesh, around Mathura–Vrindavan. It is considered to be the land of Krishna.
Vredenburg manuscript	An illustrated Buddhist text dated 1118
Vrindavana	A small town in the Mathura district of Uttar Pradesh. It is the site of an ancient forest which is the region where, according to early texts, Krishna grew up.
warraq	A page maker in a Mughal atelier
waslis	Layered sheets of handmade paper
yaksha	A broad class of nature-spirits, usually benevolent, who are caretakers of the natural treasures hidden in the earth and tree roots
Yashoda	Krishna's foster-mother
yogini	A female mendicant or seeker of spiritual knowledge
yuga	In Hindu thought, an age; a long epoch of time within a four-age cycle
zanjeer-e adal	The legendary chain of justice installed by the Mughal emperor Jahangir
zar-kash	A craftsman in a Mughal atelier who works with gold wire

COMPILED BY THE EDITORIAL TEAM, PENGUIN BOOKS INDIA

FURTHER READING

Over the years many scholars have written on Indian painting, and a complete list of their works can be very, very long. What appears below is a selection drawing attention to some of the writings most directly related to the present work and to the chief sources that it draws upon. For a fuller reading list, the reader might like to turn to *Masters of Indian Painting*, edited by Beach, Fischer and Goswamy.

Abu'l Fazl 'Allami. *The A'in-i Akbari by Abu'l Fazl 'Allami*. H. Blochman, trans. Calcutta: Asiatic Society, 1927.

Ahluwalia, R. *Rajput Painting: Romantic, Divine and Courtly Love from India*. London: British Museum Press, 2008.

Aijazuddin, F.S. *Pahari Paintings and Sikh Portraits in the Lahore Museum*. London: Sotheby Parke Bernet, 1977.

Aitken, Molly Emma. *The Intelligence of Tradition in Rajput Painting*. New Haven: Yale University Press, 2010.

Ambalal, Amit. *Krishna as Shrinathji: Rajasthani Paintings from Nathdwara*. Ahmedabad: Mapin Publishing, 1987.

Andhare, Shridhar K. *Chronology of Mewar Painting*. Delhi: Agam Kala Prakashan, 1987.

Archer, Mildred. *Company Paintings: Indian Paintings of the British Period*. London: Victoria and Albert Museum, 1992.

Archer, W.G. *Indian Paintings from the Punjab Hills; A Survey and History of Pahari Painting*. London and New York: Sotheby Parke Bernet, 1973.

——. *Visions of Courtly India. The Archer Collection of Pahari Miniatures*. Washington DC. International Exhibitions Foundation, 1976.

Bagchi, Jhunu. *The History and Culture of the Palas of Bengal and Bihar, c. 750–1200 AD*. New Delhi: Abhinav Publications, 1993.

Barret, Douglas, and Basil Gray. *Painting of India*. Geneva: Skira, 1963.

Bautze, Joachim. *Lotosmond und Lowenritt: Indische Miniaurmalerei*. Stuttgart: Linden Museum, 1991.

Beach, Milo C. *The Grand Mogul: Imperial Painting in India, 1600–1660*. Williamstown: Sterling and Francine Clark Institute, 1978.

———. *The Imperial Image: Painting for the Mughal Court*. Washington DC: Freer Gallery of Art, Smithsonian Institution, 2012.

———. *Mughal and Rajput Painting*. Cambridge: Cambridge University Press, 1992.

———. *Rajput Painting at Bundi and Kota*. Ascona: Artibus Asiae, 1974.

Beach, Milo C., Ebba Koch and W.M. Thackston. *King of the World: The* Padshahnama*: An Imperial Mughal Manuscript from the Royal Library, Windsor Castle*. London and Washington, DC: Azimuth Editions and Arthur M. Sackler Gallery, 1997.

Beach, Milo C., Eberhard Fischer and B.N. Goswamy, eds. *Masters of Indian Painting* (Vols I & II). Zürich: Artibus Asiae Publishers, 2011.

Bibliothèque nationale. *A la Cour du Grand Mogul*. Paris: Bibliothèque nationale, 1986.

Canby, Sheila R. *Princes, Poets and Paladins: Islamic and Indian Painting from the Collection of Prince and Princess Sadruddin Aga Khan*. London: British Museum, 1998.

Chaitanya, Krishna. *A History of Indian Painting: Rajasthani Traditions*. New Delhi: Abhinav Publication, 1982.

Chandra, Pramod. *The Tuti-Nama of the Cleveland Museum of Art and the Origins of Mughal Painting*. Graz: Akademische Druck u. Verlagsanstalt, 1976.

Choudhury, R.D., and Naren Kalita. *Manuscript Paintings from Kamarupa Anusandhan Samiti*. Guwahati: Kamarupa Anusandhan Samiti, 2001.

Coomaraswamy, Ananda K. *Rajput Painting*. London, 1916. Reprinted Delhi: Motilal Banarsidass, 1976.

Craven, Roy C. Jr, ed. *Ramayana: Pahari Paintings*. Bombay: Marg Publications, 1990.

Crill, Rosemary. *Marwar Painting: A History of the Jodhpur Style*. Mumbai: India Book House and Mehrangarh Publications, 1999.

Crill, Rosemary, and Kapil Jariwala. *The Indian Portrait, 1560–1860*. London: Nation Portrait Gallery Publications, 2010.

Cummins, Joan. *Indian Painting: From Cave Temples to the Colonial Period*. Boston: Museum of Fine Arts, 2006.

Dalrymple, William, and Yuthika Sharma. *Princes and Painters in Mughal Delhi, 1701–1857*. New Haven: Yale University Press, 2012.

Das, Ashok Kumar. *Mughal Painting during Jahangir's Time*. Calcutta: Asiatic Society, 1978.

Das, Ashok Kumar, ed. *Mughal Masters: Further Studies*. Mumbai: Marg Publications, 1998.

Dehejia, Vidya. *Devi: The Great Goddess. Female Divinity in South Asian Art*. Washington DC/ Ahmedabad: Arthur M. Sackler Gallery in association with Mapin Publishing, 1999.

Diamond, Debra, Catherine Glynn and Karni Singh Jasol. *Garden and Cosmos: The Royal Paintings of Jodhpur*. Washington DC: Arthur M. Sackler Gallery, Smithsonian Institution, 2008.

Doshi, Saryu V. *Masterpieces of Jain Painting*. Bombay: Marg Publications, 1985.

Ducrot, Vicky. *Four Centuries of Rajput Painting: Mewar, Marwar and Dhundhar Indian Miniatures from the Collection of Isabella and Vicky Ducrot*. Milano: Sikra, 2009.

Dye, Joseph III. *The Art of India: Virginia Museum of Fine Arts.* Richmond, Va/London: Virginia Museum of Fine Arts/Phillip Wilson Publishers, 2001.

Ehnbom, Daniel. *Indian Miniatures: the Ehrenfeld Collection.* New York: Hudson Hills Press, 1985.

Falk, Toby, and Mildred Archer. *Indian Miniatures in the India Office Library.* London: Sotheby Parke Bernet, 1981.

Fischer, Eberhard, B.N. Goswamy and Dinanath Pathy. *Göttinen: Indische Bilder in Museum Rietberg.* Zürich: Museum Rietberg, 2005.

Glynn, Catherine. 'Early Painting in Mandi'. In *Artibus Asiae* 44/1, 1983.

Goswamy, B.N. 'Pahari Painting: The Family as the Basis of Style'. *Marg* monograph, Mumbai, 1968.

———. *A Jainesque Sultanate* Shahnama *and the Context of Pre-Mughal Painting in India.* Zürich: Museum Rietberg, 1988.

———. *Nainsukh of Guler: A Great Indian Painter from a Small Hill State.* Zürich: Museum Rietberg and Artibus Asiae, 1997.

———. *Essence of Indian Art.* San Francisco: Asian Art Museum of San Francisco, 1986.

———. *Indian Paintings in the Sarabhai Foundation.* Ahmedabad: Sarabhai Foundation, 2010.

Goswamy, B.N., and Eberhard Fischer. *Pahari Masters: Court Painters of Northern India.* Zürich: Artibus Asiae Publishers and Museum Rietberg, 1992.

———. *Wonders of a Golden Age. Painting at the Court of the Great Mughals: Indian Art of the 16th and 17th Centuries from the Collections in Switzerland.* Zürich: Museum Rietberg, 1987.

Goswamy, B.N., and Caron Smith. *Domains of Wonder: Selected Masterworks of Indian Painting.* San Diego: the San Diego Museum of Art, 2005.

Guy, John. *Palm-leaf and Paper: Illustrated Manuscripts of India and South-east Asia.* Melbourne: National Gallery of Victoria, 1982.

Guy, John, and Deborah Swallow. *Arts of India: 1550–1900.* London: Victoria and Albert Museum, 1990.

Haidar, Navina Najat, and Marika Sardar, eds. *Sultans of the South: Arts of India's Deccan Courts, 1323–1687.* New York: The Metropolitan Museum of Art, New York, 2011.

Hodgkin, Howard, and Terence McInerney. *Indian Drawing.* London: Arts Council of Great Britain, 1983.

Hutton, Deborah. *Art of the Court of Bijapur.* Bloomington and Indianapolis: Indiana University Press, 2006.

Jahangir, Nuruddin. *The Jahangirnama: Memoirs of Jahangir, Emperor of India.* Trans. and ed. Wheeler Thackston. New York, Oxford University Press and the Arthur M. Sackler Gallery, 1999.

Khandalavala, Karl. *Pahari Miniature Painting.* Bombay: New Book Co., 1958.

Khandalavala, Karl, and Moti Chandra. *New Documents of Indian Painting: A Reappraisal.* Bombay, Prince of Wales Museum of Western India, 1969.

Kossak, Steven. *Indian Court Painting: 16th–19th Century.* New York: Metropolitan Museum of Art, 1997.

Kramrisch, Stella. *Painted Delight: Indian Paintings from the Philadelphia Collections.* Philadelphia:

Philadelphia Museum of Art, 1986.

———. *A Survey of Painting in the Deccan*. Hyderabad: Archaeological Department of H.E.H. the Nizam's Government, 1937.

Kuhnel, Ernst, and Hermann Goetz. *Indian Book Painting from Jahangir's Album in the State Library in Berlin*. London: Kegan Paul, Trench and Trubner, 1926.

Leach, Linda York. *Mughal and Other Indian Paintings from the Chester Beatty Library*. London: Scorpion Cavendish, 1995.

Losty, Jeremiah P. *The Art of the Book in India*. London: British Library, 1982.

———. *Paintings from the Royal Courts of India*. London: Francesca Galloway, 2008.

———. *The Ramayana: Love and Valour in India's Great Epic: The Mewar Ramayana Manuscripts*. London: British Library, 2008.

Lyons, Tryna. *The Artists of Nathadwara: The Practice of Painting in Rajasthan*. Bloomington: Indiana University Press, 2004.

McInerney, Terence. *Indian Painting, 1525–1825*. London: David Carritt, 1982.

Mittal, Jagdish. *Sublime Delight through Works of Art from the Jagdish and Kamla Mittal Museum of Indian Art*. Hyderabad: Jagdish and Kamla Mittal Museum of Art, 2007.

Mitter, Partha. *Indian Art*. Oxford University Press, 2001.

Ohri, Vishwa C. *On the Origins of Pahari Painting: Some Notes and Discussion*. Shimla: Indian Institute of Advanced Study, 1991.

———. *The Technique of Pahari Painting: An Inquiry into Aspects of Material, Methods and History*. Shimla and New Delhi: Indian Institute of Advanced Studies/Aryan Books International, 2001.

Okada, Amina. *Indian Miniatures of the Mughal Court*. New York: Harry N. Abrams, 1992.

Pal, Pratapaditya. *Indian Painting*. Vol I. Los Angeles: L.A. County Museum of Art, 1993.

———. *The Peaceful Liberators: Jain Art from India*. Los Angeles: Los Angeles County Museum of Art, 1994.

Poster, Amy G. *Realms of Heroism: Indian Paintings at the Brooklyn Museum*. New York: Hudson Hills Press in association with the Brooklyn Museum, 1994.

Randhawa, M.S. *Basohli Painting*. Delhi: Publications Division, Ministry of Information and Broadcasting, 1959.

———. *Kangra Paintings of the* Gita Govinda. New Delhi: National Museum, 1963.

Seyller, John. *Workshop and Patron in Mughal India: The Freer Ramayana and Other Illustrated Manuscripts of 'Abd al-Rahim*. Artibus Asiae Supplementum 42. Zürich: Artibus Asiae Publishers, 1999.

Seyller, John, and Wheeler Thackston, eds. *The Adventures of Hamza: Painting and Storytelling in Mughal India*. Washington DC: Freer Gallery of Art, Smithsonian Institution, 2002.

Shiveshwarkar, Leela. *The Pictures of the* Chaurapanchasika. New Delhi, 1967.

Singh, Chandramani. *Art Treasures of Rajasthan*. Jaipur: Jawahar Kala Kendra, 2004.

Skelton, Robert. *Indian Miniatures from the XVth to XIX Centuries*. Venice: Neri Pozza Editore, 1961.

Skelton, Robert. *The Indian Heritage: Court Life and Arts under Mughal Rule*. London: Victoria and Albert Museum, 1982.

Stronge, Susan. *Painting for the Mughal Emperor: The Art of the Book, 1560–1660*. London: Victoria and Albert Publications, 2002.

Sumahendra, Dr. *Miniature Painting Technique*. Jaipur, 1990.

Topsfield, Andrew, ed. *Court Painting in Rajasthan*. Mumbai: Marg Publications, 2000.

Topsfield, Andrew. *Court Painting at Udaipur: Art under the Patronage of the Maharanas of Mewar*. Artibus Asiae Supplementum 44. Zürich: Artibus Asiae Publishers, 2002.

———. *Paintings from Mughal India*. Oxford: Bodleian Library, 2008.

Topsfield, Andrew, ed. *In the Realm of Gods and Kings: Arts of India*. London: Philip Wilson, 2004.

Verma, Som Prakash. *Mughal Painters and Their Work: A Biographical Survey and Comprehensive Catalogue*. Delhi: Oxford University Press, 1994.

Welch, Stuart Cary. *India: Art and Culture 1300–1900*. New York: Metropolitan Museum of Art, 1985.

Welch, Stuart Cary, ed. *Gods, Kings, and Tigers: The Art of Kotah*. Munich and New York: Prestel, 1997.

Wright, Elaine, Susan Stronge and Wheeler Thackston. *Muraqqa': Imperial Mughal Albums from the Chester Beatty Library*. Alexandria, VA: Art Services International, 2008.

Zebrowski, Mark. *Deccani Painting*. London: Sotheby's, 1983.

INDEX